HAU
KT-179-319

WITHDRAWN
C016041533

NO BETTER FRIEND

Also by Robert Weintraub

The Victory Season

The House That Ruth Built

NO BETTER FRIEND

One Man, One Dog, and Their Incredible Story of Courage and Survival in WWII

ROBERT WEINTRAUB

JOHN MURRAY

First published in Great Britain in 2015 by John Murray (Publishers)
An Hachette UK Company

1

© Robert Weintraub 2015

The right of Robert Weintraub to be identified as the Author of the Work has been asserted by him in accordance with the Copyright, Designs and Patents Act 1988.

Maps drawn by David Lambert

All rights reserved. Apart from any use permitted under UK copyright law no part of this publication may be reproduced, stored in a retrieval system, or transmitted, in any form or by any means without the prior written permission of the publisher, nor be otherwise circulated in any form of binding or cover other than that in which it is published and without a similar condition being imposed on the subsequent purchaser.

A CIP catalogue record for this title is available from the British Library

Hardback ISBN 978-1-444-79693-3
Trade Paperback ISBN 978-1-444-79694-0
Ebook ISBN 978-1-444-79695-7

Printed and bound by Clays Ltd, St Ives plc

John Murray policy is to use papers that are natural, renewable and recyclable products and made from wood grown in sustainable forests. The logging and manufacturing processes are expected to conform to the environmental regulations of the country of origin.

John Murray (Publishers)
Carmelite House
50 Victoria Embankment
London EC4Y 0DZ

www.johnmurray.co.uk

For my family, in particular my mother, the first (and still foremost) Judy in my life

Courage is not having the strength to go on; it is going on when you don't have the strength.

—Theodore Roosevelt

Contents

A Note to the Reader

Multiple place-names are referred to or spelled the way they were during World War II, and have changed since. This is the case for some large places on the maps, such as Siam (now Thailand), as well as several small ones, such as the cities, towns, and villages in Sumatra, most of which are spelled slightly differently today.

NO BETTER FRIEND

Prologue

The two friends huddled close together, each of them the other's saving grace in a world gone to hell.

It was June 26, 1944. The friends were prisoners of war, having been held by the Japanese on the remote, mostly forgotten island of Sumatra since early 1942. They were now crammed into the hold of a ship, the SS *Van Waerwijck*, that the Japanese were using to transport POWs from one camp to another. The hold was several feet below the surface of the South China Sea, and the men crushed together on the floor were desperately trying to breathe in the fetid air. The temperature hovered near one hundred degrees. The pair of buddies had managed to gain purchase on a ledge near a porthole, which provided a hint of relief from the airless void below. But the slow crawl along the Sumatran coast elongated the amount of time they spent in the punishing heat.

Both were painfully thin, suffering from malnourishment throughout their two years of captivity. They had been reduced to eating rats and snakes to stay alive. Diseases like malaria and beriberi stalked them every day. They suffered frequent beatings and threats of death. They were sent on brutally hard, often pointless work details and endured the kinds of situations that caused horrible feelings of depression, abandonment, and apathy in even the strongest-minded of prisoners.

There was nothing terribly unusual about POWs suffering horribly at the hands of their Japanese captors. All across the Pacific theater, Allied captives were experiencing similar punishment. But there was one thing unusual about this particular duo of prisoners.

One of them was a dog.

* * *

Her name was Judy, and her life had already seen more than its share of adventure and dangers long before she found herself aboard that "hell ship." Judy was a purebred English pointer, a fine brown-spots-over-white example of this sporting and noble breed. But unlike most pointers, Judy showed from her first days that she preferred to be in the thick of the action rather than merely point to it for the benefit of others.

She was born in a kennel in the British section of Shanghai in 1936 and spent the next five years as the treasured mascot of a Royal Navy gunboat crew patrolling the Yangtze River. In 1939, Judy's ship was transferred to Singapore as the British Admiralty prepared for war in the Pacific. Not long after that, in the summer of 1941, Frank Williams arrived in the Lion City, having just turned twenty-two years old and serving as a leading aircraftman in the Royal Air Force. Many disasters later, man and dog eventually met at a POW camp—and were inseparable thereafter. Frank had even risked his life to ensure Judy was granted official POW status.

Frank was a committed caretaker to the brave and crafty pointer, but his protection provided a thin veneer that could only go so far in the everyday reality of being held by the Japanese—as was proven when the POWs were herded onto the *Van Waerwijck*.

Noon passed, and the heat and humidity in the hold were stupefying. Rivers of sweat dripped from the sardined mass of bodies—more than a thousand in all. The floor slopped and sloshed as the ship plowed through the waves. If it weren't for the sliver of air that passed through the porthole and onto her face, the fur-lined Judy may well have succumbed to the heat even more quickly than the men.

Then there was a sudden flash of light, followed immediately by a tremendous explosion almost dead center amidships. Fires erupted throughout the hold, and the torpid lump of prisoners leapt to life as if electrocuted. The men were just beginning to sort out what had happened when a second, even larger explosion ripped through the hold.

The ship had been struck by torpedoes. Their origin, tragically enough, was a British sub that had no idea the steamer carried a cargo of Allied POWs. Because of this accidental friendly fire, dozens of men were killed outright, and the remaining hundreds would surely join them if they didn't find a way through the burning, twisted wreckage in the hold.

From his perch near the porthole, Frank had a clear view of the mayhem, and it chilled him to the bone. The cargo from the deck had crashed down upon the POWs, killing and injuring many and creating an industrial obstacle course that limited the chances of a quick escape. For a man carrying a dog that weighed about fifty pounds, it would be impossible.

So Frank turned to Judy, noting that the faithful dog hadn't run off in the chaos and was remaining calm under extraordinary pressure. Frank picked her up, gave her a quick last hug, and shoved her halfway out the porthole. The pointer looked back with an expression of confusion and sadness, and, perhaps, given her history of close scrapes, a glimmer of "Here we go again."

"Swim!" Frank yelled to Judy, while giving her one last push that sent her flying out the porthole. Below, the ocean was roiling and filling with oil and debris from the dying ship. The screams of the stricken filled the air. In a second, maybe two, the dog would be swimming for her life amid the wreckage.

And her best friend was still trapped inside the sinking *Van Waerwijck*.

Judy tumbled through the air as the water raced up to meet her.

CHAPTER 1

Mascot

In September of 1936, two British sailors went looking for a dog. They were sailors on the HMS *Gnat,* one of the flotilla of gunboats that flew the Union Jack up and down the Yangtze River, protecting shipping, repelling pirates, and serving the interests of the crown, in whatever capacity that might take. The boat was in Shanghai for its annual refit and repair, but the job was mostly finished. The two officers had time to squeeze in one last important shore activity before resuming their patrol.

The men of the *Gnat* were in a quandary. Several other gunboats had animals on board as mascots—two cats on the *Bee,* a parrot on the *Ladybird,* even a monkey on the *Cicala.* Recently, the *Gnat* had encountered another gunboat, the *Cricket,* on the river, and their mascot, a large boxer-terrier mix named Bonzo, had put on such a show of barking and bristling that the men of the *Gnat* felt at a loss without a mascot of their own to answer in kind.

After much discussion, the officers of the boat decided to get a dog of their own. So the two gunboatmen, Lieutenant Commander J. M. G. Waldegrave, who was skipper of the *Gnat,* and Chief Petty Officer Charles Jeffery, the ship's bosun, meandered over to the Shanghai Dog Kennels in the British settlement, looking for a proper specimen to represent their ship.

They fell in love with Judy straightaway, especially when she leapt into Jeffery's arms when he whistled a hello in her direction. She wasn't a puppy anymore, but neither was she fully grown. A short time later, she officially belonged to the Royal Navy, having been legally adopted by the service rather than by any one member of it. Her new home would not be one of the grand houses or apartments that dotted the British settlement. She would not have a yard to romp in, trees in which to hone her natural instinct to hunt and "point out" game, or children to play with. Instead, Judy would become the mascot and best friend of a group of hardened sailors on board a steel warship.

Before the sailors left, an Englishwoman, Miss Jones, who ran the kennels, gave the sailors some background about their new and remarkable dog.

For the first few months of her life, she didn't even have a name.

The puppy was all warm fur and cold nose, one of a litter of seven wriggling, mewling pups born to a regal purebred English pointer. She lived—for the moment, anyway—in the Shanghai Dog Kennels, boarder of pets and unclaimed pups for the bustling Chinese city's British denizens. It was February 1936. Shanghai shivered under a damp cold, and an icy wind whipped through the streets that separated the city's eclectic combination of modernized western buildings and ramshackle slums.

There were five thousand British residents in Shanghai, and it seemed as though each had a dog to call his or her own. Breeds capable of large litters were favored, which accounted for the many pointers in the city. Miss Jones was present when one of her beautiful English pointers gave birth. The pups were kept at the kennels until they could be given away, generally an easy process in the English settlement.

One of the puppies, her coat a sparkling white dotted with liver-colored spots and splotches, her head, ears, and snout entirely brown, continually scraped about the perimeter of the fenced-in area where the newborns played. While the others stuck close to their mother, rolling happily in the dirt, this restless bundle of energy was already trying to escape.

Which she did, three weeks into her young life.

Lee Sung, a woman who lived and worked at the kennels, had a daughter, Ming, who often helped with the dogs after school. She was the first to notice the pup was missing, a fact confirmed by her mother, who carefully cleared the other dogs from the area in an attempt to find the escapee. What she discovered instead was a hole under the fence, dug by this restless dog. The pup had then jumped over a short wall and was now at large on the streets of Shanghai, one of the largest, busiest, noisiest cities in the world.

The horns of the motorcars, the buzzing of the horseflies, the alternately high and guttural notes of Shanghainese, the extremely tonal language spoken in the city—so many sights and sounds would have overloaded the senses of any visitor to the city. The blurring of the bicycles, the bamboo construction platforms climbing dizzyingly into the air, the endless stream of people, and the smells, in particular, were surely overwhelming. Dogs smell the world in much the same manner that humans see it, and a journey onto the streets of Old Shanghai was an olfactory wonderland. Smoke emanating from various storefronts, chimneys, and mouths. Soot flowing from the numerous factories that lined the area. The outpouring of petroleum distillates, cooking and heating oil, burning rubber, charcoal embers—the very air itself textured and subdivided into zones of precise aromas.

But in short order the pup would have lost interest in the incredible sensory overload in favor of zeroing in on the all-important job of foraging for food. Shanghai is historically one of the world's best eating cities, but famine had swept the land in 1936, and the great metropolis was feeling the lack of food. Shanghai in the 1930s was, far more than today, a leafy place full of greenswards, but the pup instinctively headed for places where there were people—and where there weren't other, larger animals.

At such a young age she would have been desperate for her mother, for guidance, warmth, and, most of all, milk. Newborn dogs in general are wanderers by nature, eager from the first to explore their surroundings, but their innate tendency is to return to mama. Why this curious pup made such an effort to escape and leave the bosom of family and shelter is unknown. But she would prove to be a most unusual dog, so it is only fitting that her first action was to push the envelope. She was lucky it didn't cost her her life. Too small and inexperienced to kill anything herself, she managed to survive on scraps pulled from garbage dumps and the odd handout from passersby. Her liver-and-white coloring dulled, and her ribs protruded from her body.

Food was difficult to come by, but in a stroke of great fortune, the young pointer was given a lifeline. She stumbled upon the back door of a general store run by a man known only as Mr. Soo. There were plenty of such shops on the western side of Shanghai, where the Brits, Americans, and Germans maintained their "quarters." They sold a hodgepodge of items to westerners and locals, including herbal remedies, birdcages, soups of various flavors, religious artifacts, household knickknacks, and good luck charms. Soo sold whatever he came across that would turn a profit, however small. He didn't make much money, but it was better than hauling lumber or pulling whites across the city on a rickshaw.

It was early spring by now, but the city remained chilly. One bitter afternoon, Soo went behind his shop to discard some trash in the alley. His attention was caught by the sound of high-pitched crying, and he noticed movement among the cardboard detritus. There was a small dog, only several weeks old at the most, whimpering and looking at Soo with huge, watery brown eyes. It was clear that the dog was very hungry and quite cold. So Soo went back inside and brought the dog some scraps of food, which she downed immediately.

For the next few weeks, perhaps as long as three months (precise details aren't known), Soo kept the dog alive by providing her with food and a place inside the shop to safely bed down at night. Here, the pup could hide from the nocturnal predators who were desperate for something to eat—a group that included many citizens of Shanghai. A Chinese proverb, born of the nation's long, sad history of famine, states, "If its back faces the sun, it can be eaten." That surely included dogs.

But when the first calamity of many in this particular canine's life fell upon her, it wasn't the result of attempted predation. Instead, it was plain cruelty. And it came courtesy of an enemy she and her friends would grow to know all too well.

Japan was at the end of a period of intense military growth and shipbuilding, and the country was ready to flex her regional muscle. Having already occupied Manchuria and cowed Korea into subjugation, Japan now set her sights on the Chinese mainland. The Imperial Navy had shelled Shanghai in 1932; it was the most critical city in the country from a military perspective, due to its strategic control of the Yangtze River. The two countries brokered a tentative peace shortly thereafter, but Japanese warships were a frequent sight on Chinese waterways, and their sailors were often found in Shanghai bars, drinking Tsingtao beer or the local rice wine. The western nations patrolled the river as well, and United States and Royal Marines and sailors were also regular visitors to these establishments. The uneasy peace between the powers often exploded into drunken brawls of east against west, with the burly, fist-fighting westerners taking on the more agile Japanese, who countered with karate moves known by all in military service.

On a rainy day in May, a group of Japanese sailors from a gunboat that had anchored in the Yangtze participated in a pub crawl up and down the Bund, Shanghai's riverside carnival. They wandered into Mr. Soo's nearby shop, perhaps to find some light food to go, perhaps to purchase a prophylactic for the rest of the night's frivolity, or perhaps to obtain some painkillers in anticipation of the next day's hangover.

The sailors, dressed in full uniforms, began squabbling over something with Soo. In short order, voices were raised, tempers flared, and the Japanese men began to beat Soo, who was in no condition to battle a group of young men primed for combat. When Soo was broken and bleeding, the sailors lost interest in him and began to demolish his shop. They were in the final stages of destruction when the pup, frightened by the noise yet curious when she heard the yells of her benefactor, wandered in through the back door.

If this were a Hollywood story, the dog would bare its teeth, snarl menacingly, and scare away the bad men, then attract medical help for the old man. But in reality, the frail little beast could barely summon the agility to scamper away from the kick of one sailor, and the missile hurled by a second. A third Japanese sailor managed to snag her by the neck, and he brought the pup out the front door and onto the street.

The dog was crying madly, scared and in pain, but the sailor ignored her yelps. He held her, arms outstretched, then punted her like a football across the street and into a pile of debris. The group of *funanori* (Japanese sailors) then resumed their drunken revelry and disappeared.

They could not know that the dog they had treated so barbarously would survive many more travels and travails, and even become a minor thorn in the side of the Japanese war machine. As it was, the free kick left the sad little pointer near an abandoned doorway, where she crawled and collapsed, too hurt and frightened to move any farther. She merely sat and whimpered.

But her placement was fortuitous, for after a time her soft mewls were heard by a little girl walking past the doorway. It was none other than Lee

Ming, the daughter of the Shanghai Dog Kennels employee Lee Sung. Ming recognized the wayward pointer immediately, even though weeks of street life had left the little dog in poor shape.

"Oh little one, where have you been?" she asked the dog, who clearly remembered the little girl as well, though she could barely summon the energy to wag her tail.

Ming picked up the dog carefully, buried her in the folds of her raincoat, and took her back to the kennels, which were only a few blocks away.

Miss Jones was there, tending to several animals in the courtyard.

"Look who I found!" Ming displayed the prodigal puppy with pride.

"Goodness! Is that our missing pointer?" Miss Jones exclaimed. After looking at her closely, she confirmed it was the same pup whose interest in the outside world had nearly killed her. "It really is the one that ran away. I think we should give her a bath and a good dinner, don't you?" she asked Ming.

They examined the dog, cleaned her, and gave her some much-needed food. The little dog lay peacefully while she was poked, prodded, and gently scolded by the women for being too curious and adventurous for her own good.

At one point, Ming murmured to her, "You're okay; there, there little *Shudi*."

"Why did you call her *Shudi,* Ming?" Miss Jones asked.

The little girl lifted the pup and wrapped her in a blanket, where she promptly closed her eyes and fell asleep in Ming's arms.

"I've always called her that. *Shudi* means peaceful. Look at her." The exhausted pup realized she was being talked about, opened a lone eye to ensure all was well, and went back to sleep.

"Doesn't she look peaceful?"

"Indeed she does," said Miss Jones. "And that shall be her name—Judy."

For the first time since she had slipped out of her cage perhaps months before, the little pointer was at last safe once more, complete with a new name. It is somewhat surprising that she was so quick to embrace humans—even well-meaning ones—after her treatment at the hands of the Japanese sailors, but as the noted dog trainer Jennifer Arnold has said, "The only indication of lack of intelligence in dogs I've ever seen is their willingness to forgive us for so much."

Her mother and siblings were gone by now, but she no longer had to worry about scrounging for her next meal. Ordinarily, she could look forward to adoption and a comfortable life with a loving family. She found instead a life full of adventure, dangers, and wonderment, and more friends who thought of her as family than she ever would have met in the backyard of a Shanghai manse.

By the time Judy came aboard the *Gnat* in 1936, China had been mostly reunited under the banner of General Chiang Kai-shek and his Kuomintang (KMT); only the ragtag Communist army led by Mao Tse-tung remained to combat Chiang. But the larger threat stemmed from the Japanese. The Land of the Rising Sun had augmented its naval presence on the Yangtze while sending thousands of troops and much of its airpower to recently conquered Manchuria. The Japanese were clearly spoiling for a fight. When they weren't fighting in bars, relations on the river between sailors of east and west remained mostly cordial, but tensions were mounting. And the Chinese were caught in the middle, often resenting the westerners but abjectly fearing the Japanese.

Despite the growing sense that war was coming, service in China was not high profile by Royal and U.S. Navy standards—there was little of the esprit of the mainline battleships and destroyers that ruled the oceans elsewhere. Discipline wasn't as severe on the gunboats, and the sailors' relationships with the local Chinese, the crew of other ships, and each other was more relaxed and humane than it was in other quarters of the globe.

This less stringent attitude allowed Judy to flourish as a beloved member of the crew aboard the *Gnat,* a status she would repay with her service.

Thirteen gunboats served in the Yangtze Flotilla under Rear Admiral Lewis G. E. Crabbe. The *Gnat* was part of the Insect class of gunboats, small and maneuverable in order to navigate the varying widths and depths of the river, but potent as well, armed with several big guns, including antiaircraft cannons. Originally designed to show the flag and intimidate the Austro-Hungarian Navy on the Danube, the gunboats proved especially well-suited for action on the powerful currents of the Yangtze.

Western gunboats had been sailing on Chinese waterways since the late 1850s. The Treaty of Tientsin, which ended the Second Opium War in 1858, lifted commercial restrictions on western traders in China (which was the war's main aim, despite the narcotic title). The foreign merchants, operating deep in the Chinese interior, needed protection, so the treaty contained a clause permitting western warships to ply the Yangtze, which reached a thousand miles into the heart of the Middle Kingdom. The Brits were the pioneers, but American and French boats swiftly followed.

The turn of the century saw an explosion in the presence of western fleets in China. The British sent a pair of brand-new ships, *Woodlark* and *Woodcock,* designed for river piloting and fighting. Along with the American and French vessels, there were ships guarding German, Italian, and Japanese interests. They added to the immense commercial traffic floating up and down the crucial artery, turning the Yangtze into a picturesque riot of colorful sails and masts, darkened only by the black coal smoke from the more modern ships. From elegant junks to rickety sampans to creaky steam-driven paddleboats to the intimidating iron hulks of the gunboats, a pleasant afternoon could be passed lying on the riverbank and watching the regatta cruise past.

By the 1920s, China was riven by internecine fighting among potent warlords, each of whom carved out a fiefdom and held on to it tenaciously. Merchant steamers passing through their territories were expected to pay tribute, and they were often pirated and looted regardless of whether they complied. The warships were kept busy protecting the merchants and were often confrontational (the movie *The Sand Pebbles,* starring Steve McQueen as a sailor on an American gunboat on the Yangtze, centers on this period). In one notable incident, several British steamers were captured by troops belonging to the powerful warlord Yang Sen. The gunboats shelled Yang's base in the city of Wanhsien, killing up to five thousand Chinese in the process of freeing their merchant marines. In the wake of the fighting, there were major riots in multiple cities, and the gunboats had to come to the rescue of harassed westerners until matters eased late in the summer of 1926.

On Judy's first afternoon in the Royal Navy, many of the *Gnat*'s men were killing time in the mess belowdecks when the upside-down head of the coxswain appeared through the hatch. He was grinning like a demented imp.

"All hands on deck in ten minutes!" he boomed.

Once assembled, the crew was introduced to their newest member.

According to Charles Jeffery, the bosun, Lieutenant Commander Waldegrave stepped forward. "As you know," he began, "the ship's canteen committee recently voted for us to take on a pet. I have studied your very interesting suggestions, most of which I have had to disregard as either impractical or perverse, and decided our ship's pet should have three qualifications.

"Because we can do with some female companionship, the first qualification is that it be a female. Second, she would be attractive, and third, she should have to earn her keep.

"From this point on, future shooting parties going ashore to hunt will no longer be able to return aboard with just one duckling while stoutly averring they shot down twenty-three, only to have lost them in the brush!"

At that, the quartermaster led Judy out to the men. She was on a lead, and in the memory of most of those present, she looked a bit apprehensive. But when a mighty cheer went up in her honor, she broke out in a grin—tongue out, jowls up, tail wagging furiously—that would become a familiar sight aboard the *Gnat* in the years to come.

"Here she is, gentlemen," Waldegrave said. "Meet the first lady of the gunboats—Judy of the Royal Navy."

Because her mother, Kelly, had been owned by a family from the Sussex region of England, she was known in the official kennel records as "Kelly of Sussex." Her litter was referred to this way as well, so in the Royal Navy archives, Judy was officially called "Judy of Sussex."

Jeffery, who served as a "buffer" between deck officers and crew, called her just that in his diary entry from that first day of Judy's embarkation on the *Gnat:* "Judy of Sussex is a thoroughbred pointer coloured brown and white. She is the most lovable creature. As the Captain and I had been the ones to buy her for the ship's company, he decided I should keep her forward so that she would not get too familiar with the men and so spoil our chances to train her for the gun."

Alas, this quickly proved impossible, as a later diary entry notes:

"The ship's company love and treat Judy as a pet, and I am delighted that the men share her. But of course our chances of making her a trained gun dog are very small."

Pointers are a hunting breed, commonly known as a "gun dog." The English varietal descends from the Spanish pointer, a dog that is the result of the fusing of hounds and spaniels. Specifically, the pointer was bred to stiffen and train its gaze and posture directly at hidden game (mainly birds). Previous hunting dogs had bounded into the bush to flush out game, but the act of pointing allowed the hunter to get his bearings, check his weapon, and ready himself before the dog went tearing into the trees to send the poor quail or duck scurrying into the air. Naturally, hunters using pointers saw their success rate skyrocket and their bellies fill as a result. The breed's aptitude as a hunting companion was enhanced by its friendly disposition and clear intelligence.

The Spanish pointers were bred into existence sometime in the seventeenth century by members of the Hidalgo aristocracy, proud and masterful sportsmen and landowners who created the dog in their image, according to Ernest Hart's history of the breed. "Sleek but powerful, noble and fleet in the field, the Spanish dog on point was like a statue of mottled marble, a piece of sculpted beauty molded by the hands of a master who produced the ultimate in balance and clean-cut muscular elegance."

The English version was crossbred with foxhounds to be much lighter and of greater stamina than their powerful sprinter cousins from Spain. It took some doing, and for a long while the resulting English pointers lost the easygoing personality and turned "ferocious," according to many sporting guides of the eighteenth century. Eventually, the sharp tinge was bred out of the English pointer, and the breed regained its pleasantness to man. But one remnant of the fiercer early pointers remained in the new version—a tremendous drive and competitiveness. On the hunting ground, this was shown by the animal's intensity and attention to detail in doing the job of pointing out game. Owners were dazzled by the breed's focus and determination when "on duty."

In Judy's case, that natural ability to point out birds and other game would never be developed. But that drive and determination would be the compelling characteristic of her life. This was particularly noticeable in her eyes, a deep liquid brown that shone with intensity. Dogs, unlike most animals, actually look humans in the eye when interacting. When Judy gazed upon her two-legged friends, the look radiated intelligence and fervor.

As a hunting companion, though, she was a failure. Pointers mature early, and Judy's crucial first experiences were spent not at the side of a hunter who taught her to point, but on the streets of Shanghai, alone, constantly searching for food to keep her alive. The officer's head mess boy, a Chinese lad, noted this instinct at an early stage of Judy's time on board the *Gnat*. He told the officers that the only time Judy went rigid and "pointed" in the proper manner was when she smelled dinner cooking. Judy would then stiffen and turn her attention toward the galley.

CHAPTER 2

Dog Overboard

Before Judy could save anyone aboard the *Gnat,* she required saving herself.

The still-growing pointer had been aboard the vessel for about six weeks, happily exploring every nook and cranny. There were a few areas, like the wardroom and the bridge, that were off-limits except by special invitation, and she quickly learned to avoid those. She also learned very early on that the Chinese cooks and mess boys didn't welcome her in the galley—they thought her unclean, but also saw her as potential dinner.

Perhaps there was a bit of prejudice in Jeffery's diary entry of October 14, when he wrote that "Judy, the lovely lass, just barely tolerates the Chinese crewmen on board," but the opinion was based in truth. The kitchen workers and the dog agreed to give one another a wide berth.

Otherwise, Judy roamed freely, without a leash. She had been given an official ship's book number, allowing her full status as a member of the crew, and she could be found at any given time with the gun crews while they were at work, high up in the foredeck with the lookouts, or below with resting crewmen—just about anywhere she could find company. Pointers are very sociable animals, and Judy in particular, after her lonely hardship on the streets of Shanghai, seemed to welcome companionship.

Her "quarters" were an open box and a ship's blanket, which at first were outside Jeffery's quarters but soon were moved all over, both by sailors and by Judy herself when the mood struck. The crew would stop and laugh when their dog would pull her box with her teeth across companionways and up and down gangways—even pushing it down ladders when the need arose.

Life on the gunships was unusual for the crew. It was an out-of-the-way posting, utterly without glamor, and, even by naval standards, short on comfort. The gunboats usually patrolled alone or in pairs, but due to the contour of the river, they never patrolled in large groups or as a combined fleet. That meant a refreshing lack of signals and semaphore emanating from the flagship. For the most part, the men who served aboard the gunboats relished this bit of freedom from ordinary naval operations. These men loved the ships and the job—and this was due in no small part to the outsourcing of menial duties, such as cooking, cleaning, and scrubbing the decks, to Chinese contractors who were paid a small fortune by local standards to keep the gunboats crisp and sparkling. As such, the men, while frequently bored, seldom developed the resentments of the average tar, who bristled at being told to "swab the poop deck, sharpish."

The total crew on board was roughly three dozen at any given time, made up of two or three officers, six or so petty officers, and twenty rank-and-file seamen. Six full-time Chinese workers were part of the official crew, with as many day laborers on board to assist.

The living quarters were backward in contrast to most naval vessels. On the gunboats, the officers lived up front near the bow, with the men behind them. The quarters ranged from comfy to brutal, depending on rank. One American officer described the disparity on the USS *Elcano:* "The Captain's Quarters [*sic*] were fairly commodious for such a small ship...and because of the hull conformation, shaped like the end of a bathtub. The skipper enjoyed the luxury of a tub and flush toilet, but lesser officers used a small steel cubicle on deck, barely large enough to squeeze into, which housed shower and archaic sanitary facilities."

Those boxy structures combining toilet and shower were standard issue on the gunboats, regardless of nationality. They were in the stern, or back, of the boat, meaning waste was easily disposed into the river. A female guest aboard a British gunboat once queried after their purpose, and an officer replied, "That, Madam, is where we deal with our secret papers."

The ships were oddities in their own right. Instead of exhaust funnels running the length of the ship, the river vessels had them side by side, offering a look that was hardly the aquiline sleekness most navy ships preferred to show. The typical gunboat was about 250 feet long, 36 feet high at the beam, and displaced around 650 tons. The term "gunboat" was mostly literal—they were basically hulls with a sheet of iron welded on top, with only the bridge, the masts, and the guns sticking out. An Insect-class vessel like the *Gnat* was armed with two six-inch artillery guns, a twelve-pound antiaircraft gun, and six Maxim .303 machine guns. It was a powerful sting, diverse enough to shell coastal targets, ward off air attacks, or strafe shipping or boarding parties, depending on the threat.

The river they sailed upon was and is one of the world's great bodies of water. The name Yangtze has no meaning in the local tongue. It was probably a mistaken derivation of Yang-tzu, which was an old name for the important river city of Chinkiang. Foreigners in the town likely heard the name and assumed it applied to the great stream on which the city sat. *Yang* means "ocean" in many common dialects in China, so it's possible the titanic river was given this title to properly credit its immensity. But more likely it was a gaffe by westerners, known locally as *gwailos*. Most Chinese call it *jiang,* simply, "the river."

For those whose lives it shaped daily, the Yangtze was indeed a singularity that was as all-consuming as the earth or the sky. It comes streaming ice-cold and crystal clear from the mountainous Tibetan plateau, conflates with the Min River to become navigable about one thousand miles inland, and turns an ugly shade of brownish-yellow, a hue brought on by sediment, pollution, and excrement. It flows through a series of deep gorges (in the area of the notorious Three Gorges Dam, completed in 2012) that hamper all but the smallest ships before tumbling in a wide, roiling clamor toward Shanghai and the east coast. In all, the Yangtze flows nearly four thousand miles—though precise measurement is tricky, as the silt deposited at the river's mouth pushes it thirty to forty feet farther into the East China Sea each year. Regardless, it is the longest river in Asia and the third-longest in the world, trailing only the Amazon and the Nile. The Yangtze Delta has traditionally been the nation's heartland and heartbeat, providing as much as a quarter of China's GDP.

The gunboats patrolled a six-hundred-mile stretch of the river between

Shanghai on the eastern coast and Wuhan to the west. They occasionally sailed beyond this area, but as the Japanese threat grew in the 1930s, the Yangtze fleet stayed closer to Shanghai. As Angus Konstam, a historian of the gunboat fleet, wrote, "To the ancient Chinese, the river was the home to a great underwater dragon, whose changes in mood explained all river disasters, from flooding to shipwreck, stranding or piracy. The job of the Yangtze gunboats was to keep an eye on this dragon, and to protect Westerners from its wrath."

Judy quickly grew friendly with the majority of the crew, from Waldegrave on down to the tars. Before long, however, she chose a favorite crewman to hang out with, the first of several men who would take the role of her best friend. His name was Able Seaman Jan Cooper, a low-ranking hand who often assisted in navigation or helming. On the *Gnat,* however, Cooper's main role was to be in charge of the fresh water and food locker, and he was also the ship's butcher, so it was no surprise that the perpetually hungry Judy preferred his company. On many Royal Navy vessels, the tankey, the moniker given to the seaman in charge of the tanks of water on board, was considered the second most important position, just after the captain, given his control of the stores. Tankey was an appropriate nickname for Cooper, who was built like a short, stout tank, with thick, powerful forearms and a deep chest.

Tankey Cooper would be responsible for feeding Judy her one meal per day and ensuring that the crew didn't slip her extra table scraps. She needed to be kept in fighting trim, Waldegrave ordered, and Cooper was the man who had to scold his crewmates, even those who outranked him, when they tried to give the dog extra tidbits. Bars of chocolate were a definite no-no, as cocoa products tend to sicken dogs, though Judy, a true omnivore, was seldom finicky. The Chinese gunboats were unusual in that they kept beer on board, and every man had a daily ration. It was quickly discovered that Judy had a taste for the lager, so it was on Cooper to keep her sober as well.

In her early days on board the ship, Judy enjoyed visiting the steel plates at the front of the boat, as far forward as one could get. There were guardrails protecting the crew from being tossed in the ship's path, but a man or a dog could easily circumvent them and venture out onto the edge.

Unfortunately, the steel was also slippery, which was why crewmen seldom ventured onto its surface without a safety line. Judy was a surefooted beast, but she discovered the perils of the outboard plates the hard way one November morning.

Jeffery, the bosun, was walking forward when he noticed Judy slip under the guardrails and onto the steel. Suddenly, the *Gnat* lurched forward and to port to avoid some rocks, and the motion threw Judy off balance. Legs skittering desperately, she slipped and slid off the *Gnat* and into the muddy Yangtze.

"Man overboard!" Jeffery yelled, not stopping to consider the finer points of species distinction in the face of emergency.

"All stop and full astern!" commanded Waldegrave.

This was no ordinary dunking. Several men from western ships had been lost after falling into the river, which was particularly fast-moving, nonbuoyant, and murky. Villagers along the Yangtze drowned regularly in its cloudy depths. Chairman Mao plunged into the Yangtze at the Wuhan Bridge in 1966 in order to prove his vitality and capability to lead the nation through the Great Cultural Revolution. Surviving a dip in the river was considered an achievement even for a strong swimmer.

And pointers, unlike retrievers or hounds, aren't natural swimmers.

The *Gnat* quickly stopped, maneuvered itself to face up-current, and launched one of its small powerboats. "The captain knew what was required and did just that," Jeffery later recorded. Three men jumped into the powerboat: Leading Seaman Vic Oliver, an unnamed engine man, and a Chinese boy named Wugle who was in charge of keeping the boat at the ready. Despite the hurried operations, Judy was already a small dot far downriver, her brown head barely distinguishable against the muck of the water.

The current was running at about ten knots, and the water was choppy from a strong offshore breeze. It took about five minutes for the powerboat to catch up to the frantically paddling dog, pass her, turn in its wake, and power slowly upstream to her. When the boat was alongside Judy, Wugle reached over to grab her collar. But either he wasn't strong enough to pull her aboard or Judy unexpectedly wrenched in his grasp, because Wugle suddenly went overboard too.

Now Oliver had to make a double rescue—and decide which of his swimming crewmates to pull aboard first. He chose the dog, both because she had been in the water longer and because he was disgusted with Wugle, later calling him a "silly boy" in the official debrief (stronger, more prejudiced epithets were used with his fellow crewmen when off the record). Wugle spat up a great mouthful of muddy water but appeared in no imminent danger of going under, so Oliver first made for the whining dog, who seemed to be ready to meet the bottom.

Holding the tiller between his legs, he and the engine man avoided Wugle's mistake and used four hands to grab the desperate dog and haul her onto the powerboat. With Judy shivering but safe, Oliver puttered over to Wugle, and he too was rescued. The crew of the *Gnat,* watching from afar, gave out a mighty yell when the rescue boat turned back and made for her mother ship.

Oliver, tiller still between his legs, sent a semaphore message over the water to the *Gnat*—"Judy's christening completed."

When they returned aboard, Wugle went for a long bath, while Judy, caked in mud, was ordered to be disinfected. Jeffery handled bathing duties, noting that the dog was "scared and shivery at first, but I talked to her and walked her around the ship. She kept next to my bunk that night and the next day was quite okay."

The dunking in the Yangtze was entered into the official logbook as a "Man Overboard and Away Lifeboat" incident, even though it had been a canine that had gone over. Meanwhile, Judy had learned a valuable lesson. From that point forward, she stayed off the steel outboard plates and refused to approach the guardrails when the boat was offshore. Even when going ashore on the gangway, Judy was "on alert," according to a bemused Oliver, "ears at the cocked position and all systems at the ready." One dip in the dangerous river was enough to teach Judy that she didn't want another.

Soon after her fall into the water, the young pointer showed her systems were indeed "at the ready" in an important way. Judy had yet to prove her worth as a hunting dog, but she had been helping the crew in another area instead. "Cess boats" or "floating cesspits" were a constant hazard on the Yangtze. These were open boats that carried barrels of feces and urine out of villages for dumping in remote areas, and the slightest exposure to their overpowering stench could infect a ship for days, as though sprayed by a skunk (how the Chinese crews served aboard these sewer ships was a mystery to the western gunboat crews). Very early on in her service aboard the *Gnat,* Judy proved her strong nose was in working order. Whenever a cess boat approached, and she could sense it coming before it came into human vision, she began to bark and run in circles, her irritation rising to a crescendo. Her early clamoring allowed the crew to batten down hatches and portholes, ensuring that the rank odor didn't remain part of the voyage once the ships passed one another.

Judy wasn't necessarily barking a warning, though her human friends took it as such. Smell is incredibly important to a dog's moment-to-moment existence. Dogs have a sense of smell far more powerful than that of humans, perhaps millions of times more powerful. Next to a dog, a man might as well not have a nose.

The German biologist Jakob von Uexküll coined the term *umwelt* (OOM-velt) to characterize an animal's world and how a creature sees things, in order to differentiate it from what we as humans perceive the animal to be thinking or sensing. From Judy's *umwelt,* or point of view, the powerful odor from the shitwagons wasn't bad, or even something to be avoided. Indeed, to a canine, scat and urine are powerful message senders, relaying much about the creature that left it behind. Judy was no doubt overwhelmed by such a potent pile of messages and was creating havoc simply to convey her difficulty in processing it all, or her excitement at the idea. To the men of the *Gnat,* however, the barking allowed them to give the disgusting vessels a wide berth. This no doubt disappointed Judy, but in the eyes of the crew, it made her invaluable.

Judy's sensory powers took on an importance of a different magnitude shortly after her dunking in the river. The *Gnat,* like all the gunboats, rarely operated at night, leaving only one or perhaps two men as lookouts while the ship was at anchor between dusk and dawn. On this day, the ship was just above the port city of Wuhu, about fifty miles inland from Shanghai, in a spot where the river narrowed appreciably.

Around three a.m., while the crew snored away, Judy jumped up from her box in the front of the boat and began barking furiously at something in the night. Not hesitating, the night watchman switched on the *Gnat*'s powerful Aldis searchlight, which illuminated a pair of junks drifting downstream toward the navy vessel.

They were river pirates, following their favored means of attack. The two ships flanked their prey while secured to each other by strong rope. When the pirates were on either side of the vessel, the rope would catch on the bow, and the junks would be swung right alongside. The pirates would then leap aboard the targeted ship, kill or incapacitate all aboard, and loot at will.

This time, however, the element of surprise had been lost, thanks to Judy. The watchman fired a pistol shot, which brought the pajama-clad crewmen out of their racks and on deck, small arms at the ready, while others manned the deck guns. As the leaders of each pirate vessel jumped onto the *Gnat,* one on each side, they were swiftly cut down, falling back into the river. Waldegrave ordered a long burst of fire from the ship's main machine gun as a warning, and that the ropes that were holding the junks in place be cut. Meanwhile, Judy kept up her ferocious barking and bared her teeth at the nearer junk. The pirates abandoned the attack and drifted into the dark, hoping for less-prepared prey the next time out.

The jubilant sailors cheered their alert mascot. Sniffing out open-air latrines afloat on the river was one thing, but this was quite another. Judy had saved the ship by sensing danger. How exactly she had picked up on the silent approach of the pirates was a mystery, though the extreme sensitivity to danger could easily have been traced to her days as a puppy navigating the mean streets of Shanghai. Regardless, Judy's ability to recognize approaching trouble in advance of her human friends would become a common occurrence in her life.

The crewmen gave Judy extra rations and much TLC as a reward, though they chalked up the repulsion of the pirate attack to a source other than her bared fangs—one member of the crew had appeared on deck clad only in a scarlet-colored pajama top, fiercely waving a fire axe, his bottoms having remained below.

That was surely more frightening than any angry dog.

CHAPTER 3

Shore Leave

Tankey Cooper was determined to teach Judy how to be a proper pointer, so he tried to pass along the techniques required for her to be an asset to the ship's hunting parties. Re-provisioning with fresh game was essential for the gunboats, and the *Gnat* was slackening in its ability to procure some of the region's plentiful poultry for her stores.

But while Cooper had a strong desire to teach, Judy did not have an equal inclination to learn. Despite the long hours Cooper spent with the animal, demonstrating what Judy was supposed to do by getting down on all fours himself alongside the ship's chicken coops and "pointing" in a rigid manner, the lessons didn't take. She would just hop around her friend, playing rather than studying. "I think she took the whole thing as entertainment," Cooper recorded.

One afternoon, he took Judy ashore for her first real test, working on the assumption that once she was out in the field, natural instincts would take over. The lone time she pointed in perfect form, like something right out of the manual, came early in the hunt. Unfortunately, instead of directing the men's shotguns at a bird, she was pointing right at Tankey. With a frenzied shout of "Don't bloody shoot!" Cooper managed to avoid disaster.

On another attempt, Judy disappeared into the brush, presumably to flush ducks or quail. She was gone for a long time, and Tankey eventually went off to search for her. A little ways on, he heard a heartrending howl, the likes of which he'd never heard from the dog. He crashed through the forest, following the sounds.

Then he saw her, a picture of abject misery. She had plunged into a large pool of mud or perhaps quicksand, Tankey couldn't tell which. In his haste to rescue his friend, he plunged into the mire himself, only realizing what he had done once he was in up to his chest.

It turns out it wasn't mud—it was an open-air cesspit. First Judy and now Tankey had waded into a gargantuan pile of shit. Here then was proof that in Judy's *umwelt,* the excrement was interesting, not off-putting. Unfortunately, it was also deep, and now she was trapped. And her whining had drawn her friend into the filth as well.

The two bodies moving through the pit had broken the thin scum that had hardened on the surface, revealing the gooey mess below. An overpowering stench rose from the cracks, to the point that both man and dog were in danger of passing out and falling into the slime, perhaps to their deaths.

His stomach rebelling and his nose curdling, Cooper managed to gather himself, grab Judy by the collar, and haul them both out of the pit, before collapsing on the dry ground.

The revolting mess covered him to mid-thorax. His shoes squelched with a disgusting noise. He couldn't stand to breathe through his nose. Slime covered his bare arms and hands and could not be wiped off on the grass. Judy was in even worse shape, covered up to her neck in the vile goop. Virtually all of the white of her coat was rendered invisible.

Their fellow hunters refused to get within twenty yards of Tankey and Judy as they traveled back to the ship. Their only companions were a buzzing cloud of flies that followed them to the water. As they approached the *Gnat,* they noticed the quarantine flag was flying from the yardarm, the ship's bell was tolling, and sailors were bellowing, "Unclean! Unclean!" It took several days of scrubbing before either crewman or mascot was considered worthy of welcome back into proper ship's company. And Cooper, for one, now had newfound appreciation for the Chinese crews that manned the floating cesspits.

Judy's pointing surely needed work. Still, by this stage, it was clear to the gunboatmen that their mascot was something special. "She seems to develop a human brain as she gets older," Jeffery wrote in his diary. "She seems to understand every word. When she gets dirty she comes to me and hangs her head. If I call her a bad dog she drops her ears and then she grins. If I call her a dirty bitch she whines and grovels at my feet. Then I pat her on the head and she knows all is forgiven. Lovely dog."

Judy's intelligence and alertness paid off in another unexpected way soon after her failed hunting expedition. One day, while anchored not far from Shanghai, Admiral Sir Charles Little, the senior naval officer (SNO) for the Royal Navy, came aboard the *Gnat*. Everyone tidied up and presented themselves for a full-blown Admiralty Inspection. As Tankey put it, the SNO was there to "give them the works"—find every dust bunny, loose thread, and untucked sheet on the boat.

As the men stood at attention on deck and beside their bedding, the tension grew. Little made it a point to find flaws and dress down several of the crew. Then he came to Judy, who was sitting at "attention," tongue hanging out in a manner that made her appear to be grinning broadly. Next to her were her neatly folded blanket, two tightly coiled leads, and a spare collar marked "Judy."

The SNO looked the dog up and down, checked out her gear, then, stone-faced and silent, moved on to the next crewman.

The day went on to include various tests of seamanship and emergency drills. About the only A+ the *Gnat* received was on its man overboard techniques, which they recently had a chance to practice with Judy. As the day dragged on, nerves frayed, and the men were closing in on exhaustion.

Suddenly, Judy, who was on the bridge, began barking ferociously. The crew feared the admiral would come down harder on them due to the racket, so they urged their dog to shut up. But she kept right on, her barking growing in intensity—and she began to point, like she was meant to do in the bush when a partridge was nearby. Some wondered if a floating cesspit was approaching.

The officers followed her outstretched nose out to the sky, where, for the first time, they noticed the outline of an airplane. As it got closer, they saw it bore Japanese markings. The scout plane dipped low, passed right over the bow, regained altitude, and flew off, disappearing into the distance.

Only then did Judy cease barking.

Radar was by that point in development under top secret conditions back in England, but here was a lowly mascot who could do the job for a pittance of the budget granted the scientists back home. "Remarkable," said Admiral Little. "Sound vibrations, presumably. The time may be coming when we all need a Judy on the bridge."

Judy would become an early-warning system in the days and years ahead, able to sense incoming aircraft—usually those with hostile intentions—well ahead of the crew of her ship. But what made her react by barking and pointing? It's possible that her instinctual response to a flying creature was kicking in at last. We know a plane is far different than a bird, but Judy didn't. To her, this was merely something that Tankey Cooper wanted her to point at, which she did. As it happened, her choice of objects to point toward was far more valuable than the occasional quail.

Whatever the biological reason for Judy's response, the incident lifted the tension and the admiral's desire to continue the inspection. With a ruffle of Judy's ears, he called a halt to the drilling. Once Little departed, the *Gnat* continued upriver toward its destination of Hankow, a strategic port city deep in the heart of the Yangtze Delta (part of a triumvirate of cities that make up modern Wuhan).

It was time for some shore leave.

When given a choice, the crew preferred to head out on the town in the "Paris of the East." Shanghai at the time was home to about forty thousand westerners in a city of ten million. The large majority were White Russians, who fled in force to China after the revolution of 1917. Despite the small population, the western *gwailos* controlled almost half of the sprawling city—appropriately enough, the western half. And it was the westerners who helped transform Shanghai into a modern metropolis, introducing inventions such as electricity and trams. British and American businessmen made a great deal of money in trade and finance, and Germans used Shanghai as a base for investing in China. At the time, the city accounted for half of the imports and exports of China.

Shanghai, a bustling city of endless entertainments, was the center of the action in East Asia. More worldly and diverse than the British protectorate of Hong Kong to the south, Shanghai catered to both sophisticates and lumpen proletariat. In the years leading up to the Second Sino-Japanese War, life in the British concession was a curious admixture of lively Asian city mores crossed with traditional English rural village life.

There were tennis and cricket clubs, tea services every afternoon (which the locals took to with enthusiasm), and, of course, pubs. And one of the ways the British concession stood out—and also contrasted with local values—was the keeping and cultivating of dogs as pets.

So it was that Judy was always welcome when she accompanied her fellow *Gnat* crewmembers out and about for whatever the night offered. Sometimes they visited a local establishment on the river, where overturned cardboard boxes served as chairs. Other times they were patrons at the highfalutin bars at the swank Park Hotel or Shanghai Race Club, where Judy's special status as an official member of the Royal Navy permitted her entry. Both scenes were central to the social whirl in the 1930s. The sailors were often provincial, unschooled types, educated in the fine points of navigation and perhaps river diplomacy, but not much else. But even if they didn't mix easily with the sophisticates who danced the night away at the Park, they were still right there alongside the swells at the hippest spots in "Shangers."

Gould Hunter Thomas, an American oil worker who captured his memories of old Shanghai in a memoir, noted, "People go and go and go in this town with many spending half their salary or more for entertainment." This was certainly true of the gunboat sailors, who had to cram weeks' worth of enjoyment into a night or two before getting back out on the river.

Since the British were used to having alcohol on board the gunboats (as were the other European sailors, who all had wine in their ship's stores), their sailors didn't go quite as ballistic as their American counterparts, who were eager to revel in the bacchanalia on offer once they were set loose upon the town. A "run ashore" for the Yanks—or as they called themselves, the "River Rats"—usually meant a freewheeling, two-fisted, epic bender that hopefully concluded with a penniless stagger back to the ship mere moments before she weighed anchor.

One American gunboat officer recalled, "After a long, dark, rainy winter, and with everything ashore knee-deep in mud, every man had squirreled away the equivalent of a half-bucket or more of silver dollars, burning to be invested in some way or other." The squalid dive bars and "gentlemen's clubs" of the Bund were always happy to put that cash into a treasury bond of some sort for the River Rats. As one of them put it, "The most of it goes for likker [*sic*] and wimmen [*sic*]. The rest I spend foolishly."

Bar brawls were legion and would break out over the slightest insult to ship or country. The river patrollers all knew one another very well, regardless of which ship or navy they were in, and the fights were often fueled more by tribal ritual than actual anger. The fisticuffs would ensue between nationalities, between ships of the same fleet, sometimes between fellow sailors who had grown tired of a shipmate's company. Alcohol brought out the dog in all of them, so to speak.

That went for Judy as well, whose propensity for beer-guzzling made her one of the boys. When in Hankow, the night often began and ended on Hankow Bund, the main road in the city, at a retrofitted canteen on the ground floor of the Hongkong and Shanghai Bank building. There was a piano, a pair of billiard tables, and English-speaking Chinese servants to fetch liquid refreshments all night long. In other words, it was heaven.

It was here that Judy was inaugurated into the Strong Toppers' Club, a drinking firm the British gunboatmen started back in the early days of the Yangtze patrols. The name derived from the lager the men drank in excess, a brand called EWO, that was topped with "horsehead," a mixture of onions, local herbs, and God only knew what else. The men drank it because they were gunboatmen, and that's what a gunboatman drank. Somewhere along the line this stuff was said to make a man out of you. All in all, it was not dissimilar to the rhino horn powder or snakeskin the locals ingested to improve their vigor and virility.

To win entry in the club, a prospective member had to face three judges while holding a beer in his left hand. He then shouted out, "Here's to the health of Cardinal Puff!" (the fictional cleric was used in military drinking games like this throughout the service). Next, he had to complete an elaborate series of hand and foot placements, capped off by the downing of the lager in a single swallow. He would then repeat this for "Cardinal Puff-Puff" and "Cardinal Puff-Puff-Puff," all while trebling the limb movements and of course downing more beer. If he managed to make it all the way through three beers without an error, he was given a membership card and taught the "Strong Toppers' Lament":

Strong Toppers are we
On the dirty Yangtze
Gunboats or cruisers
We're here for a spree

Although Judy's talents were legion, she was unable to undertake this particular debauched ritual. Instead, all she had to do was bark three times on cue, a trick Tankey Cooper taught her, and she was granted entrée in the club. She would wear her membership card affixed to her collar while in the bar, and it would otherwise hang on the bulkhead over her bed on the *Gnat*.

On nights out, Judy would wander through the frivolity, munching offered peanuts, slurping spilled beer, and hopping up on the men's laps for a pet. A different canteen in Wuhu offered a delicious assortment of ice cream, and Judy quickly became enamored of the sweet stuff, always begging for a bowlful. One time, her plaintive whines went ignored, so she ambled behind the bar and pulled out a large carton of vanilla, which she dragged into the center of the room. She received her scoop in short order after that.

Inevitably, all the beer and dairy products combined to give Judy a powerful stomachache. After a typical night out, Judy would be unable to sleep through the night. So she would waddle over to the ship's dispensary, where Chief Sick Berth Attendant William Wilson would look after her. "I sometimes gave her a dose of [the children's laxative] Syrup of Blackthorn," he would remember years later.

It wasn't only in the bars that Judy offered her easy affinity and friendly rapport to the men. She also accompanied them, in particular Cooper, Jeffery, and Vic Oliver, on long runs through the countryside. When the sailors chose up sides for soccer or rugby, she was out there on the pitch, doing her level best to keep up. While she wasn't especially good at either (nor was the *Gnat*'s crew, as they would freely admit), Judy was more of a natural at field hockey. At the sight of a loose ball she would streak in, grab it in her mouth, and gallop over to the nearest goal, scoring with impunity for both sides. The men would subtract Judy's goals to arrive at a final score.

One sailor, Chief Petty Officer Charles Goodyear, served on a different gunboat, the HMS *Bee*. He was close friends with Oliver, and through him became close with Judy as well, whom he met on a night of revelry. From then on he ensured the dog would come out with them anytime the *Gnat* and the *Bee* were in port together, and he visited her on the ship many times. A favorite haunt was the Pig and Whistle, a British-style pub in Shanghai. There was a reason Goodyear insisted on returning to the bar—he was goggle-eyed over a young Russian widow who had come to China to work as a barmaid. One thing led to another, and Goodyear married the Russian woman. He made sure that Judy attended the ceremony.

But this was largely a world without women, and Judy, though not quite a replacement, offered a hint of the domesticity and companionship the men lived without during their hard tours on the river. She also provided something beyond friendship for these men: she had proven her tremendous ability to warn her friends of coming danger, be it from the air or by sea. She did it on land as well, most notably during an excursion in Kiu-kiang (now Jiujiang), a pretty little burg along the Yangtze.

Jeffery had taken Judy for a walk along a path that abutted the jungle. "We walked about a mile and turned back toward the hotel," the CPO recorded in his diary. "Suddenly Judy left me and darted into the jungle. I knew there were deer about because I'd seen their tracks. I thought she was just having some fun when I heard her yelp. I called her and she came out trembling. Before I could touch her, she ran ahead of me, keeping to the road. I stopped and looked back and saw in the bush a big leopard. I thought, 'That's what frightened Judy.'

"Only later did I wonder whether Judy had smelt [*sic*] the leopard and distracted its attention so it wouldn't attack me."

In the years to come, several others would have reason to wonder about Judy's motivations after she had saved them in one way or another.

CHAPTER 4

War

In July of 1937, Japanese and Chinese forces clashed at the Marco Polo Bridge that connected Peking to the Manchuria-China border. It was a small engagement, but it provided an excuse for the Japanese emperor to demand that China disengage from the area. (Many historians feel the incident was fabricated by the Japanese in order to instigate war.) When the Chinese refused to create a buffer zone in their territory, Japan bombed several cities and brought troops into China proper.

To the westerners partying all night in Shanghai, war still seemed very far away. The squabbling among the Asians mattered very little to the merchants and import-export mavens, so long as trade continued unabated. Writer Edgar Snow accused Americans in Shanghai of living in a "comfortable but hermetically sealed glass case." Gould Hunter Thomas thought Shanghai was "a world unto itself. Many of the foreigners here seem to have lost their home ties. On the other hand, they know less about China and the Chinese than the person who stays home and reads about it."

After touring Shanghai in this period, English writer Charles Isherwood pointed out that the bullets and artillery flying to the north had changed nothing in Shanghai:

> The tired or lustful business man will find here everything to gratify his desires. You can buy an electric razor or a French dinner, or a well-cut suit. You can dance at the Tower Restaurant on the roof of the Cathay Hotel, and gossip with Freddy Kaufmann, its charming

> manager, about the European aristocracy or pre-Hitler Berlin. You can attend race-meetings, baseball games, football matches. You can see the latest American films. If you want girls, or boys, you can have them, at all prices, in the bath-houses and the brothels. If you want opium you can smoke it in the best company, served on a tray, like afternoon tea. . . . Finally, if you ever repent, there are churches and chapels of all denominations.

But in August of 1937, the Imperial Japanese Army (IJA) was suddenly at the door, threatening to shatter the bubble encasing the Yanks and Brits in Shanghai. Attempts to defuse tensions after the Marco Polo Bridge incident failed, largely because of militarists in the Japanese high command. Full-scale fighting began in late July, and soon one million troops, backed by naval and airpower, were at the gates of Shanghai.

By late August, the Japanese had laid siege to the city. "People stood on their apartment roofs and watched Japanese dive bombers, right before their eyes, emptying tons of bombs on the Chinese trenches hidden beyond the horizon of tile and masonry," wrote Snow. "Guests at the swank Park Hotel, in the security of Bubbling Well Road, could gaze out through the spacious glass facade of its top story dining room, while contentedly sipping their demitasse, and check up on the marksmanship of the Japanese batteries." Many westerners, to whom the local Chinese population was invisible, were dismayed that the town's hopping nightlife was besmirched. A reporter for *Time* pointed out, "The roulette tables at Joe Farren's, the Park Hotel's Sky Terrace, and Sir Victor Sassoon's Tower Night Club had none of their old sparkle."

The United States rushed in the 6th Marine Regiment to protect the American settlement in the city, and thousands of westerners were evacuated. Eventually, Chiang Kai-shek was forced to move his government west up the Yangtze, and the Japanese left a demolished, depopulated Shanghai in their wake, with an estimated two hundred thousand Chinese deaths (and nearly one hundred thousand more casualties).

Nanking, the nearby capital, was treated even worse. The infamous Rape of Nanking was an inhumane atrocity. "Wholesale looting, the violation of women, the murder of civilians, the eviction of Chinese from their homes, mass executions of war prisoners, and the impressing of able-bodied men turned Nanking into a city of terror," wrote Frank Tillman Durdin in the *New York Times* just before he escaped the burning city. Another reporter who stayed in Nanking until the last possible moment was C. Yates McDaniel of the Associated Press. He wrote, "My last remembrance of Nanking: Dead Chinese, dead Chinese, dead Chinese."

The Great Powers of the west were outraged and sent strong protests to Japan, but there was no response. The militarists pulling strings behind the emperor were not about to be dictated to by colonist powers an ocean away. So the fighting continued, and despite the wanton destruction of its cities and civilians, and despite being badly outgunned, the Chinese Army proved far tougher than the Japanese had anticipated. On the Yangtze, Judy and her fellow British and American gunboatmen found themselves in a difficult position. Their countries were not involved in the war, and the ships flying the Stars and Stripes and Union Jack remained untouched for the moment. But ignoring the carnage about them was hard, particularly because the sailors had grown close to the Chinese people, many of whom were now being killed by the Japanese.

For protection, the *Gnat* teamed up with an American gunboat, the USS *Panay,* to patrol the river. The *Panay* had come on station only a few years earlier, one of the new class of American gunboats that were larger and more heavily armed than her predecessors. *Panay* was too big to navigate the water where the huge gorges segmented the river, so she spent most of her time in the main channels between Shanghai and Hankow. This suited the crew just fine, for the good times on offer in those ports offset the fact that the *Panay* was a regular target for gunfire coming from trigger-happy locals, who either mistook the River Rats for the enemy or were overeager to protect their turf. The ship's captain, Lieutenant Commander R. A. Dyer, reported that "firing on gunboats and merchant ships have [*sic*] become so routine that any vessel traversing the Yangtze River sails with the expectation of being fired upon. Fortunately, the Chinese appear to be rather poor marksmen and the ship has, so far, not sustained any casualties in these engagements."

Not even the destruction going on downstream could keep the gunboatmen from their grog, and the crew prided themselves on being able to find fun no matter where they were docked for shore leave. The companies of the *Panay* and the *Gnat* got along very well, and early in their partnership they went out for some bonding in a small riverside village bar. After mass quantities of alcohol were consumed, the sailors stumbled back to their respective ships. Tankey Cooper was almost halfway up the gangway when he noticed Judy was missing.

He asked everyone who had been ashore if they had seen Judy since leaving the canteen. Then he asked everyone who had stayed on board. He radioed the *Panay* and asked them about the dog, who had instantly won over the Yank sailors as well. "No sign of her, sorry," came the reply.

Against regulations, Cooper went back ashore and scoured the area, to no avail. He got no sleep that night and was still upset the next day when the "villager telegraph" sent word to Cooper: Judy was being held captive aboard the *Panay* after all.

Late that night, Cooper and another sailor took a sampan and crept up to the *Panay*'s rail. Showing the agility of the best pirates, they slipped on board the American vessel without being detected. After a few minutes, they returned, heavily laden, to the sampan, and silently made it back to the *Gnat*.

The next day, the *Gnat* received a signal from the *Panay:* "Boarded in the night by pirates. Ship's bell stolen."

The reply was swift: "We were also pirated—of Judy. Will swap one bell belonging to USS *Panay* for one lady named Judy, property of officers and ship's company of HMS *Gnat*."

The exchange was made within the hour. The point was made as well—no one dared abscond with such a beloved member of the *Gnat*'s crew.

Such revelry came to a halt a couple of weeks later, when the Japanese began attacking the gunboats in earnest. Nanking was in her death throes, and the last of the Chinese resistance fled the city on December 11. The worst of the atrocities followed in the wake of this collapse. The *Panay* was concerned with the fate of the American citizens still in the city. The gunboat signaled farewell to the *Gnat,* which went upriver to escort several cargo steamers. The *Panay,* amid mass chaos and with bombs dropping all around her, evacuated the fourteen remaining Americans from Nanking, including embassy staff. Also rescued was a pair of newsreel cameramen, Norman Alley of Universal News and Eric Mayell of Movietone News. Now under the direction of Lieutenant Commander James J.

Hughes of New York, the *Panay* then sailed upriver several miles to safeguard the progress of three U.S. oil steamers carrying crude for Standard Oil (along with dozens of company employees fleeing Nanking).

On December 12, Japanese aircraft were ordered to attack "any and all ships" sailing the Yangtze above Nanking. This order was considered so aggressive that the navy, whose airplanes controlled the skies over the river, asked for it to be confirmed. "Bomb away" was the reply, and at about one thirty p.m., the sound of approaching aircraft was heard on the American ships. Judy was not on board to bark a warning that the inbounds were hostiles, but Lieutenant Commander Hughes assumed the large American flags painted on the white hull and bridge of the ship would protect them from any attacks.

Not so. The three Japanese bombers and nine fighters bombed and strafed the quartet of American ships with murderous intent. All four ships were sunk in the attack. Three crewmen of the *Panay* were killed and forty-three more were wounded, along with five of the civilians she was evacuating. The newsreel men captured dramatic footage of the attack and, after they had abandoned ship and been rowed ashore, the sinking of the *Panay*. The hulks of the vessels destroyed during the attack remained burning and visible along the shores of the great river for weeks.

Angry recrimination and negotiation followed. The Japanese accepted responsibility, though they claimed the attack was unintentional (two British merchant ships and two other British gunboats were fired upon the very same day, which made the "Who, us?" statements of the Japanese seem suspect). An indemnity of $2 million ($33.5 million in today's cash) was paid to the United States, but the money did little to soothe frayed relations. Hostilities between Japan and America truly began that day.

This was the most stressful of several tense moments to follow between the invaders who wanted to exploit China and the western powers who claimed rights to be there. Japanese officers became a common sight aboard the *Gnat* and the other gunboats, particularly following any episodes where sailors intervened on behalf of the Chinese in one fashion or another. Judy often greeted these visiting Japanese with bared teeth and snarls, not having lost her anger for the people who had first treated her so badly back in Shanghai when she was a pup. It got so bad that Judy had to be confined belowdecks when a Japanese representative came aboard.

The *Panay* bombing and the tensions that followed were both a fitting end to what had been a fraught 1937 and a sharp foreshadowing of the devastation that was to come in the near future. In some respects, the eventual atomic destruction of Hiroshima and Nagasaki came as a direct result of the sinking of the *Panay.* But the full-scale war that sucked the western allies into the Pacific conflict was still over the horizon. In the meantime, Judy would take advantage of the relative peace that existed to follow her natural instincts.

CHAPTER 5

Amour

Judy was considered dear by pretty much everyone she encountered who was not Japanese. And she didn't discriminate against other Asians—she grew especially close to some of the Chinese who spent time on and around the *Gnat.* One of her favorites was a Mr. Sung, aka Joe Binks, who was the official procurer of provisions and supplies for the Royal Navy in Hankow. His position was known as "compradore," and it was a posting of considerable prestige and importance. Joe not only ensured the boats got all the grub, grog, and gunpowder they needed, but also served as an all-purpose fixer and occasional Father Confessor to the swabbies.

Joe would often bring his four children on board when the *Gnat* docked at Hankow, and it was here that Judy was first able to play and romp with kids. Dogs often have a special relationship with human children, generally because their smaller size allows for a more equal footing. And after considerable time spent in the company of grown men, it was a special treat for Judy to nip at the youngsters' heels, chase the balls they threw for her, and bask in their unadulterated love.

A woman known as Amah, as well as her children, also vied for Judy's affection. Amah directly translated to "servant" in the local tongue (elsewhere in Asia it can mean "maid" or "mother"), but this woman was much more of an entrepreneur, having bargained for and won the right to serve as the *Gnat*'s all-purpose boat. Amah ferried people and goods to and fro, carried excess supplies, fished for fresh provisions, and carried workers who cooked on board or painted the forever muddy hull.

When Amah became a regular alongside the *Gnat,* Judy had a consistent group of children with whom to have fun. Indeed, Judy spent almost as much time aboard Amah's large sampan as she did on the *Gnat.* The seamstress aboard Amah's sampan also held Judy in a hypnotic spell, apparently due to the soft melodies that she sang while fixing the dress whites or cargo pants of the sailors. Judy would trot next to "Sew-Sew" as she traveled between the warship and Amah's sampan.

But Judy was closest with four of the sailors aboard the *Gnat:* CPO Jeffery, who had plucked her from the kennel back in Shanghai; Bill Wilson, who treated her when she overate, suffered a hangover, or fell into the muck; Vic Oliver, who had saved Judy from the river; and Tankey Cooper, who made sure Judy got her meals.

Alas, by mid-1938, all four of Judy's pals had rotated off the *Gnat* and onto other ships in the fleet. Tears flowed as each man left the ship and the mascot he had come to love. They ruffled Judy's ears and received a warm lick from that ever-smiling mouth one last time. This was no ordinary farewell to a cute but ultimately forgettable dog. Indeed, all four men would carry memories of this exceptional pointer for decades, well into the stage in their lives when they recalled little else of their days spent patrolling the Yangtze.

Judy displayed her sadness at each friend's departure, but the truth was that she had yet to form a truly special and uncommon bond with any human. She spread her emotions among multiple entities, as though not wanting to risk giving herself fully over to a single person.

But then love—or at least lust—entered her life for the first time.

The *Ladybird* was one of the ships fired upon by the Japanese the same day the *Panay* was sunk, but prior to that, the ship had had an outsized influence on the lives of the *Gnat*'s crew—after all, it was exposure to her giant mascot, Bonzo, that convinced the men they needed a dog of their own on board. But after Judy arrived, she had to be hidden belowdecks whenever the two ships got together, because Bonzo went crazy in her company. It was readily apparent he had taken a strong fancy to Judy; not surprising, really, when one considers the dog spent all of his time without the company of females of any variety. But Judy never reciprocated his affections—instead, she growled with anger at the terrier-boxer mutt. The *Gnat* men considered Bonzo beneath the dignity of their beloved Judy anyway, so they kept her away from Bonzo's crude advances.

True to stereotype, it took a suave French *chien* to break down Judy's walls and win her heart.

In addition to the *Panay,* a French gunboat, the *Francis Garnier,* combined operations with the *Gnat* from time to time. One day in the spring of '38, the *Francis Garnier* was anchored next to the *Gnat,* and Judy was belowdecks with her new close pal, a boyish able seaman with the surname Boniface, known throughout the ship as "Bonny." The young man had taken over the ship's stores duty from Jan Cooper, so naturally Judy gravitated to the new man in charge of the food and ale.

The sailor was trying unsuccessfully to write a letter to a sweetheart he had met in Shanghai. But Judy was acting strangely, motioning to the ladder and tugging at Bonny's leg. At last, he put down his pen and took her up on deck.

Once there, however, Judy remained coolly dismissive. Head up, tail out straight, she paraded up and down the foredeck, ignoring the sailor's calls and any attempts to play.

When the sailors looked across the water to where the *Francis Garnier* was anchored, they soon began to understand Judy's odd actions. For up on the deck of the French ship was another pedigree pointer, in most ways the spitting image of Judy—only male.

His name was Paul, and he had his forelegs up on the railing and his eyes on Judy's every move. After a few minutes, Judy scampered back down belowdecks, leaving the *Gnat* crew in stitches. "Just like a lady," Boniface said, laughing as he fed her. "Didn't even look at him, just showed herself and disappeared."

Paul may have been on a French boat, but he wasn't exactly a lady-killer. His version of savoir faire was to pratfall almost immediately in Judy's presence, legs splaying akimbo and chin hitting the deck hard. He galloped this way and that, eagerly displaying his manly qualities for the dog he loved at first sight. Judy remained coy, at times ignoring her fellow pointer, other times snapping at him with her sharp teeth.

One day, when the two ships were tied together for an officers' strategy meeting, Paul took the opportunity to show off his athleticism. He sprinted the length of the ship, his flanks heaving, his tongue lapping to one side. But the guardrails on the *Francis Garnier* didn't extend all the way around, and Paul was unable to stop his dash in time. He plunged right off the side of the ship and into the muddy river. Fortunately, he was close to the shore, and a group of villagers waded in to rescue him.

Judy was no longer prim and reserved. When Paul hit the water, she began barking and whining, and attempted to jump in after the French boat's mascot. When Paul made it over to the *Gnat* after his rescue, Judy licked his face and nuzzled him.

The ice had been broken.

Judy spent the rest of the day exploring the French ship, having been given a special "tour" by her suitor. When she came back aboard the *Gnat,* several crewmen, including Boniface, gathered around her and ordered her to sit. Years later, he remembered the speech he delivered.

"We feel that the time has come for us to have a serious talk," Bonny began. "We are, so to speak, your legal guardians, and we naturally want to do our best for your happiness. But everything must be done properly and according to the rules and the finest navy tradition."

Judy cocked her head and licked his palm.

"Paul is a very nice dog, with a pedigree too, and they are a very nice bunch over on the *Francis Garnier.* So with our permission, you can get engaged today, and married tomorrow!"

The group cheered, and Judy seemed to understand something good was afoot, for she began to run in an excited circle.

"Remember," Boniface continued, "the first puppy will be called Bonny."

One of the men, the ship's electrician, pulled out a small anklet he had designed just for the occasion and slipped it over Judy's front left leg.

"And that," he said, "is your engagement ring."

Just after lunch the next day, the men of both ships gathered on the deck of the *Gnat* for the ceremony. They were lined up and dressed in their full formal attire. A small group of curious Chinese watched from shore. The two dogs were led out by the tankeys of either ship—Bonny of the *Gnat* and a sailor named LaPointe from the *Francis Garnier.*

Boniface boomed out, "I now pronounce thee . . . ," then looked at the sea of smiling faces for inspiration. "Dog and dog? Dog and bitch? Paul and Judy? What?"

The first lieutenant from the French gunboat called out, "Just pronounce them as one!"

Bonny did just that, and the two dogs were then free to consummate their marriage.

Paul remained aboard the *Gnat* for three days, and he and Judy were seldom seen, cozied up as they were in their specially constructed "love nest" in the forward mess. After seventy-two companionable hours, Paul was led back to his ship, protesting loudly all the way.

Shortly thereafter, Judy was plump with puppies. She began moving more carefully as she gained weight, going out of her way not to disturb the lives growing in her pregnant belly.

After the standard canine gestation period of nine weeks, Bonny came sliding down the ladder to inform his dining colleagues that Judy had given birth. Her litter numbered thirteen puppies, three of which, the extreme runts, didn't last through the day. The other ten suckled happily, quickly growing tubby thanks in part to the extra milk and grains constantly being fed to them by the steady stream of visitors to the *Gnat,* who were all eager to see the new additions to the crew.

Paul was out of sight for a while, until the *Francis Garnier* returned from operations and caught up with the *Gnat*. Upon their reunion, the proud parents were led on exercise walks, with the ten pups, all on a leash of their own, following closely behind. The French sailors reported that Paul had been acting oddly over the past few weeks, as though aware he was missing out on an event of great importance.

One dog worked out just fine for the gunboat, but eleven were too many. The pups swarmed the ship on their chubby legs, gnawing on slipcovers, ammo belts, canvas sails, and everything else that wasn't metal. They also left puddles all over the boat.

Inevitably, Lieutenant Commander Waldegrave made the difficult decision—the pups had to go. The men of the *Francis Garnier* took several, the pick of the litter, as they weren't worried about adding to their ship's canine roster. The officials at the Hankow Race Club traded their field gun and several pans of ammo for another pup, fearing that the weaponry would lead to unwanted Japanese attention. A couple of pups went to the British Consulate, and another to the crew of the American gunboat *Guam*. The last was gifted to a Scottish engineer working aboard a river steamer who had helped the *Gnat* crew with a particularly knotty repair one day.

Judy was upset by the loss of her litter for a time, but she soon regained her wits. That was necessary, for while the "wedding" and "honeymoon" took place during a relatively quiet period in the war—well after the *Panay* incident had sparked tensions between Japan and the west—the Japanese once more began bombing the gunboats. Indeed, the *Gnat* had been missing Judy's early-warning system. On the day of the birth of her pups, while Judy was otherwise occupied, a pair of Japanese bombers had appeared suddenly overhead. Luckily, they were chased off by a squadron of Chinese fighters after dropping a few wayward bombs.

During the latter months of 1938, Japanese supremacy over the Yangtze valley was being challenged more and more by the Chinese Air Force, a motley group of planes flown by an even more diverse group of pilots—some Chinese, but many more American, British, and Russian. Indeed, the commander of the Chinese Air Force, General Claire Lee Chennault, was an American, and he would later play an important role as leader of the fabled Flying Tigers when full-scale war broke out.

Interestingly, the *Gnat* made a significant contribution to the tilting of power in the skies over China during the Sino-Japanese War. The ship's telegraphist, a man named Stanley Cotterrall, had fallen ill and was taken to the American Mission Hospital in Wuhu. As it happened, the infirmary lay directly in a heavily used flight path for Japanese bombers seeking targets on the Yangtze. Hours after Cotterrall's operation, he heard the distinct rumble of Japanese planes fly over the hospital. He prevailed upon his surgeons to let him go to the roof to signal ships in the area that trouble was on the way. "What's the point of having a telegraphist here if you don't make use of him?" Cotterrall said to his skeptical doctors. The gunboatman then taught Morse code and fundamental telegraph operations to several of the hospital staff, and western shipping suddenly had an early-warning system in place. Between these signals and Judy's barking, the *Gnat* was never caught unaware, and Chinese planes always appeared in the nick of time, much to the frustration of the Japanese.

Meanwhile, Judy continued to fight her own personal war against the

Japanese. One morning in October of 1938, she went for an exercise run along the water with Boniface and another sailor, Leading Seaman Jack Law, when they encountered a Japanese soldier on patrol duty along the boardwalk. Usually, the sailors were able to divert Judy from the armed Japanese men she loathed, but on this occasion, she didn't have her usual reaction. She walked up to the soldier with bowed head and ducked tail, and began sniffing at his boots.

The soldier reacted with unusual anger, screaming and kicking at Judy. Judy didn't scamper away, though. Instead, she rose up, hair on end, and began growling ferociously at the soldier. The Japanese sentry stepped back, pulled on his rifle's bolt action, and leveled his gun at Judy.

There was no question of the soldier's intent, and Law reacted instinctively. The burly Law raced to the soldier, picked him up, and threw him in the river.

After ensuring the man didn't actually drown, the crewmen and Judy hightailed it back to the *Gnat.* For several days, Japanese diplomats and officers visited the ship's wardroom for high-level negotiations over the incident. Finally, after the downing of many glasses of rum and sake, an agreement was reached. The Japanese would forget about the manhandling of their soldier, and Judy would be confined to the ship while in the Hankow anchorage from then on.

CHAPTER 6

War Dogs

By the summer of 1939, war was rapidly approaching in Europe. Though fighting had been going on for some time in China, the Royal Navy had only just decided to upgrade their military presence in the region. That meant a new posting for Judy and much of the *Gnat*'s crew. The aging Insect class of gunboats was augmented by bigger, faster, more powerful boats, with names like *Dragonfly, Scorpion,* and Judy's new billet, the HMS *Grasshopper. Gnat* would see duty in Africa ahead, winding up as a stationary port defense boat in Egypt during World War II.

The new generation of gunboats scarcely got a chance to safeguard the Yangtze. On September 1, Germany invaded Poland, touching off the official start of World War II. The British Admiralty, foreseeing a future Japanese-German alliance, opted for the conservative strategy of pulling the gunboats out of China and back to the empire's strongest position in Asia, the citadel at Singapore.

For the first time in her life, Judy would be leaving China. The *Grasshopper* sailed into the East China Sea and turned south. She would never return to the city of her birth.

The initial voyage to Hong Kong wasn't a particularly treacherous one, but for the pointer, accustomed as she was to the relatively gentle conditions on the river, the oceanic cruise was torture. Seasickness affects all mammals, not just humans, and Judy spent much of the trip puking her guts out. The crew tried to help her by withholding food and demanding she take her daily exercise, but it wasn't until the final eighteen hours of the trip that Judy got her sea legs and returned to her usual joyful self. "She's eating like a horse," recorded the coxswain in the ship's log. After a short stopover in Hong Kong, the *Grasshopper* proceeded to its new home.

The British colony of Singapore, a diamond-shaped island only fifteen miles long and twenty-five miles across, was both a relief and a jarring reminder of life in the "real navy." Judy and the sailors left behind China's active war zone for a peaceful, almost hedonistic city, where pleasures like two sets of doubles and Singapore Slings at the fabled Long Bar in the Raffles Hotel were far more important than preparing for hostilities. In that sense, Singapore resembled the carefree days enjoyed by the westerners in Shanghai before the Japanese put an end to the frivolity. It was, in the parlance of the sizable British population, the land of "stinks, Chinks, and drinks"—an intoxicating blend of exotic Asian culture, cloying humidity, heavy alcohol consumption, and poor sewage treatment.

At the same time, the gunboatmen were no longer free to zip up and down the Yangtze as virtually independent operators. They were now serving on an active and vitally important Royal Navy base, and the first few weeks of regular salutes and snap inspections came as a shock to the crew. Shirts had to be tucked in (and worn in the first place), stubble had to be removed daily, and the boat needed to be spotless at all times. Judy, too, felt the change. While no superior officer took displeasure at the thought of her serving as mascot, her movements were strictly prescribed, and she could no longer wander with complete impunity to all areas of the ship, or carouse with the same indifference to the next day's consequences.

War was inching closer to enveloping the world in its death grip. Soon enough, Judy once again would be hearing the sounds of guns at full roar. But halfway around the world, other dogs were already finding themselves in the thick of it.

The use of dogs in warfare probably dates to at least the seventh century BC, when the war dogs of Magnesia helped fight the invading Ephesians. During battles, the dogs (a surviving epitaph shows that one was named Lethargos) were released to initiate the combat and break the ranks of the invaders, then were followed by a cavalry charge. Two centuries later, the Persians used a bit of psychological warfare with dogs, bringing hundreds of the animals to the front lines in order to unsettle their Egyptian opponents, who saw the animals as gods. Dogs were on the battlefield at Marathon and Thermopylae, and they served alongside the Roman legions across the empire.

In more modern times, dogs have been present for nearly every engagement, major and minor, the world over. In the American Civil War, dogs marched with soldiers singing the "Battle Hymn of the Republic" or "Dixie." There is a memorial to a Boston terrier named Sallie on the hallowed grounds of the Gettysburg Battlefield National Monument. The mascot of the 11th Pennsylvania Volunteers, Sallie stuck with the boys of the unit from inception through the fight at Gettysburg and all the way to 1865, when she was shot and killed in Virginia. Hundreds of thousands of visitors each year read the following inscription describing the value dogs added to the units in the War Between the States:

TO SOLDIERS FAR FROM LOVED ONES,
THEY WERE A FRIENDLY FACE FROM HOME.
TO THE WOUNDED, HOPE;
TO THE DYING, A FINAL SOLACE.
TO THE VETERANS, THEIR MEMORY WAS
EVERLASTING.

Many dogs served without achieving such lasting fanfare. In April 1862, a lone female passenger detrained in the small Tennessee town of Shiloh. The last time Mrs. Louis Pfeiff had heard from her husband, he had been about to march into Shiloh, where the Army of the Tennessee under Ulysses S. Grant was invading the western front of the Confederacy. In the bloodiest battle of the war to that point, the northerners took Shiloh. But Lieutenant Pfeiff of the 3rd Illinois Infantry had disappeared. So his beloved took the train from Chicago down to Tennessee to find out for herself what had happened.

She searched among the roughly twenty thousand dead and wounded men, to no avail. She was about to give up and return home when she spotted her husband's dog trotting toward her. The small pooch had been in combat with her master, and now she led Mrs. Pfeiff away from the town to a remote field, all the way to the unmarked grave in which Louis was buried. Asking around, Mrs. Pfeiff discovered that the dog had been there when Louis was shot, stayed by his side until he died, and then faithfully kept watch at the grave site for twelve days. The dog then took the train back to Chicago with Mrs. Pfeiff.

World War I was far more dangerous terrain for dogs (and humans) than even the Civil War had been. The advent of the machine gun, poison gas, and the battle tank took its toll on the sizable number of dogs that roamed the trenches. Two breeds in particular were common, especially on the German side. Doberman pinschers and German shepherds were both native to the land of the kaiser, and the Imperial German Army used plenty of them. They were highly intelligent and easily trainable, attributes that made them excellent guards. In addition, their dark coats allowed the dogs to slip across the nighttime terrain without alerting the enemy. Both sides also used terriers trained as "ratters" to comb the trenches for vermin. But mainly the dogs served as sentries, scouts, and messengers, as well as mascots. Some twenty thousand dogs were recruited from the Battersea Dogs Home in London alone for the express purpose of fighting on the western front.

A Boston terrier by the name of Sergeant Stubby was one of the few dogs brought across the Atlantic by American forces. Stubby initially served as a mascot, but his role grew significantly from there. He was a stray in New Haven, Connecticut, living off scraps of garbage, when he chanced upon the Yale University parade grounds where the soldiers of the 26th Yankee Division were training to go fight in Europe. An infantryman named John Conroy adopted him, named him Stubby for his truncated tail, and made the dog mascot of the force. In what would become a common scenario involving dogs and the soldiers who loved them, Conroy was too enamored of Stubby to leave him behind when it was time to ship out. So he smuggled the terrier aboard his troopship, and Stubby was soon running through the trenches of France, his nose in the mud.

Stubby took shrapnel at the Battle of Seicheprey, the first blooding of the war for American troops. After convalescing, the dog fought on until the war's finish. He was with the Yankee Division at famous battles like St. Mihiel, the Marne, and Château-Thierry. The dog wasn't spared the horrors of war—he was gassed, wounded a second time, and even caught a German spy mapping trenches in the Argonne Forest. After the war, Stubby received many awards and accolades, including a gold medal from the Humane Education Society. The pugnacious little terrier became a celebrity upon returning to America: he led multiple parades, met three different presidents (Wilson, Coolidge, and Harding), was offered free food for life by the YMCA, and stayed in five-star hotels.

The *New York Times* saw fit to run an obituary when America's most famous war dog passed on in 1926. It read, in part:

> On Feb. 5, 1918, he entered the front lines of the Chemin des Dames sector, north of Soissons, where he was under fire night and day for more than a month. The noise and strain that shattered the nerves of many of his comrades did not impair Stubby's spirits. Not because he was unconscious of danger. His angry howl while a battle raged and his mad canter from one part of the lines to another indicated realization. But he seemed to know that the greatest service he could render was comfort and cheerfulness.

Stubby lives on at an exhibit dedicated to him at the Smithsonian.

By the Second World War, canines performed all manner of exploits. The first dogs to make an impact during World War II were rescue animals in England that scoured the rubble in the wake of the Blitz, locating and saving hundreds of victims. They became national heroes for their work. The U.S. and British armies also trained dogs to be paratroopers, dropping them into hot spots across Europe. In the Soviet Union, dogs were used as an eerie preview of the coming kamikaze attacks (and later human suicide bombers). Explosives were strapped to their bodies, and the dogs were sent to scurry under invading German tanks, destroying both the tanks and themselves in the process.

They were scouts, messengers, mine sniffers. They detected ambushes on Pacific islands and in European mountain passes. But most of all, every dog that spent any time with troops in the field became a treasured friend, sharing the special bond that only exists between brothers under fire.

At the time of Pearl Harbor, the sled dog was the only working type to be found in the U.S. Army. But that changed quickly, as guard dogs in particular were needed to defend suddenly vulnerable installations, such as factories and arsenals, especially on the coasts. Shortly thereafter, the War Dog Program was instituted to provide thousands of canines for use overseas. The British reported that their dogs in North Africa were easily frightened and disoriented by artillery fire and heavy bombing. So the first thing trainers did was attempt to desensitize the dogs to the deafening noise of the modern battlefield.

The specialized training paid off, and many dogs went on to perform heroic deeds under fire. Chips, a mixed breed (a little husky, some collie, and some German shepherd), was part of the first War Dog Detachment to be sent overseas with American troops. One of his initial duties was to stand guard outside the rooms in Casablanca where President Roosevelt and Prime Minister Churchill discussed strategy in 1943. He then traveled from Africa to Italy to France and to Germany, seeing combat at every stop.

It was in Sicily in 1943 when Chips spotted an enemy pillbox (a concrete dugout where several troops could fight from within), broke away from his handler, and attacked the machine gun crew inside. He seized one man, then forced the entire four-person crew to surrender.

In recognition of his service, the theater forces awarded him the Silver Star and the Purple Heart, and his unit unofficially awarded him the Theater Ribbon, with the arrowhead for an assault landing and a battle star for each of the eight campaigns in which he participated. Not everyone was as blown away by his bravery, however. After the war, the Pentagon decided that awarding citations to dogs was "contrary to Army policy" and stripped Chips of his medals. That may help to explain why Chips reacted to meeting General Eisenhower by biting him.

Wolf was a Doberman, and a brave one. He was leading an infantry patrol in the mountains of northern Luzon in the Philippines when the scent of the enemy wafted past his powerful nose. His warning allowed the men to take favorable positions on a hillside. In the ensuing firefight, Wolf took shrapnel wounds but stoically stayed quiet, not allowing the Japanese to lock in on where the soldiers were located. Wolf then led the withdrawal, sniffing out ambushes three different times. At last, they made it to headquarters, where Wolf was rushed into emergency surgery.

Alas, his wounds were too severe. Wolf, U.S. Army War Dog T121, died on the operating table.

Some of the dogs mixed heroism with other human characteristics. The ultimate example was Sinbad, the mascot of the Coast Guard cutter *Campbell.* He became famous enough for his exploits on and off the ship that *Life* magazine profiled him in December 1943, describing his lineage as "liberty-rum-chow-hound, with a bit of bulldog, doberman pinscher, and what-not. Mostly what-not."

The *Campbell* escorted ships carrying vital matériel to the Allies in Europe, hunted submarines off the U.S. East Coast, and rescued drowning sailors from torpedoed ships. Sinbad was along for all of it, on board as the cutter plowed through frosty North Atlantic seas.

Sinbad was indeed brave and capable. During a twelve-hour battle with the Nazi submarine *U-606,* the American ship sustained heavy damage. Most of the crew were taken off, but a hardy few stayed on board and patched the hull, keeping her afloat as the water rushed through the multiple holes punched in her side. Sinbad was one of those who remained, sensing the morale boost he could offer. "If Sinbad is aboard, the *Campbell* will stay afloat," promised the captain. And indeed, the cutter made it back to port.

It was this sort of dedication to duty that earned Sinbad an actual rank in the Coast Guard, that of chief petty officer (dog), complete with all the necessary enlistment forms and other official paperwork, uniforms, and even his own bunk—which he usually eschewed, preferring to snuggle up at the feet of the crew in their racks.

In the finest tradition of the rambunctious seaman, Sinbad caused plenty of trouble, but made up for it by coming through when it mattered. "Sinbad is a salty sailor but he's not a *good* sailor," wrote *Coast Guard* magazine. "He'll never rate gold hashmarks nor Good Conduct Medals. He's been on report several times and he's raised hell in a number of ports. On a few occasions, he has embarrassed the United States Government by creating disturbances in foreign zones. Perhaps that's why Coast Guardsmen love Sinbad; he's as bad as the worst and as good as the best of us."

And like many sailors, of every era, Sinbad enjoyed his time ashore. Truly, the dog was something of a drunk. Sinbad loved to belly up to the bar for a whiskey and a beer, usually getting served before his mates. He seldom hung out with the officers, preferring the company of the crew, who worshipped the little dog that spent nights curled in their bunks. Even though Sinbad would drink a lot on his nights out, the ship's doctor would give him—along with the other hungover crewmen—an aspirin the next morning and off to work he would go.

Sinbad's rough edges only increased his popularity. Newspapers in the United States and Europe followed his every move. In Ireland, society pages trumpeted the news every time the *Campbell* pulled into one of the country's ports. A biography of his life, *Sinbad of the Coast Guard,* became a bestseller. Sinbad was a four-legged version of the barfly Norm from *Cheers*—in waterfront dives in a hundred ports in a dozen countries, everyone knew his name. They all toasted Sinbad when he appeared at the bar, barked once, and lapped up his libations. And someone else always paid the tab.

Sinbad's enjoyment of liberty got him in trouble on multiple occasions. He was banned from setting a paw in Greenland after drunkenly chasing a prominent farmer's sheep. He was "arrested" in Sicily by the shore patrol for unruly behavior. Once, when he was late arriving back to the ship, the *Campbell*'s fed-up captain pulled out without him. Sinbad barked furiously, then jumped in the sea and began swimming after the ship. After much begging from the crew, the captain swung around and picked up the soaked CPO Sinbad. He was busted in rank several times after episodes like that, but he always won his way back into the hearts of his superiors.

Unlike Sinbad, most dogs that saw combat were all business. Thanks in large part to the formation of the 2nd and 3rd War Dog Platoons, which were trained specifically for combat against Japan, war dogs performed more reliable service in the dense jungles of the Pacific than the open lowlands and snowy mountain trails of Europe. War Dog Platoon training began at Camp Lejeune, North Carolina, with seventy-two dogs and one hundred ten men, and advanced work continued in California, en route to the Pacific.

The Pacific War was largely the province of the Marine Corps, so War Dog Platoon operations mostly fell to the jarheads. Marines who became handlers rarely signed up to do so. Most came to the program by accident; they had joined up to fight and kill the enemy, not play fetch. Many had never owned or handled a dog. Some were even afraid of the intimidating Doberman pinschers. But with training and exposure to the dogs, they became convinced of not only their meaningful role in the war but also their unswerving bravery and loyalty.

The first taste of combat for some of these war dogs came at Guadalcanal. The platoon originally consisted of twelve scout dogs, twelve messenger dogs, and a mine detection dog, along with twenty-seven men. Experience proved that it was the scouts that had the most impact, so the proportions were altered—eighteen scouts to six messengers, with the mine dog dropped altogether (hiding mines on the coral and lava of the islands was difficult, mitigating the powerful noses of the sniffers).

Perhaps their finest hour came during the 1944 Allied invasion of Guam. Dozens of Dobermans of the 2nd and 3rd War Dog Platoons helped in the liberation, working side by side with marine recon scouts who went in ahead of the main invasion body, as well as search-and-destroy scouts who cleared the island of pockets of resistance. The work was incredibly dangerous: twenty-five Dobermans were killed during the invasion.

"These dogs lived in foxholes with their men," said William Putney, commander of the 3rd. "Their handlers killed three hundred and one enemy soldiers with the loss of only one of my men on patrols. So the fact that these dogs were killed instead of us and kept us from ever being ambushed or surprised at night makes them heroes in my mind."

The first Doberman to be killed was named Kurt, taken by a Japanese grenade. He was buried in what would become a war dog cemetery on Guam, adjacent to the marine cemetery on a beach called Asan. Two dozen dogs followed Kurt, including a dog named Cappy, who had just pointed out a spot where a Japanese platoon was hiding when he was shot dead. His handler, Private First Class Stanley Terrell, ran to the dog's side to cradle the bloody corpse.

"Some photographer came up," Putney recalled. "Terrell looked at me, tears running down his face. I said, 'Go take your pictures somewhere else.' "

After the war, Putney acted to repay the dogs for their service. His first act upon returning home was to lobby the military to "detrain" the war dogs and make them available for adoption by families. Few civilians were inclined to take the dogs home, however. The Dobermans and other breeds were thought to suffer from "junkyard dog" syndrome, meaning they would attack at the first household provocation. Putney felt this was nonsense, and he fought for the right to reindoctrinate the dogs to civilian life, much as the soldiers themselves needed adjustment after combat. In the end, he was successful—of the 549 dogs that returned from war to his program, a mere 4 weren't able to become household pets.

Often, the dogs were taken in by their handlers, as they had already faced life and death together. If they hadn't been adopted, the dogs would have been put down, so it was an opportunity for the handlers to reciprocate and save the lives of their dogs.

In 1989, Putney, who had become a veterinarian in Los Angeles, returned to Guam and found the war dog cemetery in disrepair, the grounds choked with weeds. Outraged, Putney contacted the U.S. naval station on Guam, and officials there agreed to host the cemetery's new location. Putney also donated a memorial to the new cemetery and commissioned a sculptor to carve a bronze likeness of a Doberman atop the monument, with the title "Always Faithful."

The memorial reads in part:

INSPIRED BY THE SPIRIT OF THESE HEROIC DOGS
WHO ARE THE EMBODIMENT OF LOVE AND
DEVOTION

A dog that truly embodied those qualities was Gander, a massive Newfoundland from the eponymous eastern Canadian province where they were first domesticated. Male Newfies average about 140 pounds (though one once tipped the scales at 260), and Gander was a large example of his breed, so he wasn't a dog to be trifled with. But Newfies are known as gentle giants for a reason—they seldom use their muscular bulk for intimidation or fighting.

Gander's best buddy was a diminutive corporal in the Royal Canadian Rifles named Fred Kelly. Gander became the company mascot and, much like Judy, ingratiated himself thoroughly into the lives of the soldiers. Given Gander's bulk and Kelly's lack of it, the pair were roughly the same size. In fact, it was sometimes hard to tell them apart, especially when Kelly wore black. This would prove to be particularly helpful when the human got orders to travel across Canada without his beloved dog. No dogs were supposed to travel with the military detachment, but the battalion was determined to take their mascot with them. Camouflaging a dog the size of a small horse would take some doing.

First, the men cheekily added Gander to the official ranks under the disguise of "Sergeant Gander" before leaving. As a member of the battalion, Gander would be issued rations, a uniform, even a kit bag. Most important, for the moment, he was given a seat on the train west. When roll call was taken at the station, Corporal Kelly yelled, "Here!" when Sergeant Gander's name was called. Then two of his buddies pretended to scuffle when Kelly and Gander were about to board the train, distracting the officers at the platform. Without much trouble, man and dog, corporal and sergeant, were headed west toward the Pacific.

For three days Gander lay quietly on the floor and did his business in a private spot Kelly built in the washroom. Though the massive dog didn't get a chance to run or exercise, he was able to stay under the radar for the entire trip to British Columbia.

On October 28, the Canadians boarded the troopships for the long haul to the Far East. Gander and his battalion were to travel on the HMCS *Prince Robert,* an escort vessel. As they approached the gangplank, a dozen or so men formed a tight circle around Gander in an effort to hide him. The deck area was a hive of activity, but the Newfie was spotted by some stevedores, who blew the whistle. One of the regimental officers told the soldiers to get rid of Gander, but shortly thereafter, the officer was seen holding his small dog as he prepared to board. Risking court-martial, Kelly and his buddies howled in protest. The only differences here were size and, it seemed, rank. The officer caved in the end, and

Sergeant Gander was allowed to board the ship. He and Kelly were off to Hong Kong.

The journey took nearly a month. It was hot and uncomfortable much of the time, thanks in part to a water shortage aboard that required strict rationing. But Gander was beloved by the men, and he served as an excellent distraction from the coming conflict that weighed heavily on their minds. Most were young men, some as young as sixteen. They were small-town kids from a wintry environment, many of whom hadn't ever traveled beyond their home province or even town. Now they were headed to a place utterly alien to what they knew, potentially facing death on the opposite side of the globe. With every wag of his tail and slobbering lick of his tongue, Gander reminded them of the life they had been living until a short time ago.

On November 16, 1941, the *Prince Robert* arrived in Hong Kong. The city was known as the "fragrant harbor" in the local tongue, and the battalion was assaulted by the powerful aroma that permeated the air. Huge crowds turned out on the Kowloon side of the water to greet the soldiers as they disembarked, and once the local children realized Gander wasn't a bear, they went crazy for him.

The Japanese struck just three weeks later. The Royal Rifles, including Kelly and Sergeant Gander, were ferried to Hong Kong Island, where they prepared to battle the invading forces pouring south from China. The Japanese landed on the north side of the island on December 18, and Kelly and his fellow Canadians quickly found themselves in the thick of things. Gander was left to his own devices as the men fought off the attack. Incredibly, the humongous dog faced down Japanese soldiers himself by rising up on his hind legs to his full height and growling ferociously. Though they were carrying rifles, the onrushing soldiers didn't shoot Gander but invariably turned and ran from this wild creature they came to refer to as the Black Devil. The Canadians would report this news with astonishment to their superiors.

Throughout the attack, Canadian troops were driven away from the beach and farther inland. By the early hours of December 19, they had been pushed up into the hills above the landing sites. Kelly, worried that his friend's luck would run out, found an empty pillbox and told Gander to stay put. Then he ran off to continue the fight a few hundred yards away.

To flush out the Canadian troops, the Japanese infantry tossed bushels of grenades at their positions. The defenders would attempt to catch them and toss them back down the slopes before they exploded, a most deadly game with no room for error. A group of seven troops under an officer named Captain Garvey were engaged in just such action close to Gander's pillbox. After several grenades were safely thrown back, a "pineapple" landed in the center of the group. For a moment, everyone stared at the grenade in stunned disbelief.

Suddenly a streak of black fur dashed in and seized the sizzling grenade. It was Gander! None of the men had known he was there, and at the time, they didn't realize what was happening. The dog ran off with the grenade, getting about twenty yards from the men.

Then the grenade exploded.

The gentle giant was killed instantly. Did he truly know what he was doing by snatching the grenade and racing it out of harm's way, or was he merely acting on instinct? Gander had been cooped up in the pillbox for a while and may have been letting off some steam when he saw the chance. However, he had been in the thick of fighting for hours, so it wasn't as though he was merely looking for some play—he would have been aware of the danger, if not the particular nature of the deadly orb he grabbed.

The seven Canadians whose lives had just been saved managed to retreat and fight on. But they were so pressed by the Japanese advance that they had to leave Gander's corpse behind. Kelly wasn't far away, but at the time he was unaware of Gander's bravery or his fate. It wasn't until several hours later that word of what had happened was passed to him. He was too busy fighting for his life to be mournful in the moment, but as the hours passed, Gander's body lay between the forces for all to see. The shambling, sturdy dog that had scarcely left Kelly's side across a continent and then an ocean was now a carcass being pecked at by crows.

"I could see that he was dead and I hated that I couldn't go near," Kelly recalled later. "To think he was gone hurt me so much, and I'm not ashamed that I cried. I missed my old pal so much. That damn dog was a friend to us all."

On Christmas Day, Hong Kong was surrendered to the Japanese. Kelly, Garvey, and thousands of others were taken prisoner. The men of the Royal Rifles never got a chance to collect Gander's body.

Gander's story was mostly forgotten until 1996, when a group of veterans were discussing the heroics of Sergeant Major John Osborn, who won Canada's first Victoria Cross of World War II. Osborn had pounced on a live grenade, saving several of his comrades' lives. One of the men exclaimed, "Just like that goddam dog!" The tale was passed up the chain, and four years later, Fred Kelly accepted the Dickin Medal, the highest honor an animal can win for military service, on Gander's behalf.

"This is the best day of my life!" Kelly exclaimed.

Gander had no better friend than Fred Kelly. Several months before their relationship was forever ceased, while man and dog were bonding back in Newfoundland, a soldier arrived in Asia, one who was destined to become Judy's closest friend.

CHAPTER 7

Frank

Once in Singapore, Judy met two new crewmates. The first was a monkey purchased by one of the *Grasshopper*'s new sailors while on shore leave. Judy had been ashore herself, staying with a customs official whose three children had met and fallen for the dog while touring the ship. As often happened during the ship's service time in Singapore, Judy was allowed to live in the local family home for up to a week. It was a nice change for her, and she became well-known among the British in government service in the Lion City.

When Judy returned to the ship, she was greeted by her new primate crewmate. Most activity stopped to watch the two animals greet each other. The monkey, named Mickey, was attached to the upper deck by a length of chain. Upon seeing Judy for the first time, Mickey said hello by leaping on her back and trying to ride the pointer like a jockey would a thoroughbred.

Judy desperately bucked and bowed, trying to shake her rider free. When Mickey firmly clamped on, Judy sat down and howled miserably, to peals of laughter from the crew. Abashed, the monkey slid off and put one arm companionably around Judy's neck, but the dog wasn't having any of it. Noticing the lead Mickey wore, she trotted down the deck until Mickey's chain stretched taut. Unable to follow, it was the ape's turn to wail when he saw Judy skip to the other end of the boat and disappear into an open hatch.

For the next few days, Judy ignored the monkey. Then a new petty officer appeared at the gangway. He gave his orders to the sailor at the deck and stepped aboard his new ship for the first time. Imagine his shock when his first greeting came from a monkey, who flew through the air, landed on his shoulders, and snatched his cap right from his head. But George White, as he would prove again and again in the years to come, was not shaken easily. A career navy man, married, and a little over thirty, White silenced the laughter of nearby crewmen by grabbing Mickey, wrenching his cap back, and hurling the monkey to the deck.

Judy appeared from the shadows of the hull. As White later remembered it, she "appeared to be laughing her fool head right off." From that moment, White would become Judy's closest companion on the *Grasshopper.* Mutual irritation with the monkey brought them together, and neither would be unhappy when Mickey was put off the boat, unable to handle naval duty and the rocking waves of the ocean.

The next eighteen months were relatively quiet for Judy, White, and the crew of the *Grasshopper.* The ship mostly shuttled between Singapore and Hong Kong during this time, and a trio of men captained her. Lieutenant Commander Edward Neville was skipper for fourteen months before he was transferred; Lieutenant Commander Robert Aldworth took over in April 1940 but retired after only a few months; and on September 21, 1940, Commander Jack Hoffman took over the bridge. Hoffman came to the *Grasshopper* from a trawler called the HMS *Wolborough,* so this was a step up in class for him. A hindrance to his career had been his vision. Hoffman was severely nearsighted. Despite this handicap, Hoffman was a solid officer, and he would play a significant role when the war finally reached Singapore.

Meanwhile, in the summer of 1941, another Englishman turned up in Singapore. He was a fresh-faced, newly minted leading aircraftman of the Royal Air Force by the name of Frank Williams. It would take some incredible circumstances to bring this boyish twenty-two-year-old into Judy's life. But when it happened, an inseparable bond would form that would last a lifetime.

Francis George Williams was born in London on July 26, 1919, the second son (after David Jr.) to a family that would eventually number six children. Soon after his birth the family moved south to the island city of

Portsmouth. The Williams clan lived in a modest home at 38 Holland Road in the beach neighborhood of Southsea, at the southerly tip of Portsmouth, a short trip across the English Channel from the Isle of Wight. Southsea was a popular tourist destination. Vacation guides across England encouraged people to "Come to Sunny Southsea," and its beaches were packed during the summer months, before rough seas and plummeting temperatures sent visitors scurrying back home.

According to tax records, the head of the household at 38 Holland Road was a Mary Ann Langrish, which indicates the Williams family shared the residence with Mary Ann and her daughter, Alice, and perhaps others. This was hardly an unusual arrangement for the time. In September 1928, when Frank was only nine, his father, David Arthur Williams, passed away. Frank, who idolized his dad, was bereft. In the custom of the time, the corpse was washed, prepared, and kept right there in the house for weeks, allowing anyone who wished to pay respects until the stench was too much for the living to bear.

Portsmouth was almost as densely populated as London at the time. The seafront city was home to a citizenry yoked to the ocean: Royal Navy seamen and officers, shipbuilders, dockworkers, fishermen, ferrymen, and merchant seamen filled local pubs like the Herd, the Polar Star, and the Ship & Castle with tales of narrow escapes and of the ones that got away—both fish and females. Fabled Admiral Horatio Nelson stayed at the George Hotel on the Portsmouth waterfront while preparing the HMS *Victory* for battle with the combined French and Spanish navies representing Napoleon. He sailed from Portsmouth on September 14, 1805, and handed his enemy a resounding defeat at Trafalgar five weeks later, giving his life in the process and becoming Britain's greatest naval hero. The *Victory*'s anchor sat just off the harbor's esplanade as tribute. The atmosphere of manly hard work and heroism was an intoxicating brew for a youth who grew up without a father.

Life for Frank's widowed mother, Jean Agnes Williams, and the large family was difficult. While they weren't in abject poverty, money was tight. Jobs were scarce, and kids as young as ten worked long hours on the dockyards. But Frank was steadfast. As an example, he saved for two years to scrimp together enough money from odd jobs to afford a bicycle.

Perseverance was drummed into him from a young age, and he had both an ability to withstand difficulty and a will to overcome things that would serve him well in the years ahead.

Not all was Dickensian grimness, however. According to local histories of the period, boys of Frank's age spent many hours "mudlarking," scavenging the harbor seafloor at low tide for treasure. They enjoyed watching Portsmouth Football Club matches at nearby Fratton Park, where kids perched on a wall that ran around the playing area, many of them knocked off it by errantly kicked balls. There were weekly fireworks displays at the South Parade Pier and youth dancing at the Empress Ballroom. Tex Ritter and Flash Gordon films were regular attractions at the Rex Cinema, where kids took advantage of the fact that there was only a single employee to take tickets and handle concessions—they sneaked in the back door in droves.

Men peddled fresh shellfish in wheelbarrows along the streets of Southsea, while others sold water from bottles tied around their waists, hectoring locals to "Have one for the road!" "There were no supermarkets then," recalled Ruth Williams (unrelated to Frank) in a Portsmouth oral history of the period. "Every neighborhood had its own co-op market and butcher. My mother would go up Albert Road [the main shopping district of Portsmouth] sometimes, just to go somewhere."

The death of Frank's father had driven him inward, and the young man was shy and quiet, his reticence likely not helped by the tumult of the crowded home or the local schools, which had a reputation for tough discipline and violent hallways. But he became bewitched by the atmosphere of the docks, and he was amenable to the life lessons passed along by the briny, wizened men who stumbled out of the dockside pubs and proudly strolled Portsmouth streets in their uniforms. There was always a replacement father figure, if only a transitory one, who would encourage his dreams of a life at sea.

Around this time someone had snapped a photo of a young Frank smiling and saluting while wearing a seaman's cap and uniform, indicating an interest in the maritime life from an early age. And so it was that in the spring of 1935, at the age of sixteen, Frank joined the Merchant Navy (the equivalent of the U.S. Merchant Marine). He packed a small bag, hugged his mother, brothers, and sisters, and took a train to Wales, where he reported to a dock in Cardiff. His new home was a ship called the SS *Harbledown,* a cargo steamer of the J & C Harrison line of London about as long as a soccer field. Cadet Williams was given an official ID number (#163338) and maritime health insurance through a local insurer. On his information card he gave his eye and hair color as brown, and, mysteriously, his complexion as "fresh."

His uniform hung from his slender frame, but his cap was set at the requisite jaunty angle as he boarded his ship. For a boy who loved nothing more than to take long, often punishing bike rides, who was already showing a wanderlust that would last his entire life, the lure of the open sea and the adventures promised by a life among the waves was irresistible.

The Merchant Navy had been around since the seventeenth century, transporting goods to and from the ports of the British Empire, but had only been given its formal name by King George V after the First World War. Now Frank served aboard a ship transporting food and matériel to ports around the world, though mainly across the Atlantic to the United States and Canada. There are photos of the *Harbledown* docked in Wilmington, North Carolina, from this period, and Frank later related that he enjoyed port of call in Vancouver during this time so much that he would later move his family to the area. But while little remains of the ship's travels or Frank's time aboard her in the historical record, a note on his memorial website captures what an extraordinary—if unromantic—experience life on board the *Harbledown* must have been. "Although this was a tough life for a young man," it reads, "it included two outstanding benefits that would make it all worthwhile for him... he survived many an exciting adventure and he traveled to the farthest corners of the world."

Though Frank enjoyed life at sea, he had also dreamt of flight—of dancing among the clouds where only the birds and the gods dared go. This was no doubt fostered by the fact that the nascent aviation industry had come to Portsmouth early on. In 1933, Airspeed Ltd. opened its aircraft factory in the city, and citizens could watch the company's air taxis and test flights of new planes virtually every day. Visions of flight never left Frank's mind for very long, even as he was rolling upon the open ocean. He left the Merchant Navy after two long voyages, and he was back in England during the summer of 1939, when the warning signs of war with Germany were flashing as brightly as the neon marquees on the

West End. Prime Minister Neville Chamberlain had guaranteed Polish independence, while Adolf Hitler had drawn up invasion plans. On June 22, 1939, just over two months before German troops raced across the border, setting the stage for the Second World War, Frank enlisted as a noncommissioned officer in the Royal Air Force. He was scarcely a month shy of his twentieth birthday. After a medical checkup, he received his serial number and was welcomed to the service.

Alas, he was too tall to fly.

Denied his dream of becoming a pilot, he received training to track the flights of others, becoming a radarman. He would have started training at the nearby RAF base in Tangmere, near Chichester, in southern England. The base would become famous for its role in the Battle of Britain, as most of the fighters who met the Luftwaffe over the English Channel took off from Tangmere.

The crucial, unlikely success of the RAF against the Germans was helped in great measure by a scientific breakthrough—radar detection. The English had been on the forefront of the technology since 1935, when a receiving station easily picked up the radio waves that rebounded off a Heyford biplane bomber flying eight miles away. The advantage was obvious: it gave the English the ability to detect incoming air attacks when they were far off and to vector interceptor places to the right position. Hard work on the new technology allowed for British pilots to be uncannily in position to strike German bombers. Use of the radar systems was a closely guarded secret, to the point of parody. When Commander John "Cat's Eyes" Cunningham was asked by the press how he managed to shoot down twenty Luftwaffe bombers over the English Channel in nighttime action during the Blitz, he responded that it was his steady diet of carrots.

In 1940, with the United Kingdom drained from battling the Nazis, it was decided to secretly bring the United States up to date. In late September, aeronautical scientist Henry Tizard led a mission to the States to marry America's industrial might with the British discovery. Tizard was surprised to find that U.S. Navy research had led to similar breakthroughs, and the technology on both sides was closer than expected. The decision of the two nations to share science was an early signpost in the special relationship that would only grow closer as the war progressed.

Frank began training as an aircraftman first class (AC1), then was promoted to AC2 and on to leading aircraftman (LAC). What that meant in practice was that he was a radar mechanic—an installer, a troubleshooter, a repairman—though the term "radar mechanic" wasn't used in Britain until 1943 (radio direction finding, or RDF, was renamed radar—radio detection and ranging—during the war, as that was the United States' preferred acronym).

After intensive training on the complicated electronics of radar and the intricate mechanical interfaces within the planes themselves, Frank arrived in Singapore, most likely aboard the *Athlone Castle* as part of convoy OB 340 on July 13, 1941, after stops in Cape Town and Bombay (it's possible he was aboard a ship that arrived slightly earlier via Durban, South Africa). The man who arrived in Singapore had filled out some from the time he served on the merchant ship, thanks in part to a strict military fitness regime and a more consistent diet, though he was still quite lean. In photos he seems boyish, with apple cheeks and a twinkle in his smile, eyes shining bright with optimism.

That good cheer would soon be severely tested.

His unit, called a RIMU (radar installation and maintenance unit), was established at a rubber plantation in a place called Ponggol Point, in the far northeast section of Singapore. Three miles east of the original RIMU in Singapore, Ponggol was, in the words of fellow radarman Stanley Saddington, "isolated, small, and ill-defended." Conditions were primitive. There were three huts, all used for operations. The men lived in tents and dined in a mess made of a few equipment boxes. There was no power source—save the small generators used for the RDF—no running water, no machinery. Road access was minimal. There were only about a half-dozen armed guards to protect the fifty or so officers, mechanics, and operators at any given time.

The RAF in Malaya and Singapore had other problems as well: there were few spare parts, not enough support staff on the ground, badly situated airfields that were quite vulnerable to attack, and an inadequate number of trained pilots. Meanwhile, the planes the radarmen like Frank serviced and directed were mostly a spent force of antiquated Brewster Buffaloes, which were slow, poorly crafted, and ill-equipped to combat more modern fighters.

So while Judy and her mates on the *Grasshopper* adjusted to the highly regulated life of the proper navy, Frank adjusted in the opposite direction: after his cutting-edge training with state-of-the-art gear paid for by a bottomless research budget back in England, he found himself making do in the jungle with substandard equipment—what could be found of it, that is.

And though Frank and his future best friend were both in Singapore, they never saw each other. They were close by in terms of distance (the naval base and Ponggol Point were separated by less than twenty kilometers) but leagues apart in terms of prestige. Airpower was still in its infancy and not taken particularly seriously by large segments of the British military, which was historically enthralled by sea power. A low-ranking RAF man wouldn't have much, if any, business at the naval base, nor would he be particularly welcome there. And the top secret nature of Frank's work ensured that he kept his contact limited to his small circle of radarmen.

Judy, on the other hand, spent her time either at sea or docked at the brand-new Royal Navy base at Sembawang, on the far northern edge of the island. The immense dry dock—at the time the largest in the world—was paired with a huge floating dock, comparable in size to the one at Pearl Harbor. Plans to build the base had been in effect since the early 1920s, but only when the Japanese invaded China did the Admiralty actually begin construction. When it at last opened in 1939, just in time for the *Grasshopper,* along with her sister gunboats *Dragonfly* and *Scorpion,* to dock there for the first time after leaving China, the construction costs had neared an incredible 60 million pounds, or the equivalent of 5.3 billion U.S. dollars in today's money.

The price tag was an enormous testament to Britain's naval power (power that had enabled the country to rule the world's seas—and a sizable chunk of the land—for two centuries). Boats left the base via the Johore Strait, the narrow strip of water, about the width of the Mississippi River, that separated Singapore from Malaya (now Malaysia), and huge batteries of fifteen-inch guns lined the Strait to defend the base from attack. Sembawang was the anchor of Britain's war plans in the Pacific, and as a result, Judy was entrenched in the heart of her country's military complex.

As war raged in Europe, military planners stayed up late imagining how conflict with the Japanese would play out. As 1941 eased from summer into fall without a noticeable decline in Singapore's equatorial heat and humidity, tensions between the west and the empire mounted. Economic sanctions aimed at isolating Japan over its aggression in China began to push the increasingly militaristic government in Tokyo into a corner. Scrap metal, rubber, and, most crucial of all, petroleum exports to Japan were cut off. In response, Japan set its sights on the material-rich lands of Southeast Asia, most of which were under colonial sway. The nation announced the Greater East Asia Co-Prosperity Sphere, a mouthful to say and even harder to swallow for the west. In essence, the Japanese lay claim to the huge amount of food, minerals, and oil in Singapore, Malaya, the Dutch East Indies (modern Indonesia), and several other western-dominated countries. Any nation standing between Japan and its right to strip those places clean would be considered an enemy. They backed up the rhetoric by seizing French Indochina (now Vietnam) in July of 1941, ratcheting up predictions of imminent war.

Yet Singapore remained a city determined to enjoy the fruits of peace, even as Japan loomed and Europe was convulsed by war. Singapore's multistory entertainment centers, known as Happy World and Great World, made up for their generic names by hosting a dazzling variety of fun, including theaters, dance halls, cafés, and nightclubs. Meanwhile, the Long Bar at the Raffles Hotel served as the unofficial headquarters for off-duty military men and the women they danced with.

With such fun at their fingertips, most westerners in Southeast Asia fervently hoped conflict could be averted. Indeed, Singapore was hardly on a war footing—the entire British garrison, including those aboard the navy ships, was ordered to take daily snoozes between one and three p.m. Content to nap in their supposedly impregnable citadel, called the Gibraltar of the East by Prime Minister Winston Churchill, few in Singapore believed the Japanese would dare attack them.

The plain truth was that the bulk of the British officers and enlisted soldiers in the Pacific felt out of sorts and left behind—they wanted to be back in Europe, fighting what they perceived as the real enemy. The United Kingdom had become electrified during the Battle of Britain, brought together by German bombs and Churchill's oratory. Nearly seven thousand miles away from London, those trapped in the Pacific theater weren't nearly so motivated. One report by an American journalist noted that the Brits he talked to in Singapore cared little about fighting the Japanese. "They want action, but against the Nazis," he said.

Ultimately, the Japanese were mainly considered an empty threat, unworthy of worrying too much about. Most believed they were bluffing, trying to extract some economic relief from the west without actually challenging its military might. The Brits took notice of how the Imperial Japanese Army had struggled to conquer the ragtag Chinese and dismissed them as a credible threat. Notions of racial superiority also led to underestimation of the Japanese. They were written off as nearsighted, incompetent in strategy, and unethical slaughterers of innocents. Most believed that one British soldier was worth ten Japanese. "Those Japs can't fly," one naval officer assured his mates, according to one reporter on the scene. "They can't see at night and they're not well trained."

"They have rather good ships," said another, "but they can't shoot."

Meanwhile, as had been the case in Shanghai, the garish Singapore lifestyle continued unabated. One American lieutenant took in the scene at the Long Bar, watching the handsome British military men with slick hair and "carefully tended mustaches" dance with "gay, effervescent British girls" decked out in expensive fashions. "Is there a war going on here?" he snorted. In August, an American journalist named Cecil Brown arrived to cover the impending action. The British customs official who greeted him at Singapore's Kallang Airport airily dismissed any threat of war with Japan. "We've had these Jap scares before," the man explained. "They are an old thing by now."

Nevertheless, Churchill decided a little show of force couldn't hurt, so he sent one of his fleet's best capital ships, the battleship *Prince of Wales,* along with the smaller but lethal battle cruiser *Repulse,* to Singapore. *Wales* was well-known for her role in the fight against the fabled German dreadnought *Bismarck* seven months earlier, in May of 1941. She had been heavily damaged, and her sister ship, HMS *Hood,* the pride of the Royal Navy, had been sunk by the mighty *Bismarck,* which was eventually sent to the bottom herself. Any ship that stood toe-to-toe with the behemoth of the Atlantic was thought to be more than a match for the

Japanese. A junior officer, Lieutenant Geoffrey Brooke, recalled the dominant feeling on board was that "at last we were going to get a little relaxation!" The battle group arrived in Singapore on December 2 to much fanfare and chest-puffing.

The British were sure this would cow the Japanese. But almost unnoticed was the fact that an aircraft carrier meant to accompany the *Wales* and *Repulse* had been damaged en route and left behind for repairs. The carrier would be missed far more than any of those cheering the arrival of the capital ships on that bright December Tuesday realized.

CHAPTER 8

Force Z

The time spent in Singapore, a little over two years, had been an oasis of calm for Judy the pointer. She had adjusted to the new captain of the *Grasshopper,* Jack Hoffman. She had her new close pal on board, Petty Officer George White, who neatly stepped in for Tankey Cooper and Bonny Boniface to ensure she was well fed, groomed, and looked after. More important, she had at last gotten used to life without shrieking airplanes descending from the heavens or angry Japanese servicemen brandishing arms at her.

But on December 8, 1941, war reentered her life.

The surprise attack on Pearl Harbor brought the United States and Japan into direct conflict at last, a fait accompli to many since the advent of Japanese muscle-flexing in Asia, the attack on the *Panay,* and the severe economic sanctions inflicted by the Roosevelt administration. It was already the following day in Asia when news of the attack circulated around Singapore. The sheer audacity and logistical triumph of the bombings froze the blood of the British command, namely the top military commander, Lieutenant General Arthur Percival, and colonial governor Sir Shenton Thomas. They wondered whether an attack on Malaya, Siam, and Singapore itself could possibly be next.

They didn't have to wait long to find out. Bombers appeared over Singapore early the morning of the eighth, raining death on the sleeping city. The *Grasshopper* and the other gunboats immediately weighed anchor and pulled out to sea so as not to remain sitting ducks for the bombers.

The *Grasshopper* shot round after round of antiaircraft fire at passing planes, but she seldom scored hits or even caused the pilots to change course. Judy barked her warnings when the planes were approaching, then stood stoically as the guns roared, despite her acute hearing. She had experienced loud blasts while in China, though it had been several years since she had witnessed intense action. Her performance during the Japanese invasion proved she was as unflappable as ever.

Compared to Pearl Harbor, and the damage inflicted in the Philippines and elsewhere in Southeast Asia, the destruction wasn't as severe in Singapore. But the impact on the psyche of the locals was immense. There had been a palpable lack of worry in the military, the government, and the citizenry. Now that untroubled front had been badly damaged. And it only got worse when reports of Japanese troop landings in Siam reached the city.

The gunboats lacked sufficient speed and firepower to do anything about the troop landings, but the *Prince of Wales* and the *Repulse* were on station. They sallied forth toward Siam on December 8, buoying the spirits of Singaporeans both local and British. The flotilla was code-named Force Z. On board the *Prince of Wales* was a young officer named Ian Forbes, a lieutenant from Scotland who would later join the crew of the *Grasshopper* and who had already been forced to abandon ship in the Atlantic naval war, jumping off a sinking escort vessel downed by German bombers into the icy waters off Norway.

Aboard the *Repulse* was Cecil Brown, the American correspondent. During the two-day journey to Siam, he played with the ship's kitten and longed for some action to write about. It came shortly before eleven a.m. on December 10. The ships had no friendly air cover, preferring radio silence so as not to tip off their position. An aircraft carrier would have given them invaluable eyes and striking power in the sky, but theirs was back in the Atlantic undergoing repairs. As it was, few navy men had yet to grasp that airpower was about to become the critical weapon in oceanic combat, particularly in the Pacific. A Japanese scout plane spotted the ships, and soon afterward, wave after wave of Mitsubishi G3M bombers (known as Nells) appeared and began to pound Force Z to smithereens. Brown's reporting captured this first instance of airplanes battling ships in the Pacific, noting how the Nells swooped in "like moths around our flaming guns," coming in "so close you can almost see the color of the pilot's eyes" before dropping their bombs and torpedoes.

A bomb found the *Repulse,* twenty yards astern of Brown's position on the flag deck. Fifty men were killed instantly in the blast.

"Bloody good bombing for those blokes," one gunner remarked.

The initial attack ended at eleven fifty-one a.m. by Brown's watch. Exactly ten minutes later, a shout: "Here they come again!"

Prince of Wales had already been hit several times when Brown saw the death blow to the *Repulse* coming, staring in numb fascination as the torpedo beelined straight toward him, striking the boat close to where he stood. "It feels as though the ship has crashed into dock," he reported. "I am thrown four feet across the deck but keep my feet. Almost immediately the ship lists."

The crew began to abandon the *Repulse*. One man, an eighteen-year-old Australian midshipman named Peter Gillis, dove from the top of the air defense control tower, some 170 feet above the water, into the churning main and swam away. Another misjudged his leap and smacked into the side of the sinking ship, breaking every bone in his body, "crumpling into the sea like a sack of wet cement." A third dove directly into one of the *Repulse*'s smokestacks and was incinerated.

Brown sat down amid the chaos and carefully took off his new, very comfortable shoes, made for him by a Chinese cobbler days before. "I carefully place them together and put them down as you do at the foot of your bed before going to sleep," he later wrote. Brown, who had been covering hostilities since the war began in 1939, was too seasoned a reporter not to assume his own death. He found himself paralyzed, unable to leap to his potential salvation. His mind couldn't absorb what his eyes were witnessing—"two beautiful, powerful, invulnerable ships are going down." Brown found himself unable to jump, to "hasten the inevitable," as he put it.

At last Brown shook himself into action and jumped the twenty feet into the ocean, his camera swinging wildly from his neck. He landed not in a salty splash but in an oily thud. The reporter in him forced a look at his watch, which was still ticking. It read 12:35, eighty minutes after the first bomb had streaked through the azure sky to pierce the *Repulse*'s hide. The oil sickened Brown with every gulp of petrol-infused water he swallowed. His life belt, airless but sodden with oil, choked him at his waist and pulled taut the preserver arms around his neck, making Brown believe he would die by strangulation, of all things. A ring on his left hand, a gift from his wife, Martha, while on honeymoon in Florence, came loose. Brown clenched his left fist tight so it wouldn't slip away into the abyss, and stroked only with his right arm as he swam.

He looked back to watch the *Repulse* sink to the bottom. *Prince of Wales* followed a short time later. In a little over two hours, the entirety of major British sea power in the Pacific had been eradicated. The Japanese had lost all of four aircraft, and the British had lost any ability to stop Japanese landings, bomb them from the sea, or move masses of troops or refugees.

In his memoir, Churchill recalled the loss of Force Z:

> In all the war, I never received a more direct shock.... As I turned over and twisted in bed the full horror of the news sank in upon me. There were no British or American ships in the Indian Ocean or the Pacific except the American survivors of Pearl Harbor, who were hastening back to California. Over all this vast expanse of waters Japan was supreme, and we everywhere were weak and naked.

Brown was narrowly saved from death by a passing lifeboat. A barrel chested marine named Morris Graney, shirtless and coated with oil, grabbed ahold of him and pulled him to safety.

"I want to rest down there," a delirious Brown babbled, pointing at the water.

Graney slapped him across the face, and admonished, "Now, none of that. You stay right here with me."

Glassy-eyed, Brown squinted through his blurring vision and saw two other men perish in the boat. Other survivors pushed the dead off the raft in order to make room for the living.

Brown was nearly naked when he made it aboard a rescue ship, but he held on to two precious items—his wedding ring and his notebook. He made it back to shore to send reports of the sinking of Force Z to America (for CBS, *Collier's,* and *Newsweek*)—accounts so intense and immediate that they would win him a Peabody Award and the profound respect of his fellow correspondents. Upon his return to Singapore, Brown raced to the cable office in borrowed slippers to crank out his initial report. The overly officious employees there at first refused to let him use the office typewriter (Brown's was at the bottom of the ocean), so he wrote the first passages by hand. They wouldn't let him sit, either, so he made history while standing up.

From their radar stations, Frank Williams and his RAF compatriots had detected the blob of the ships of Force Z as they sailed proudly out of Sembawang. Alas, they detected little else. Radar was supposed to bring an advantage to the British that never materialized. Instead, problems plagued the effort to combat the Japanese in the sky. There were large gaps in the network, which meant the enemy planes would disappear while they did their damage over Malaya. The craft would reappear as they departed the scene. The equipment had been installed in a hurry, and "certainly did not function as effectively as it could have done," in Frank's recollection. Construction of radio towers was difficult to achieve, especially in Malaya, due to local bureaucratic and labor issues. Refitting and replacing parts was rendered nearly impossible by the highly classified nature of the program and the distance between England and Singapore. And the placement of Frank's unit in the rubber plantation proved wrongheaded. The radarmen in Ponggol attempted to cover hundreds of miles of surrounding airspace with thirty-foot telegraph poles instead of standard hundred-foot towers. These poles barely peeped over the rubber trees, severely limiting their range and causing a "drastic reduction in our performance," according to Stanley Saddington, one of Frank's fellow radarmen. The effective range of the station was roughly 30 percent of optimal.

Unfortunately, the speed and ferocity of the Japanese advance would thwart the RAF's ability to improve their craft. In short order, the Japanese attained complete air superiority. The Buffaloes of the RAF were no match for the enemy. More modern Hurricanes arrived too late to make a difference. After severe losses, the remnants of the air force were evacuated to Java. An American pilot named Arthur Donahue, who joined the RAF to fight the Battle of Britain, was sent to Singapore in time to see the aftermath of the brief fight over the city. "The beautiful hangars and terminal buildings of what had once been a great airline base were barren and empty, with windows gone, walls gashed and torn.... The vast concrete aprons were torn and pitted with bomb craters, as was the entire field. The saddest sight of all was the remains of several Hurricanes and Brewsters... sorry-looking, smashed and twisted wreckages, mostly burned-out, the victims of bombing and machine gun attacks. It was heartbreaking."

Donahue wrote in his memoir, *Last Flight from Singapore,* about a moment when he walked in on his commander yelling at someone over a telephone. "I refuse to have anything more to do with air raid warnings!" the officer shouted. "You might just as well leave the warning on permanently!" Indeed, the radar stations were issued a standing order to "Regard all aircraft as enemy." But that meant the failure of the radar section was compounded—they were usually unable to track incoming raids in a timely fashion, and even when they did, there were no friendlies who could step in and do anything about the enemy. The RAF sent most of its intact planes to Java before they could be destroyed. Frank and the other radarmen were left behind, rendered impotent.

If the situation was bad on the water and in the sky, it was dire on the ground, where the British (along with units from Australia, New Zealand, India, and Malaya) were being swiftly and shockingly overrun. Lieutenant General Tomoyuki Yamashita, like his naval comrade Admiral Isoroku Yamamoto, the mastermind of Pearl Harbor, held doubts about the war his nation had embarked upon—but when pushed into duty, he proved a cunning, brilliant ground commander. Yamashita developed a plan that was the Pacific equivalent of the more heralded German blitzkrieg of France and the Low Countries. Using bicycles to move equipment and troops through the thick jungle, and light tanks to overwhelm resistance, Yamashita's 25th Army (along with three other powerful battle groups) defeated the complacent, outmanned British defenses, killing or capturing some fifty thousand soldiers in six weeks of lightning war.

It was a feat that earned Yamashita the memorable sobriquet the Tiger of Malaya.

The Japanese may have had a tremendous battle strategy, but they were aided by British ineptitude, overconfidence, and poor planning. The Japanese threat was taken so lightly that none of the Commonwealth soldiers had even undergone jungle combat training. Instead, the entire defense was built around the giant artillery pieces that commanded the sea-lanes approaching the island. The guns defending Singapore were so enormous they took up an entire island called Blakang Mati. But as it turns out, they were facing the wrong way. The Japanese were coming over land, not by sea, a development that seemed to have escaped anyone's imagination. To add to the problems, the great coastal artillery was outfitted only with antiship ordnance. There were no exploding shells designed to break apart into small pieces, which is vital for killing infantry. So even when they were finally turned, the guns were largely ineffective, despite being fired incessantly at the enemy.

The very idea of Singapore as an invincible fortress was exposed as mere propaganda from London. Truthfully, the garrison there was hardly bulwarked like the Asian Maginot Line it was hailed to be. The city itself boasted few fortifications. Several *Prince of Wales* sailors recalled that on their first day ashore before sailing to their doom they taxied the length of the island and didn't see any defensive positions. Meanwhile, Japanese intelligence had so thoroughly penetrated both the civilian and the military apparatus in Malaya and Singapore that they knew precisely where and how to strike. General Yamashita actually turned down the offer of an extra division during invasion planning, dismissing it (correctly) as not necessary.

As had been the case with Force Z, the British were caught fighting the last war, unprepared for modern innovations in combat. By the time they realized their mistakes, it was too late. Penang fell on December 19. Kuala Lumpur, Malaya's capital, on January 12. Siam and Malaya were almost completely in Japanese hands by the end of January, and the advancing IJA was threatening to shove the Brits right from their citadel into the South China Sea. One retreating infantryman put the stunning turn of events quite succinctly. "It's true that one British soldier is worth ten Japanese ones. Unfortunately, they have eleven."

With the *Prince of Wales* and *Repulse* at the bottom of the ocean, the gunboats *Grasshopper, Dragonfly,* and *Scorpion* were pressed into nonstop action, usually at night, as sailing under daylight was far too risky.

All three ships had taken on new crewmen—survivors of the sunken capital ships. The gunboats performed highly dangerous missions to attack Japanese transports and bombard coastal positions. These were mostly unsuccessful—the *Grasshopper* and her sisters carried too light a punch to do more than irritate the Japanese. A far more important and all-too-frequent mission was to evacuate soldiers, often from the battered 11th Indian Division, cut off by the advancing IJA in Malaya. At one point the *Dragonfly* and *Scorpion* saved an entire two-thousand-man brigade that was about to be annihilated and ferried them to Singapore. The sailors were at action stations virtually around the clock, eating at their posts, snatching naps in twenty-minute chunks when possible. Judy felt the urgency and went without her usual allotment of food and sleep.

While they were running rescue missions under cover of night, Judy and the *Grasshopper* were sitting ducks during the day, surviving only by zigzagging about and hoping the Japanese would concentrate their raids on larger, more important targets. The small size of the gunboats made them hard to hit and easy to ignore—they were no threat to Japanese landings or shipping, and thus were relegated to "targets of opportunity" status by the Japanese airmen.

It isn't known for sure if Judy went ashore with rescue parties to bring survivors to safety on the boats. Her early-warning capabilities would have been invaluable to warn the rescue parties of approaching enemy patrols, but she was also too beloved to be risked in such hostile jungle. On one occasion when Judy was certainly not present, a sailor from the *Dragonfly* named Les Searle was shot in the leg during a rescue mission on the Malayan coastline. Despite the wound, Searle, a Portsmouth native like Frank Williams and George White, helped a group of cut-off sappers (frontline combat engineers) make it back to the ship in one piece. Searle was cooped up in the infirmary for several days, and Judy made frequent visits to see him, brightening his stay and that of the other wounded. Searle had certainly heard about the *Grasshopper*'s brave mascot and had seen her around the docks from time to time, but little did he know that he would become a key figure in Judy's story in the days to come.

Judy was also proving to be reliable in terms of knowing when not to bark. When the *Grasshopper*'s guns opened up to shell inland targets,

Judy stoically remained quiet, never once seeming affected by the massive roar. Likewise, when the gunboat was creeping stealthily along the coast, snooping for soldiers to rescue or targets to attack, Judy never gave away their position with an untimely bark, whine, or collar-jingling scratch of her neck. The pointer who had confronted death practically from birth was, unsurprisingly, proving to be quite a war dog.

By the new year, Singapore was under siege, a hellish landscape of explosions, panic, and despair. "Ain't we got no air force, sir?" murmured one young soldier to his commanding officer. "That young lad's reproach became more and more the reproach on all lips as the days went by," wrote Lieutenant F. E. W. Lammert in an official report filed to the War Ministry. "The Japs had the sky to themselves and they rained bombs on us night and day, relentlessly, diabolically. You could almost hear their staccato laughter as their racks were unloaded. To them all Singapore was a military objective and they tore the city to pieces."

The city was indeed reduced to rubble by unceasing shelling and bombing. The naval base at Sembawang was evacuated. Refugees streamed toward Keppel Harbor at the southern end of the island, hoping for any way off Singapore before the inevitable capture. Rape, torture, and beheading were well-known by-products of successful Japanese invasions, and the people of Singapore, including what remained of the British Army, were desperate to avoid such a fate.

The end of January saw Japanese forces at the far side of the Johore Strait, ready to push across and conquer the supposedly unconquerable fortress. Artillery could now reach virtually all of Singapore. Meanwhile, sympathetic civilian snipers in the city picked off British officers in the streets at night. Deserters prowled the waterfront, robbing civilians at gunpoint.

At the Raffles Hotel, the band played on, but according to Australian correspondent Athole Stewart, no one danced, as "the rumble of artillery could be heard above the music."

The British severed the Johore-Singapore Causeway that connected Singapore to Malaya on January 31, but just over a week later, it had been repaired enough by Japanese engineers to allow the first troops of the IJA to occupy northern areas of the city. A sense of doom set in over British military command. Churchill issued a directive from London to stand fast until the end and destroy everything of value in the path of the Japanese. But when the *Empress of Asia,* a converted luxury liner repurposed as a troop transport, was sunk in early February with soldiers and matériel meant for relief, Singapore was out of hope.

Massive evacuation by sea was impossible—there simply weren't enough boats to do it. Some three thousand spots were open on the boats that were available, including standing room aboard fishing vessels. Rear Admiral E. J. Spooner allocated eighteen hundred places to army soldiers, several hundred to Royal Navy and RAF ground staff, and the rest to members of the civil government—the bureaucrats who ran the colony. Most of the operation was kept secret to avoid mass panic and swamping of the boats. The lucky folks granted a lifeline off the embattled island were given little warning—they were radioed and told to proceed for Keppel Harbor forthwith.

That included Frank and his fellow radarmen. Exactly why they had remained in Singapore to this stage is something of a conundrum, as any possible advantage radar may have gained was long since gone, and many of their RAF colleagues were already in Java. Likely it was due to the anti-evacuation policy of the brass and Governor Thomas, who were eager to avoid losing face and crippling morale with pell-mell retreat. So although he should have been safe (for the moment, anyway) on Java, Frank was still at Ponggol Point. He and his comrades destroyed their equipment, lest the secret material fall into enemy hands, carried away what they could, and bobbed and weaved their way south, dodging enemy mortar rounds the whole time. The good news was that they knew they were ticketed for a ride away from the fighting.

General Percival greatly feared that the Japanese would replay the wonton sacking of Shanghai and Nanking in Singapore, an event that would have horrendous repercussions for the city's large Chinese population in particular. This worry, and the fact that the enemy had taken control of the reservoir, influenced his decision to surrender sooner rather than later, despite Churchill's order to fight on.

To ensure that the IJA wouldn't go on a drunken rampage, Percival ordered an island-wide destruction of all alcohol stocks. He then prepared to officially wave the white flag on February 15. (He was ultimately taken prisoner, as was Thomas and most of the other top-ranking military and civilian personnel, and spent the war in Changi Prison).

The gunboats would be at the forefront of the evacuation, doing what little could be done. Commander Hoffman and the skippers of the other gunboats were ordered to Keppel Harbor and informed that they would be leaving Singapore for the final time on February 13. Hoffman was told he should prepare to take on refugees, both military and civilian, and was put in overall command of the ad hoc escape. When the *Grasshopper* arrived, Hoffman and his crew discovered people, many of them armed, savagely attempting to board or commandeer any fishing boat, ferry, or floating wood they could find. Through the dark nights of desperation, Judy stood watch at the gangway, barking furiously when dangerous gangs approached the *Grasshopper* or *Dragonfly*.

Not everyone was eager to flee, though. The *Singapore Free Press* put out an edition on February 11, complete with full local and international coverage, along with a front-page editorial encouraging readers to stay "determined and defiant." Another journalist who stayed as long as possible—indeed, he was the last western reporter to leave Singapore—was C. Yates McDaniel, the plucky Associated Press correspondent who had witnessed Japanese atrocities in China. The thirty-five-year-old McDaniel had, like most of his colleagues in China, found his way over to Singapore and Malaya to cover the fight there. He dodged bombs and artillery shells while careering through Singapore's streets until almost the very end, bearing witness to the one-sided nature of the conflict and the suffering of the local populace.

His final filing, datelined February 12, is a masterpiece of immediacy and fortitude:

> The sky over Singapore is black with a dozen huge fires this morning as I write my last message from this once prosperous, beautiful and peaceful city.
>
> The roar and burst of cannonade of bursting bombs which are shaking my typewriter and my hands, which are wet with nervous perspiration, tell me without the need for an official communique

that the war, which started nine weeks ago and 400 miles away, is today in the outskirts of this shaken bastion of empire.

I am sure there is a bright tropic sun shining somewhere overhead, but in my many-windowed room it is too dark to work without electric lights.

Over the low rise where the battle is raging I can see relay after relay of Japanese planes circling, then going into murderous dives upon the soldiers, who are fighting back in a hell over which there is no protecting screen of fighter planes.

But the Japanese are not completely alone in the sky this morning! I just saw two "wildebeasts"—obsolete biplanes with an operating speed of about 100 miles per hour—fly low over the Japanese positions and unload their bomb burdens with a resounding crash.

It makes me rather ashamed of myself, sitting here with my heart beating faster and faster than their old motors, when I think of what chance these lads have of getting back in their antiquated machines. If ever brave men have earned undying glory, than these RAF pilots have on this tragic morning.

There are many other brave men in Singapore today. Not far away are anti-aircraft batteries in open spaces—they must be, to have clear fields of fire....

Pardon the break in continuity, but a packet of bombs just landed so close that I had to duck behind a wall that I hoped would—and it did—screen the blast.

But those gun crews keep on fighting, their guns peppering the smoke-limited ceiling every time the Japanese planes come near, and that is almost constantly.

The all-clear has just sounded—what a joke! For from my window I can see Japanese planes hedge-hopping, not a mile away.

A few minutes ago I heard one of the most tragic two-way telephone conversations. Eric Davis, Director of the Malayan Broadcasting Corporation, urged the Governor, Sir Shenton Thomas, to give permission to destroy an outlying broadcasting station. The Governor demurred, saying the situation was not too bad, and refused to direct the order. Davis telephoned the station in question, instructing them to keep on the air but to stand by for urgent orders. We tuned in on the wavelength of the station in question. In the middle of the broadcast in Malay, urging the people of Singapore to stand firm, the station went dead.

Henry Steele of Richmond, Surrey [England], Army Public Relations Officer, who has seen us through a bad situation from the Thai border to Singapore, just told me I had ten minutes to pack up and leave.

For a fortnight I have been the only American newsman in Singapore. But when Henry says go, I go, so goodbye from Singapore.

Definitely last—

Don't expect to hear from me for many days, but please inform Mrs. McDaniel, Hotel Preanger, Bandoeng, Java, that I left this land of living and dying.

CHAPTER 9

Flight

Keppel Harbor was a miasma of humanity, an admixture of fleeing refugees of all types—retreating soldiers, stoic government workers, terrified Chinese, stunned colonial families. All they had known before was a sandcastle before the rising tide. Some staggered along with everything they owned; others carried nothing save the clothing they wore.

Matrons dressed for high tea commingled with nearly naked refugees. Grim men with rifles fought for places in line with mothers clutching crying babies to their bosom.

All had their eyes on the prize—a place aboard one of the motley group of ships that swung at anchor off the harbor's Clifford Pier, waiting to take them away from the rampaging Japanese. Wave after wave of refugees crushed toward the improvised fleet of rescue vessels—the ones that remained afloat, that is. Dozens of small craft had been sunk in recent raids on the harbor, their masts sticking above the shallow breakwater.

It was February 12, 1942. A little more than eight months earlier, British forces retreating from the Wehrmacht avoided obliteration on the beaches of France when a makeshift flotilla of rescue ships hauled more than three hundred thousand troops from Dunkirk across the English Channel to England. In Singapore, similar heroics would be performed by a makeshift flotilla of 183 ships that formed a Dunkirk in miniature that, unfortunately, had nowhere nearly similar results. But the incredible drama, bravery, and fortitude displayed over the coming hours, days, and weeks would dwarf even the exploits in the English Channel.

The biggest of the rescue vessels were the gunboats—*Grasshopper* and her sister ships, *Dragonfly* and *Scorpion.* Aboard the *Grasshopper* Judy watched the chaos below from the foredeck. If the mayhem made her particularly nervous, she didn't show it. She sat quietly near the rail, occasionally walking slowly to the other end of the ship, only to return, as if transfixed by the naked emotions on display on the pier.

Her senses would have been assaulted by the noise and especially the odors of the harbor. Black smoke palled, blotting out the blazing sun. An evil smell permeated the pointer's nostrils, one that had the nearby humans, with their distinctly poorer olfactory sense, making futile attempts to clamp their nostrils shut. The usual waterfront stench of rotting vegetation, fish, and fuel was mixed with the reek of raw sewage—thanks to the destruction of the sewer system—and the overpowering redolence of the bombed-out city. Scorched rubber, melted steel girders, lumber turned to ash, and the decomposing victims of the Japanese assault competed for the honor of severest assault on the senses. All around, people retched, overcome by the horrible stink.

Meanwhile, the bombs continued to fall, many right there on the docks. Long stretches of stifling inaction, as the Royal Navy attempted an orderly boarding and escape, were punctuated by dizzying moments of horror as Nells suddenly appeared above. The shriek of the bomb's approach would join with the screams of the refugees. And then the explosion, often quieter or less dramatic than many expected. Many bombs missed badly, exploding in the harbor, sending up fountains of dark water, or in the city behind them, adding to the whipping flames. But some struck the dock area, and the moans of the newly wounded and soon-to-perish added to the macabre scene.

Through it all, Judy retained her preternatural calm, occasionally running under the steel cover of the bridge when the sound of falling bombs cut through the air. Judy was no stranger to the horrible sensations of war and misery. She had seen plenty of suffering and shots fired in anger during her years in China. Whether that tempered her reaction to the mayhem in the harbor is impossible to know for certain, but it seems reasonable. Canine temperament is as individual as human disposition, and Judy had already proven to be cool under fire and capable of military-grade self-control. It isn't surprising that she wouldn't let the madness get to her.

One of the first boats to flee the harbor was the *Scorpion,* which had actually left on February 10, departing early after being roughed up badly by the Japanese during the previous weeks. One of her crewmen was Charles Goodyear, the sailor who was close enough to Judy to invite the dog to his wedding back in China. Now the pointer stood with her front legs on the rail as the *Scorpion* slipped away and barked warmly at Goodyear as he waved from his boat to the *Grasshopper.*

It was the last anyone saw of him or his ship. *Scorpion* was damaged by Japanese aircraft and subsequently sunk by surface ships as it drove for Java.

Two smaller civilian steamers that had been refitted for military use left the night of the twelfth as darkness settled over the harbor. The *Kung Wo,* a dilapidated vessel that had once been a ferry on the Yangtze River and had frequently passed Judy when she was on board the *Gnat* in more peaceful times, had been converted to a minelayer by the Royal Navy and was now a key part of the evacuation process.

In the previous weeks, *Kung Wo* had been bombed repeatedly at the naval base. Only three lifeboats remained on the vessel, and these were perforated by shrapnel and bullets. Several forward-thinking people actually refused to come aboard due to the lifeboats' horrendous condition.

Of the 140 who did board her were a group of reporters, including McDaniel, who fled to the docks immediately upon filing his final report from the bombed-out city, along with the British PR man Henry Steele, Australian Atholo Stowart, and a young, exceptionally pretty Chinese woman named Doris Lim. Doris was the assistant to Wong Hai-Sheng, better known as Newsreel Wong. Wong had gained worldwide acclaim for his photo and film coverage of the brutal Japanese onslaught in China. His photo "Shanghai Baby" showed an abandoned infant crying out amid the bombed-out wreckage of a railway station, and it was displayed across the globe as a primary example of Japan's barbarity.

Wong had already left the doomed city in order to get some images out to the west. Doris, who had grown up in an American convent in Shanghai and spoke perfect English, had stayed behind to evacuate some equipment and continue on in her other job, spying for the British. She had been an intelligence agent in China during the invasion and had fled to Singapore, one step ahead of the Japanese, who knew who she was and what she was doing.

Now she was getting out of Singapore one step ahead of them once more. But it was not without incessant attempts from the Japanese to stop her and the many others trying to evacuate, as they sent more bombers over the harbor. Stewart captured the scene in an article syndicated across Australia:

> We waited two hours on the pier. Dive bombers and high-level bombers were now coming over. The end of one alert scarcely passed before another was heralded by the wailing dingo-voiced sirens. The crump of bombs as they fell on the wharves of Keppel Harbour mixed with the staccato crack of the anti-aircraft guns. The crowd on Clifford Pier went down on its collective face with one accord, just as a congregation at prayer. Their prayers could not have been more fervent had they been in church. Blasphemous utterances took on the cogency of real supplication.

Even as the reporters on the pier recovered from the bombing, Doris, dressed in a blue shirt and trousers, won over the men with her unflappable demeanor. "(She) treated the whole thing as a sort of lark," recalled Geoffrey Brooke, a *Prince of Wales* survivor who had joined the *Kung Wo* as a member of her bridge crew. He was one of roughly two hundred men pulled from the water after Force Z was sunk who joined other ships during the escape.

Once the *Kung Wo* got out to sea, the reporters having dug in and helped shovel coal into the burners along with the skeleton crew, they were bombed once more. Two hits from Japanese bombers left a "hole quite definitely 'Made in Japan,' " according to Stewart. Fortunately, they were close enough to a small island to scurry onto it when they abandoned ship. *Kung Wo* listed but didn't sink, and was anchored while help was sought.

Another small liner that had been requisitioned by the Royal Navy called the *Vyner Brooke* slipped out of Singapore on February 12. She had been bombed repeatedly since the war began. Several weeks of evasive maneuvers made her crew, in particular her captain, R. E. "Tubby" Borton, quite adept at avoiding airborne danger.

Vyner Brooke was something of a hybrid between a large private yacht and a small passenger steamer, about 250 feet long and 45 feet wide. Reports vary on how many passengers she could comfortably accommodate, but all agree that the huge number of frantic evacuees overloaded her capacity. Nevertheless, Borton took aboard everyone who turned up at his gangplank on the night of departure. In all, 330 people, most of them civilian women and children, boarded the ship.

That included the last sixty-five Australian army nurses (known in the Aussie army vernacular as "nursing sisters") left on the island, the only ones who hadn't made it out with their colleagues on a ship called the *Empire Star.*

The nurses, under the command of Chief Matron Olive Plashke, had braved exploding ordnance to gather letters home from Aussie soldiers left behind. The nurses wept as they accepted farewells from the soldiers, who cried freely as well, hugging the sisters as tightly as they would their own families, whom they were certain they wouldn't see again.

They then ducked as the same bombs that Athole Stewart described fell on them. A Royal Navy officer supervising the evacuation noted the exceptional bravery and calm the nurses displayed under fire:

> The air raids were causing heavy casualties among the evacuees. To the noise of the guns were added the cries and screams of the wounded and dying. Smoldering and dismembered bodies lay everywhere among the pathetic remains of scattered, burst-open suitcases. It was essential to calm and succor the survivors if complete panic was not to set in. These brave nurses are always the first to answer the calls for assistance and by their bearing and spirit were in stark contrast to some of the opposite sex.

As dusk fell, the nurses were taken to the *Vyner Brooke.* One remembered her first impression as being of a "small, sinister-looking dark grey ship."

This was a woman with a name—Vivian Bullwinkel—to match her

fantastic story of survival. Vivian (never Viv—her friends called her Bully) was twenty-six years old, a native of a South Australian copper mining town called Kapunda, about fifty miles northeast of Adelaide. Physically, she had little in common with the cartoon moose that is her namesake. A superb high school athlete, she was tall and slim, indeed lanky, with blue eyes and short, straight hair that curled slightly in the tropical humidity. She had flat feet that kept her out of a nursing position with the Royal Australian Air Force, but the Army Nursing Service had no such qualms.

Notionally, she held the rank of lieutenant. "She is not an excitable person at any time," wrote fellow nurse and POW Betty Jeffrey in her memoir, *White Coolies*. Vivian's dispassion was a trait that would serve her well in the coming hours.

Captain Borton steered the ship into the middle of the harbor to await darkness and a chance to escape to sea. All around the ship, people in small groups paddled canoes and other small craft, plaintively calling out pleas to come on board and be saved. *Vyner Brooke* was already dangerously overcrowded, so Borton, his Malay crew, and the Aussie nurses could only shut their ears and try to ignore the heartrending cries.

At roughly ten fifteen p.m., the ship slipped out of the harbor, leaving the flaming skyline behind. They had arrived in a far different Singapore almost exactly one year earlier, and enjoyed the cosmopolitan, energetic city greatly—many of them, like Bullwinkel, hailed from small towns in the Australian bush. Now they were fleeing this "never to be forgotten scene," as Jeffrey recorded, members of a defeated force leaving their beloved new home, which lay in ruins. A group of nurses began to sing "Waltzing Matilda," but the poignancy of the moment overcame them after a single verse, and the ship fell silent.

The next day broke to even more urgent and awful conditions in Keppel Harbor. Judy and the others on board the *Grasshopper* awoke to the sounds of a city on the verge of being conquered. The tremendous thunderclap of an artillery barrage landing nearby spilled man and dog from their beds at dawn. Japanese bombers appeared regularly overhead, flying with total impunity over the harbor while taking the time to also strafe clusters of citizens wherever several were clumped together in the open. Shots rang out at random, fired by rifles belonging to fleeing British and Aussie soldiers, Japanese invaders, and civilian snipers. And every so often, the guns on the decks opened up in feeble riposte to the onslaught that was ending British control of the city.

But the most disturbing cacophony of all was not generated by weapons but by people, desperate refugees in even greater numbers than the day before, any hopes of riding out the attack shattered by the endless pounding of explosives and the inability of the British military to fight back. Judy was used to the sounds of conflict by now. Gunfire and bombs had become part of her natural landscape.

But the distressed keening of the men, women, and, worst, children on the pier must have disturbed her greatly. Judy was used to bringing smiles to the faces of the humans in her midst; that was especially true of children. Now she could only watch helplessly, her tail sunk between her legs, as youngsters cried and screamed all around her.

Around mid-morning, the order was passed to the gunboats to take on passengers and ready to leave that evening. Judy immediately sprung out of her depressed reverie and began excitedly hopping about as the first of the refugees piled onto the gunboat.

The boarding of the *Grasshopper* was anything but standard and orderly. "Embarkation," reported one sailor in the aftermath, "was a case of individuals climbing onto the boat and being pulled on board by those already on the ship." The gunboat wound up carrying as many civilians as could reasonably be crammed on board. Precise figures are impossible to verify, and estimates from those on the scene vary wildly. Some put the figure at about fifty, others at one hundred fifty, or about three times the number of sailors that made up the standard complement aboard the ship, not counting the other military types aboard. The truth is likely in the middle, probably on the higher end. There were nurses; engineers; an elderly couple from New Zealand, Mr. and Mrs. Lampen-Smith, whose son had evacuated on a different ship; several intact families; and many others (even a half-dozen Japanese prisoners under close guard by an intelligence officer named Lieutenant H. M. Clarke)—all of them shell-shocked at the turn of events.

Merely nine weeks before, all had been well. They lived peaceful lives concerned with family, friends, careers, education, and fun. With sickening speed, all of it had been wrenched away by the invading Japanese. Hopes and dreams were gone, along with much of their possessions and their sense of place. Now survival was all that mattered, and that was on the razor's edge and would remain so in the foreseeable future.

It was George White's job, as chief of the ship's stores, to scramble to find a way to feed the new mouths on board. Most of his day had been spent organizing, scrounging, and pleading for as much food and water as he could possibly muster. Of course, the various other tankeys were doing likewise, so there wasn't much to add to his storeroom. A strict rationing would have to be set, that much was certain. Nevertheless, White managed to greet each passenger upon boarding with a cup of tea and a slab of chocolate.

Meanwhile, Judy was doing her best to settle the civilian horde. She was seen constantly nuzzling up to the many crying, frightened children, hoping to give them a familiar and friendly sight, and "personally greeted virtually everyone on board," according to White.

A few slips down on Clifford Pier was the *Grasshopper*'s fellow transfer from the Yangtze River, the *Dragonfly. Dragonfly* boarded roughly 150 British soldiers and 75 more Malay crew, for a complement of 225 (as with *Grasshopper,* accounts of her precise passenger list vary, as the chaos at the harbor prevented accurate accounting). She was under the leadership of Commander Alfred Sprott and Lieutenant Sidney Iley. *Dragonfly* carried more retreating servicemen than did the *Grasshopper,* including the scattered remnants of a company of East Surrey Regiment troops, just fourteen left out of nearly two hundred that had been in the original ranks.

At the same time the gunboats were told to take on passengers, similar orders were given to the numerous smaller ships that the Royal Navy had been using as a jerry-built fleet since the destruction of Force Z, including a pair of Royal Navy auxiliary patrol boats that had buddied up to evacuate personnel and civilians. They were the SS *Tien Kwang* and the HMS *Kuala,* tanker steamers that had been repurposed for military usage. Frank Williams and his fellow RAF radarmen were on their way to escape aboard the *Tien Kwang* even as the orders to stand by for evacuation were sent.

It hadn't exactly been a glorious war thus far for Frank Williams. His action essentially consisted of endless troubleshooting of secret radar systems that weren't yet up to snuff, while his air force was chased from the sky by the Japanese. Now he was retreating madly from an army he and the rest of his countrymen had scoffed at mere weeks before.

On the morning of February 13, the radarmen were waiting at the Raffles Library for evacuation instructions when the word came down at eleven a.m.—head for Keppel Harbor, posthaste, and prepare to be shipped away from the burning city. The official Air Ministry report details their orders. "Great care was to be taken to avoid observation, no kit or bedding was to be carried, only arms and rations sufficient for four days, and the last mile of the journey was to be made on foot in groups of not more than ten men."

Upon their hasty arrival at the tumultuous pier, the RAF evacuees were pointed toward the *Tien Kwang,* and Frank waited in a long line while he and the other 265 radarmen prepared to board, along with numerous army personnel and a handful of civilians, mostly Chinese employees of the Bank of China. At this point, Frank would have been within a short distance of Judy, who stood watch over the scene from the *Grasshopper,* but he never saw the pointer. The *Tien Kwang* was anchored not far offshore, and all day long, men were ferried to her gangplanks.

As they boarded, several men noticed the aftereffects of action on the *Tien Kwang*'s superstructure—several ragged gashes and buckled steel. The *Tien Kwang* had spent the previous weeks as part of antisubmarine screens for other ships. She had racks of depth charges in the hold, as well as a four-inch gun in the bow. She was "a tiny vessel," according to Saddington, "just a few hundred tons, with one squat funnel, and she was in some need of a coat of paint."

Tien Kwang was skippered by Lieutenant W. G. Briggs of the Royal Navy. She was a 731-ton ship, just shy of 200 feet long, and scarcely 30 feet across, not much room for Frank and his colleagues, all of whom were under the command of a squadron leader named Ray Fraser. The military men "wore cork life jackets or rubber air bags," recorded one of the Chinese evacuees, Wang Hua-Nan. "We had barely enough space to sit on deck with our backs against each other." Also evacuating on *Tien Kwang* were seven female doctors who had stayed behind until ordered out of Singapore, in addition to a smaller number of servicemen and nine Japanese prisoners. By the time she set sail, "every nook and cranny of the little ship was occupied," remembered Saddington.

Morale among the retreating forces was vaporizing. Aboard the *Tien Kwang,* Fraser, the stout, middle-aged group captain in charge of the military men, yelled at Frank and the other RAF men that the ship they were on was a flat-bottomed riverboat, and any substantial movement of passengers was likely to capsize her. Therefore, he added dramatically, anyone moving around would be shot. One RAF man muttered in response, "Get fucked."

Next door to *Tien Kwang,* the other converted steamer, *Kuala,* loaded up to bursting. Her complement was much more diverse, including nurses, Public Works Department employees, and motley civilians, twenty-six of them European, according to an official count made by H. J. Page, the director of the Rubber Research Institute of Malaya, who was on board.

Kuala was larger than *Tien Kwang* and likewise stuffed with refugees and whatever belongings they could squeeze on board; in all, she sailed with between five hundred and six hundred people. Her commander was Lieutenant William Caithness, a burly 225-pound Scotsman from Aberdeen.

At five fifteen p.m., the scream went up: *"Take cover!"* There was mass confusion as Nells appeared above and sent down several bombs that exploded close to where the two ships were loading. A group of people waiting to board, most of them destined for the *Kuala,* were killed, either by direct fire or as a result of nearby automobiles exploding in the fiery aftermath. Despite the carnage, or perhaps because everyone was simply numb to it, boarding continued shortly thereafter. Saddington noted, "The tin hat of an airman had a jagged hole in its brim but the man himself was unscathed. I pondered his chances of safely reaching home to display this memento of what must have been a very lucky escape."

The *Tien Kwang* and *Kuala* pulled out of the harbor first, at six fifteen, an hour after the deadly attack. The two ships weighed anchor and painstakingly wound their way through a harbor choked with shipping and mines.

Judy's boat, the *Grasshopper,* seemingly fully laden, began to pull out into the crowded harbor but was ordered back to the dock when a fresh wave of refugees rushed up to the jetties. Though every inch of the boat teemed with escaping people, the ship's crew hastily reorganized the haphazardly strewn luggage and shifted the passengers around to make more room. Even as the light faded, Japanese aircraft continued to scream overhead, heightening the chaos and adding urgency to the boarding process. Then artillery was added to the mix. "We came under fire from a gun firing from the direction of the Swimming Club, to the east of town," remembered a civilian refugee named J. A. C. Robins. "We could see the flash, then hear the report, followed by a bursting of the shell in the sea nearby. We were never hit—we were a lucky ship." When the gunboat was stuffed beyond capacity and to the point of dangerous overcrowding, Hoffman at last ordered the *Grasshopper* away from the docks for good. Screams from the helpless unfortunates left behind to the Japanese trailed the boat as it powered into the harbor.

The *Dragonfly* was tasked with waiting until the last moment to board soldiers racing to the docks in mad retreat. A Welsh crewman named W. J. Long, known as "Taff" for his origins near the Taff River that runs through Cardiff, was detailed with a few other sailors to head out into the chaos to find the men assigned to flee on his gunboat. "We were issued rifles and bayonets and climbed on to the jetty," he wrote years later.

"Bullets were striking the galvanised sides of warehouses, whether fired by friend or foe we had no idea. It was eerie with the numerous fires casting flickering shadows everywhere. Pungent smoke rose and wafted in dense pockets and visibility was such that imagination made one see an enemy that wasn't there—or were they?"

Miraculously, Long and his party found the soldiers, and they took off running for the *Dragonfly,* chased by mortars landing on the pier. Shrapnel flew indiscriminately. "On arriving, everyone in the party threw their weapons over the guardrail and clambered aboard with a few well-chosen words of relief," Long remembered.

Dragonfly pulled up its gangway even as the last of her officers came storming up with a final group of soldiers, explosions going off all around them. On the bridge, Lieutenant Iley screamed, "We can't wait any longer! Cast off forward! Cast off aft!" But no one got to the aft line, so the revving gunboat yanked free from the jetty, the rope breaking with a resounding twang.

The *Grasshopper* started to trail her out of the dark harbor, but then was radioed back to perform an odious task. She fired upon and sank several small, abandoned, often half-submerged craft of all sizes that dotted the area, thus denying them to the enemy.

Finally, at twelve thirty a.m. on the fourteenth, it was time to leave. Hoffman turned out to sea and made for the *Dragonfly* at flank speed. The two gunboats formed a mini-convoy, with the *Dragonfly* taking the lead. Out ahead of the gunboats, *Tien Kwang* and *Kuala* were tacking a different course in the same direction.

The destination for all the ships, including the dozens of other small vessels that streamed away from the maelstrom of Singapore, was the city of Batavia, that evocatively named capital of the Dutch East Indies. City and country have since been renamed Jakarta and Indonesia, but the romantic name, one that calls to mind long ocean quests for priceless spices, remains one of the few elements of the colonial period that induces nostalgia and not winces. Batavia was on Java, the island in the Indonesian archipelago where the chain curves east below Sumatra. A large western presence there promised immediate safety and the likelihood of larger ships for escape to India, Ceylon, or Australia. Sumatra itself was to be avoided—the largest island in the chain was far too close to Malaya and Singapore. Its loss to the Japanese was a given, simply a matter of days.

Ordinarily, sea travel between Singapore and Batavia took place in the wide channel off the west coast of Borneo before hanging a hard right turn at the large island of Tanjung Pandan for the last leg to Java. But these weren't ordinary times. Japanese airpower ruled the skies over the area so completely that any vessel larger than a rowboat in the open sea would be shortly spotted, reported, and sunk. Meanwhile, the enormous espionage network of sympathetic locals the Japanese had built in Singapore ensured the enemy knew the details of each departing vessel, down to their serial numbers.

So *Grasshopper* and the other escaping ships needed to stick close to the riot of islands that dot the waters south of Singapore like droppings from Jackson Pollock's brush. These hundreds of volcanic nose cones, just some of the more than thirteen thousand islands that composed the Dutch East Indies, made up several sub-archipelagoes, including the

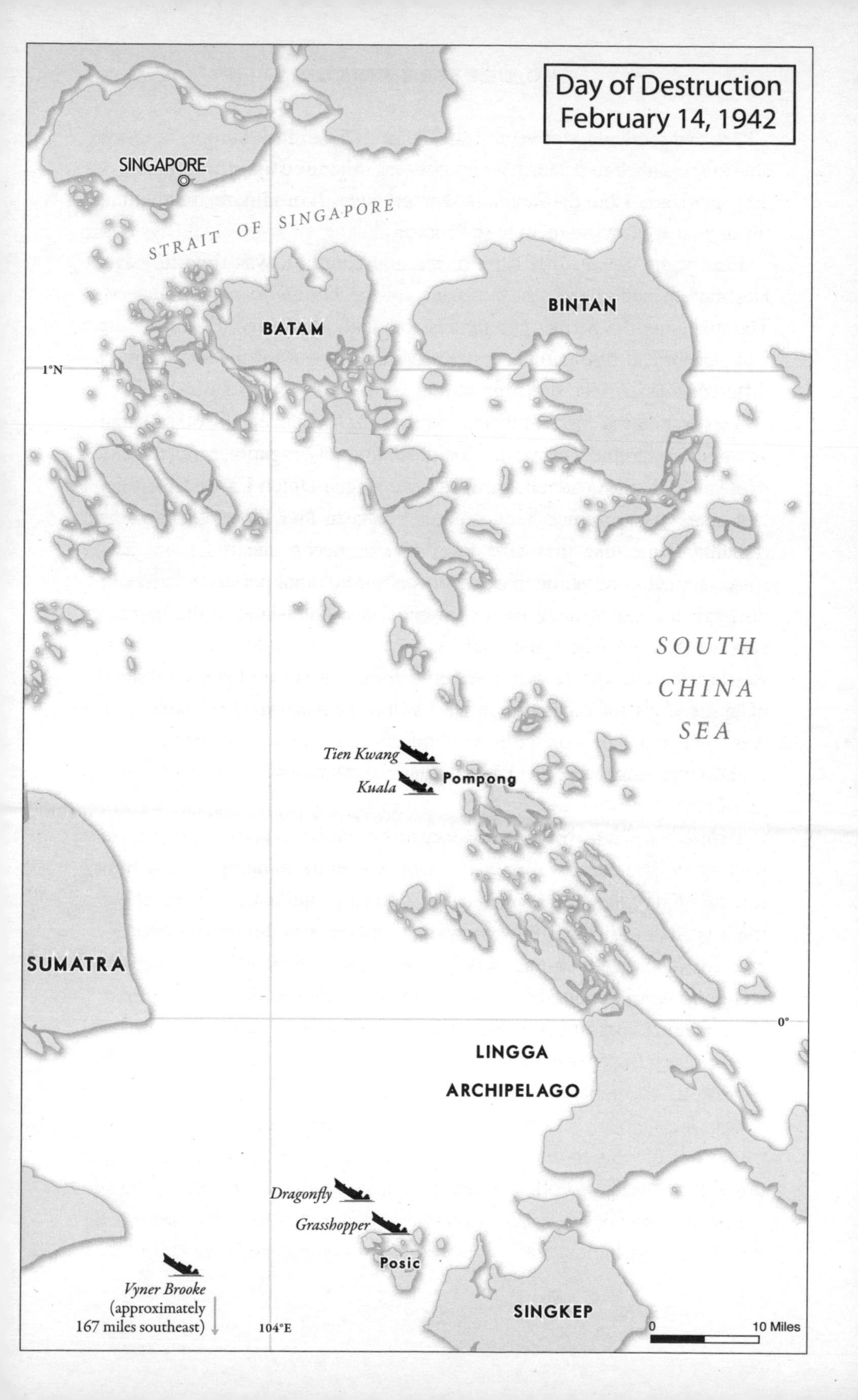

Day of Destruction
February 14, 1942
SINGAPORE
STRAIT OF SINGAPORE
BATAM
BINTAN
1°N
SOUTH
CHINA
SEA
Tien Kwang
Kuala
Pompong
SUMATRA
0°
LINGGA
ARCHIPELAGO
Dragonfly
Grasshopper
Posic
Vyner Brooke
(approximately
167 miles southeast)
104°E
SINGKEP
0
10 Miles

Riau and the Lingga. They ranged from small to microscopic, and were mostly uninhabited. Many were enclosed in jungle, which would provide crucial cover from the Japanese spotter planes during the daylight hours. The plan was to race across open water during the inky blackness of the ocean night, then anchor close to shore just off one of the myriad islands as the sun peeked over the horizon—preferably an island with tall trees overhanging the beach. The fleeing ships would then hide all day under this canopy, before getting under way and making for the next island by the stars. With luck, the ships would be unloading in Batavia before the Nells ever caught sight of them.

As they pulled out to sea, the crew and passengers on all the ships looked back at the Gibraltar of the East. Huge flames shot up from the oil reserves kept offshore, now exploded to keep them from the Japanese. Black smoke rose over the shattered city. Occasionally, a searchlight swept over the coastline, picking out attacking bombers in the dark skies. It was a scene from Dante's "Inferno," one that none of the survivors would or could ever forget.

Frank took note of the carnage he was leaving behind. He re-created the scene to Dutch authors H. Neumann and E. van Witsen years later:

> The red glow of the burning harbor installations and barracks, the fires in the cities and the thick smoke clouds illuminated by the continuous fire beams of the artillery and exploding grenades, provided a ghostlike scenery that was visible miles away. When we slowly sailed past the oil and gasoline supply tanks that were set on fire on the island of Pulau Boekoem, every detail of our ship was clearly visible because of the heavy glow caused by the burning of the enormous supplies in contrast to the dark night sky. It was a great relief to feel the chilly wind of the sea when we left this inferno.

CHAPTER 10

Day of Destruction—February 14, 1942

The wind howled through Judy's ears as the gunboats pushed hard under the comforting cloak of darkness. They cleared the Riau Archipelago, which includes the now-popular tourist island of Bintan, in the wee hours, and as the first streaks of red were spotted coming up over Borneo, they weren't in sight of land. The convoy was in a tricky position—the small islands they required for cover weren't immediately apparent, yet they would be sailing through ocean that would be heavily patrolled by the Japanese.

The pointer should have been deeply asleep, but the noise and crowds and palpable fear on board kept her from doing anything but brief snoozing. She curled up near George White on occasion, but just as often lent her comforting presence to the many scared civilians on board. The ship was packed from stem to stern with people, most dirty, unshaven, and disheveled, all exhausted by their ordeal. They slept anywhere they could find an unclaimed spot. "I tried three different places to sleep, none of which were really better than the others," wrote J. A. C. Robins, who had made it onto the *Grasshopper* before it departed Singapore. Dogs tend to reflect the emotional weather of a given room or person they are close with, but in this case, Judy, as befitting her background, was the stoic naval officer providing succor to scared passengers.

On the *Grasshopper* bridge, Hoffman conferred with Ian Forbes, who had joined the gunboat after having escaped from two sinking ships, including the *Prince of Wales*. The men discussed their best course of action. They decided they had no choice but to press on at full speed toward Java—and when good cover was spotted, they would head for it. The sun rose, and with it the dread aboard the gunboats. As the new day began, Japanese flight operations were winding up, and scout planes were taking to the sky. Bomber crews were breakfasting, likely confident of the damage they would inflict that day. The reality that this could well be their last day on earth permeated the ship, crew and passengers alike. The strong among them buried the thought and carried on. For about two hours, the gunboats made good, undetected progress, but a few minutes past nine a.m., their luck ran out.

After her fitful night, Judy had been quiet as day broke, content to make her way around the deck and lie panting in the heat. But now she began a sharp bark. The crew knew what that meant and began to scan the skies. Sure enough, a Japanese seaplane appeared promptly above. These were mainly used for reconnaissance duty but carried a couple of bombs aboard, generally so the pilots could have a chance to sink some tonnage and boast about it with other combat pilots.

The seaplane immediately commenced a dive attack, dropped one bomb at the *Grasshopper* that missed badly, then turned and tossed another bomb at *Dragonfly.* This one was a much better attempt, exploding close enough to the gunboat to cause slight, but not critical, damage to her bow. The seaplane disappeared, but that was small comfort to those on board the gunboats—the seaplane's big brothers now knew where they were, and a mission to sink them was being planned and sortied even as the damage was assessed.

Due south from the *Grasshopper* and *Dragonfly* lay the Lingga Archipelago, which was anchored by Singkep, an island at the bottom of the chain that was only about twenty-five miles east of Sumatra. Curving in a gentle northerly arc were dozens of the sort of small isles that would potentially provide cover from the incoming bombers. The boats throttled up as fast as they could muster in the direction of these spits of land.

En route, a ship was sighted, a small military launch known as a Fairmile. On board were Scottish troops of the Gordon Highlanders, a fabled regiment that had seen many of its troops captured in France. The Malayan portion of the Highlanders would see many more men perish as

POWs than in combat. The launch settled in behind the gunboats and tried to keep pace.

By eleven thirty land had been spotted, and the gunboats closed to within two miles of the island of Posic, a tiny extension of lava and sand that scarcely poked out of the water. It would be a poor option for cover—other islands in the Lingga chain were much better for hiding. But there wasn't much choice at this point, especially when Judy began barking again.

Bombers soon appeared in formation out of the south. "Aircraft off the port beam!" someone shouted. Some witnesses to the attack identified the bombers that appeared over the fleeing gunboats as the Nells that were so often spotted over Singapore, but Forbes, a more reliable plane spotter, reported that these were actually "Army 97 bombers," aka the Mitsubishi Ki-21, known by the Allied forces as the Sally (a later version was dubbed the Gwen). Originally it was known as the Jane, but General Douglas MacArthur had objected to any enemy plane sharing a code name with his wife. Whatever the nickname, Judy was spitting her fire at them, and the antiaircraft guns did likewise.

But there were far too many planes (one *Dragonfly* sailor counted 123) coming in far too fast for any possible defense. Having passed over the ships, they broke formation and attacked in the standard nine-plane groups that had become all too familiar to the sailors and civilians alike (especially Forbes, who had seen these deadly precision attacks up close two months earlier aboard the *Prince of Wales*).

The Sallies began their attack runs from between two and four thousand feet above the water, and came in five-minute intervals. Hoffman and Iley began zigzagging their respective ships madly in the direction of Posic, hoping to round the island and find any semblance of cover. Wave after wave of bombers shrieked overhead, drowning out the screams of the civilians and Judy's angry yelps. At this point Forbes showed off his uncanny survivor's sense. "For some reason I changed position [on the bridge] at the last minute a couple of paces to port," he recounted after the war. It would be a fortuitous swap. A glancing blow hit the *Grasshopper,* shrapnel slicing through the bridge, grazing both Hoffman and Forbes and blasting the spot that Forbes had vacated moments before. "Where I had just been was riddled with large holes. I only got a small graze on my right forearm. I began to realize that I had a charmed life."

Knowing the *Grasshopper* carried civilians, including women and children, Iley turned the *Dragonfly* sharply away from Posic and out to sea in order to draw fire away from the innocents. It was a brave piece of work, but futile—there were more than enough Sallies to chase both ships.

Grasshopper avoided bomb after bomb, but *Dragonfly* wasn't so lucky. She took a direct hit amidships, a blow that practically split the boat in two. "The entire ship," reported one survivor, Army Captain R. L. Lyle, "aft of the smokestack, was just a mass of twisted metal, and the stern of the ship had completely disappeared." Two other bombs connected near the front of the ship, including an explosion that laced the bridge area with shrapnel and debris.

Commander Sprott and Lieutenant Iley may or may not have been killed at this moment—no one who saw their deaths lived to talk about it. Regardless of the exact moment and cause of death, they perished, Sprott at forty-eight, Iley only thirty, a world away from home.

Officially, forty crewmen were reported killed, including Malayan crew, in the explosions that ripped the *Dragonfly* asunder. Plenty of others remained alive, but desperate. There wasn't much time, as *Dragonfly* was going under fast. She was burning badly in the bow and was splintering down the middle. Several sailors launched a lifeboat and a couple of circular flotation devices called Carley floats. Many men clung to the floats, including a reconnaissance unit soldier named Lance Corporal Hollard, who lived to report the sinking. Several wounded men were heaved into the sea without apology.

The *Dragonfly* flopped over on its back, or "turned turtle," in Hollard's vernacular, and sank. "She slid below the sea," wrote Taff Long, who had managed to jump overboard, "carrying with her the bulk of the ship's company and nearly all the odds and bods we had picked up in Singapore. This all happened in about ten minutes."

The water was thick with thrashing men, making an inviting target for the Sallies, who twice returned to shoot the waterborne men with their machine guns. Long saw them coming and dove as deep as he could to avoid the fire. "As God as my witness—I could hear the bullets hitting the water with a 'zip zip zip,' and I could see the bubbles rising as they penetrated beneath. If I ever prayed I prayed then." Several more men were hit, including Captain Gingell of the East Surrey Regiment, who was wounded but not killed. He clung to the side of a Carley float and eventually made it ashore onto an uninhabited island. At least a dozen or so others were killed.

While *Dragonfly* went under, *Grasshopper* was busy trying to avoid the same fate. She had evaded dozens of bombs, and in so doing had steamed well away from her sister ship, which had run for its life in the opposite direction. The key to the evasive action was Forbes, who served as Hoffman's guide dog. "Commander Hoffman was unable to see the aircraft owing to his defective eyesight," Forbes remembered, "so I told him when the bombers were at the point of bomb release and which direction to con the ship to lay her at right angles to the stick of bombs." But the percentages were heavily weighted against Judy's ship. The Sallies kept coming and coming. Survivors of a tugboat that had already been sunk nearby watched the drama from one of the islands. For nearly two hours, bombs exploded alongside the plucky gunboat, enveloping the ship in geysers of water. Time after time, the *Grasshopper* would pop from the drenching with her antiaircraft guns blazing away.

"We avoided between fifteen and twenty attacks," reported Forbes, but at last the falling explosives found the *Grasshopper,* the greenish-blue plumes of water replaced by a bright orange tongue of fire. Half a mile out from Posic, a bomb smashed into the mess deck on the aft, or rear, side of the boat. As it happened, this was where a great number of civilians had taken refuge. By sheer ill fortune, after numerous misses, the bomb that finally struck hit home in a most sensitive spot—among helpless people not wearing uniforms.

Several dozen people were killed outright in the blast. Judy had been with these folks most of the night and had been seen heading belowdecks when the bombing attack began in earnest.

The nearby magazine, or armory, was threatened by the fire that spread from the ruined mess deck. Forbes raced to the scene to see if the magazine could be flooded, which would prevent the explosives inside from cooking off and ripping the *Grasshopper* into small pieces. To his dismay, it would be impossible to flood the hull because bomb damage had badly twisted the one area where water could be let into the gunboat without it spreading elsewhere and sinking her. The *Grasshopper* was in imminent danger of exploding at any minute.

Forbes sprinted back to the wheelhouse to inform Hoffman of this unfortunate state. The skipper ordered the lifeboats lowered, and all remaining civilians left to board them, with his officers as guides. Then Hoffman stayed on the bridge and rammed the gunboat as close to the shore as he could. Though she had a shallow draft that had made her so useful back on the Yangtze River, the *Grasshopper* couldn't quite make it all the way to the beach. She caught and held on a sandbar about one hundred yards offshore. Hoffman ordered abandon ship, and the officers began screaming at everyone left on board to head over the side and into the waist-deep water.

Beached, the *Grasshopper* sat at a shallow angle in the water, low enough that much of the fire was extinguished by the sea, so the danger of explosion was lessened. But the Sallies hadn't given up. Blood was in the water, metaphorically, and they pressed the attack on the now-stationary gunboat. Twice more, the bombs fell, but again missed. "The aiming must have been poor to have missed a stationary target offering no resistance," Robins remembered. Both the gunboat and the passengers who had leapt overboard remained unscathed. This included the Japanese prisoners on board, who "acted magnificently" in Forbes' words. "All pretense at guarding them was dropped, and they went around calmly and efficiently helping the wounded."

One last strafing run commenced, this time with just machine gun fire threatening the survivors, but if anyone was killed in this attack, it wasn't recorded. "We reviled the Japanese for this last brutal attack on women and children," Robins wrote. Mostly the bullets plowed up sand and tree roots. The Fairmile launch came screaming up the beach as well, grounding itself under a hail of gunfire. The Scotsmen on board flopped over the side and raced up the beach toward the cover of the jungle.

At last, the Sallies disappeared into the clouds. The survivors popped their heads up and looked around. The immediate release of endorphins that came with the realization they had survived was quickly leavened by the dawning awareness of their situation. They were marooned on a tiny island, with no food or water. Several people were wounded, and there were two hugely pregnant women among the survivors. There was also a blind civilian, tended to at all times by her daughter. These people had made it through the bombing, but staying alive and getting rescued were hardly things to be counted on at the moment.

A civilian survivor named John Duke, who had been wounded during the attack but managed to swim a good distance onto Posic, later described the scene on the beach in a letter to his wife.

> *There were about 100 people ashore, mixed bag, including... Naval ratings, Flying, Naval, and Military officers, about six women, six Japanese pilots who had been brought down... funny looking blokes, their straight black hair was uncut and stuck out all round like gollywogs [then a popular character from the label of Robertson's Jam with black skin and unruly curled locks, today a racist symbol akin to Aunt Jemima].... I hadn't a shirt at that time, only a lifebelt. We couldn't light a fire as the smoke would attract further bombing.... To sleep on the hard ground at any time to one who is not used to it, who is over 50 years of age, is an ordeal, but to one who is wounded as well was an agony which I do not believe I shall ever forget.... Later that night someone took compassion on me and gave me a shirt and later I got a dead man's shorts.*

Amid all the mayhem, no one noticed that Judy wasn't on the beach.

Meanwhile, steaming well to the north of Judy was Frank Williams, for whom sleep also came only in fits and starts. He crouched against the railing near the front of the converted steamship *Tien Kwang,* surrounded by more than 250 of his fellow evacuating RAF radarmen. Another former civilian vessel turned navy escape ship, the *Kuala,* rode alongside and somewhat lower in the water, as she was more heavily laden with refugees than was Frank's ride out of Singapore.

Passage through the warm and moonless night was mostly uneventful, despite the loss of one of *Tien Kwang*'s engines. They had left Keppel earlier than the gunboats, but they were slower boats and had taken a path farther east of the more heavily traveled sea-lanes toward Java. By the first inkling of dawn, the ships were well north of the gunboats. But more important, they were within sight of a small island that looked like it would make for a good hiding spot for the suddenly nocturnal refugees.

The island was a tiny piece of coral called Pompong (sometimes called Pom Pong), though granting it island status was being generous. Forty-five miles south of Singapore, Pompong lies about the same distance nearly due north of Posic, where the gunboats had run aground, in the Lingga Archipelago. The largest islands in the chain, Singkep and Lingga, which lay to the southeast, would have balked at including such a nothing little spit if they could have.

But Pompong's miniature geography was attractive to Caithness and Briggs, the skippers of the small flotilla. It wasn't a natural place to seek harbor, it wouldn't be on most maps the Japanese might have, and it wouldn't be easily spotted from above.

The *Tien Kwang* and the *Kuala* anchored in a small, horseshoe-shaped bay at five forty-five a.m., between two and three hundred yards offshore, with *Kuala* slightly closer to the island. On the *Tien Kwang,* several men volunteered to take the lifeboats and go ashore to collect tree branches, vines, and shrubbery in order to camouflage the ships, a duty Saddington deemed "a useless operation. It would have taken a week to cut enough branches to cover the two ships."

Unfortunately, there was a hitch in the plan—the *Kung Wo,* the converted minelayer that had ferried C. Yates McDaniel, Doris Lim, Athole Stewart, and the other newsmen out the day before, and been promptly bombed by Japanese warplanes. Its slightly damaged hulk lay roughly three miles away, anchored and abandoned off another speck in the sea called Banka Island. In the dark, neither Briggs nor Caithness had seen the *Kung Wo,* or they would have looked elsewhere for cover.

The damaged ship was a candy-coated beacon for the Japanese. They made right for it, and at eleven o'clock, seven planes arrived to blow her to smithereens. Watching from their own deserted island, the ship's crew removed their caps as their vessel vanished. "With it went all I possessed," recalled Stewart. But he and his fellow reporters were more fortunate than the passengers on the two converted steamships. While one bomber dropped its stick of bombs on *Kung Wo,* another came in low over Pompong and spotted *Tien Kwang,* despite her concealment.

Radio calls went out, and in a matter of moments, seventeen bombers were overhead, sniffing blood. *Kuala* took the brunt of the initial damage. Bombs blasted the stationary target, with direct hits on the upper bridge, the stokehold (where the boilers were fed with coal), and the engine room. The ship exploded into flames, the fire stretching from stem to stern. Scores were killed instantly.

Caithness was blasted from behind, taking shrapnel in the neck while the entire bridge seemed to fall on top of him. He thought for a terrible moment that he was paralyzed, but when the shock wore off, he struggled from the wreckage. Nearby were five of the stunned but uninjured women doctors, including Dr. Jean Lyon and a Dr. Crowe (two others were killed in the attack). Caithness led them to the gangway, which he struggled to lower. It took five minutes, but Caithness finally dropped the gangway into the sea and shoved the women down it, telling them to wade or swim ashore.

The small dinghies the *Kuala* carried were on Pompong with the brush-gatherers, and there were few life belts or rafts. If they hadn't been able to swim, they would have been in trouble—but all five made it to land. They were followed into the ocean by as many of the survivors as could make it over the side. The water around the burning ship was alive with splashing, frantic bodies.

One male passenger, a Captain Hancock, the governor of prisons on Malaya, was among the first to escape the burning ship. According to Caithness' account, Hancock went down the gangway but inexplicably turned back toward the mortally wounded *Kuala* and yelled something at the dazed civilians laboring ashore about trying to extinguish the blaze. His wife lay dead inside the wreckage, but it is possible, even likely, that Hancock didn't know this, or perhaps was in shock as a result. Saving the ship was an impossibility by that stage, but it mattered not—Hancock was never seen again.

One of the officers appeared with a boat from the island and brought as many people as possible to safety. Many had been killed by the explosions already, but there were still at least two hundred people to rescue. There wasn't a tremendous current, so most who made it out of the flaming wreckage made it to shore—but that was only half the battle. There was no beach to speak of on this side of Pompong, just a litter of rocks that made scrambling to safety difficult.

The Japanese above noticed the struggle and turned to deliver bombs right on top of the humanity swimming for their lives. A group of roughly twenty women who had alertly dove off the *Kuala* when the bombs first struck were tiptoeing along the rocks, aiming for the cover of the trees beyond, when a low-flying pilot saw them. He immediately banked into an attack run and hurled a stick of bombs at them. The explosions scythed the women down like wheat.

What had recently been an idyllic Pacific setting was turned into a slaughterhouse. Dead and dismembered bodies were strewn everywhere.

One survivor, an American architect named Stanley Jewkes, wrote in his memoir of rescuing innocents from a watery grave. His lifeboat drifted into

> a young mother [who] had probably been in the water for an hour or so, hanging on to the rope with her right hand. Cradled in her left arm, with its head barely above the water, was a baby girl about a year old. A little boy of three years clung to his mother with his arms clasped tightly around her neck. They were not more than five feet from the red-hot starboard bow of the minesweeper. The tide, which was now running fast, was dragging the rope out at an angle. We found them as we rowed the lifeboat around the bow of the ship looking for any remaining survivors before returning to the shelter of the trees on Pom Pong Island. Japanese planes were still circling overhead, dropping more bombs. Flames had spread through most of the ship, and were playing around the mid-ship depth charges. Ammunition in the ship's magazine was exploding like Chinese crackers, as it had been for the past hour. We expected a violent explosion to occur at any moment. Carefully and with difficulty we lifted the mother and her two children over the lifeboat's high gunwale.

Even those who reached the shore found it was not necessarily sanctuary. A British nurse named Molly Watts-Carter managed to clamber past the rocks and onto land, finding a cluster of fellow survivors there. "With a small group of seven men I was making a steep hill climb from the beach when the Japs returned.... One bomb fell very close to us, killing all my companions and miraculously missing me. I was however numbed by the blast for about fifteen minutes and could not move."

A government employee named Oswald Gilmour had a similar experience. "A soldier gave me a hand to get up the sharp rocks out of the water, then we both dived for the jungle as the planes were heard again.... I made a frantic effort to reach an overhanging piece of rock for cover. I managed this, but just in time.... A bomb fell... when I got up, the trees around were seared and torn and half a dozen soldiers near me had been killed."

Meanwhile, the bombers turned their attention to *Tien Kwang,* the smaller of the two vessels. "Abandon ship!" screamed Briggs from the bridge, an order echoed by Fraser to the men on deck and below. Swiftly afterward, a follow-up order—"Take your shoes off before you go in!"

Everyone aboard dove into the water, seemingly all at once. Many first tossed over the side anything that could possibly float, including Wang Hua-Nan, who grabbed an armchair and heaved it into the salt water, hoping it would help get him the short distance to shore, as he could not swim.

They had just started swimming for Pompong when the first bombs fell. None hit the ship, which turned out to be a disaster—they exploded in the water atop the men instead. Those not incinerated in the explosions had their bodies wrecked by the concussion of the bombs going off.

Other aircraft added machine gun fire to the storm of steel, raking the desperate swimmers with bullets, killing an unknown number of them. All the Japanese POWs were killed in the initial attack. "I remember especially the screams of the women," Saddington wrote in his memoir. "Men also no doubt cried out but it was the women's voices which carried across the water."

Frank recalled the moment years later by noting, "The lifeboats were destroyed and we were forced to jump into the water. We had to swim about three hundred meters to reach the shore, hoping that the exploding bombs scattered the nearby sharks. The water between the ship and the shore was filled with drowning men when the second wave arrived for the deathblow. The squadron... made a reconnaissance flight of the battered ship, turned in a wide arc and released their remaining bombs over the drowning men at mast height. Dozens died in this cowardly attack."

But Frank wasn't one of them. The exact sequence of events is lost to the chaos of the attack, but it appears Frank was closer to the island than many of his fellow swimmers, either because he was stronger in the water or his seamanship, honed by his time in the Merchant Navy, allowed him to get overboard quicker and in better position than the others. It might well have been mere fortune. Whatever the cause, he escaped the worst of the effects of the bombs and was able to stagger on to Pompong in one piece.

Another RAF man named Williams survived—John Williams, who wrote about the attack after the war. "I had forgotten to take my glasses off, but by a miracle they had not been dislodged. I pocketed them and struck out for shore. I was shocked by the scenes around me. Women and children from the *Kuala,* mutilated and burned in the water, struggling and screaming, some drowning, others attempting to reach the shore of the island."

One man refused the order to go over the side; he was an electrician and engineer for the Malayan government named Charles Baker. Baker had evacuated aboard the *Kuala,* but rowed over at first light to the *Tien Kwang* when asked to have a look at the conked-out engine that was puzzling her crew. The attack commenced just after he descended belowdecks. When the order to flee came, he yelled to the engine room crew that if the ship wasn't sunk, she would need her engines to be working. So they stayed and made the fixes, and when no bombs landed, Baker let out a sigh of relief.

He made his way back topside when someone yelled to him, "Look at your bloody ship!" *Kuala* was burning furiously, on the verge of destruction. Baker dove into the ocean as another wave of bombers swooped in. Giant waterspouts erupted as the explosions went off. Miraculously unhurt, Baker made for the burning *Kuala* to try to save some of the documents he had been transporting since evacuating his post in Malaya weeks earlier, but the fire was far too strong. So Baker turned toward Pompong. He was headed for a clump of women struggling in the water when the burst from a falling bomb rattled him, causing his false teeth to fly out and "sink forever."

Toothless, he pulled three women to shore by their life belts.

Moments later, the *Kuala* slipped away. The bombs that hit her engine room had destroyed the steam pipes required for firefighting, so there was little anyone could do to save her. Caithness and his navigation and gunnery officer, Lieutenant Frederick George, ducked in and out of the flames to search her entirely before abandoning ship. Satisfied there was no one left alive, they jumped off as the ship broke apart and sank.

For whatever reason, the fickle ocean currents were stronger by the *Tien Kwang* than they were a few hundred yards away, where the *Kuala* survivors weren't badly affected. Wang Hua-Nan and his armchair missed landfall and drifted past "numerous floating bodies, both living and dead" out to sea. His armchair soon broke apart. "I succeeded in getting hold of two headless European corpses, both of which had life jackets on and were within my reach," he later wrote in a letter to his friend George K. C. Yeh. Wang used a special money belt he wore for secreting banknotes to tie himself to the dead bodies, then floated for hours in waters "infested with sharks and crocodiles."

Another raft carrying thirty civilians from the *Kuala* was swept past Pompong and out into open waters, but mostly, it was the surviving radarmen off the *Tien Kwang* who were unable to reach shore. Some would drift for days, eventually washing up on other islands or getting picked up by fishing skiffs. Far more perished a watery death before salvation arrived. Lieutenant Briggs and most of the *Tien Kwang* crew made it to Pompong Island, but that was not the case for the majority of the RAF personnel. Frank was extremely lucky. Of the 266 radarmen aboard, 179 were killed in the attack. Only thirty-four of them would eventually reach safety in Ceylon. The other fifty-three, Frank included, would suffer a different fate.

The *Vyner Brooke* was farther south of the carnage, having had a full day's head start on the others. Her decks full of Australian nurses, including Vivian Bullwinkel, the ship had made it through the previous night without being spotted. But on the stroke of eleven o'clock on the morning of the fourteenth, as drenched survivors of the mass sinkings elsewhere in the area collapsed on shore and the dead lapped in the surf, a Japanese spotter plane appeared from nowhere, raked the starboard side of the boat with machine gun fire, and vanished.

Captain Tubby Borton knew the Bangka Strait as well as any skipper in the region and figured he could use the extra room to maneuver his way to safety. He decided to make a break for it. Just before two in the afternoon, Borton spotted a small island at the entrance of the strait and made for it, rather than enter the waters between Bangka and Sumatra. But the shelter proved futile, for they were spotted moments later by a flight of Nell bombers, who launched their explosive cargo at the *Vyner Brooke*.

Borton engaged his hard-earned strategy for staying afloat under bombardment, zigzagging furiously, carefully watching the Nells line up and take turns dropping their bombs. When he saw a bomb loose from its rack, he hauled the wheel hard over. By employing this tactic, the *Vyner Brooke* managed to avoid twenty-nine bombs thrown her way.

But the thirtieth went directly down the ship's funnel, exploding in the engine room. From that moment, the *Vyner Brooke* was doomed. "There was a terrific bang and after that she was still," recorded Betty Jeffrey. Several more on-target bombs killed many aboard and removed any hope of rescue. Borton ordered abandon ship, and the nurses moved to evacuate the civilians still alive inside the badly damaged vessel.

As they attempted to move the living toward the lifeboats that weren't demolished in the bombing, panic began to break out on deck. Then a high-pitched voice, one that belonged to a female but not one of the Australian sisters, cut through the pandemonium. "Everybody stand still!" the voice commanded.

The authority in the voice was so absolute that there was a moment of silence as all movement stopped. Then the voice came again, slightly lower in tone: "My husband has dropped his glasses."

Despite their immediate future prospects, everyone laughed at the chutzpah involved. But the smiles faded as everyone went onto the water. Vivian didn't know how to swim, so she checked and rechecked her life belt until the *Vyner Brooke* was almost on her side. She took off her shoes, dropped into the water, and made for a nearby lifeboat that was overturned and partially submerged. As Vivian grabbed a stray rope and held on for dear life, another nurse nearby boisterously began singing "We're Off to See the Wizard." Everyone joined in, their voices carrying over the wreckage, even as *Vyner Brooke* went under the waves and vanished. It was two twenty-five, a mere fifteen minutes after the attack began.

Vivian's boat, along with the majority of the nurses who survived the ocean, washed up on an island called Bangka (not to be confused with the far smaller Banka, where the *Kung Wo* survivors, including C. Yates McDaniel and Doris Lim, washed up), a relatively large piece of land east of Sumatra. Vivian ended up as part of a large group that included two dozen nurses and a dozen servicemen, plus some civilians. They were all huddled together on a beach called Radji, debating what to do next. Not long after that, the Japanese arrived.

It was a company-sized unit of IJA soldiers. They marched the men down the beach and around a headland, out of sight. Left on the beach were Vivian and twenty-two other women, all nurses, save one elderly civilian.

"There are two things I hate the most, the sea and the Japs, and now I've got them both," spat one of the ladies.

As everyone laughed, the sound of gunfire erupted in the distance, off past the headland where the men had been led. The nurses looked at each other, aghast—there was little doubt about what had just happened.

Indeed, the servicemen and male civilians had been massacred—made to tear their clothing to use as blindfolds, then gunned down by machine gun fire and repeatedly stabbed with bayonets. On the brink of the killing, one man muttered, "Here's where we get it in the back."

"Well, I'm going to give it a go, then," replied a sailor named Ernest Lloyd, a stoker who had also survived the sinking of the *Prince of Wales*, only to be blasted by enemy munitions into the sea once again.

When the anticipated slaughter commenced, Lloyd managed to race into the water and survive the hail of gunfire sent his way (he was hit twice, but superficially). He later swam back to the beach, which had become a charnel. Lloyd's luck soon ran out—he was later recaptured and held as a POW for the duration of the war. But he kept his life, one of only two men to do so.

After a few minutes, the Japanese detachment shuffled back through the sand toward the women. They plopped down companionably in front of the nurses and began to clean their rifles and bloody bayonets. They remained expressionless, and the women matched their stoicism. There was no sound save the metallic clicks of rounds being chambered. There was nowhere to run, no point in resistance. As a unit, the Australian women gracefully accepted their fate. "Chin up, girls, I'm proud of you and I love you all," said an older nurse.

"We all knew we were going to die," Vivian told the *Canberra Times* after the war. "We stood waiting. There were no protests." Some historians believe that evidence points to the fact that the women were raped, although Vivian never admitted as such.

But there was no doubt about what happened next. The soldiers motioned for the nurses to stand and began to push the women into the ocean. The surf was knee-high, and several ladies stumbled as the waves crashed. The Red Cross sashes they still wore became drenched. All Vivian could think of was that she was about to join her late father, wherever he was. When the women had waded into water that reached their midriffs, the Japanese opened fire with rifles and a heavy machine gun.

"They just swept up and down the line, and the girls fell one after the other," Vivian recalled. All were shot in the back and disappeared into the water. Vivian was hit as well, just once, and by a miracle the bullet hit her in the fleshy spot over her left hip. The force threw her facedown into the water. She was thoroughly exhausted from the last two days, she swallowed salt water that nauseated her—and, of course, she still couldn't swim.

Yet she was not dead.

Fully realizing that any movement would bring a hail of bullets, Vivian forced herself to remain motionless, floating randomly with the current. She held her breath, badly wanting to vomit. The surf action pushed her closer to shore, and it was all Vivian could do not to kick away from the beach, to put distance between herself and certain death. But with a majestic will, she played dead, somehow sneaking occasional, hastily sucked breaths while staying facedown in the water.

She couldn't hear properly over the crashing surf, but after a while she perceived a stillness from the beach. She worked up her courage and, chancing everything, poked her head up and looked around.

"There was no sign of anybody," she remembered. "There was nothing. Just me." Vivian stumbled ashore, her wound having been stanched by the long immersion in salt water. Semi-coherent, she tottered off the beach and into the jungle, where she collapsed. "I don't know whether I became unconscious or whether I slept," she said later.

Vivian awoke at first light, dreadfully thirsty. She discerned movement through the jungle. Japanese troops were on the beach. "My heart went to the bottom of my feet," she recalled. She rolled into some brush and remained silent until the soldiers left. After they moved on, Vivian at last could get some water from a nearby spring. As she greedily gulped it down, a voice sounded behind her.

"Where have you been, nurse?"

A startled Vivian soon recovered her poise. The voice was faint but the accent unmistakable. It was a British soldier from Yorkshire named Private Patrick Kingsley, who, although badly wounded, had survived when the men had been shot and bayoneted.

Amazingly, two of the three people to survive the massacre (including Ernest Lloyd), were now together. But they were hardly safe. Bangka Island still teemed with Japanese soldiers and natives unwilling to cross the men with the guns. Vivian and Kingsley pushed into deeper jungle, where the nurse, despite her own pain, not to mention the mud, slime, insects, rain, and soul-killing humidity, tended to the soldier, binding and rebinding his wounds, treating them with coconut innards, ensuring he got enough water and food to live, and keeping him from crying out when he slipped into delirium. It was perhaps her most extraordinary bit of heroism yet.

Vivian and Kingsley managed to remain hidden in the jungle for twelve days. But their prospects worsened by the hour. Finally, famished and having abandoned hope of miraculous rescue, Vivian and Kingsley realized the time had come to take their chances and surrender. They clung to the idea that the Japanese would let them live—that they wouldn't waste ammunition on such a miserable pair of prisoners. Kingsley agreed to the plan but asked for a short reprieve.

"I'll be thirty-nine tomorrow," he whispered, "and I'd like to think I had my thirty-ninth birthday free."

"Time is no object," Vivian replied, and the next day they celebrated his birthday in the jungle.

Then the hardy pair at last surrendered to the Japanese. Vivian was sent to a women's prison camp on Sumatra. Sadly, her heroic efforts to keep Kingsley alive were in vain, as he died shortly thereafter.

The Japanese officer responsible for ordering the massacre was traced to the Manchurian front in the waning days of the war, but he committed suicide before he could answer for his war crime.

The nurses and servicemen slaughtered on Bangka were just some of the many thousands killed as part of the Japanese destruction of the evacuation fleet. An estimated five thousand people fled Keppel Harbor, with about 75 percent killed or captured. Of the myriad ships large and small that had managed to desperately escape Singapore on February 12 and 13 (one official count put the number at forty-four, though some small craft weren't included), at least forty were sunk by Japanese planes and warships. Countless civilians and military personnel alike were drowned, burnt, shot, punctured by shrapnel, or otherwise died a cruel, mostly anonymous death.

As for the fortunate survivors, like Judy and Frank, their travails were just beginning.

CHAPTER 11

Posic

The *Grasshopper* and *Dragonfly* survivors gathered on the sandy beach of Posic, one of a group of atolls just north of Singkep. The area was small, quickly giving way to dense jungle that pressed upon the shipwrecked, one "thick with closely packed trees from which hung a tangled mess of thorns," Robins wrote. "However careful one was it was impossible not to get scratched." Posic appeared to be uninhabited, but Hoffman ordered the lone whaler carried by the gunboat to be manned and sent on a circumnavigation of the small island to make sure. He then barked at Forbes, who had just survived his third sinking of the war, to "Go and get help!" Forbes grabbed a Malay officer and an interpreter named Macfarlane and set off on foot.

After a few hours, it was apparent that there was not only no one living on Posic, but also no fresh water on the island. This meant the survivors faced few options, none of them good. They could wait on the sand as long as they could until they were captured or died of thirst, or they could cram as many women as possible into the small whaler and have the men swim for it, hoping to survive the sharks and the current until they found another island—one that hopefully had water. Neither plan held much appeal.

White had seen most of his stores destroyed during the bombardment, but the superstructure of the *Grasshopper* remained above the waves, and he hoped something belowdecks survived the attack. Hoffman asked White if he would go check out the ship once the whaler returned from its exploration. White shook his head at the delay and volunteered to swim over to the ship at once, thus breaking his policy of never volunteering for anything. Time was of the essence here. He immediately regretted his decision as he walked toward the surf. A dead shark, longer than White by about three feet, lay on the beach. It wasn't clear if the monster fish had been killed by exploding bombs or taken down by an even larger shark, but whatever the cause of death, White was unnerved by the sight. Ever stalwart, he peeled off his shirt, hoping that this would be his lone sighting of toothy predators of the deep.

Setting his personal best in the freestyle, White covered the hundred yards or so to the *Grasshopper*. He made his way below, pushing into the officers' quarters. Chest-deep in water, White recovered several things of value floating about, including pots, pans, and cutlery. But the only ingestible item he discovered was an unopened bottle of whiskey. He opened it and took a slug of Dutch courage. "For medicinal purposes," he whispered to himself.

He made his way to the forecastle deck, where the ship's lockers were. In near darkness, slogging through the water, White's mind began to drift into the unknown, and he suddenly felt quite afraid, despite the warm alcohol in his veins.

Then he heard an inhuman whine, almost a moaning. The warmth of the whiskey rushed from his body, and his hairs stood on his head. "I've never been that scared, even when the bombs were falling," he later said. But despite the frightening sound, duty called. He had to push through to the last portion of the locker area to complete his search. Gathering all his courage, he went into the room at the end of the partially submerged hall, when the moan was heard again.

This time, however, White's fright was replaced by elation, for he recognized the noise—it was Judy!

In the chaos and hubbub of the bombing, sinking, and rush for survival, no one had taken note of the ship's canine crewmember, not even White himself. During the attack, Judy had instinctively gone below to take cover. She had been in this room, which was near her usual sleeping berth, when a bomb's concussion caused several of the ship's lockers to slew madly against the wall. They didn't fall entirely, which would have crushed the dog. Instead, they trapped her in a small pocket against the bulkhead, where she could sort of stand in the water, using the sunken gunboat's angle of repose to her advantage. But she couldn't escape. White followed the noise to the fallen lockers and ran his hands behind them. He felt wet, matted fur, then a dry ear, and then a cold nose. Judy licked the hands, not knowing or caring who they belonged to.

White managed to pin himself against the lockers, and using his weight as a lever, he moved them enough for Judy to escape the trap and splash into the open area beyond. White lifted her into a gentle carry and went up the ladder to the deck. He suspected the poor dog was hurt, scared, and exhausted. The ordeal of the sinking had nearly done him in, he reckoned. What chance did a dog have?

To his amazement, after a moment, Judy stood up, furiously shook herself dry, and ran over to White, eagerly licking his face and ready to play. To the sailor, Judy's relief was palpable. White recalled that he didn't know whether to laugh or cry as Judy licked him.

"You silly bitch," he said to her. "Why didn't you bark? I'd have come for you a lot sooner."

Then man and dog returned to the deck of the *Grasshopper,* where White yelled the first good news of the day to the survivors.

"Hey, I found Judy! She's alive!"

A cheer rang out from the beach.

White constructed a makeshift raft from loose timber and piled the few treasures he could salvage aboard it. He was on his knees, trying to steer the unwieldy craft with Judy standing next to him. It was awkward, and White was doing his best to manage the current when Judy suddenly barked loudly and jumped into the drink.

She swam strongly in circles around the raft. White was puzzled by her behavior until he saw a dark shadow pass under him, sweeping the sea floor. His first thought was that a Japanese submarine had somehow found them. Then he realized he was watching a large shark, most likely a deadly tiger shark, cruise by.

Judy kept barking. She would have been a tasty snack for the mammoth shark, but either he wasn't hungry or he was disquieted by the ruckus. Either way, White sped for the nearby beach and soon ran aground, with Judy bounding from the surf just ahead of him.

"I was quite sure Judy had sensed the danger and did what she could to protect me," White later wrote. "She was clearly at the shark's mercy, but true to her nature, she dove right in regardless." The incident was similar to the one back in China, when Judy had warned Charles Jeffery away from a prowling leopard.

Having looked out for White's life in the surf, Judy now turned to the rest of the survivors. She began running up and down the beach, actively sniffing the sand, at times running into the water, which was receding at low tide. After a while, one of the marines looked up from the fire he was building to yell to White.

"Hey, Chief, I think your dog has found a bone or something."

White went over to where Judy was furiously digging at the sand. Expecting her to have found something that appealed only to dogs, he was shocked when a burble of water popped up from the wet sand.

"Water!" he yelled. "Judy's found us fresh water!"

Indeed, a small well of lifesaving water erupted into a geyser when White joined Judy in the digging. He and several men caught as much as they could in the pots he had rescued from the *Grasshopper,* and the haul was rationed among the group. There was enough to make cocoa and rice for dinner. One of the party lifted his cocoa. "To Judy," he toasted. In response, she looked around at the mention of her name, wagged her tail, and went back to snoozing, snuggled neatly between a pair of survivors.

Their most immediate worry was appeased, but the group remained unsure of what to do next. As Hoffman pondered the issue, a small whaler approached the beach and ran ashore. It was Les Searle, the sailor from the *Dragonfly* who had been wounded during a rescue mission in Malaya a few weeks earlier. Judy ran right to Searle when she saw him talking to the *Grasshopper* officers, remembering her favorite patient from the infirmary back in Singapore. Fully recovered from his wound, Searle had been sent on a recon mission to see if there were other survivors nearby, and he was overjoyed that Judy and the others were alive.

He reported that the *Dragonfly* was beneath the waves, and that a few of the survivors were on the next atoll over, about three miles from Posic. No officers had made it, and there were several wounded men (many of the wounded had already been lost). There was no Judy to find them fresh water, so they were on the verge of perishing from thirst.

Hoffman and White organized a party to bring the *Dragonfly* survivors to join the group on Posic and share their life-sustaining victuals.

But there were now more people under Hoffman's watch, which meant more mouths to feed.

The first night was spent shivering in the surprising cold and listening to the baleful cries of the wounded. The only light came from the still burning *Grasshopper,* a blaze that intensified into the wee hours of the morning. Robins described how the fire "had now got a firm hold and was burning fiercely, the flames making a lurid glow through the trees. Small arms ammo was going off continuously, occasionally shells would burst and seemed to whistle away into the distance. We felt uncomfortably close to her. After an hour or two of this there was a terrific explosion as the magazine blew up, the air was filled with sparks like a gigantic fireworks display and a shower of burning material came down on the trees around us."

If White hadn't gone aboard and discovered Judy, she would have perished in the blast.

Another man joined the party the second day—Taff Long, the sailor from the *Dragonfly* who had dodged the bullets in the water. He had been in the water overnight, landing on Posic on the fifteenth. He was weak from vomiting seawater, his shoulders and back were rubbed raw by his life belt, and he was nearly mad from thirst—but he was alive. He stumbled into the mob of ragged survivors on the beach. "What a shambles!" he recorded.

> Wounded people were lying everywhere. There was no medical supplies—there was no food and precious little water. What water they had had been found by Judy, the Pointer bitch that had been the *Grasshopper*'s mascot.... There were half-a-dozen dead who had been laid some distance away as there were no tools to bury them. It had been decided to throw them in the sea and hope the tide would take them out.... I found myself a space in the sand and settled down for the night.

At this point Forbes, probably feeling invincible, decided to push his already remarkable luck. He was granted permission to swim to a promising island nearby, one he had seen during the attack, to seek help. Macfarlane and the Malay sailor, whose name is lost to history, went with him. It was a tremendous roll of the dice, but Providence and the currents were in their favor, and they reached the island. When they hauled themselves up on the beach they were swiftly accosted by natives, who were "of a mind to put me to death," Forbes later recounted. But the Malay man managed not only to talk the locals out of killing them (given the hundreds of languages spoken along the island chains, merely being understood was a minor miracle), but also to lead the three to yet another island, where they were welcomed with beer by a Chinese man. Eventually the village headman there said he would take on the wounded from Posic.

So Forbes returned to Posic with a group of local tongkangs (native fishing craft), and the worst of the wounded were ferried to the headman's village. Of equal import was the intelligence Forbes had picked up from the headman. The island of Singkep, the largest in the local chain, was the site of a Dutch colonial government office, and rumors were flying that a rescue operation was centered there. Forbes reported this to Hoffman and said he was ready to venture on in search of a better option than the far smaller island he had just left. Hoffman grunted his permission to depart, and Forbes sailed off with the village priest and his son to Singkep.

When this excitement had passed, there was little the others could do but wait and hope the indefatigable Forbes could deliver. Night fell with oppressing suddenness. The only light came from the stars, which shone brilliantly over the ocean, seemingly close enough to touch. The nurses on Posic were overwhelmed with tending to the remaining wounded, so White was recruited as an ad hoc nursing sister. Judy did her part to sustain spirits as well. Then the daughter of the blind woman who was part of the group came to White with troubling news—the two pregnant women, both Dutch, were about to give birth. Exactly why they weren't evacuated with the wounded isn't recorded, but presumably it was thought that their pregnancies were too far along to risk the open-sea journey, and they preferred to give birth on solid land—even land as remote as Posic.

As it happened, there was an experienced midwife among them. White had helped deliver a baby on board a navy ship during the Spanish Civil War and he felt comfortable doing it again. The nurses couldn't be spared, so off he went, with only the blind woman's daughter as an assistant. Fortunately, nature took its course, and all went well. Two boys were delivered safely and were baptized in the sea the next day. The grateful mothers named their newborns George and Leonard (White's middle name) in his honor.

For four more days, the survivors clung to life, living basically on coconuts and the water Judy found. "The wounded were pitiful to see and suffered greatly," according to Long. The beach camp was virtually overrun by ants, tiny sand lice, and biting fleas. The insects made life miserable for the group, who were also plagued by bold spiders and thieving lizards that went directly for the dwindling food supply. But worst was the ever-present threat of poisonous snakes. Several species of dangerous reptiles teemed across the atoll, including coral snakes, banded kraits, and several varieties of cobras and pit vipers.

Judy became a lone sentinel in the fight against the snakes. Almost hourly she would leap up and engage an unseen threat in the sand or the nearby tree line. She would buck about like a bronco, using her exceptional quickness to stay away from the flashing fangs. Generally, the reptile would retreat, but if it didn't, Judy would strike with her paw or teeth until the snake was dead. She would then scoop it up and deposit it at the feet of a horrified human survivor. At least a few made for a decent dinner. Judy was doing her part, but if rescue didn't come soon, the group would either perish or be forced to sail the whaler into the unknown, a few people at a time.

Then, salvation. At last, as night fell on the fifth day after the *Grasshopper* was sunk, a shout went up. "Boat!" A large tongkang was headed to shore. When it landed, one of the men aboard explained that the irrepressible Ian Forbes had browbeat the Dutch controller on Singkep into sending this boat, the largest available, to the rescue. Under cover of darkness, the remaining survivors were ferried off Posic in waves, destination Singkep.

Thanks to fortitude, blind luck, and the superhuman nose of a dog named Judy, they had survived being cast away on a desert island. But their hardships were only just beginning. Deliverance was still a long way off, and the Japanese could undo their efforts at any moment.

CHAPTER 12

Pompong

Frank Williams was enduring plenty of adversity of his own. Like Judy, he was stranded on an uninhabited island with scores of wounded, many of them civilians. Rescue would be problematic, given the number of castaways and the prowling Japanese, hungry for more targets. Indeed, the *Tien Kwang,* which had been damaged by concussive impact from the bombs but not actually hit by any, still swung at anchor just offshore, and several times during the day bombers returned to finish her off. Remarkably, none connected with a knockout blow. But many of her steel plates had loosened and been yanked askew, and she was in imminent danger of sinking.

Frank assisted in the first order of business, which was to carry the wounded to a clearing in the jungle about one hundred feet above sea level. One female survivor later described the area in the following way: "In normal times it would have been an ideal picnic site; now it resembled a small battlefield." Pompong Island was about half a mile long and three-quarters of a mile wide, bisected by a spiny backbone of rock that loomed roughly four hundred feet over the water. The land rose steeply out of the ocean, and the rocks that plagued the abandoners of the boats made getting in and out of the sea difficult. There was only one small beach, fronting a lagoon dubbed Rocky Bay. It was here the doctors, some of whom nursed personal injuries sustained in the attack, and surviving nurses set up the island hospital.

One patient in need of immediate attention was Caithness, skipper of the *Kuala*. It wasn't until he was abandoning ship that he had noticed a pain in his belly. He felt under his blouse with his fingers, and when he pulled them out they were crimson with blood. He had been badly wounded on his side, and the paralysis he had shrugged off on the bridge now partially returned, rendering him unable to swim. He managed to slide down the gangway and hang on to a side ladder. Another officer paddled in on a lifeboat and grabbed him, but he couldn't haul Caithness, who was six foot two and powerfully built, into the boat. The others on the lifeboat held the captain above water as they made for Pompong. He immediately collapsed upon landfall and was unconscious for the next three days.

Just over six hundred people had made it to safety in two main groups, and they now collected to form a huge party. Everyone was in need of food and water. A group of crewmen took one of the small boats and rowed over an oil-slick sea out to the *Tien Kwang* to raid her for victuals and medical supplies, including morphine, aspirin, and tins of fruit juice. They also found an RAF sergeant named Chippendale, terrified but unhurt, cowering in the hold. Man and gear were brought back to the island. The men tested the seaworthiness of the craft but determined the ship wasn't long for sunlight. Bowing to the inevitable, the men widened the gaps that were allowing the ocean to trickle in, and soon the *Tien Kwang* disappeared beneath the surface and settled on the bottom.

(Frank himself remembered to the Dutch authors Neumann and van Witsen years later that the *Tien Kwang* "was hit multiple times during the first attack and was heavily battered amidships. The engine room had been destroyed and the bridge was a mess." This account contradicts multiple reports from other witnesses, all of whom recounted their stories far closer to the event than Frank, who was reflecting on this in 1970. Given the chaos of the moment, it is easy to understand the confusion—the bombing did damage the ship, after all—but it seems clear from the evidence that Frank was wrong and the *Tien Kwang* wasn't struck by bombs in the first wave.)

There were plenty of tins of bully beef and biscuits on board, but there was no fresh water, save three small beakers that had been on the lifeboats. A party was formed to search for potable water, and a small spring was found near the sandy beach. It "slowly but regularly dripped drinkable water," Frank remembered, though another survivor, a Dutchman named

H. van der Straaten, reported it was "badly contaminated." Regardless, it kept the survivors alive for days without any disease epidemic.

Wing Commander Farwell, RAF, took charge of the military men, and Reginald Nunn, the head of the Public Works Department (PWD), was elected to command the civilian government workers. Nunn was universally respected, as was his wife, Gertrude, who was on the island as well, but Farwell was not looked at so fondly. Charles Baker, the government electrician who had lost his false teeth in the attack, said of him, "Of all the damn fools I have met he was the worst." According to Baker, who was quite familiar with the ship's innards, *Tien Kwang* might have been saved, but instead Farwell's bluster and indecisiveness cost them the ship. "He bawled and shouted" — mainly in a power struggle with Nunn — "and due to this man we didn't get off to *Tien Kwang* until eleven thirty." By then it was too late.

The *Kuala*'s chief engineer built a lean-to canopy of branches and vines to give the wounded some relief from the blazing sun. But despite the ministrations of the women doctors and some thirty nurses from Singapore Hospital ("They worked liked Trojans," according to Baker), the suffering at Rocky Bay was great. Caithness would later record that "one poor man asked Lieutenant Briggs to shoot him as he was a mass of raw flesh, but Briggs had not the heart to do it. Mercifully it was only a matter of a few minutes before he passed away for which Briggs said 'Thank God!' "

An RAF man, identified only as Bryn B., wasn't so fortunate, as John Williams recounted. "(His) stomach had been gashed open by a bomb and his bowels literally spilled out. Still conscious, in terrible pain, he implored someone to put him out of his agony. . . . Bryn's request was carried out by one of his comrades."

One man required his leg to be amputated, and a brigadier general nearly died from a hand wound. He lost three fingers but held on for the moment. An RAF officer named Hogg lost an arm; stoically, he said, "This should be worth a few pints at the Local when I get home." A Eurasian girl, just sixteen years old, died of peritonitis after suffering a belly wound. A newlywed named Mrs. Hawes was crippled for life by shrapnel that severed her sciatic nerve. But amid the pain and hideous suffering, there was a glimmer of light, as there had been on Posic: there was new life amid all the death. A baby was born to a Mrs. Jones, whose husband worked for Borneo Motors in Kuala Lumpur. The newborn boy's crying was drowned out by the wails of anguish from the wounded.

Frank spent a good deal of his first day on the island working with other parties on the unenviable task of moving the many corpses that washed up on the beach. There wasn't much deep soil to work with, and the men often had to go well into the jungle to find proper resting places, generally leaving the bodies in heavy bush when unable to dig holes.

The RAF men separated into their own group and clustered near the spring. Virtually everyone was shoeless, having lost their footwear in the attack, so even walks were difficult. There wasn't much to do except watch the clouds pass across the azure sky and count the minutes until chow time, which would momentarily soften the rumbling in their stomachs. And little could distract them from the painful cries of the wounded, the soft weeping of the many women on the island, and the realization that they were in deep trouble.

Rations were enforced, and each survivor was given two cups of water per day. Baker estimated this volume as enough to fill "half a cigarette tin." The bully beef was plentiful, but as it wasn't known how long it was needed, twelve people would split a tin apiece twice a day, along with some condensed milk and two biscuits. The diet kept the survivors alive but had many scurrying for the bushes to violently relieve their bowels shortly after meals.

The first night passed uneventfully, given the situation, though the bitter cold caught the lightly dressed survivors off guard and added to the overall misery. Campfires were ruled out, as they had been on Posic, for fear of attracting enemy aircraft. The people slept clasped tightly to one another for warmth. Apathy set in as morale plummeted. One of Oswald Gilmour's friends asked him, "How long do you think we should give it before throwing ourselves into the sea?" John Williams remembered the stench. "The smell was overpowering—mostly from corpses that were being washed up and gangrene from some of the wounded."

Despite the hardship, the leaders were optimistic that the plethora of islands in the area and the hard-to-miss attack would ensure rescue. It was Sunday, February 15, and plenty of prayer was heard around Pompong that morning. As if in response, a British sailor soon puttered up in a local tongkang. It was Lieutenant Commander Anthony Terry, first officer from the *Kung Wo,* the ship that had drawn Japanese attention from above and led the bombers to the *Tien Kwang* and *Kuala.* As with Ian Forbes and so many others in the immediate area, Terry was a survivor of the *Prince of Wales* sinking two months earlier. Like the rest of his fortunate former shipmates, Terry had been pulled from the roiling sea, given a fresh uniform, and posted on to a new ship. And, like Forbes, Terry had now had another ship blown out from under him. While the passengers of *Kung Wo* (including C. Yates McDaniel, Athole Stewart, and Doris Lim) were in the process of being evacuated, Terry was scanning the area for others who had survived the onslaught. There wasn't much room left in the tongkang, but Terry took the six youngest and most badly wounded survivors, mostly burn victims, with him, eventually getting them to Singkep.

"It was a disastrous image," Frank remembered, "seeing children wounded and burned this heavily. I often wondered what became of them."

Soon after Terry left, some other tongkangs from neighboring islands began to arrive, bringing fruit and a bit of meat to the starving survivors, which helped get them through the day.

Wing Commander Farwell had left with Terry for Singkep early on Monday the sixteenth in order to arrange rescue efforts, leaving the seamen and Nunn in charge. Terry had already arranged for more substantial evacuation means while on Singkep, and late on the sixteenth, help arrived—a steamer a bit larger than the *Kuala* appeared on the horizon. Saddington, who knew Morse code, signaled the vessel into the bay strewn with debris. This was the *Tanjong Pinang,* with room for two hundred evacuees. She had been one of the few ships to escape Singapore on Black Friday to make it safely to Sumatra. En route, the captain, a Royal Navy reservist from New Zealand named Basil Shaw, had seen the destruction around Pompong and resolved to return after "dumping his lot." Good as his word, he had returned, though he would ultimately make a fateful mistake.

Shaw came ashore to confer with Briggs, skipper of the *Tien Kwang,* who advised the Kiwi to head back to Sumatra's nearest port, Tembilahan, which was but one hundred miles away. From there the women, children, and wounded could be transported to larger ships on the west coast, and then on to India or Ceylon. But Shaw insisted on sailing for Batavia, where he claimed he had business to attend. He gave Briggs charts of the local waters, left some malaria medication and brandy, and returned to his ship.

It took four hours to load the two hundred survivors onto *Tanjong Pinang,* which was rather fast given that the boarding took place in near pitch blackness. The only lights came from the ship several hundred yards offshore and a few lanterns used to traverse the jungle and the sharp, oily rocks. Almost all of the women and children, including the nurses, wives, and newborn baby, were carefully led over the rocks to waiting launches, which took them to the *Tanjong Pinang.*

Gertrude Nunn, who had been a celebrated choral singer before the war, got as far as the embarkation point before she stopped and asked for her husband. "Rex, I don't want to go if you aren't coming," she said, using her pet name for Major Reginald Nunn, and she persuaded him to let her stay. She was thus the only woman still on Pompong when the *Tanjong Pinang* departed at three a.m., heading south.

The steamer would never reach its destination. It was shelled by a Japanese warship the following night, which sank it nearly instantly. There were precious few survivors. One was Molly Watts-Carter, the British nurse almost obliterated by Japanese bombs on Pompong. She jumped over the side when the first searchlight hit the *Tanjong Pinang.* Ten others, including five British women, three Malay boys, a Chinese woman, and an Englishman, wound up in a raft with Molly. They drifted aimlessly through the South China Sea, north of Java, for several days. Some of the Brits went mad, slipping off the raft and disappearing into the ocean. On the fourth day, one of the Malay boys suddenly seized the Chinese woman, strangled her, and threw her into the water. Two others perished on day five. The curtain was dropping steadily on the rest when land was spotted. The indomitable Molly tried to pull the raft in by swimming and hauling, but the current betrayed them again, and soon they were back in open water.

All seemed lost when a searchlight pierced the early morning gloom. It was a Japanese cruiser. Molly was pulled from the sea and placed on a stretcher. "The Japanese treated me very well and soon revived my flickering life in me with food and brandy," she reported.

Molly was one of only a handful to survive the sinking (Captain Shaw, surprisingly enough, was one of the others). No one knew what happened to the *Tanjong Pinang* for a long time. Years later, a secret report to the British command could only assume "that those still listed as missing must now be presumed to have been drowned and their next-of-kin notified accordingly." It was a horrific end for the hundreds of innocents that had survived one sinking only to face another just days later.

The remaining men (and sole woman, Gertrude Nunn) on Pompong knew nothing of this tragic turn of affairs. By Tuesday the seventeenth, the lack of food was beginning to wear on the survivors who remained on Pompong, even though there were far fewer of them to feed. The men lay around, hungry and listless. "Any exertion needed considerable willpower," according to one man left on the island. John Williams remembered, "We seemed condemned to one of two fates, either to die of starvation or to be found by the Japs and summarily disposed of, as were other parties in similar circumstances. We were fairly weak and mostly lay down whilst a few kept lookout in the rather forlorn hope that another friendly ship might come to our help."

Wang Hua-Nan, the banker who survived the sinking of the *Tien Kwang* by tying his money belt to two headless corpses, had been picked up by a local islander and brought to a village where several other Europeans were still recovering from their ordeals at sea. The village headman wasn't keen on helping any more *hongmao* (slang for "westerners"), but Wang convinced him that many *tongsennen* (native islanders) were still swimming for their lives beyond the reef. "He responded to my appeal, and many sampans were dispatched. In [*sic*] midnight, they came back nearly exhausted and brought to us over twenty persons more." None were members of his family, but one of them was Ray Fraser, the senior RAF man from the *Tien Kwang*. He told Wang of the situation on Pompong. The next day, Wang arrived on Pompong himself in the headman's boat. He was informed that all of his family and many colleagues from the Bank of China had been evacuated aboard the *Tanjong Pinang*.

It would be more than a year before he discovered their unfortunate fate.

Wang gathered as many men as he could, got back in the headman's boat, and returned to his island. About ninety minutes later, a small Japanese fishing craft motored into sight at Pompong. At the helm was an Australian man named Bill Reynolds. Having just retired from government service in Malaya, the sixty-year-old Reynolds had stolen the fishing boat a week earlier in Singapore and survived the passage to Sumatra, towing other damaged vessels en route. When he was informed of the desperate straits on Pompong, he volunteered to go get them. The vessel, which Reynolds renamed the *Krait,* took seventy more of the walking wounded off Pompong, including Caithness.

Seeing the *Krait* shove off with its first round of evacuees knocked some of the men out of their lassitude. The RAF men retained total discipline and stayed put, as ordered. But the seamen and the civilians had had enough of Pompong. Electrician Charles Baker went off in one of the lifeboats with several others, including Lieutenant George from the *Kuala.* They stocked the boat with eight tins of beef and a cask of water, then carefully picked their way across the rocks and made for Singkep. After a few hours they stopped at a tiny island where they saw some swimmers. They asked for—and received—four hundred coconuts. Such brass paid off, and they reached Singkep that night, presumably not having eaten all of the coconuts.

Some of the locals who delivered food to the survivors had also towed small craft to Pompong. These weren't particularly suited for open-sea voyages, but many of the stranded had run out of patience. Those who left on these boats often weren't as lucky as Baker and George had been. Several bankers drifted off course and spent weeks at sea, but they ultimately made it to India. Three others were at sea for five full weeks before being captured by the Japanese and sent to a POW camp at Palembang in Sumatra.

At last, on February 20, as Frank and the other servicemen (mostly RAF radarmen) left on Pompong could think of nothing except their own hunger and despair, salvation arrived in the form of a Royal Navy lieutenant with a memorable name: Sjovald Cunyngham-Brown. A sandy blonde with a confident, almost cocksure air, he had skippered the *Hung Jao,* a small vessel that had evacuated a few fortunate refugees from Singapore to Sumatra. Told of the castaways on Pompong by Basil Shaw, the captain of the doomed *Tanjong Pinang,* Cunyngham-Brown, who had plied the waters of the region for years, thought it best to go to Singkep, round up a bunch of junks, and then proceed to rescue them. Shaw instead went straight for the island and on toward Java, and paid the price.

Cunyngham-Brown's method proved more fruitful. He stopped first at Banka to pick up the last of the *Kung Wo* survivors, including Geoffrey Brooke and an Australian engineer named "Tommo" Thompson, and then was off with his quartet of ships to Pompong. Frank and the other airmen piled aboard, smashed like lemmings into the hold of the forty-foot boat, and they hunkered down for the overnight trip.

In an account given many years later, Frank said he left Pompong on a boat helmed by a "Lt. Comm. Cunningham-Brown [*sic*], R.N., from Lee-on-Solent (England)" for a trip to Singkep to "find coconuts and water," though Singkep was a far more important destination than merely a pit stop for sustenance. "How we managed to maneuver that vessel remains a mystery to me," he remembered of the tongkang, hardly anyone's first choice for a desperate voyage on the open ocean. Then there was the continuing threat from airplanes with bloodred suns painted on them. "Two times Japanese airplanes passed over us, but they let us be," Frank said. At least Frank was off Pompong, and soon enough, he arrived at Dabo, the main port city of Singkep.

The junks that saved Frank from starvation came courtesy of an incredible effort by not just Cunyngham-Brown but by a Malay named Tongku Muhammed Mahyiddeen. Tongku had been on board the *Kuala* but was washed away by the current after leaping overboard to escape the bombing. He hung on to a log for some seven hours before getting picked up by Malay fishermen. He promptly set to work organizing rescues on surrounding islands, but due to unfortunate miscommunication with some British soldiers, he thought all his fellow survivors on Pompong had been evacuated. On December 16 he encountered Wing Commander Farwell in Singkep, who disabused him of this notion. Shortly thereafter, he met Cunyngham-Brown, who told Tongku of his desire to mount a rescue force.

Tongku went to a nearby Malay village and arranged for four long junks and men to sail them. It took some brass-knuckle negotiating, complete with threats of retribution (and a promise to steal their opium), but these boats ultimately took the last of the survivors off Pompong for good.

The official British report of the incident praised Tongku effusively: "Without these unceasing efforts of a Malay among Malays, there is little doubt that the plight of the survivors would have been much worse, and they owe a great debt to the initiative and energy of Tongku Muhammed Mahyiddeen." Cunyngham-Brown was also considered a hero for the days following the fall of Singapore, though he would be captured after several more days of derring-do and sent to prison, where he would encounter many men who owed him their lives.

As with Judy and the *Grasshopper* survivors, Frank and a large number of others had not succumbed to the specter of death that hovered near them while marooned. But they were all still a long way from safety.

CHAPTER 13

Sumatra

Singkep Island was a relative monster of a landmass compared to the tiny atolls and spits of land in the area, measuring nearly as large as Singapore itself. It was a key way station for those who survived the fall of Singapore and the Japanese onslaught in the nearby waters. For the white soldiers and civilians, the Dutch administration there was far easier to deal with than the indigenous islanders, who, when not outright hostile, carried more than a whiff of Schadenfreude at their plight. The Greater East Asia Co-Prosperity Sphere carried the motto "Asia for the Asians," and while none of the locals felt especially attached to that propaganda, the plain fact was that these white colonials had been humiliated by an army that looked more like the natives. This feeling took hold in the region, and even after the Japanese were defeated, most of Southeast Asia threw off the yoke of their colonial overlords in Europe.

Singkep was prized by the Dutch (and soon enough the Japanese) for its copious deposits of tin, which was mined across the island. But it would be another element that would later take on great—and top secret—importance to the western world and make Singkep a significant spot on the map. Immediately after the war, the Dutch made a covert agreement with the United States and Britain to allow them to mine deposits of a radioactive mineral called thorium from Singkep, one of the few places in the world it was found. Thorium was a critical element in the construction of nuclear weapons, and the cache enabled the American effort to stay well ahead in the arms race with the Soviets.

That was far into the future as of the late winter of 1942, when the war in the Pacific was off to a bleak start for the Allies. All that mattered to the survivors of the *Grasshopper* and *Dragonfly* was that they were off of Posic and hopefully headed toward safety. Judy rode up front on the tongkang that took her to Singkep, nose pointed ahead, scanning for the enemy, or perhaps just enjoying the ocean breeze. After many hours at sea, the tongkang pulled up to an exceptionally beautiful beach. The passengers disembarked and walked a short distance to the main port city of Dabo, where the Dutch administrator held court. The man seemed to be a godsend. He took the wounded and placed them in a decent hospital, though it was up to the indomitable nurses to continue their care, as the Dutch medical staff had been evacuated already. He fed the group their first decent meal since they had left Singapore nearly a week before.

He also passed along a tantalizing rumor—on Sumatra, in the western port city of Padang, there were British, American, and Australian ships waiting to take survivors to safe havens in India and Ceylon, perhaps even Australia.

The massive island (the world's sixth largest) to the west loomed large in everyone's imagination. The heavyweight of the Dutch East Indies, Sumatra straddled the equator and contained vast swaths of unexplored wilderness, most of it rainforest, along with towering mountains, fast-flowing rivers, hostile creatures and natives, and, of course, marauding Japanese, who were landing invasion forces even as Judy was finding water on Posic. Sumatra stretches so far north that its topmost point is a short boat ride across the Malacca Strait to the Siamese-Malaya border. Its southernmost tip reached practically into Batavia. And as the western gateway to Southeast Asia, control of Sumatra directly threatened India and Ceylon on its Indian Ocean flank. In other words, Yamashita and his jungle-taming army were bound to conquer it quite soon.

However, Sumatra also had advantages for the escaping refugees of Singapore. The sheer breadth of the island meant there were lots of places to hide. The Dutch had set up rudimentary but reliable enough transportation systems, mostly bus and short rail lines, and large sections of Sumatra were navigable along its rivers. And there was nothing to the west of Sumatra but open ocean and the British forces in Ceylon and India. As the waters to the east of Sumatra (the South China Sea) were thoroughly dominated by the Japanese, this represented the only real hope of escape.

This renewed possibility of freedom ignited the appetites of the survivors, and Judy ate right along with them. All-they-could-eat veggie stew and rice might not have been the richest of banquets, and for a dog it was hardly on par with a good meaty bone, but it tasted great after the rationing of the past week. The escapees mostly slept outside at Singkep. The officers and the women had been put up in the swankier digs, mostly Dutch clubs, but these supposed places of elegance were so overrun by mosquitoes that finding a spot with a hint of breeze was preferable, even if it meant a dirt mattress.

Judy and the Posic group, Frank and the Pompong group, and many other evacuees from Singapore, most shell-shocked from enemy attacks and dripping wet from abandoning ship, all washed up at Singkep in dribs and drabs. Judy and Frank would have overlapped in Singkep on February 20, when the *Kuala* and *Tien Kwang* contingents arrived to join the *Grasshopper* and *Dragonfly* group, who had arrived before dawn. At first, there seemed to be an assumption that Singkep would be a good spot to lie low for the time being. It was too small for the Japanese to worry about, with bigger fish such as Sumatra and Java there for the taking, and at least there was food, water, and shelter.

Frank never laid eyes on Judy, as the two main groups of rescued survivors don't appear to have intermingled on Singkep—with one notable exception.

On February 20, Commander Hoffman of the *Grasshopper*, along with *Kuala* survivors Major Nunn; Charles Baker, whose quick thinking and bravery under fire had evidently made quite an impression on Nunn; and a few other high-ranking officials like Brigadier Archie Paris met with the Dutch controller of Singkep. Paris was the commander of the 11th Indian Division in Malaya, an outstanding if offbeat officer who never appeared at his headquarters without his two Irish setters by his side. He was considered an expert on jungle warfare (despite recent events) and had been ordered by the British command to flee Singapore ahead of the Japanese invasion rather than stand and fight. He had been on Singkep for a few days, having picked his way across the frightful waters on a yacht (the dogs, alas, were left behind).

The Singkep administrator may have been helpful to the downtrodden and hungry masses that washed up on his shore, but by the time the officials and officers gathered in his office, he was eager to rid himself of the Brits, saying there was little food on Singkep for the escapees, especially with "two thousand hostile coolies" (native islanders) to feed. Help might come to Singkep, he told Hoffman, but then again, it might not. "He had a very pessimistic outlook," Baker recorded. "He finished his speech by asking us to keep order and not to loot."

On that cheery note, many of the escapees made plans to get to Sumatra. That meant another sea voyage, mere days after the lot of them had been aboard larger boats that were sunk in traumatic fashion.

What the Singapore evacuees would do when they reached Sumatra remained an open question. All they had to work on was the unsubstantiated rumor that salvation lay on the other side of the island. Even if they survived the perilous crossing between Singkep and Sumatra, roughly five hundred or so kilometers of wilderness still stood between them and rescue (including the Barisan mountain range, which towered over Padang on the western side). Eventually, the survivors would cross Sumatra from east to west by three main routes. The southern route, through the large town of Djambi (now Jambi) was fastest, as it was a straight shot across the island from there to Padang. But the area was closed quickly by advancing Japanese forces, who made surprise landings at Palembang on December 14 and were working their way north. Only the earliest refugees who made it to Sumatra made it across this way.

Another route, some 460 kilometers north of Djambi, went through a town whose name would become infamous to Judy and Frank—Pakan Baroe. At the moment it was the hub of a good trail west, one that arced down on well-maintained but little-used roads to Padang. The relative few who crossed Sumatra in this fashion found themselves steaming west on board evacuating ships. But because this route was well to the north of Singkep, it required a far longer passage over the Japanese-dominated waters to reach it.

The majority of the escapees used the middle passage. This route meant travel up the Indragiri River to Rengat, a fair-sized village eighty miles inland, which was as far as the river could take them. From there, vehicles carried them across the harsh interior of the island to Sawah

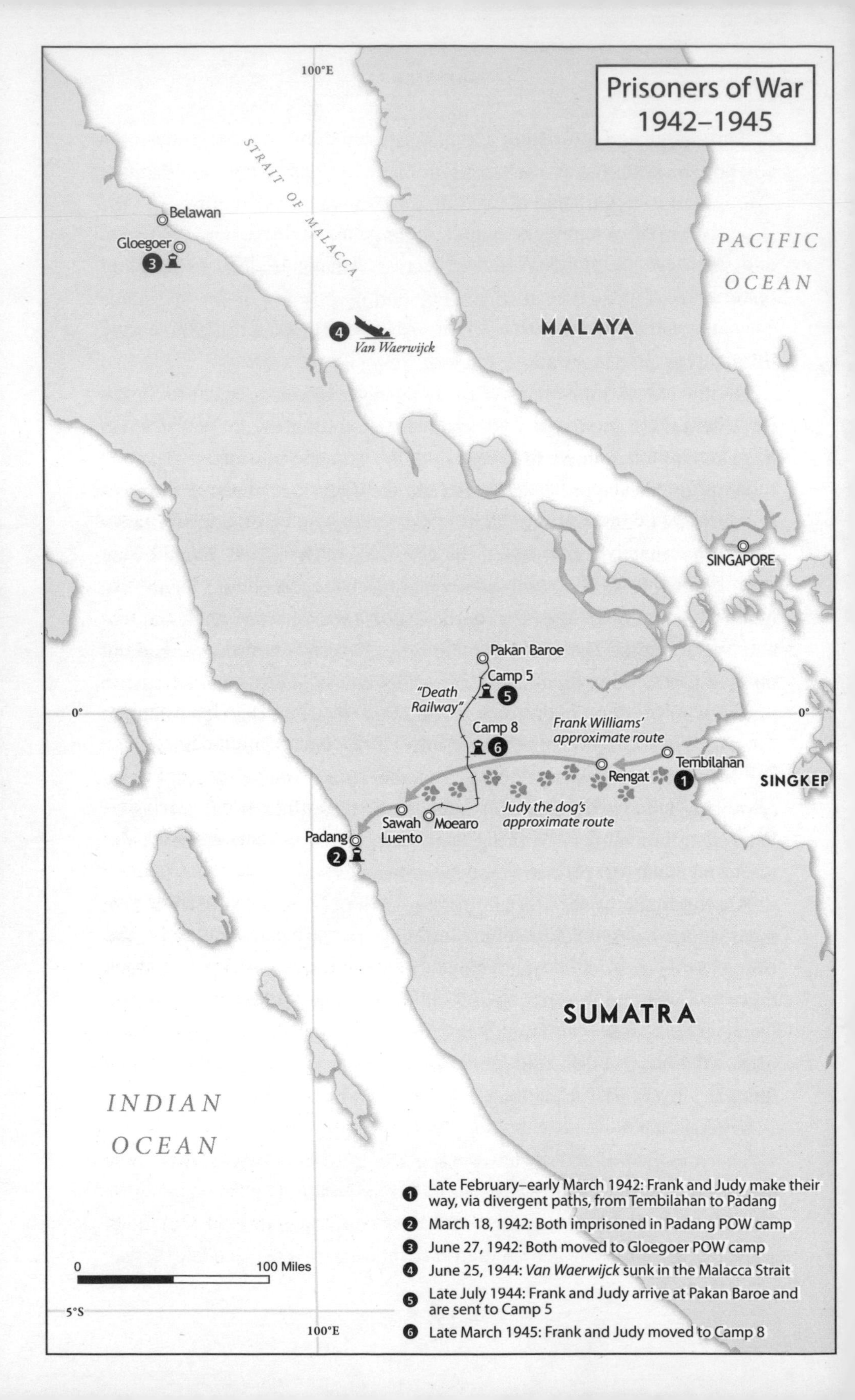

Prisoners of War
1942–1945
100°E
STRAIT OF MALACCA
Belawan
Gloegoer
3
PACIFIC
OCEAN
4
Van Waerwijck
MALAYA
SINGAPORE
Pakan Baroe
Camp 5
5
"Death
Railway"
0°
0°
Camp 8
6
Frank Williams'
approximate route
Tembilahan
Rengat
1
SINGKEP
Judy the dog's
approximate route
Sawah
Luento
Moearo
Padang
2
SUMATRA
INDIAN
OCEAN
0
100 Miles
5°S
100°E
1 Late February–early March 1942: Frank and Judy make their way, via divergent paths, from Tembilahan to Padang
2 March 18, 1942: Both imprisoned in Padang POW camp
3 June 27, 1942: Both moved to Gloegoer POW camp
4 June 25, 1944: Van Waerwijck sunk in the Malacca Strait
5 Late July 1944: Frank and Judy arrive at Pakan Baroe and are sent to Camp 5
6 Late March 1945: Frank and Judy moved to Camp 8

Luento, a railhead more than a hundred miles from Padang. Trains then covered the final distance to the port of Emmahaven in Padang, winding through the mountain passes and down to the sea.

In an excellent example of organizing capacity under duress, the Dutch and British would quickly make this central passage quite an efficient operation, complete with headquarters and hospitals at each major stop. Because of their efforts, many more survivors made it to Padang and thence to the Indian subcontinent than would have otherwise.

But the assistance across Sumatra benefited those refugees who got to the island quickly. By the time Judy and Frank arrived in Singkep, the Sumatran setup was winding down, with the higher-ups assuming that most of the survivors who needed to get to Padang had already passed through. While most of the shipwrecked had managed to get to Sumatra straightaway, Judy's group had been on Posic for several days, and likewise Frank was on Pompong until the very end. The many others who had tasted the striking power of the Imperial Japanese military and arrived on Singkep earlier were eager to get moving, wanting to light out in the direction of safety as quickly as possible.

The fear led many civilian and army and air force types to head straight for every available boat, despite the fact that they were landlubberly. "If a full and frank account of the army's attempts at navigation were compiled," opined one top secret report written in the aftermath, "much of it would be very humorous." One soldier stole a local fishing vessel and noticed an odd-looking piece of wood sticking out of the hull. He yanked it free, not realizing this was a makeshift stopcock, a valve that was preventing the sea from filling the craft. The boat nearly sank before he was able to wedge it back into place. Another spent hours making an anchor, then threw it into the water for the first time without tying it to the boat, thus losing it. The waters off Sumatra were heavily mined by the Japanese, and many other makeshift sailors were lost when they sailed directly into the strange-looking lumps in the water.

Others, especially those with naval backgrounds, were more fortunate. Charles Baker and Lieutenant George, having opted to leave Pompong in their own fashion (with great success), did so once more. They again traveled by native craft and made good time to Padang, where they were evacuated to Ceylon on March 2. George, alas, would be killed roughly two months later when his new boat, the HMS *Tenedos,* was bombed off Colombo.

That particular gruesome irony—surviving one life-threatening mess against the odds, only to perish shortly after in a separate action—was all too common for the escapees from Singapore. Commander Hoffman, too, took off on his own from Singkep, though in his case it was a matter of importance—he was needed in the fight. Brigadier Paris and Major Nunn went separately (Paris infamously told the *Grasshopper* and *Dragonfly* survivors to "stick together" before slipping off, leaving them to fend for themselves), sailing in a boat provided for them by the Dutch administrator. They all got to Padang in short order, to be greeted by the indomitable Ian Forbes, who had braved rough seas and the ever-present threat of attack to evacuate a dozen Dutch officials to Sumatra and then crossed to Padang via the Djambi route. He and Hoffman found passage on a steamer to Java, where they went aboard the bridge of yet another Royal Navy command, the destroyer HMS *Stronghold,* and returned to challenge the Japanese mastery of the waves.

Days later, on March 2, 1942, *Stronghold* was sunk in action during the Battle of the Java Sea, as the Japanese invaded Batavia and the surrounding areas. Hoffman was lost, as were all but fifty aboard. One of those fortunate few was Forbes, who incredibly survived his *fourth* sinking in under two years. This time he was picked up by the enemy, to be held in a POW camp in Celebes, another island in the Dutch East Indies (now called Sulawesi), for the rest of the conflict. But he survived that too, going on to become the British naval attaché to Sweden after the war and being awarded the Distinguished Service Cross for his bravery and unsinkability.

Calling Forbes the human Judy isn't too far from the truth.

The survivors of the *Grasshopper* and *Dragonfly* who remained behind had an ace up their sleeves, or so they thought. As his last order of business, Hoffman had arranged with the administrator to leave the wounded in Singkep and to provide a junk for the rest to get to Sumatra, complete with Chinese crew. Even so, it took prolonged convincing by a multilingual officer from New Zealand named Eustace to persuade the captain to sail. At last, on the twenty-first, they boarded the junk and made for Sumatra.

It was at this stage that Judy said good-bye to another close companion. For George White decided, in what he later called "something of a lunatic choice," to split off from the group making its way to Sumatra. Instead, he and a handful of others opted to try to make the subcontinent directly, with an attempt to sail from Singkep for India and the safety provided by the British colonial presence there.

"I was firmly convinced that there was no longer safety in numbers and that the Japanese would eventually round up all refugees and escapees," White recalled later. "I also decided I was not going to be around when they did so."

Part of White's thinking, as he would later write, was connected to his closeness with the pedigreed pointer he had come to love. Since he was convinced the group heading for Padang was going to die in one fashion or another, that meant in all likelihood he was going to either be forced to watch Judy die "after all she had been through" (which he didn't know the half of, having only met her in Singapore), or he would die in front of Judy. He wasn't sure which was worse. So by trying this foolhardy escape across the Indian Ocean, at least he would spare himself and Judy that fate.

"She seemed to understand all that was going on and licked my hand before I turned away," White later recorded.

So as Judy was taking a last prowl around Singkep before departing on her voyage west, White slipped away, along with two other rescued sailors, the Aussie engineer Tommo Thompson, who had been on the *Kung Wo* and helped rescue Frank from Pompong, and an able seaman from Liverpool named Tancy Lee (White never identified them by the names their mothers gave them). Unlike Baker, White had quite a positive view of the Dutch administrator. "He was a wonderful man," White writes—though like all the other British accounts, no one saw fit to record his name ("We called him Dutchy" is the best White can manage). The kind feelings didn't help, though, as the by-now-exasperated Dutchy turned away their request for a boat and told the trio they were fools for not having stuck with Judy's contingent, which was off to Sumatra. Soon after, though, he changed his mind and provided White transport north to the nearby tiny island of Selajar. Two army men, named Lamport and Fixter, joined them for the journey.

On Selajar they began several weeks of hiding in the jungle, in mangrove swamps and in isolated inlets, anywhere the Japanese weren't. At last, White and his mates made it to a local village on the nearby island of Pinobu, where they met a Chinese gentleman ("and I do mean 'gentleman,'" White noted) who fed them fish eyes and gave them a boat, a fixer-upper that the men took a while to patch before putting it to sea. The Chinese man's son, a fifteen-year-old boy who had been at the English school in Singapore, supplied another crucial gift. He tore a page from his school atlas, one that had a detailed map of the Indian Ocean.

With this page and nothing but a pencil and ruler as his navigation equipment, White laid out a plan to sail north through the Malacca Strait and then west for India. "It's only two thousand six hundred eighty miles!" White exclaimed to his dubious mates.

Off they went, pushing away from land on April 11, 1942, in a twenty-five-foot vessel, carrying spare fuel, water, rice, bananas, a bottle of gin, a rifle, a blanket, a watch, and a pistol with no ammo. Hardly enough supplies to take them back to Singapore, much less sail nearly the width of the continental United States.

"Weather good. God be with us," was the first recording in White's log of the journey.

Almost immediately, Fixter insisted on being dropped off, having considered the seeming futility of the epic voyage in front of him. White pleaded with him to stay, but the young soldier wouldn't be persuaded.

"He was in tears—so was I," White wrote. "It's a terrible thing to see a man cry, but none of us were feeling very strong at that time—and I think we all had a feeling that a wrong decision could easily mean death, his or ours."

It turned out to mean his. The remaining men gave Fixter their remaining money, which Fixter tried to refuse until it was pointed out there would be no need for cash in the middle of the Indian Ocean. White dropped Fixter off in a wooded creek on the Sumatran coast, where he hoped to join up with Judy's group. As White feared, Fixter was taken captive by the Japanese and was sent to a prison camp in Siam, where he perished from disease.

The four men pushed north without him. After a few days, the boat cleared Sumatra and turned left, heading into the immensity of the Indian Ocean. "We set a northwesterly course," White told the *Portsmouth Evening News* in 1945, "because it was obvious that if we sailed on in this direction we were bound to make a landfall somewhere on the Indian coast." They had already had several close calls with the Japanese along the way, but of equal concern were the nasty boils erupting on Able Seaman Lee's body, Tommo Thompson's increasing fever, and the discomfort of relieving themselves at sea. "It was pretty grim," White recalled, "having to hang on to your chum as he squatted over the stern, but it had to be done. I always had the fear that a shark would make a sudden snatch at what it thought was dangling bait!"

"We had our good days and our bad days," White said later, but by their fourteenth day at sea, conditions were dire. Their fuel supply was down to the dregs of the last drum. Thompson was in the grips of malaria, alternately shaking violently and spiking with fever. Lamport cared for him as best he could, but without treatment, the Aussie would surely die. And now Lamport's health was failing. No one slept much, least of all White. A steady rainfall threatened to swamp the small vessel. White's sketchy log (jotted in tiny print on the atlas page) kept a terse drumbeat of the problems. "Raining hard all night...had to stop and anchor...working on leak, doubt whether we shall be able to do it...pumping every three hours...can't make any hot drink...pumping every watch."

There had been no sightings of anything save breaching whales for days. White fretted that he had driven them in circles around Sumatra, or worse, somehow missed India, a very possible occurrence given that he was navigating with a page from a schoolboy's atlas, now soaked through with seawater. If he had somehow bypassed the subcontinent, there was nothing beyond until the African coast, a landfall they would surely never reach.

"I prayed like mad while I boldly foretold that we would sight land within the next twenty-four hours," White remembered. "I didn't say *what* land, but it cheered everyone up."

White's bluff, or perhaps his appeal to a higher power, paid off the next afternoon, when they indeed spotted terra firma, an occasion noted laconically in White's log as "land sighted." Sure enough, they had found

India—a seaside village in the south called Pulicat, where a friendly beam from the village lighthouse guided them in. White had unerringly brought them to a spot a mere twenty-three miles from the British naval station in Madras. The overworked engine, coaxed masterfully by Thompson through twenty-five hundred sea miles of duty, at last conked out some two hundred yards from shore. Natives pulled the exhausted men through the breakers and onto the beach. "I had a marvelous meal as soon as I got into British quarters," White remembered. "Bacon, eggs, tomatoes, everything I wanted. And I was violently ill after it."

It was an incredible journey, one of the most amazing acts of seamanship in modern nautical history, right alongside William Bligh's voyage after being set adrift from the HMS *Bounty*. But alas, it was not without casualty. While White, Lee, and Thompson survived the war, Lamport was taken straight to the base hospital, where he died of paratyphoid.

Meanwhile, Judy proceeded to Sumatra.

The junk's Chinese crew meant the sailors didn't have to work to sail the ship, but they could hardly relax. Between the patrolling Japanese, the mines, and the tricky currents, disaster could befall them at any moment. Fortunately, junks like the one they were aboard were common enough in those waters, and for the time being, the Japanese still had bigger targets to hunt.

With a stroke of good fortune, the two-day passage to Sumatra was uneventful. Judy, now without White to cuddle up to, rediscovered Les Searle, and made him and his group of pals her new favorites. One of those pals was ironically named Williams—Len Williams, an officer from the *Prince of Wales* who had come to serve on the *Dragonfly*. Searle's clique also included a large Scotsman named John "Jock" Devani, an accomplished scrounger and "the bravest man I've ever known," according to Searle. Judy curled up alongside these sailors for much of the boat trip, her nose between her paws, for once too tired to do much in the way of warning or morale building. Taff Long and Lieutenant Commander Eustace were on board as well, as was a badly wounded stoker from the *Dragonfly* named Farley, who insisted on coming with them rather than staying behind in Singkep with the others who were injured.

Everyone aboard breathed easier when they reached Sumatra and cleared the mouth of the Indragiri River to sail inland. It's unknown why, but the Chinese skipper didn't take them to the largest village on the Indragiri, Tembilahan; instead, he took a turn and left them when the river was no longer navigable for his boat. Judy and the escapees found passage up to Rengat anyway, where the overland transport system across the Sumatran interior to the railhead of Sawah Luento had been in operation for nearly two weeks.

But crucially, Judy's group never found any motorized transport that would help them traverse the island. It seems the main problem was that they had left a hairsbreadth too late from Singkep, or had been delayed just enough by the failure to stop at Tembilahan. Lieutenant Commander Eustace searched high and low for any officers or controllers still on the scene, but they had all hopped aboard the last of the vehicles heading west. And there was no heroic figure like Anthony Terry or Bill Reynolds willing to make round-trips to ensure their safe passage. "The Indragiri escape organization was closing down by the time we arrived and after a while Eustace explained that it was every man for himself," Long reported. Incredibly, some people they did encounter in Rengat were the six Japanese prisoners who had set out aboard the *Grasshopper* from Singapore, all still under the watchful eye of Clarke, the intelligence man.

Judy's group apparently didn't make time to stop at the rest house in town, either, where they would have been able to bathe, sleep, and eat in as much comfort as they had seen in Singapore. The *Kung Wo* survivors, including Doris Lim, Athole Stewart, and C. Yates McDaniel, who passed through Rengat earlier, took advantage of the hospitality. They gorged on rice, gigantic prawns, and beer, though Stewart recalled that he "would have given much for a single cup of Australian-made tea instead of the liquor."

Instead, Judy's group met up with some locals who gave them some food. The locals also showed them the river path that would take them across Sumatra from Rengat—on foot, roughly 170 arduous miles through some of the thickest, creepiest jungle on the planet.

A group of fifteen navy men, including Searle, Devani, and Long, no doubt feeling desperate to move on, with the specter of the Japanese hovering just over their shoulders, made off from Rengat immediately, Judy by their side. Farley, the badly wounded stoker, was unable to come with them this time—he was simply not up to the punishment ahead. The group left him with some nurses who remained at their station (all subsequently to be taken prisoner). Had they delayed in the village longer, they may have stumbled upon some sort of vehicle heading west. But in their minds, said vehicle may well have been a truck full of Japanese troops. No one wanted to take that chance. Instead, they disappeared into the jungle, swallowed up at the edge of the village by the overgrown greenery.

The jungle that stood between Judy, the other survivors, and what they hoped was safety in Padang averaged sixty inches of rainfall a year and teemed with a nightmarish creature-scape that seemingly contained every creepy-crawly that could do harm. Various vipers, cobras (including the spitting cobra), and kraits slithered under logs and rocks, while in the trees, the largest snake in the world, the reticulated python, waited to snatch prey from the night and implode their organs with its bone-crushing squeeze. Among the arachnids in the jungle, the scorpion-tailed spider was particularly ghoulish, with its long, spiky appendage trailing off its standard eight-legged body.

Then there were the mammals. The enormous wilderness contained everything from colossal (and easily riled) Sumatran elephants to dangerous-when-confronted tapirs and rhinos, from the beautiful clouded leopard and its fierce relative the black leopard to the world's only venomous primate, the slow loris (which is actually quite quick when scared). There was an abundance of deer, apes, civets (similar to bobcats), and smaller game. There were even bears—sun bears, the only species that doesn't hibernate, given its tropical range. Sumatra was also one of the few habitats of the orangutan, that orange-haired primate so close to man in many ways—indeed, the very name *orangutan* is translated from the native language as "forest person."

The most dangerous of all the mammals were the Sumatran tigers, which were yet to have been hunted to near-extinction. Though their numbers were dwindling (countless animals were killed during the war), they still stalked the forest interior, which Judy and the escapees would come to witness firsthand.

And, of course, there were crocodiles, lots and lots of crocodiles. Of all the natural threats in the jungle, they posed the greatest threat to man and dog.

The flora the group encountered was likewise outsized, unique, and dangerous. The clear-cutting that marks the Sumatran rainforest today hadn't yet begun in earnest, leaving the wild growth nearly as pristine as it was when the first settlers appeared on the island. Beautiful rare orchids grew under towering bamboo trees anchored by roots one POW compared in size to "large aircraft tail fins," while in the undergrowth carnivorous plants called monkey cups snacked on unlucky insects.

The group found the river (more of a stream at this point in the jungle) soon enough, as it ran only a few hundred yards from the outskirts of the village, though already any signs of civilization had been wiped from view by the growth. As soon as they turned west, Judy took point position and ranged ahead of the party, on the lookout for any potential danger. She was easy to spot, as someone had slipped a navy cap onto her head just before setting off.

"What a sight we must have been leaving Rengat," remembered Long. "Some with no shoes—ragged, filthy shorts, some with native clip-clops.... We had no money—no soap—no provisions."

According to Les Searle, Judy felt like the group "belonged to her." The way she acted, he said later, was as though she was single-handedly responsible for the safe transit to Padang. She was tireless in the jungle, loping from front to back, sniffing madly, testing the soundness of the terrain, ears perked up for any crashing sounds rumbling out of the darkness.

They had enjoyed the sight of the jungle slipping past while on the boats to Rengat, but Judy, Searle, and the others now found themselves in its heart. Walking was extremely difficult. The heat, already in the nineties, was amplified by the intense humidity. The survivors' clothes were soaked within minutes and wouldn't dry the entire journey. Huge roots or overgrown branches regularly blocked their path. The lush, pretty green carpet near the jungle floor was merely camouflage for the thick, sucking mud that was everywhere. The gooey muck was full of leeches, which attached themselves greedily to exposed skin and could only be detached by flame. If a leech is pulled off once it has attached itself, there is not only pain but also an open wound to contend with. In that climate, the wound would fester into a tropical ulcer in no time. Devani found a leech attached to his groin early on in the march and had to grit his teeth and singe the bloodsucker off, managing not to permanently alter his manhood in the process.

Judy was crucial in finding solid ground on which to walk. As the party's ranger, she took it upon herself to find the best pathway, and her barks signaled the group to follow her lead—indeed, to stay in her footsteps where, at times, the walkable land was as narrow as Judy herself.

On the second day of the trek, the survivors had their first brush with the dangers of the jungle. A short time after breakfast, Judy was running ahead as usual when she stopped short and growled loudly. Everyone froze. After a moment, a large crocodile sloshed into the water off the path about twenty feet in front of the pointer.

Before any of the survivors could thank Judy for the heads-up, she continued her barking, chasing the croc up the river. She may have been trying to scare off any attack, or merely showing a bit of territorial dominance, but whatever the reason, Judy got a little too close to the enormous reptile, which turned and lunged at her, wrong-footing her. With a midair twist, Judy managed to miss the slashing jaws by a millimeter ("I thought for sure she was dead," Searle would later recount), but the croc raked her across the shoulder with its claws. She yelped and backpedaled furiously. The crocodile took the opportunity to escape instead of pressing the attack, but it most likely could have bitten Judy in half had it chosen to chase her.

Jock Devani was the first of the party to reach Judy and eyeball the damage. The croc had cut a six-inch slice into the dog, though miraculously it wasn't especially deep. There was blood, but it was just an oozing that could be patched up with the limited first aid supplies the group possessed. Knowing how important Judy was to the success of this trek to safety, the group stopped to carefully tend to Judy when they reached an abandoned warehouse a couple of hours later. But the animal that had survived a dunking in the Yangtze, angry Japanese soldiers and sailors, a ship bombed out from under her, and a desert island wasn't about to let a prehistoric beast end her life.

Judy was so energetic and seemingly unaffected after being patched up that Devani felt comfortable enough to leave her side and go on a scrounge mission, and it paid off mightily. He came across a case of Marmite, a sticky brown food paste used as a spread. Its salty, at times overpowering flavor made it an acquired taste (its marketing tagline was "Love it or hate it"), but to Devani and his group it may as well have been caviar. High in potassium, the Marmite would replenish salts lost via the unstoppable sweating, at least a bit.

Otherwise, the men could hear their stomachs growling. "We lived either off the land on bananas, pineapples, etc. when we came upon them, or went hungry," wrote Long. "When we reached a native village we either depended on their generosity for a meagre gift of rice or, failing co-operation, took food by other methods. We were desperate men."

Judy wouldn't require much medical attention, but soon the other members of the party began dropping like flies. A twisted ankle here, symptoms of malaria there, exhaustion everywhere. The unit had to stop to fashion stretchers from trees and roots in order to carry the afflicted. Any momentum from the boat rides had long since evaporated, and utter fatigue settled over them. The single-file trekkers started to stretch out dangerously, forcing Judy to double back to encourage and safely guide the stragglers, using even more energy.

Whenever anyone began to flag, Judy was there to bark, wag her tail, lick muddy faces, whatever it took, despite the fact that she herself was caked in muck. She would disappear into the distance ahead and return with (mostly) edible small animals, often flying foxes, to add to the meager rations on hand. On several other occasions, she sniffed out crocodiles lying in ambush and barked until they moved on (not getting nearly as close as before, however; of that she made sure).

At one point, deep into the slog, Searle heard a ferocious growl unlike any he had heard before. Assuming it was Judy, he whistled for her and set off toward the noise, hoping she wasn't hurt again. Judy appeared, but behind him. She was actually chasing after him and was barking furiously in her accustomed manner. Wondering what had been the source of the original growl—and not wanting to find out—Searle began to back away slowly. There was a flash of brownish orange to his left, and the crashing of brush. Judy kept up her cacophony as Searle moved with speed back to the group. While he could never be positive, he was convinced he had just had a close encounter with the rare but deadly Sumatran tiger. He was also certain it had been Judy's barking that prevented the beast from attacking. It was a similar incident to what had happened with Charles Jeffery in China and George White in the waters off Posic—Judy drawing the fire of a deadly beast with her aggressive displays, potentially forestalling a predatory ambush.

The naval refugees wandered on a circuitous path, following the river for the most part while getting course corrections along the way from villagers encountered at the water's edge. "We climbed and descended mountains, waded through swamps and small rivers and finally reached the railhead in a sorry state," Long wrote. At last, after roughly three weeks of exhausted trudging through the rainforest, the group had straggled into Sawah Luento, a town of about fifteen thousand inhabitants—and site of the train that would take them the final fifty miles into Padang. Searle and Devani were in about as good condition as anyone in the group, and they could barely move another step. Had they needed to walk the rest of the way, they may all have perished in the jungle.

Frank Williams and his fellow survivors wound up in Sawah Luento well before Judy's group, via a far less grueling yet still perilous path. The remaining men of the *Tien Kwang* and *Kuala* had been taken off Pompong to Singkep by Sjovald Cunyngham-Brown and the Chinese sailing the junks. The local rescuers had refused to take them directly to Sumatra, probably because the Japanese landings there had begun. But the RAF men were assured there would be readily available boat traffic from Singkep to Sumatra and, eventually, Padang.

A key player in these movements was Bill Reynolds, the aging but tireless Aussie, whose boat *Krait* continued to ferry survivors toward safety. After his work getting the wounded off Pompong, Reynolds took nearly two thousand people between Singkep and Sumatra, bringing most of them to Rengat. According to a postwar history by the British War Department, "During his trips, Capt. Reynolds kept his passengers entertained with his stories, and his wit and cheerfulness made him an ideal rescuer. What he lacked in navigational skill he made up in sheer guts and undoubtedly did a very stout job of work."

When there were no more people left to ferry, Reynolds piloted *Krait* around the eastern coast of Sumatra, despite the prowling Japanese and the mines, and wound up in Padang, where he caught transport to India and safety, the *Krait* tied up alongside the cruiser that took him out of harm's way.

Had Frank and his cohorts been brought to Sumatra by Reynolds, they would more than likely have made it safely off that island. But Frank's RAF contingent was too numerous for Reynolds to consider transporting. The Dutch administrator ("Dutchy") instead found some locals to pilot them across the strait in a flotilla of tongkangs and junks. The Chinese captain was not nearly so eager to leave the comforts of Singkep for the dangers of the sea, and he put them off for two critical days. At last he was persuaded to set sail from Singkep, a decision apparently assisted by the gift of a box of opium, and Frank and about three dozen others sailed off on a rickety but sizable tongkang painted to look like a sea dragon. Two sinister eyes drawn in bright red on the bow stared down any rivals.

They cleared Dabo's harbor on February 20, one week to the day that Frank and Judy had escaped from Singapore. It seemed a lifetime ago already. The two-day voyage to Sumatra was mostly spent in the steaming belowdecks, as most of the remaining RAF men, including Stanley Saddington and a Kiwi named C. R. Knowles, along with a few other Singapore refugees on board, stayed out of sight, lest they attract the attention of passing Japanese ships or airplanes. "A couple of [British] sailors dressed as Chinese crew" were the only ones Frank remembered risking a trip up into the fresh air until night fell. John Williams remembered peering up through the hatch and seeing the captain prepare and smoke his opium.

The voyage brought them to the mouth of the Indragiri River. It was a difficult spot to find amid the mangrove bushes, but the captain apparently did, and turned in to float upriver. Geoffrey Brooke got there on a different junk just ahead of Frank's boat. He remembered the slow progress against the tide:

> [The passage was] marked by the ponderous ascent of large birds of the crane variety, and groups of wild pig beating hasty retreat from stretches of mud into the thick jungle which crowded each side.

> Peculiar fish with fins that looked like rabbit's ears scurried about in the slime and once we saw a crocodile. Eventually the sun was extinguished by a black fretwork of trees and so was our interest in Sumatran fauna, or anything else.

Frank would have done this same voyage a day or two after Brooke. They would have stopped at a small fishing village built on stilts, where, tacked to a wall of a hut, were orders from a British major on exactly how to proceed. A Eurasian was the headman of the village—he offered food to Brooke but pointed out that several thousand people from Singapore had already been through and had nearly emptied the larder. So Frank, arriving after Brooke, not only didn't fill his belly but also would have realized that time was running short.

The unease no doubt mounted at Tembilahan, the main stop on the Indragiri. The English officer in charge, Captain Ernest Gordon, asked Brooke how many were in his party. "Sixty, with two or three junk-loads to follow." Gordon was surprised. "That's awkward," he said to Brooke. "We thought we were about at the end." Indeed not, for a day or two later Frank's junk showed up. The men gorged on coconuts (which gave everyone the runs), eggs, and rice, and slept in a warehouse where "dozens of rats swarmed the walls," according to John Williams. The beat-up old tongkang was showing signs of cracking, so Gordon arranged to have it towed farther west upriver by a landing craft.

Their next stop was a rubber estate at a village called Ayer Muluk (also called Moelik or Iyer Molek). Rain had started to descend in torrents. The men squelched through the mud to brick huts once used for processing rubber, where they were given soup before sacking out. The long crepe rubber sheets that remained inside were used as bedding, so they "slept like hibernating caterpillars," according to one escapee.

At this point, the situation with the tongkang had reached crisis. The rotten wood was sodden, and water was shooting up from the bottom. Frank and a few other men decided the time had come to swap vessels, and they managed to find an unclaimed motorboat big enough to carry them. It proved to be a wise decision, for while they slept in the rubber huts, the tongkang sank to the bottom of the river. In the morning, as Frank pushed the motorboat off the dock, he could see the unmistakable red eyes painted on the bow staring upstream. "It gave the impression of a prehistoric water monster," Frank recalled.

The group went on to Rengat, where, while puttering along on the river before actually entering town, there was apparently a fateful moment that portended much. In a tantalizing detail from the interview Frank gave to Neumann and van Witsen in 1970, Frank said it was here that he caught his first-ever glimpse of Judy, the pointer that would become his best friend. "I did not know who she was or where she came from," he remembered. "Only later was I told that she was one of the survivors of the HMS *Grasshopper.* I remember thinking, 'What on earth is a beautiful English pointer like that doing over here with no one to care for her?' . . . I realized that even though she looked thin and frail she was a true survivor."

He records nothing else, no special pang in his soul at seeing Judy, who would have been just a passing fancy, notable only because it was unusual that a dog was in such close company with other British servicemen. But the frisky female pointer apparently made enough of an impression on him that he remembered the momentary sighting decades later.

Unfortunately, this raises any number of questions. Judy's group of Posic survivors, it will be recalled, were also running late in their desperate lunge for Padang. But when they got to Rengat, it was after the last of the motorized transport had headed west. It was "every man [and dog] for himself [or herself]." There is nothing in Frank's recorded interviews that illuminates exactly why the Posic group that included the pointer was forced to walk into the jungle and all the way to Sawah Luento, and Frank's group from Pompong was not.

The lone clue may come from Brooke. In his memoir he recalled several days of anxious waiting in Rengat as the officials in charge scrambled to find trucks or buses. At last, Brooke was placed in charge of an old steamboat that pulled two barges, laden with half the men in Rengat. They puttered along at walking speed, scarcely one knot. "The bank could just be seen to be going past!" Brooke wrote. But the next day, they rounded a bend in the river to see a large encampment of servicemen. Several buses had indeed been rounded up, and the Rengat stragglers put aboard—and there was plenty of space for those on the barges, including Brooke.

Clearly, Frank and his party got on one of these buses. If indeed Frank had seen Judy at Rengat, and there is no reason to believe he was mistaken, the only logical explanation is that during the period before the buses were found, Judy's group of sailors got discouraged and set off walking. Once in the jungle, the odds of running into the others was impossibly small.

When Frank did arrive at Rengat, the rain was still hammering down in sheets. John Williams, who arrived shortly before Frank, remembers a friend noting "it wouldn't much matter if we did fall in the river now, we couldn't get any wetter." Right on cue, Williams wrote, "As he spoke he missed his footing and into the river he went, to the amusement of all."

In Rengat, some of the organizational capabilities of the British and Dutch were still in effect. Frank and his friends were put up in a schoolhouse that was overrun by mosquitoes who "gave them a hearty welcome," according to an after-action report. There was a small customs warehouse that processed and kept track of the refugees passing through. Parties were organized with a leader for the trek onward. A kitchen run by the Dutch fed them soup and rice—hardly filling, but better than nothing. And there was the hospital, as there now was at all the major outposts along the central route. They were modestly equipped, but they provided quality care for the walking wounded.

The Dutch were evacuating their personnel at the same time but provided as many vehicles as they could. Everything that moved—bus, truck, jeep, or oxcart—eventually wound up in Sawah Luento. It was hardly first-class transport. "For the most part they were incredibly ramshackle," noted a British report on the evacuations, "yet they tirelessly made journey after journey carrying full loads." The drivers screamed around the tight mountain passes, leaning on their horns the whole way, seemingly about to plunge over one chasm or another at any moment. At one stage in the journey was a river that required a winched ferry to cross. Using a wire and handwheel, the ferryman slowly and painfully hauled man and vehicle to the other side. "We arrived in one piece," remembered a British artilleryman named John Purvis. "I don't know how we did it."

From Sawah Luento, a train left for Padang every afternoon, winding through the mountain passes that guarded the seaside town. The train was "a tall, ancient thing," according to Brooke, "and we climbed up to the carriages via several steps." Brooke recalls a pleasant journey on comfortable cushions, but most other contemporary reports tell of badly overcrowded cars, with doors and windows left open to provide a modicum of moving air for the suffocating passengers. Frank was on one of these trains, one that left Sawah Luento on March 7 or 8, bound at last for Padang.

Almost exactly one week later, midday on March 15, Judy and the Posic group emerged from the jungle into Sawah Luento. Rumors were flying all over town of the impending arrival of the Japanese. No one had actually seen anyone in the uniform of the Imperial Army or Navy, but it was considered a matter of days—even hours.

The disheveled men and their injured but hardy dog startled a boy who was playing in front of his hut. He thought it was the advancing Japanese, but when he saw Judy, his terror turned to a smile, and he walked with the party all the way to the train station. "We were overjoyed to be informed that a train could take us to Padang that very afternoon," recalled Long.

For Judy and the men who had somehow survived the hellish trek across Sumatra, the relief at closing in on their holy grail, Padang, was palpable. Because they were so late getting to Sawah Luento, the vast majority of escapees had already made their way to the sea—but that at least meant the train wasn't as cramped as it had been the last few weeks. They were making great time at last, and they were *sitting down*.

Optimism replaced the specter of death that had hung over the survivors ever since the Japanese dive-bombers had destroyed their gunboat. The group could practically taste the ocean breeze, imagine themselves leaning over the rail of a safe and sturdy ship, and feel the comfortable bed they would lie upon in India or Ceylon or wherever, so long as it was far from the infernal Japanese and this war. Not that any of them were cowards—every one of them would have gone back to fight immediately if asked. They just needed a short respite. And they were so close to getting one.

CHAPTER 14

Padang

If the docks at Keppel Harbor during Singapore's dying moments as a free city were the very picture of chaos, the scenes at Emmahaven Harbor, Padang, during late February and early March were little better. In some ways, Padang was worse. Though there had been bombs falling on evacuees in Singapore, the order maintained by the British military, in the main the Royal Navy, had been exemplary. Comparatively, the naked displays of humanity's worst impulses under intense duress were far more prevalent at Emmahaven.

Having survived extreme trials at sea and over land, the escapees that descended upon the waiting ships were, understandably, impatient to finish the drill. The men and women grappling for passage were driven by the primal urge for safety, and the fragrance of this panic permeated the docks. These people desired nothing more than to be taken far from the Japanese invaders. The race to board the few available ships, including a pair of Royal Navy destroyers along with three cruisers and civilian vessels of varying sizes and seaworthiness, resulted in mayhem unworthy of a military operation—even that of a bedraggled, multiservice force in disgraced retreat. Officers ditched lower-ranking men to secure places on the departing vessels. Violent arguments broke out over the dwindling berths. The Dutch administrators and local citizenry were flabbergasted by the unmilitary displays.

Upon war's end, a secret report on the Sumatran experience was prepared by the British War Ministry. It pulled no punches in describing the horrific behavior displayed in Padang.

> The behaviour [*sic*] of our troops from senior officers to privates was in many cases deplorable.... An accepted rule was that all should go forward in the order of arrival in Sumatra, each considering he was just as worthy an escaper as the neighbor and had just as important a fund of knowledge and experience to carry away. In other words the average individual had no desire to be evacuated before those who had won the boat race but stuck up for his own place in the evacuation. However, when he saw staff officers jumping ahead of him, heard of telegrams ordering surplus medical and PWD personnel forward in priority, saw civilians who travelled with the military organization only when it was the quickest means of transport going ahead on their own, his anxiety was very noticeable.

In a different section of this report the tut-tutting practically leaps from the page. "In Sumatra, until men came along who put their own personal safety last, those who had a finger in any organization very often managed to do the work to their own benefit. This was especially true in Padang where it was frequently noticed that those 'on the spot' managed to get on board ships after a shorter wait than the rest."

Meanwhile, the situation was exacerbated, at least in the minds of the British and Dutch, by a group of rampaging Australians, many of whom had deserted in Singapore and found their way to Padang, pulled in by the gravitational force of rumored escape ships. They turned lawless once there, stealing from soldiers and civilians alike, ransacking the homes of Dutch controllers looking for valuables to hawk, and selling weapons (mostly pilfered) to locals, a high crime in the minds of the Dutch. The marauding Aussies also got drunk and shot off their guns at random, which—in addition to their thievery—made for a lack of safety in the streets of Padang.

A different postwar, top secret British report on the performance of the Dutch in Sumatra noted that their overall assistance was very good "before disgraceful scenes [from Commonwealth soldiers] which attended departure of... ships for Ceylon.... They were so annoyed at this subsequently it was reported that their aim was to be clear of everyone as quickly as possible."

* * *

The selfishness and dishonorable conduct reached its nadir with the escape of the SS *Rooseboom,* a Dutch steamer bound for India. Brigadier Archie Paris, who had been granted special status to leave Singapore early, had escaped on a private yacht owned by one Scottish soldier, Major Angus MacDonald, and skippered by another, Captain Mike Blackwood. The favoritism appeared to go to Paris' head. He shoved his way onto the *Rooseboom,* commandeering the entire officers' quarters on board for himself, MacDonald, and Blackwood, along with a handful of select staffers—many of whom were pulled out of order ahead of those who preceded them in the queue. Loud complaints were voiced and everyone involved was left with a sour taste in their mouths, especially the lower ranks passed over for boarding. Many swore to themselves "they will not take orders from such men in the future," as the aforementioned report noted in its synopsis.

Others used their pull to bully their way aboard, including Major Reginald Nunn of the PWD and his wife, Gertrude, who earlier selflessly had stayed on Pompong Island instead of fleeing on the doomed *Tanjong Pinang.* Doris Lim found her way onto the ship as well. The other reporters had left on a boat to Australia to chase the war, but she preferred to sail for presumed safety in India. The *Rooseboom* pulled out for Batavia on February 27, chased by the catcalls of the angry people left behind.

Three days out of Padang, just past midnight on March 2, a Japanese torpedo slammed into the *Rooseboom,* taking most of the five hundred passengers on board to the bottom—including Reginald Nunn, who managed to shove his steadfast wife out of their cabin porthole before succumbing. As with the *Tanjong Pinang,* which took survivors off Pompong Island only to be sunk on the way to safety, an apparent ship of salvation had been turned into a vessel of death.

Brigadier Paris and the *Rooseboom*'s captain took charge of a twenty-five-foot wooden lifeboat that was overburdened with about eighty survivors, including a barefoot Doris Lim and Gertrude Nunn. But there were no paddles to propel them, leaving the passengers at the mercy of the current. Days turned into weeks, with no land in sight. Paris could do little to prevent most of the survivors from going mad from thirst and hunger; scores would hurl themselves into the water to end their suffering. Both Doris and Gertrude sat topless in the baking sun, uncaring of propriety, desperately using their shirts as makeshift shade.

Still alive on the raft was a dogged Scottish soldier named Walter Gibson. Gibson had survived the Battle of Slim River in Malaya, where the Japanese had shocked the British by utilizing tanks along a jungle road at night, shattering an entire division. Fleeing into the bush, Gibson and a band of fellow Argyll Regiment soldiers worked their way to the coast, disease and hunger dropping several of them en route. Taking to the sea, Gibson was in the vanguard of the refugee armada that soon would dot the waters off Singapore. Amazingly enough, he had made it all the way to Padang, only to be confronted once more by the overwhelming might of the Japanese military.

Despite shrapnel wounds and a broken collarbone suffered in the torpedo explosions, Gibson saved himself from drowning and made his way onto the raft, one that would be fated to wander aimlessly across a thousand miles of ocean. Once again he would watch as his fellow survivors perished one at a time.

Brigadier Paris slipped into a coma and died a week after the sinking. Captain Mike Blackwood went the next day. Major Angus MacDonald guzzled a cask of brandy he hallucinated to be water, went mad, and slipped over the side. The Dutch captain was killed—stabbed—by one of his own engineers, who apparently had been nursing a grievance for months.

As if the natural attrition wasn't bad enough, the death rate was aided by a gang of five renegade soldiers who began systematically murdering the weak and dying and throwing them off the raft to extend the meager rations. Gibson, despite his injuries, led a group of a dozen or so of the other survivors to confront the quintet. "It's them or us," he said to the others. As they charged across the boat, the soldiers met them with broken bottles and the sharp lids torn from cans of bully beef.

"We struggled, stumbled and rolled, wrestling at the bottom of the boat," Gibson wrote in his memoir. "We did not seem to put them overboard one by one so much as to rush them overboard in a body." Several attempted to grab on to the gunwale and pull themselves back into the raft, but Gibson and his mates hammered their fingers until the five killers had slipped beneath the waves.

At one point, sensing they all were about to meet their Lord in person, Gertrude Nunn decided to hold a prayer service. By some miracle, there was a waterlogged Bible on board. Gertrude's face was blackened by the sun, her voice hoarse with thirst and weakness. But she led the others through the Lord's Prayer and several hymns, including "The Lord Is My Shepherd." Gibson wrote that the other men were inexplicably drawn to her, a feeling a psychiatrist later explained to him. "You were all overcome," the doctor said, "by that urge that seizes every man when he is in danger—the urge to return to the safety of the womb. To all of you, Mrs. Nunn personified the mother."

She died the following day.

Days later, Gibson tried to commit suicide, but upon leaping into the sea with another soldier, he panicked and thrashed back onto the raft. His compatriot was never seen again. He spent the next several days clinging helplessly to Doris Lim. At one point, the last stirrings of his humanity bubbled to the fore, and as Gibson confessed later, he "was seized by the male urge." He began to fondle Doris, weak as he was.

"Please let me die in peace," was her reply.

After more than three weeks at sea, there were but two white men, including Gibson, left on the raft, along with four Javanese and Doris.

Then the Javanese battered the other white soldier to death and ate him.

"Blood dripped from their faces," Gibson wrote, "as, still chewing, they grinned horribly at us. One of them shouted at us and proffered something he held in his hands." It was a hunk of the dead man's flesh. Gibson rightfully feared he was next to be cannibalized, but the raft ran aground, at long last, before the Javanese could kill him for food.

They had landed on Sipora, a small coral island only a hundred miles from where they started in Padang. They had drifted for twenty-six days and a thousand miles, only to land right back in the laps of the Japanese. They were swiftly captured. Gibson was sent back to Padang to become a POW.

The Japanese knew all about Doris Lim's espionage activity, and they tortured her (as though her recent travails weren't torture enough) but spared her life. She too was sent to a POW camp, at a cement factory outside of Padang, where she helped to run a clinic. Despite everything that had happened to her, Doris remained fetching, and men in the area began to court her. To gain her freedom, she returned their ardor, and eventually undertook a marriage of convenience with a local Chinese farmer.

One day late in 1944, husband and wife argued, and the farmer stabbed Doris repeatedly, killing her. She had survived war zones and shipwrecks, weeks adrift at sea and hiding in the jungle. But just as it appeared she was relatively safe, death found her, courtesy of the man she lived with. The husband was given all of one year in jail as a sentence.

On March 7, just before Frank's train pulled into Padang, the SS *Pelapo* pulled up her anchor and sped away from the port of Emmahaven with fifty servicemen of varying ranks aboard. Unbeknownst to Frank, Geoffrey Brooke, and the others arriving at roughly the same time, she would be the last escape boat out.

If they were to be stuck waiting, at least Padang made for comfortable idleness. The streets were paved, and the shops were well-stocked, as befit a town of sixty thousand inhabitants. As Stanley Saddington of the RAF would recall, Padang had "all the signs of a well-run and peaceful little town." Towering green mountains up to twelve thousand feet high flanked the city, adding even more beauty to a landscape already featuring an ocean view. There was also a suburbia of sorts, with villages well away from the city center. Some men frequented them, finding "generous (and pliable) Dutch daughters," in Saddington's words. The officers were housed in fine hotels, the Centraal and the Oranje, with a local boy to cater to their needs, while the rank and file made do with an old gymnasium. Discipline had been restored to the town after the riotous days of port chaos and nights of Australian rabble-rousing, and the evenings were eerily quiet thanks to an enforced curfew. Schools had canceled classes, performing arts centers shut down, and government services ground to a halt.

With Padang now relatively calm, the first thing that Frank and the RAF men did upon arrival was to report to the few remaining British officers left at the makeshift headquarters at the Eendracht Club. The officer in charge was a Royal Marines colonel named Alan Warren, a tall, ramrod-straight man with a black mustache and "great force of personality," according to Brooke. Warren asked for volunteers to help the Dutch fighters defend the town. Almost everyone, Frank included, submitted their names for service, but the Dutch commander politely turned them down. The Brits didn't have any jungle fighting experience, it was explained (of course, some of them did, albeit the slapdash effort to combat Yamashita in Malaya wasn't something they wanted to highlight on their résumés). They would need to be equipped with arms and gear that couldn't be spared, and their recent experiences escaping Singapore had left them far from match-fit. Few of the RAF men put up an argument on this score.

The Kiwi C. R. Knowles, for one, would come to the realization that the Dutch show of force was just that—a show, a pretend exercise for morale purposes. "We later fully realized that it was not intended that there should be any worthwhile resistance," he reported long afterward. The word had come through the jungle from the Japanese—resistance was futile and would be punished. Should the city be declared "open," it would not be bombed. The Dutch authorities agreed. So the only planes that flew over Padang were reconnaissance planes—ironically, American-built Lockheed 14s, now in the hands of the Japanese.

The Dutch in charge at Padang, and indeed throughout the Netherlands East Indies, struck the other westerners as a curious lot, worthy of both admiration and scorn. All were impressed by their colonization techniques; for example, unlike most British serving across the empire, virtually every Dutch administrator was familiar with local tongues and customs. They "went native" far more readily than Brits and Germans tended to in other parts of the world.

Then there was the matter of bravery. The same report that noted the Dutch disdain for the behavior evinced at Emmahaven also sharply contrasted their fortitude with that of the Brits. In words that must have stung proud Englishmen to write, the report noted, "The Dutch...stayed at their posts although the Japs were rapidly advancing northwards. This was in sharp contrast to the British in Malaya, where officials were evacuated back to Singapore as danger approached."

At the same time, the Dutch were cursed by soldiers from the Commonwealth for their haughty attitude, their lack of apparent verve in fighting the enemy, and their embrace of Realpolitik when it came to capitulation. During a particularly low moment, a brawl broke out between British and Dutch soldiers, and an English colonel attempting to separate them had his jaw broken. Later in the war, the POWs from the Netherlands would be dismissed as virtual conspirators, model prisoners who rarely attempted resistance or sabotage.

But in Padang, most of the Dutch and English seemed strangely accepting of their fate. Propaganda radio broadcasts trumpeted that all of Java and Sumatra were already in Japanese hands. This was untrue, but those in charge in Padang swallowed it whole, giving in prematurely to the inevitable. While it was probably the prudent move in the big picture, many of the escapees found themselves stuck, a frustrating position after their incredible efforts to get to the port. They slept fitfully, with their boots on, ready at a moment's notice to flee. But the word never came.

One ship, a British cruiser, was circling offshore for nearly a week, awaiting the code signal to approach. But the British consul had burned the codebooks in anticipation of the enemy taking the town. Because of this act, no alternative plans to rendezvous elsewhere could be made. When Frank and the boys learned about this, their anger at the ineptitude of their commanders, already sky-high, reached new levels. Frank had already spent months scurrying from one radar malfunction to another while his air force was embarrassed over Singapore, a prelude to the swift fall of a supposed British stronghold. Now his military couldn't even radio a rescue ship steaming just over the horizon.

The last men to escape Padang snuck away on March 8, as Frank was just getting his bearings in the city. Eighteen men had been ordered to make a break for it by Colonel Warren, as they were deemed more useful continuing the war effort elsewhere than exposing themselves to the mercy of the invaders. The group comprised sixteen British officers, including Brooke and Clarke, the intelligence man, having handed over his Japanese prisoners at last by direct order from Warren, along with a pair of "Asiatics." Disguised as locals in straw hats, they made a run for it under cover of darkness in a small fishing boat, their spare fuel hidden under palm fronds. The group was nevertheless spotted and strafed from above by one of the Lockheed reconnaissance planes, but they managed to make it, amazingly enough, to Ceylon.

When word of this midnight run found its way to those left behind, it built upon the injustices witnessed during the boarding of the escape ships. What made those men more valuable? Why were their lives to be spared, with the others offered up for capture and (they assumed) certain death or imprisonment without a fight? These decisions are the essence of war, and the men who acknowledged this aspect of military reality accepted their fate with equanimity. Frank never recorded his feeling on the subject one way or the other, but he was hardly a grizzled veteran suffused in the spirit of the bayonet. It's likely he and the men his age and rank were royally pissed, though he wasn't the sort to complain much about it.

It was a surreal situation, one made even crazier by a small earthquake that shook the city while the men waited for deliverance. After scrambling out of Singapore, getting off Pompong, and managing by hook and by crook to cross Sumatra to this promised oasis, Frank and the other men now were sitting around, helplessly waiting for the other shoe to drop. There would be no fight to hold the city; instead, the Dutch concentrated on preventing anyone from slipping away. There were small native craft and tugboats scattered about, in much the manner of Keppel Harbor, but the Dutch made them off-limits. "To our dismay," Frank recalled, "the civilian harbor authorities refused to transfer ownership of these boats to us out of fear of Japanese retribution. They even disabled them." A handful of men beat the system by volunteering to patrol the harbor to prevent boats from being stolen. Once on the job, these men found a boat they could handle and set out to sea.

One group of twenty-five or so men, including artilleryman and former stockbroker Lieutenant John Purvis and an Australian sergeant and engineer named Stricchino, managed to steal a junk and hit the high seas. But after six weeks they were waylaid by a Dutch vessel, which took them back to Padang as they had been ordered to do by the Japanese. "After all we had been through this was a most heartrending moment," Purvis later recounted. "And I am afraid the tears rolled down my cheeks as I told them that it was all over because we had been betrayed by the Dutch."

Into this setting of hopelessness bounded Judy the pointer.

"There's the sea!" someone yelled when the train carrying the *Grasshopper* and *Dragonfly* survivors crested a hill to show Padang glistening on the shore of the Indian Ocean. "What a sight!" remembered Long. "The first ray of hope for nearly a month." After an overnight journey, the train clanked into the station early on the morning of March 16. The engine hadn't even stopped before the group was helping each other off and bombarding anyone they passed with questions about getting out on the next ship.

It was a grizzled old local man who broke their hearts. "The last ship left already—you just missed it." Technically, it had been nine days since the *Pelapo* had disappeared over the horizon, which is not exactly "just missing it." But the essence of the old man's statement was spot-on. After all this group had been through, the critical delay at Singkep and Rengat had cost them everything.

When the men reported in to a startled Colonel Warren, he sympathized with their plight, but he was also blunt. Don't consider fighting—the surrender is already arranged. Don't try to steal local watercraft—it would be suicidal. Feel free to return to the jungle (but that was hardly an option after the walkabout they had already taken).

The survivors seemed to collectively sag at the knees. "Despondency and despair descended on all," recalled Long. According to Searle, Judy seemed to sense the depression that hovered over her friends, an intuition of which dogs are fully capable. It was one of the evolutionary advances that led to domestication: humans enjoyed having another creature around that could comprehend their emotions. Judy likely would have tried to be extra friendly and attentive during this period, despite her exhaustion, in order to lift the spirits of her human companions. It was behavior both perfectly habitual and totally in character for this particular pointer.

Hoping against hope, the band spent the night at the dock, scanning the sea, desperately trying to wish a friendly boat into existence. But none came. They were ordered to move en masse into the Dutch school. Many other westerners, including Frank Williams and Peter Hartley, a twenty-one-year-old Royal Army sergeant who had escaped by stolen boat as Singapore fell, were down the street in the Chinese school.

It was Judy who was first aware of the long-dreaded arrival of the enemy. She was lying in the center of the small classroom she had claimed, head resting on forelegs in her natural repose, staring at the door. Searle was drifting in and out of sleep in the corner. He was one of a handful of men who had remained armed throughout their long trek, and he had refused the entreaties from the officers and the Dutch to surrender his sidearm. A few men had rifles as well. Searle had argued bitterly with the others who agreed to disarm and become passive prisoners. He wanted to storm the guards of the small boats and take them by force. "To hell with the Dutch," was his thought.

But the brass had decided to cooperate. The Dutch authority had saved Searle and the others back in Singkep, so it was a difficult leap for the survivors to suddenly turn on their hosts now, even if it meant impending capture by the Japanese. If Searle was to be honest with himself, he had to admit that he didn't think his small band of beaten-down men with pistols were capable of taking the boats in the first place. And even if they had taken them, capture or death at sea seemed the likely result. Searle and the others would be forgiven at that point for thinking, *If only we had gone with George White when we had the chance.*

So the survivors huddled in the elementary school, awaiting the inevitable. When Judy stood up and began to bristle, her lip tensed in a silent snarl, everyone in the room knew that their time was up. Motorcycles were heard, and she started to bark. Searle tore a piece of cloth from his pants and slipped it through Judy's collar, pulling her closer to him.

A Japanese colonel and his staff soon entered the room with a flourish. The officer had thick glasses and a professorial air, but his sharp staccato burst of words established his immediate command of the situation. He pointed to Judy and said something in Japanese that no one caught, abruptly turned on his heel, and left. Searle and the others with guns were disarmed, and then they were left alone to ponder their fate.

The colonel went to the Chinese school next and took visible glee in smashing a portrait of General Chiang Kai-shek to smithereens. He next proceeded to the office of the head Dutch administrator in Padang, where Colonel Warren gave his impressions:

> They strode purposefully in with the air of conquerors, kicking their legs in front of them, their muddy boots striking heavily on the floor, their curved swords jangling as they walked.... These were good fighting men, crude, fierce, proud and confident. There was little about the undersized, myopic Jap in this bunch with the broad flat, yellow faces and long whispy [*sic*] mustaches.

All night Judy's group discussed their situation. Everyone had heard the fates of those unfortunate enough to be taken by the Japanese. The Shinto culture that held sway in the IJA at the time sneered at military types who chose surrender over death, and thus the Japanese held little respect for POWs. Japan never ratified the Geneva Conventions, notifying enemy countries through its Foreign Affairs Ministry that the Conventions would be applied mutatis mutandis, i.e., changing only that which needed to be changed. It was an open-ended statement that allowed the Japanese to do whatever they pleased to those who had been captured. Indeed, many defendants at later war crime tribunals knew nothing of the Conventions and were ignorant of the crimes they had committed.

The men in the schools assumed they would be tortured, the women raped, and as for Judy—well, any horror that could be imagined seemed plausible. In the end, they were sure all would be killed. Apprehension, truculence, and despair were the dominant emotions in the Dutch school that night. Judy stuck close to Searle and remained silent.

Frank didn't record his feelings upon capture, but one thing is certain—these Japanese soldiers would have been the first he had encountered up close so far in the war.

On March 17, Judy, Frank, and the rest left behind in Padang were officially taken prisoner by the invading Japanese army. In the race to escape, they had fallen just short of the finish line.

CHAPTER 15

Imprisoned

The next day, March 18, the Japanese took stock of their prisoners. The first thing the invaders did with their human bounty was separate the women and children, who were put into their own camp. Then the men were sectioned into four distinct groups—British, Aussies, Dutch, and officers of all nationalities—and marched through town to the main Dutch army barracks. Roughly a thousand men took part in this humiliating funhouse mirror of the classic send-off parade that is an important rite of passage for any soldier set to march off to war.

The men keenly felt all eyes upon them. Their defeat was thorough, their humbling complete. They were dirty, ragged, washed-out. The soldiers among them felt unworthy of their code of honor. The civil servants wondered how things had gone so wrong. There was no love along the route for any of them. Dust from the streets swirled in their faces, the Japanese guards prodded them with their rifle butts, and the local citizenry snickered behind their backs as they passed. The Dutch colonial masters had gotten their comeuppance. The British, supposed guarantors of safety in Southeast Asia, had been whipped in record time.

Peter Hartley, the young Royal Army sergeant whose memoir *Escape to Captivity* detailed his imprisonment in deeply moving prose, felt the eyes on him and the shame well up. But national pride kept him and his mates from caving in. "The knowledge that we were British... acted as a goad which forced our heads up and made us march with almost the precision of guardsmen. Even the wounded fought to overcome untold ago-nies, rather than falter in their step and be humiliated by being abused or kicked by the guards."

Upon arrival at the Padang barracks, the prisoners were confronted with hundreds of hysterical women. This was the main shelter for the wives and children of native troops in Padang, and now they were being forcibly punted from the rooms for defeated westerners, those who had previously lorded their "superiority" over the locals. Their protests were mixed with the crying of their small children and the screaming of the Japanese, who slapped, kicked, and clubbed the families out of the building.

Judy, whose dealings with these strange shouting soldiers included a formative kick in the stomach when she was a pup, likely gazed upon the violence and found her hatred of these men, so different in attitude and even scent from her friends, reinforced.

When the local families had been fully evicted, the POWs settled in to the barracks. Each group of 250 had a one-story building to themselves, set in a rectangle around a large common courtyard that was big enough to house a football pitch. There was a gymnasium, wraparound verandas, and an old canteen, complete with billiard table and balls. A Ping-Pong table offered the chance for regular tournaments. J. A. C. Robins, who survived the *Grasshopper* bombing, wrote about winning "twenty cents prize!" after coming out on top one day.

A POW named Anthony Simmonds kept a diary of his internment at Padang, recording his activities in a pocket day planner in small, slanted handwriting. In this journal he tersely set down the daily routine, which included "reveille 545, parade 615, breakfast 840, lunch 1240, and another parade at 430 followed by tea at 5 pm. & lights out at 930." The men were on their own for food after dark. Mornings included cleaning of the barracks and the heavily used showers (Simmonds took three a day), and there was usually an afternoon nap.

There was no thought of mass escape—most of the men were too rundown, and the jungle dissuaded such thoughts for all but a couple of desperate and hardy types, none of whom are known to have survived the attempt. Besides, life in the barracks wasn't all that bad. The accommodations were dorm rooms and large converted spaces that housed the men comfortably. Hartley even had his own "apartment," living with his buddy Phil Dobson, a salt-of-the-earth supply officer who had fled capture in Malaya with Hartley, in a small office space they had discovered. The two men cleaned out the filth and the centipedes, and turned it into a private, if cramped, room. Dobson was older, married with children, and had little in common with Hartley, a deeply religious schoolboy, other than geography; both were from the same English town, Letchworth, a few miles north of London. But it was enough to form a close friendship.

Frank lived in the enlisted British main quarters. Judy, following her nose to where there was more food, took up mostly with the officers, including Searle. As such, she didn't encounter Frank in this prison, which was sizable in both population and acreage. Judy was no stranger to any of the four main barracks, but if Frank caught sight of the dog at Padang, he never mentioned it in later interviews.

While the first thought is to wonder how the two never crossed paths in the enclosure of the barracks, it isn't too far-fetched. Searle and the others who came in close contact with the pointer kept her on the down-low for the most part, for fear she would be killed. And Frank himself seems to have been something of a loner, never mentioning other POWs to whom he had grown close (save Judy, of course) and not appearing to take much solace in the rec room facilities on offer at Padang. He was still a boy in many ways, just twenty-two years old, with little in common with the seasoned infantrymen and salty-dog sailors in his midst, and even less with the blunt-speaking Aussies and condescending Dutchmen.

Frank was thrown in among men who killed others, either from a distance or so close they could feel the final breaths leave their victims. Even the other radarmen remembered little about him in later years. He was a bit of a dreamer, still the youngster who had lost himself in the idea of flight, and an introvert, not one to call attention to himself or strike up a conversation with a stranger, even with little else to do. He was, in short, someone in need of a good friend.

Had any of the POWs known what was to come, they would have appreciated the Padang barracks for the comparative paradise it was. The towering green mountains provided a scenic backdrop for their meditations. There was none of the backbreaking labor that would later define their imprisonment. They played marathon bridge and other card games on the veranda in the mornings, slept away the brutally hot afternoons, and played nightly soccer matches in the evenings.

Most of these POWs would later have no time or energy for anything except basic survival, but at this point they considered intellectual nourishment a crucial component to making the best of their time as prisoners. The men studied languages (particularly Dutch, though Greek and Latin were favorites too), practiced math, and discussed literature. Few of them had much advanced schooling, so this was a unique, if star-crossed, opportunity to improve their minds.

Lectures on various, often arcane topics were a daily event, a good way to pass the time as well as take advantage of the wide-ranging expertise many of the POWs had accrued in life prior to this unfortunate turn of events. Robins wrote of attending a fascinating "talk by Miller on insects." Simmonds recorded in his diary almost every ad hoc seminar he attended. "We went today to hear a lecture on the original invention of the sound track in cinemas," reads a typical entry. Others included lessons on tin mining, math, bookkeeping, and business, along with "the trials and tribulations of being a bus conductor—quite amusing." Incongruously enough, he even took in a lecture on sailing.

This interregnum in Padang made up one of the few recorded Japanese POW encampments that resembled Allied POW life in Europe as "guests" of the Germans. Not that circumstances in the stalags were any picnic, but they were essentially humane. Prisoners of the Japanese were treated far more harshly, save this brief period. Indeed, according to Stanley Saddington, the Japanese kept a low profile in Padang. At one point, he was even allowed to leave the camp to go into town to visit a "corpulent German" optician and be fitted for new eyeglasses. J. E. R. Persons noted that "except for a brief period in which the Japanese threw their weight around, we have been treated far better than anyone dared hope." Simmonds wrote, "It appears that we are more like internees than prisoners of war. We even get BBC News, through secret sources."

The Dutch prisoners felt especially at home, since essentially they were. Most were living in Padang when the Japanese came, and they had houses, and often families, nearby. As such, creature comforts began to appear, including mattresses, furniture, and, most important, money, which they used to buy food from native sellers who were allowed to ply their trade in the camp and through the gates. Many Dutch even went over the walls at night to return home, a practice that became so brazen that the Japanese had to threaten to shoot one of every four POWs should anyone escape. "In retrospect I doubt whether the threat would have been carried out," remembered John Williams, "but in view of other atrocities perpetrated by the Japs, it was certainly taken seriously."

Because the Dutch lived so royally, they became targets of derision from the other prisoners. This loathing worsened as the food supply dried up for everyone who wasn't from the Netherlands. The main thing keeping them from forgetting they were prisoners, other than the armed guards, was the gnawing hunger. The Commonwealthers who had escaped in the mad dash from Singapore almost universally had lost everything in the various sinkings they had endured. They had no money to spend and nothing to trade. Since the Japanese hadn't begun work projects, the prisoners weren't earning anything either. So the food peddlers working the barracks were a particularly brutal tease.

"By force of circumstances," Hartley wrote later, "the Dutchman found himself in the position of plutocrat in a new society, while the British [and Aussies] constituted the downtrodden masses." The Dutch and Brits argued furiously over who was more to blame for their plight. "At least we fought in Malaya and didn't allow the Japs to take the bloody place by telephone," one English sailor said, trumping any Dutch counter.

So scrounging for scraps became the norm for most of the non-Dutch POWs. They rummaged through trash heaps, stood outside the Dutch barracks hoping for handouts, begged and pleaded with the vendors for advances on credit, and stole as much as possible.

Judy fit right in, as most of her time was spent foraging for food as well. She was quite an accomplished predator. Rats, snakes, lizards, insects—she killed and ate everything and anything she could find. She also became a gifted accomplice in the varied missions of "creative acquisition" the men undertook. She made it a point to accompany Searle, Devani, and a couple of other cohorts on "Market Snatch Day." Once a week there was a designated day for sellers of all varieties to set up shop in the camp (others were allowed in on an ad hoc basis the remainder of the week). The penniless sailors would browse the local buffet and make a big show of picking out specific goods. One of them, usually the ebullient Searle, would noisily haggle with the seller, distracting him or her while Devani and the others stuffed their pockets. There was also a scam in which one prisoner would pick up and inspect a large load of foodstuffs and "accidentally" drop some. Judy would swoop in, grab the food, and deliver it to a waiting Devani, who would disappear in the crowd.

In another episode, someone from the group lured one of the Japanese commander's goats (which provided fresh milk for the enemy officers) to the British compound using banana peels. Another sailor, watching from a window, managed to slip a noose around the animal's neck and haul it up to the prisoners, who ruthlessly slaughtered and devoured it. They then spent a long night dispensing of any evidence, down to the individual hairs, for the next morning. The commander, furious, ordered a complete search of the entire barracks block, but nothing was found.

John Williams remembered another rare victory in the battle against hunger. "A group of POWs supplemented their rations by a rather ingenious method. Through the bare bars of their window, they saw a number of chickens scratching around for food. They attached a bent pin to some string, and baiting the hook with a piece of bread ration, they waited until the Jap sentry was out of sight before casting their line. They successfully hooked a few birds, later to be surreptitiously cooked."

Judy, being Judy, enjoyed visiting the other barracks, especially the Australian one, as she had made friends with the *hancho,* or boss, of the group, Sergeant Stricchino—the same man who had attempted to escape with John Purvis, only to be returned to Padang after being caught by a Dutch vessel. In the Australian barracks, a manhole led to a forgotten sewage system, which allowed the prisoners to slip outside the camp. Stricchino, perhaps recognizing Judy's gift for stealth and chicanery, made the pointer part of an elaborate operation of breaking and entering. The Aussies began to raid local homes for food, drink, and various creature comforts. Sergeant Stricchino would bring Judy along to sound the warning if anyone came to arrest them.

The Aussies flaunted their thefts, appearing in front of their block lounging in lawn chairs, smoking large cigars, reading glossy magazines, and sipping whiskey. No one could figure out how this was happening, and when the Japanese confiscated the items, they always turned up the next day with more.

But Stricchino undid himself. One day he asked a Dutch prisoner to translate a book he had stolen. The man, a doctor, recognized it as an obscure medical text that had been taken from his own home! For the second time in a matter of weeks, Stricchino was victimized by Dutch collaboration with the enemy, as the doctor ratted him out. In short order, the manhole system was discovered, and Judy stayed away from the larcenous Aussies after that.

But her nighttime roaming continued, much to the consternation of Searle and his buddies. There was a small hole in a mesh window that Judy could slip her frame through, and she started going on raids in the dark in search of food. The men worried she would be shot by the Japanese or locals. Searle went to the Japanese officers in charge and stated that Judy was a full member of the Royal Navy, and thus deserving of some protection, but they laughed him away. And he and his friends weren't able to discourage the hungry dog from her forays. Matters came to a head after she came back with a half-eaten chicken, which she accidentally dropped on a snoring prisoner, a pal of Searle's named Punch Puncheon, scaring him half to death. After that the men began tying her up at night. "This isn't punishment," Puncheon assured her, "but we just don't want you to be eaten by the Japs."

After three months of captivity at Padang, rumors began to circulate around the barracks. The POWs were going to be moved to Japan, Singapore, Java. No one knew exactly, but with so much chatter, something surely was going to happen, and soon. Their low-impact imprisonment of afternoon naps and evening soccer games was coming to an end.

Finally, the word came down. The prisoners were being moved in two stages of five hundred men to the sea—specifically, to Belawan, a port city across the Malacca Strait from Malaya, nine hundred miles from Padang across Sumatra. If they were going to a port, that surely meant another sea voyage was in the offing, something that made the men blanch. Indeed, a week or two earlier, a mixed group of officers and men, including Stanley Saddington, had already been sent to Belawan and shipped to POW camps in Burma.

On the appointed days, the men moved out. The Dutch tried to take their creature comforts with them, including their mattresses and furniture, but the Japanese ruled that each man could only take a single bag. Meanwhile, Searle and some of his friends, including Puncheon and *Dragonfly* sailor Len Williams, puzzled over an important question—what to do with Judy?

Judy had remained mostly unnoticed by the Japanese until now, dodging the odd kick and rifle butt but largely being ignored by remaining mostly out of sight—though she could hardly trot past the guards and take a seat on a truck. So they decided to hide her under some rice sacks and slip her on board. When the trucks came to a halt, Judy would disappear under the sacks. It would be the first of several such subterfuges that would allow Judy to travel alongside her friends.

The transport across Sumatra was grueling, a five-day marathon of sweat and discomfort. A long caravan of trucks wound through the mountain passes, at times terrifyingly close to steep drop-offs. When they reached the equator, Frank and the other prisoners were ordered to get out of the vehicles and walk across (while Judy remained hidden under her sacks). They remounted on the other side, and the drive continued. Despite the tropical location, the nights were very cold. One truck skidded out on a steep road, sending all the prisoners inside to the hospital. Remarkably, they were visited there by a Japanese general bearing fruit and flowers, who assured them the driver would be severely punished for his carelessness and who humbly apologized in the name of the Imperial Japanese Army.

It was in many respects a memorable journey, replete with gorgeous vistas and decent food courtesy of frequent stops at local markets. Anthony Simmonds recorded eating sardines and "14 cents worth of bananas" he bought en route. Purvis remembered years later the glory of eating a buttered roll with his legs dangling over Lake Toba, a shimmering, high-altitude body of water. If only for a moment, he felt unshackled from his plight, enjoying the simple pleasures free men enjoyed. All too quickly, though, it was back into the truck.

At last, the convoy plunged out of the highlands down to the sea. With "indescribable dread," in Hartley's words, the POWs, even the navy men, looked at the "turquoise immensity" as a place they had been lucky to escape from, given how many had died fleeing from Singapore. To be back on the ocean main, on a long voyage to parts unknown, made them extremely apprehensive.

When they arrived at Belawan, Searle and his friends carried the rice sacks off the truck. In the confusion and bustle of the offloading, when they were sure no one was looking, they let Judy slip away to hide in the dock area. There was no shortage of equipment and shadows, and she was able to skulk around unnoticed. Meanwhile, the men were treated to their first speech from the Japanese commander, Colonel Hirateru Banno. He stood on a large box and told the men in perfect English that he was their father and they were his children, and they must obey him, or he would "shoot us or cut our heads off," Hartley recorded. On a lighter note he added that he hoped the prisoners would be happy in his camp, and that his fondest wish was that they would all be returned home after the Japanese won the war. Then the POWs were cattle-herded into the port quarters of the native stevedores, dark and dirty concrete one-room huts.

All Frank and the others wanted to do was sleep. Judy too was exhausted from the trip, one that was especially hot and uncomfortable for her under all those heavy sacks. But while they could ignore the dirt and the hard cement floors, they could not ignore the mosquitoes. In the thousands the insects tormented the POWs, the air throbbing with the beat of their wings.

The group had to deal with the winged assault for only a few nights. Then the Japanese announced the prisoners would be on the move again. Happily, that feared sea voyage would not happen; instead, they would be taken about a dozen miles inland to Gloegoer, a suburb of Medan, the main city in Central Sumatra (why exactly these men stayed in Sumatra while Saddington's group was sent overseas is a logistical mystery lost to time and destroyed Japanese documentation). They were crammed into piping hot railcars, with twenty men literally sitting on top of one another, a narrow slit in the door the lone source of light or air. "My god it was hot," Simmonds wrote in his diary, "with the midday sun beating down on the metal roofs of the trucks." Presumably, Judy was secreted on this stage of her journey as well, though this element of her travels has not made the historical record. The trip was short, however, and the men blinked at their new home as they emerged from the train. It was June 27,

1942. Earlier in the month, the Japanese momentum in the Pacific had been blunted at the Battle of Midway; in North Africa, General Erwin Rommel's Afrika Korps had taken Tobruk, another British military citadel; the Germans pushed deep into Russia, driving for Stalingrad and the oil fields of the Caucasus, while the Final Solution discussed at the Wannsee Conference in January was in full effect across areas conquered by the Nazis. And General Dwight D. Eisenhower had just arrived in London to take command of the Allied war effort in Europe.

The POWs knew little to none of this, however—at the moment, their world was limited to the collection of native homes and Chinese shops that made up Gloegoer, a small outpost on the main road into Medan. Here too was an old Dutch army barracks, known as Gloegoer I, which would be where most of the POWs were held. Down the road about a mile was Gloegoer II, a former lunatic asylum. It was a suitably grim and desultory place, one Frank and Judy would call home for the next two years.

CHAPTER 16

Gloegoer

Judy found Gloegoer a much harsher setting. Conditions were worse, the food even less plentiful, the guards tougher and more hostile, her friends weaker and more distracted by their own suffering. The punishment of the last four and a half months, including the sinking of the *Grasshopper,* the stranding on the desert island, the jungle trek across Sumatra, and the capture and imprisonment in Padang, had accumulated by now, wearing her down and causing her to lose weight and energy. Before the Japanese took Singapore she had weighed sixty pounds, but at least ten of that was gone, perhaps more. Her leanness was notable, her liver-colored coat noticeably faded, and her soft brown eyes took on a harder edge as thoughts of food crowded out her standard enjoyment of life.

At first, Judy stuck close to Searle, Puncheon, and the other friends she knew best. She slept near them, often hidden under bunks or in the shadows at the ends of the barracks. The guards at Gloegoer began to see her about more and more, and while some saw through her, others enjoyed the sport of attempting to kick her flanks or hurl stones at her head. Judy generally retained enough animal agility to elude these blows and learned quickly to stay mostly out of sight. Hunger, and the need to hunt for her meals, drove her into the open, especially in the spaces between the barracks and the camp perimeter. She could penetrate the fences that led to the forests where prey could be found easily enough, but getting past the patrolling guards that walked there was the tricky part. She began to shift many of her hunting forays to nighttime, when more animals were about to be caught and the guards more easily avoided. Unlike at Padang, where the men had tied her up at night to keep her close, at Gloegoer that wasn't an option.

That didn't mean she didn't have any fun. Anthony Simmonds wrote in his diary about exercising the pointer. "Much amusement this evening caused by racing the dog Judy up and down the 100 yd barrack block; even used the kerosene food tins as hurdles for Judy to jump over."

Judy's clear disregard for the Japanese, which she wore on her proverbial sleeve, was even more apparent now. "She always loped with her eyes on the guard and her lip curled upwards in a silent snarl," Searle recalled, "and her obvious hatred put her life in constant danger from a rifle bullet."

In truth, for large swaths of time Judy was largely forgotten. The prisoners who looked out for her welfare ended up being much busier than they had been at Padang. They were eventually sent off on work details that often took them away from Gloegoer for the entire day. Time in the camp was frequently spent foraging for food with increasing desperation. There wasn't much time left for proper dog care. The POWs consoled themselves by noting that Judy had proven herself a survivor many times over. If there was ever an animal the men would feel secure about leaving to its own devices, even in an enemy prison camp, it was this most resourceful pointer.

The first thing that happened to the POWs at Gloegoer was getting locked up in their barracks for a period of three weeks. They rightfully wondered if that was to be the new paradigm. If so, it was a rude awakening after the relative cushiness of Padang. On the other hand, it wasn't as though they were missing much by not being able to stroll the grounds of the camp. There were no amenities like athletic grounds and pool tables. A tiny strip of grass was put to use for occasional rugby matches, but that was the extent of the competition. There were just the long barracks, with a gravel parade ground dotted by coconut palm trees. There was nothing aesthetically pleasing about the place. Padang had had mountains, Belawan the sea. Here there was nothing but heat and dust.

The barracks had two long, raised platforms separated by a central concrete gangway. The beds were nothing more than wooden planks, six feet long and eighteen inches wide, on steel girders. The tiled roof was infested with rats, which feasted on bananas and other fruit above the men, frustratingly out of reach, though Judy would sometimes snare one. Only one side of each barracks had windows. There were three barracks to hold the Dutchmen, one for the Brits, and one for the Australians. All were crowded into an area barely bigger than a football field. They were "very cramped," according to Simmonds. "There were 199 of us in one building and 120 in another," J. E. R. Persons wrote in his diary. "Each room intended for 80 coolies not 199 Europeans."

Each man's bed space was his castle, where he slept, played cards, ate meals, received friends, read books, lay ill with malaria, everything. He had another prisoner eighteen inches away on either side. *Privacy* was not a word that carried much meaning to the captives. There were shower and toilet facilities at the end of the barracks. A POW named John Hedley recalled in an oral history that "the loos were an open drain that you squatted over and hoped for the best." Holes in the wall led to gullies outside the building that flushed away the dirty water to the sea. In time, these holes in the wall would become critical meeting points for barter activity between prisoner and native seller.

This claustrophobic hovel was the entirety of their existence for much of July 1942. Just when the prisoners began to believe they would spend the duration of the war locked in the barracks, stultifying, Banno appeared to declare that they had completed their punishment for resisting the Imperial Japanese Army and would now be treated as honorable prisoners of war. Emancipated, the POWs wandered outside for the first time to see the sights, such as they were.

Among the first things they saw was a native trader, a man granted permission by the Japanese to set up shop within the walls twice a week, selling food, fruit, tobacco, cards, paper and pencils, soap, and other crucial items. Persons wrote that he purchased and "ate so much fried rice I felt sick." In a related note, almost right away a dysentery outbreak plagued the camp.

In order to earn cash with which to buy food and other goods, the POWs would form work parties that were paid a small amount in imitation Dutch guilders created by the Japanese for just this purpose. Officers, by contrast, were granted a fixed income, and were excused from most of the initial work details. The money paid out varied widely. Hartley remembered being paid a sixpence (nine cents) a day. Simmonds put his daily wage at fifteen cents. An Aussie private named A. W. Milne worked for a year to help construct a Japanese temple shrine to the dead. He was paid thirty cents a day for his efforts. Regardless of how much a man earned, the Japanese cheekily forced him to kick back 20 percent for food and lodging.

By now some eighty thousand Japanese troops occupied Sumatra, strangling the life out of the island. As such, supply went down and inflation went up. At first, Hartley's pennies could buy him several bunches of bananas. But as stocks dwindled, by the end of Milne's project, it took three days of work to afford a single banana. And as in Padang, there was a massive inequality in the ranks. Officers made out best. The Dutchmen, who had far more cash than the average Brit or Aussie POW, could eat and groom themselves much better. And if anyone fell ill, he wouldn't be able to work—therefore, he would not get paid and wouldn't be able to eat properly, a vicious cycle that ground the men down inexorably.

Some cash-poor POWs adapted. Those who thought in terms of commodities futures bought coffee in bulk and sold it by the cup later on. Others carved pipes and chess pieces to sell to the Dutch. A pair of Aussie sheep-shearers put their skills to use setting up a camp barbershop. And the men became expert scroungers, especially while out on work parties. Anything they came across could be put to use. A tin can could be repurposed as a coffee mug, with a piece of wire twisted into a handle. Wood planks could be fashioned into a stool. A hubcap could work as a dinner plate. Though the Japanese threatened beatings for prisoners who stole from work sites, all manner of booty was brought back to the barracks nonetheless.

In a triumph of civilization, one of the earliest additions to the barebones camp was a library. Prisoners donated books they carried with them, and dozens more were stolen from nearby homes by the work parties. A large number of English works were available, including the complete works of Shakespeare, *For Whom the Bell Tolls, How Green Was My Valley,* and, no doubt a favorite of Searle and the other navy men at the camp, the Captain Hornblower novels. To keep their minds sharp, there were quiz contests and spelling bees, with teams representing the

RAF, Navy, and Army vying for prizes that almost always involved food. After winning one such contest, Simmonds exulted in his diary, "By Jove that fruit salad was good."

As they adjusted to the lack of physical recreation, which had been readily available back in Padang, the POWs took madly to another hint of high-class leisure—the widespread play of bridge. Much of their idle time was taken up with the game, usually accompanied by enormous cigars. Sumatran tobacco was both plentiful and excellent, a mainstay of colonization since the Dutch first arrived in the East Indies at the end of the sixteenth century. It made for quite a sight—throngs of emaciated and shirtless men carefully bidding and trumping in the equatorial sun while puffing on immense stogies, all enclosed by barbed wire and watched by rifle-toting guards.

The smoking came with severe restrictions, however. The Japanese were tremendously scared of the threat of fire, as there was no immediate capacity to fight a blaze, which was sure to roar out of control. Ashtrays were everywhere, and the men toted them from place to place inside the camp. The POWs were forced to smoke only in prescribed areas and at certain times, and violation of these rules almost always resulted in heavy—and sometimes ghoulishly creative—punishment. One Dutchman caught lighting up at the wrong time was forced to smoke a huge pile of tobacco without stopping until he became violently ill.

Aside from cards and cigars, life at Gloegoer was far more punishing than it had been at Padang. The Japanese were much more present—and angry. The guards were a capricious bunch, a grab bag of mostly low-ranking Japanese, with a few Koreans and even the odd native thrown in. "They would, for no apparent reason, fly into sudden and hysterical rage, and vent their spleen and fury on the nearest available prisoner," Searle recalled. "They were really unpredictable."

Every POW took beatings from time to time, for a gamut of offenses from shirking work to failure to pay proper tribute to the emperor. The worst treatment was usually given to the various heads of the barracks or work details, called *hanchos,* Japanese for "squad leader."

The *hancho* of the British barracks was Phil Dobson, Peter Hartley's buddy and roommate back at Padang. Dobson was responsible for the welfare and behavior of every man inside—and dog, as it happened, for Judy occasionally was considered to be under the purview of the British POWs in the barracks. If the guards were mad at Judy for something (usually her very existence), Dobson paid the price.

At any given moment, the scream might come from a guard outside the door.

"Hancho!"

Dobson would go pale and shuffle to meet his fate, wondering which of his men, who were forever stealing, scheming, and otherwise upsetting the Japanese, had gotten him in trouble this time. He took countless beatings for offenses he had nothing to do with. Dobson had lost his boots all the way back in Singapore, and so led his men barefoot. However, his position as hut *hancho* meant he didn't leave the camp for work duty. *Hanchos* were even more vulnerable on the work parties, where any imagined slight might set off the guards. As such, Dobson spent most of his time reading in his bunk, stoically awaiting the next time he would be summoned to answer for the actions of his fellow POWs.

This culture in which "the officer is directly responsible for his men" was encapsulated in an incident witnessed by a POW named Edward Porter, a British warrant officer and artilleryman in Singapore. Porter had been in charge of the big guns that were useless in fending off the invading Japanese. He, like Brigadier Archie Paris, was deemed important enough to evacuate early, but his ship was sunk by Japanese cruisers. Like so many others, he made his way to Padang after a harrowing journey by lifeboat, tongkang, and foot, only to arrive too late.

Porter was a frequent work *hancho,* and was slapped, punched, butted, and kicked on a near-daily basis as a result. His anger at the treatment leavened somewhat on a long drive back from a detail one day. A Japanese officer and a lone guard were up front in his truck. A staff car, possibly containing Colonel Banno, passed them. When the truck reached camp, the officer beat the guard senseless using his sword scabbard. The guard had failed to call the POWs to attention when the staff car drove past. The incident didn't make Porter's beatings any less painful, but at least he knew he wasn't alone in receiving them.

The work parties varied greatly, from hard manual labor to make-work tedium to, at times, jobs that paid off in satisfying accomplishments. Whatever the gig, it was crucial to put in the hours, not just for the negligible pay but because men who didn't work were refused full rations. If a POW was too sick to perform full work, he could do lighter functions around camp and at least get half-rations. The bedridden got nothing, which only exacerbated their condition.

One job that presented some enjoyment was clearing jungle lots to facilitate the construction of camouflaged supply depots. The men felled mammoth trees with axes, trying their best to send them falling in the direction of their guards. Shouts of "Timber!" echoed across the forest, and the POWs could take out their frustrations on the trees. Frank was often out in the forest swinging an axe, a job that at least got him out into the fresh, though humid, air. Another job that stood out for its physical release was the dismantling of an old Ford Motor Company plant in Belawan. The prisoners took to the sledgehammers, knocking down the vast works, then transporting the raw materials to the port for the Japanese to melt down and use elsewhere.

A warehouse job proved a godsend for the prisoners, who were ordered to clear a supply depot that contained all manner of parts used in constructing wireless radios. The light-fingered men stole as much as they could and secretly put together a set in each barracks. The news they received over the airwaves was virtually all courtesy of Axis propaganda broadcasts, however, so they didn't get much boost from what they heard. The Japanese realized this and thus didn't come down too hard on the POWs for this seemingly dire breach of camp rules. At one point, some prisoners complained to a gentle officer on Banno's staff named Captain Takahashi about the low quality of the newspapers they could buy from the natives. "What do you need a newspaper for?" Takahashi asked with an impish smile. "You have a wireless." Eventually, some better newspapers reached them. Simmonds recorded receiving a stack of *New York Times* from mid-1941 — in December of 1942!

Most of the other jobs weren't so fulfilling. The prisoners were forced to carry reams of wood from one end of the Belawan dock to the other, stack them perfectly, and then carry them back. They would roll oil drums across fields for no discernible purpose. They would untangle miles of rusty barbed wire, clear pathways of weeds, unload cargo from ships, sort scrap iron. "It was purely an exercise to keep us occupied," recalled John Hedley in his oral history.

But the defining work detail of the Gloegoer camp was the aforementioned temple project that paid Private Milne thirty cents a day. It took almost the entirety of the two years the POWs were imprisoned there to build the edifice, which the locals came to call the White Man's Mountain.

The building site sat a short distance from the camp, between Gloegoer and Medan. Several weeks were spent clearing an abandoned experimental tobacco plantation that the jungle was attempting to recapture. Prisoners swung curved machetes called parangs and smaller implements known as billhooks to whack away the growth. After that came the weeding, an even more backbreaking process requiring endless digging. The men's hands were blistered so badly they couldn't hold their dinner plates. Some POWs stooped for weeks after wrenching their spines over the shovel.

At first they came to the work site in rotations of fifty men, which was augmented as time passed and progress proved slow. Virtually every prisoner spent time in the fields, including Frank. Judy came often too, sometimes catching a ride by being smuggled onto the carts the men used to transport implements over to the site, and sometimes slipping over there on her own through a circuitous path in the forest.

When the area no longer belonged to the jungle, the leveling began. A couple of bulldozers could have done the job within a day or two, but the Japanese preferred slave labor. Tons of earth were shifted from one side of the fields to the other, requiring a POW to fill a pair of buckets, slip a bamboo pole under the handles, and carry them on his shoulders. After hours upon hours of this, their bodies began to rebel. Their skinny frames offered no cushion, and they had no clothes to protect the skin. The guards hovered, ensuring that every bucket was filled to capacity with dirt.

Once, Hartley was caught with half loads in his buckets. Instead of beating the small (five foot six), waifish Englishman, the guard decided to show him up. He filled the buckets to overflowing, then hoisted the pole in a display of strength. It snapped in half, dumping the guard heavily upon his keister. Hartley dared not laugh.

It was in the temple fields that the POWs distinguished themselves by nationality in how hard they worked. The Australians were mostly men called off their farms to join the service, and they carried their natural tendency to soak up tough labor to the temple project, despite the lack of protein to fuel their efforts. Other prisoners and Japanese captors alike marveled at the Aussies' capacity for grueling work.

At the other end of the effort scale were the Dutch. Under the broiling sun, parang in hand, these older civil servants and colonial bureaucrats perfected the art of appearing to work without actually accomplishing much of anything, a technique the others called "bludging." In between the two extremes were the British. The Japanese would flatter them by calling the Dutch bad workers and the Brits good workers, and in a surge of counterproductive jingoism, the sons of the Union Jack would double their efforts to show up the Netherlanders, sneering at them as they worked. The Dutch were not only unmoved by the insults, but also laughed at how easily the gullible Brits could be played.

Regardless of how much effort the POWs put into it, they all suffered out in the fields, and from more than just sore bodies. Insects ravaged them, the ants chewing up their bare feet and ankles, the mosquitoes passing along malaria to almost everyone. The sun scorched them, causing POWs to drop from sunstroke and heat prostration.

Snakes were so common that gangs of Japanese guards came specifically to the work site to hunt them, particularly the pythons (mostly blood and short-tailed pythons), which made for excellent eating. Work came to a halt when one was spotted, as prisoners and guards alike would team up to capture the constrictor, preferably alive, so it could be taken back to Gloegoer, skinned, and dropped in a boiling pot. The Japanese sent presents made from snakeskin back to their loved ones on a regular basis.

Other, more venomous snakes, especially the red-headed krait, plagued the workers. Whenever Judy found her way to the site, which was more and more often as the work progressed, she remained on alert for this deadly creature, along with the various cobras and vipers in the area, and the large marine iguanas that occasionally ventured inland. Though her time on Posic had proven that Judy was an accomplished snake-killer, she was more keen on finding rodents and turtles.

Over time, a great mound rose from the muddy earth at the temple site. The POWs transported heaps of soggy dirt from an artificial lake they created in the field in order to have more pliable material to work with. When the mud dried in the sun, it was stronger and more cohesive than a simple pile of dirt, built in much the same manner as the giant termite structures that abounded in the forest. The muck allowed for some rare fun—the prisoners hurled it at one another in impromptu mud fights and greatly enjoyed bobsledding down the pile in the metal wheelbarrows used to carry the mud up the steep slopes of the mound.

Atop the mound, carpenters fashioned the temple itself from giant beams of teak, which were hauled up by the POWs as the guards lashed them on with screams. Huge doors and a roof adorned with golden carved dragons were hammered into place. A stairwell that curved to the summit was created. When the day came at last to bless the finished structure, a Japanese priest wearing a sword and pointed shoes consecrated the temple, touching the assembled officers with the twig of a tree. Then the doors were sealed forever shut, the souls of the fallen granted eternal peace.

When all was finished, the labor had been worth it, at least from an aesthetic viewpoint. The temple glowed atop an artificial hilltop, while below were fountains, terraces, moats, and bridges, all landscaped in the classic Japanese fashion. The complex was adorned by exquisite flowers and shrubs, planted in just the right proportion to highlight but not dominate.

Like the famous bridge over the Kwai River in Siam, slave labor from POWs had constructed something of lasting value. "There were few men who worked on this job who could have failed to find some compensation for their labors in the thought that here at least was something to show for many weary hours of toil," wrote Hartley. "Here was something created in the midst of destruction, something which, even though in many ways repulsive to western eyes, possessed a certain beauty to those who could regard it without prejudice."

The Kwai River Bridge was bombed to smithereens in Allied raids but was rebuilt after the story of its cost in blood became known. The Gloegoer temple had no such afterlife. In yet another example of how being a POW in Sumatra was brushed aside by history, the temple was demolished swiftly after Sumatra was retaken, the grounds reswallowed by the jungle.

As the months passed, the food rations dwindled drastically, and not only for the POWs. The Japanese were so low at one point that, incredibly, fifty prisoners were issued rifles and five rounds apiece and told to go hunt pigs in the nearby forest. That they didn't attempt to mount an immediate armed mutiny and free the camp is testimony to how beaten down by imprisonment they were, as well as to the impossibility of true escape. It surely would have felt good to assassinate a few guards and make a run for it, but further starvation, along with likely recapture and heinous torture followed by execution, was the almost certain next stage. Better to shoot some hogs and sit tight, on a full belly.

Alas, they didn't find any boar to kill.

Escape was beyond their capacity, but that didn't prevent the Japanese from introducing a non-escape pledge the men were ordered to sign. As a point of pride, the POWs refused outright. Despite all manner of threats, no one could be persuaded to put pen to paper, so all one thousand prisoners were jammed into a single barracks and were denied food and rationed water for three days. At last, the men signed, their point proven to their satisfaction. But the momentary pride didn't help quell the growling in their bellies.

The diminished food supply went hand in hand with increased illness. At first, the POWs were surprisingly healthy, relatively speaking. While malaria and dysentery, along with malnutrition, were constant threats, only a handful of men died in the first eight months of imprisonment at Gloegoer—this despite the fact that there was a distinct lack of medical supplies available for the camp doctors. Spirits were comparatively high, although the few deaths cast "an aura of intense gloom over the whole camp for many days," Hartley wrote. In the future, the POWs would drop so quickly as to be hardly recorded, but while at Gloegoer the body count was rather low.

One of the men who died, coincidentally, was a friend of Judy's named Cousens, a private who had a job making and repairing boots for the Japanese soldiers. He thus had access to leather, which he would surreptitiously cut off, at great risk to his life and limb, and feed to Judy. Leather wasn't exactly a feast—it was tough and hard to digest—but it had nutrients she needed, so the pointer made the effort, chewing so hard she would have to hang her exhausted jaw over her forelegs and rest it afterward.

Cousens and Searle also partook in a desperate and foolhardy trek to the Japanese officers' quarters, ordinarily a trip to be avoided at all costs. Cousens, in his role as boot maker, had spotted some unguarded sacks of rice nearby, and he talked Searle, who was zombielike from hunger, into accompanying him to steal it.

Stealing the rice was "surprisingly easy," as Searle said, but he forgot about an inspection scheduled for the following day. As the guards approached the blanket where he had hidden his bounty, he was in a panic. Discovery meant a certain beating, or worse.

Then Judy sprang into action.

"I think animals have a built-in radar system which picks up all radiations of different sensations such as fear, happiness, panic, and sorrow, as in fact postmen will confirm," Searle said after the war.

That ability was most likely related to Judy's amazing capacity for smell and the way it shaped her experiences. Again, return to the concept of the *umwelt:* the dog's perspective on the world. Judy could perceive changes in attitudes from people by dint of her special sniffing prowess. Judy's uncanny ability to appear at the scene of brewing conflict wasn't particularly special for canines. What she did upon arrival, however, was.

"Judy certainly sensed the danger in that room," Searle continued, "and she also knew what to do about it. She also knew, as we all did, that the Japs had a deep fear, almost horror, of skeletons, graves, almost any evidence of death.

"It cannot, then, have been any coincidence that brought Judy charging into that room at that critical moment like a mad beast, her ears back, eyes glowing redly. And in between her bare teeth was a gleaming human skull!"

It isn't hard to believe that Judy would have learned that dead bodies, in one form or another, distracted the Japanese, those humans she recognized by both sight and smell. Whatever the provenance of her gambit, Judy completed several circuits of the room, nimbly avoiding all obstacles, and the Japanese, who were hysterical at the sight of the skull. Just when it seemed a guard would have to raise his rifle and shoot Judy to quell the disorder, she abruptly left the room as suddenly as she had burst in. The guards, still agitated and yelling in high-pitched voices, left too, the inspection forgotten. Judy had saved Searle and Cousens from a certain thrashing—and she also saved their stash of rice, which they later consumed.

Cousens wouldn't get to enjoy his victory for long, however. He fell ill with malaria and died shortly after stealing the rice. Judy would be spotted stretched out, head on foreleg, by the small lean-to Cousens had used for a workspace and where he had fed Judy the leather. "It was as if she was in mourning," Searle said.

Judy had lost a friend, and she had also lost her most reliable source of extra food. But it wasn't long until she found a replacement—one who would become considerably more to her than a mere provisioner.

In early August, Frank began to see more of the pointer whom he had briefly glimpsed in Rengat. Since then, Judy and Frank had crossed paths, generally at mealtime, when Frank would often flick her a few grains of rice or, in a special treat, a maggot, which suffused the daily bowls given the POWs. Frank didn't stand out to Judy in that way, as plenty of the prisoners slipped Judy a taste, albeit no more than that—they couldn't spare the calories. But with Cousens gone, and food scarce, Judy was out and about sniffing around the other prisoners more openly. It was dangerous behavior because it brought her into more close contact with the guards, who wouldn't hesitate to throw Judy in the same boiling pot as the pythons. But hunger was making everyone do things they wouldn't otherwise consider.

The Japanese ration of rice and vegetables was barely enough to get a man through the day. For breakfast the POWs received a watery rice they called pap, which if not accessorized by banana or other fruit was tasteless, and either way was sweated out of their system within an hour. Lunch consisted of bread rolls, at least until the flour ran out after about a year, after which it was replaced by more rice. Dinner was yet more rice, a thin soup made from barley and tree leaves, and a mysterious meat stew called ongle-ongle. It was flavorless, slimy, and looked like "frogspawn," according to one Dutch survivor. A British POW named Fred Freeman remembered that it resembled "wallpaper glue," and indeed a similar product was used in the Netherlands to post bills on walls. All of the offerings came ridden with maggots, along with sand and other inedible objects that required removal.

During the first year of imprisonment, the officers and the Dutchmen, using their extra funds, were able to scrape up enough food from outside sources to establish a modest cookhouse that supplemented the rations. The Dutch cooks could usually whip up one decent meal per day for the POWs to augment the pap and ongle-ongle. Colonel Banno even allowed them to build a vegetable garden, though once it began to sprout edible plants he reversed himself and seized it for his officers. "This caused a great outburst of wrath from all the prisoner officers," recalled Purvis. "And then the Japanese relented a little and said they would not take it all but whatever we had would be deducted from our rations. So, in the end, the camp was no better off."

One of the main shortages at Gloegoer was salt, which was keenly missed in the tropical heat—what the men sweated out was hard to replace. So parties were regularly organized to march to the nearest inlet and gather seawater to use in cooking. It was distilled as best as possible, often using charcoal filters. The salt could then be used for food, and the water itself became potable too.

Despite their efforts, hunger was omnipresent. It made the men listless, unfocused, and ill-tempered. Their stomachs were always growling. Undernourishment could blot the memory, blurring whole weeks into one continuous search for food. Many diary keepers from the period simplified their entries to "Same as yesterday." Sleep, already difficult, turned impossible with the pangs ravaging the body. Their gums bled from a lack of calcium; their skin flaked from a lack of vitamin A. Their immune systems were stressed to the breaking point.

In his diary, J. F. R. Persons tracked the dwindling supply, moving from "Food is a bit short nowadays, the midday loaf is small and the evening not enough for most, though it is sufficient for me" to "There are only two subjects of discussion—food and vengeance!" to "Feel as weak as a kitten and don't know how I shall manage a day's work but the others are doing it so daresay that I shall make the grade" within a few months.

Ironically, even the one food they did get plenty of—rice—proved detrimental. The consistent diet of white, polished rice resulted in a disease called beriberi, a defect caused by the lack of vitamin B-1, or thiamine. The rice consumed by the POWs was dehusked during the harvest, which made it last longer but removed the vitamin. A swelling in the ankles was the telltale initial symptom. Soon the sufferer would seize up from nerve paralysis, his heart would beat irregularly, his limbs would spasm, and, often enough, he'd die, unless he could get some of the pivotal vitamin down his gullet, especially in the form of eggs and enriched breads. In unfortunate cases, men developed elephantiasis of the scrotum. A POW named Raymond Smith described those struck by this particular horror: "None could wear shorts . . . and had to remain unclad from the waist down. The testicles were enlarged to roughly the size of a football and had to be 'carried' by the individual to avoid the intense 'dragging-down' pain." While the flour lasted, beriberi (the name means "weak" in Sinhalese, the language of Ceylon, and is repeated for emphasis) was rare; once it ran out, ankles swelled all over camp.

Mainly, Judy tried to forage for herself. Geckos, or *cheechahs* in the Malay parlance, so named for the sounds they made, worked the rafters for insects. Judy would stalk the lizards for hours, as she would the rats and other vermin that were everywhere. In the fields, she devoured anything she could find and kill, from immobile insect larvae to speedy flying foxes. She caught the odd frog but didn't like the taste, which suited the men—they captured the hoppers themselves and held races with them. But these were only occasional feasts—ultimately, she was forced to make do with scraps from the men.

Frank began to take more interest in Judy than he had before, now that she spent more time nosing for food among the masses. He spent a day or two observing the dog as she forlornly sniffed about the camp, searching for anything to eat. Frank wasn't aware that Judy had recently lost a human friend who fed her regularly; he just knew the dog seemed troubled and no one in particular seemed to be taking care of her.

Something wobbled in his soul. He was in a terrible situation, and it was all he could do just to survive himself. He could die or be killed at any time. But the sight of this dog wasting away, without help from any of the human friends she clearly relied upon, was intolerable to him. The kinship between man and dog, forged over thousands and thousands of years, defeated harsh practicality in Frank's heart.

So on a scalding August afternoon, Frank decided upon a fateful act. After waiting on line for the usual portion of rice to be slopped out on his makeshift plate, he sat on the ground in the open area reserved for eating meals. The men were busy shoveling the food into their mouths with their hands. Judy, as usual, swerved her way around the bodies, nosing for scraps. She recognized Frank as someone who usually had some extra morsels for her and began to wag her tail when she saw him. She sat down in front of him, almost at attention, in the manner a well-trained dog will do when commanded to sit and stay.

Her watery brown eyes gazed at Frank. He poured some of the pap into his palm.

"Come on, Judy," he encouraged. "This is yours."

The pointer remained frozen but emitted a soft whine. Frank knew instinctively what she wanted—not merely food, but a friend to share it with. He put his whole bowl on the ground and used his free hand to tousle Judy's ears and stroke her head.

"Okay, okay," he murmured. "Make yourself at home, girl."

Judy visibly relaxed and lay down at his feet. Then she vacuumed up every atom of rice in an instant.

And thus did Judy meet Frank Williams. She would spend most of the rest of her life close by his side.

While Judy had been very close to Tankey Cooper, Bonny Boniface, George White, and Les Searle, she was still very much her own dog—in the end as beholden to the food these men shared with her as to the individuals themselves. But with Frank, it was different from the start, a love story, even though the genesis of the relationship was a shared meal. Perhaps Judy sensed the depth of Frank's gesture—a starving man going hungry so that she could eat his rice—and fell head over heels at first sight.

But why did Judy, who had been a close compadre of several other men, decide that she would take this relationship to the next level? Perhaps, despite the fact that Judy's nose and stomach made most of her decisions, it was her eyes that sealed the deal. Frank was quite boyish-looking, especially for a soldier. He was twenty-three by now, with some hard living behind him, even before the war and his capture aged him immeasurably. But he retained his youthful appearance—even when he was a senior citizen, photos of Frank would capture his unique fresh-faced twinkle.

He was only six months younger than Les Searle, for example, but appeared far younger. It's possible she was attracted to Frank's adolescent features, even if they were sunken and drawn from hunger.

Of course, no one can ever know for sure just how differently Judy perceived her relationship with Frank vis-à-vis Cooper, White, Searle, and the others. It's possible that to her Frank was just another friendly sort with food to offer, at least at first, and she was following her instincts in choosing the companion most likely to keep her fed and thus alive. At this point, she was in her most vulnerable state. On the *Gnat* and *Grasshopper* she was healthy and vital, and on Posic and in the jungle her animal instincts made her indispensable. She belonged to everyone she encountered, until now. Now, she needed the help of this friendly species more than ever, and the options were few. Frank seemed like the most reliable of them, so she didn't beat around the bush. In the end, she may simply have been tired of going it alone. The dog whose very first act as a pup had been to run away from her family, and who had spent her life falling into and somehow getting out of one pickle after another, finally was ready to give herself fully to someone else.

Frank, as was his wont, wasn't particularly emotional or revealing in remembering this crucial turning point in his captivity and his life. "I decided to permanently adopt her," was his cursory description of the moment in his letter to Neumann and van Witsen nearly three decades later. But it seems quite clear, from his later statements and behavior, not to mention simple common sense, that he found himself melted irrevocably by the sight of this creature so nakedly in need of aid and companionship during these extreme circumstances. There is no record of Frank having been a dog or animal lover heretofore, but he became one now.

Whatever the truth, man and dog took this occasion to seize the moment—or, more accurately, the moment seized them. They achieved a surprising symbiosis almost right away. "I just had an immediate connection with her," Frank would recall after the war. "It was as though I could understand her every thought, and more amazingly, she could understand mine."

His connection with Judy also helped bring the shy radarman out of his shell. Judy's popularity with the other POWs transferred somewhat to Frank, as though he had begun to date an especially fetching girl. *If Judy is so fond of him*... was the prevailing line of thought. Frank began to interact more with his fellow prisoners, though his primary relationship was with his new dog.

Naturally, food was in the forefront of their thoughts at all times, so it stood to reason that one of Frank and Judy's first acts as new best friends would be to develop a scheme to help fill their bellies. On the temple grounds, the Japanese would leave fruit at the shrine instead of the western tradition of flowers. Frank taught his dog to hide in the bushes and listen for his signal as he worked. Frank would snap or emit a low whistle when the coast was clear, and Judy would dart in and swipe the fruit, which the two would enjoy back in the shadows of the forest.

Judy may have been a pointer who never learned to point, but otherwise, she was a quick study in most situations, and she was immediately extra-attuned to the shadings of Frank's voice, the angle of his stance, the sharpness of his finger snaps, and the tempo of his whistling as it changed from adagio to allegro. Her ability to learn commands was quite natural, and pointers as a breed are more receptive than most hunting dogs to their master's voice, which certainly helped Judy in her swift attachment to Frank. It was in this devout attentiveness to her new friend's every action, no matter how subtle, that the difference in this relationship from her previous ones can be seen.

The risk they ran with this larceny became apparent when one British soldier was caught stealing in a similar manner. He was ordered to pick and eat a dozen papayas. The rest of the POWs were paraded in to watch him. The man made it through four of the papayas, then indicated he couldn't go on. He was clouted over the head for his insolence and told to continue. He had a couple more, then keeled over while emptying his bowels all over himself. Still, he was ordered to keep eating. At last, half-conscious and deathly pale, he finished. "The Japs delivered their usual lecture to us and ordered him back to quarters," Porter remembered. The thief's neighbors in the barracks couldn't have been happy with the smell.

Judy's ability to elude the guards and raid the jungle for food proved to be a boon to Frank once they teamed up. Whereas before she would as often as not consume her prey fully before returning to the barracks, or bring back largely chewed extras for the men, now she refused to let go of any captured rat or snake until she brought it, often still wriggling in terror, directly to Frank. If the radarman was put off by the disgusting deliveries, he never mentioned it. More likely the idea of meat for his supper overpowered any gag reflex. He also ensured that the other men got their fair share of the bounty.

Not all of Judy's training was devoted to food acquisition. She was able to quickly learn a variety of tricks and games. In addition to the standard fare of sitting, staying, rolling over, and the like, Frank taught the dog to hide on command. Frank would snap his fingers, and Judy would disappear under a bunk, only to reappear at the far end of the barracks at a second command. Judy would stand stock-still, then tear off at full speed at a gesture or sound from Frank, only to then come to another dead stop when Frank made a different snap or whistle or nod. Other, more elaborate displays were hinted at by the POWs who remembered her, but were not detailed. The exercise regimen described by Anthony Simmonds most likely continued, though in a less energy-draining manner.

Much of this was done to combat the boredom and Sisyphean futility of camp life. Frank would ignore his work duties, at risk to himself, to spend time teaching the dog new tricks. When they had an act down pat, the duo would perform it for groups of other POWs, sometimes in twos or threes, other times in front of a barracksful of prisoners. It was what passed for entertainment in a camp devoid of frivolity, save for the Christmas shows the men mounted, like the Yuletide 1943 extravaganza *All This and Gloegoer Two!*

Clearly, their unique and hazardous situation was a huge factor in explaining why Frank and Judy clung so fiercely to each other. But as this instant kinship showed there was something deeper there as well, a primordial bond that would later prove to be almost spiritual in nature. From the first, they were as important to each other as life itself. So Frank decided to risk his in order to ensure Judy's safety with a daring, almost foolhardy gambit.

Judy's first true home, the Yangtze River gunboat HMS *Gnat*. (© IWM [Q 93287])

HMS *Grasshopper* was an upgraded gunboat that replaced the *Gnat* to become Judy's new home in 1938. (© IWM [HU 43993])

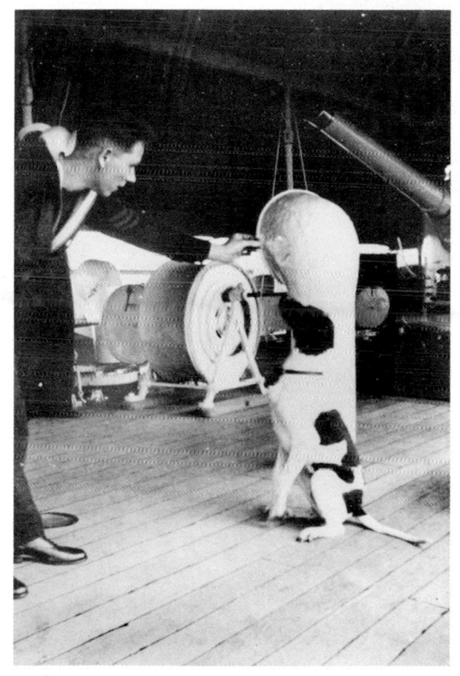

Judy shows she can follow orders as well as any sailor. (© IWM [HU 43990])

Thanks to her friendly manner and ability to warn the ship of impending dangers, Judy became a treasured member of the crew. (© IWM [HU 43987])

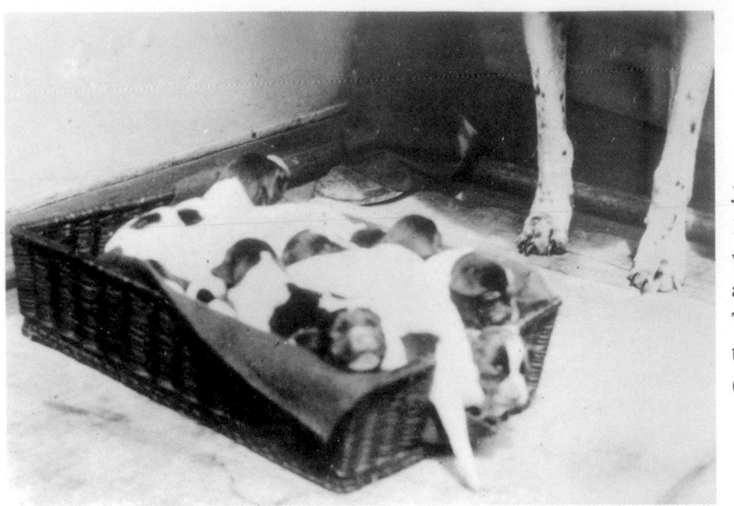

Judy's first litter, born in 1938, contained ten pups who lived. The father was another pointer, named Paul. The mother's legs are in the background. (© IWM [HU 43988])

Several of Judy's pups take a stroll on the *Grasshopper*'s deck. It was soon decided that a warship had room for one dog but no more, so the puppies were given away. (© IWM [HU 43989])

The Royal Navy battleship HMS *Prince of Wales* sallies forth for her final sailing on December 8, 1941. Along with HMS *Repulse,* the two capital ships were meant to deter the Japanese from attacking in Southeast Asia. Both were sunk on December 10. (© IWM [A 29068])

Singapore, the bulwark of British power in Southeast Asia, was supposed to be invincible, but the Japanese captured the city shortly after invading. In the final days of British rule, the oil fields near Keppel Harbor were set ablaze to deny them to the Japanese. (© IWM [FE 584])

The Japanese destroyed almost every ship fleeing Singapore in mid-February 1942. Lifeboats dotted the South China Sea in the aftermath of the destruction. (Australian War Memorial)

Survivors of the attacks on the SS *Tien Kwang* and SS *Kuala,* which included Frank Williams, on tiny Pompong Island. (© IWM [HU 105593])

Numerous survivors were plucked from remote islands and atolls and brought to (temporary) safety. This vessel, the SS *Krait,* piloted by an Australian named Bill Reynolds, ferried an estimated two thousand people in the waters off Sumatra during the chaos. (Australian War Memorial)

Vivian Bullwinkel, the lone female survivor of the Bangka Island massacre. (Australian War Memorial)

The final stage of the Sumatra crossing—the train between Sawah Luento and Padang, the coastal town that promised freedom. (© IWM [HU 1055613])

Several POWs took note in their diaries of Judy's presence at the Gloegoer camp. One prisoner even took the time to sketch her. (Image Bank WW2—Museon)

The living conditions in a Pakan Baroe camp. (Image Bank WW2—NIOD)

Lady Edwina Mountbatten — wife of the British supreme commander in Southeast Asia, Lord Louis Mountbatten — greeting Australian POWs at Pakan Baroe as part of Operation Mastiff, the massive Allied effort to liberate and treat POWs in the theater. (Australian War Memorial)

happy " till she was brought home after spending the war as an evacuee in Cornwall.

While in Cornwall she won a scholarship to a well-known school.

Her mother, who is said to be ill, in a statement read at the Toynbee Hall Juvenile Court, London, yesterday, described bringing the child home as "the worst day's work I ever did."

The girl had run into a police station and asked for help because her father was hitting her mother. She appeared as a person in need of care and protection.

The girl, who refused to return home and whose mother did not wish her to do so, was sent to a remand home

Mrs. Hepworth, arrived, said, "Are you trying to kill her?"

Mrs. Green said she was playing with Janet, and threw her on the bed so that it would "spring" her. Janet's leg must have been caught.

HAPPINESS HALL

Derelict cottages at Hollingbourne, Kent, have been made into "Happiness Hall," a new community centre.

BAPTIST PRESIDENT

Mr. C. T. Le Quesne, K.C., of London, was elected president of the Baptist Union at their annual assembly in the Bloomsbury Central Church yesterday.

MISSION IS SECRET

Brigadier Neil Hamilton Fairley, Australian Forces Director of Medicine, is coming to London on a secret Army mission.

GUNBOAT JUDY SAVED LIVES—WINS A MEDAL AND LIFE PENSION

SHE was wounded by the Japanese, saved the lives of British sailors, and then shared their hardships in prison camps.

So yesterday Judy got a "For Valour" medal and a life pension — from the Tailwaggers' Club.

She is a pedigree English pointer, and only came out of quarantine in this country yesterday after prisoners of war brought her home.

Judy was on board the gunboat Grasshopper, at the time of Singapore's fall in 1942. Jap planes smashed the Grasshopper but all the crew got safely ashore . . except Judy.

She was rescued, badly wounded and clinging to wreckage, a day later.

With the men of the gunboat she was marooned on a small island for several days . . and it was she who discovered a fresh water spring when men were dying from thirst.

They escaped to Sumatra in a commandeered Chinese junk. But there they were captured by the Japs.

Still a P.O.W. in 1944, Judy was being taken to another camp when the ship was torpedoed.

Picked up and landed at Singapore, the Japs ordered her to be shot and eaten.

Her execution was prevented by the arrival of British liberating forces. And, with other prisoners, Judy was repatriated.

To L.A.C. F. G. Williams, who became her owner in the Jap camps, the Tailwaggers' Club presented a cheque so that Judy may spend the rest of her days in peace and comfort.

A kennelmaid says good-bye to Judy and her master before they go to receive the honours Judy won in the Far East. Judy's adventures are told in the story above.

WITH 8 DOING ORGERY

IRED Scrip- g ex-choir the police to eight perfect ot away with began a life —for forgery, *Mirror* New nt.

ne, 59. Detec- the last fif- is life in the at six wealthy en with whom died or dis- riously — with from property

e the person ve died from Cline would to make out a at effect and ody cremated. e forged some n an £80,000 voman he had police of San d on him.

'LE OF

It started but someth pened to m she wasn't Next tim cushion—or where her high and h

The smoke gets in h

ONLY woman member of Bedworth (Warwick) Council, Mrs. A. E. Smith, thinks smoking at council meetings should stop.

Otherwise she is afraid councillors may yet bring pints of beer into the council chamber, undo their collars and let their dogs in.

Asking the council for a "no-smoking" rule, Mrs. Smith said the air "could be cut with a knife" at the previous meeting and gave her lasted for a we

She compla had been thr at the meetin hope we can g way of con with dignity— very little dign

But scare smoking" rule public away feated the mo to seven.

"Gunboat Judy" bids a fond farewell to one of her handlers upon her release from mandatory six-month quarantine after her arrival in England. (© Mirrorpix)

Judy is awarded the Dickin Medal, the animal equivalent of the Victoria Cross, in a ceremony in May 1946. Frank is on the right; Major Roderick Mackenzie, chairman of the Returned British POW Association, is on the left. (Getty Images)

Judy poses with other winners of the Dickin Medal. (Image Works)

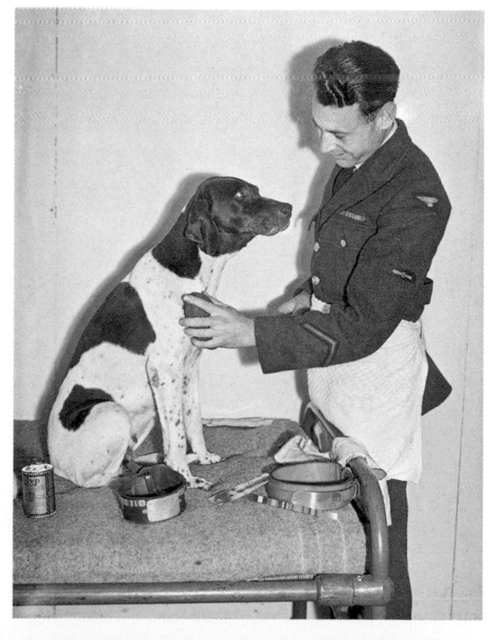

Frank grooms Judy before one of her many public appearances. (Getty Images)

Judy and Frank appear on the BBC television show *Picture Page,* hosted by Wynford Vaughan-Thomas, on September 9, 1946. (BBC Photo Library)

Two best friends pose for a portrait taken in 1948, just before they left for Africa. (Image Works)

The memorial Frank created for Judy upon her death in Tanzania in 1950. (© IWM [HU 43991])

CHAPTER 17

POW #81-A

Many considered it an Immaculate Conception. Some of the prisoners even took to calling Judy "Mary" for a spell.

Despite her gnawing hunger and the frequent danger, Judy went into heat. Then—somehow—during one of her myriad trips into the jungle in search of edibles, Judy had an encounter of the kind she hadn't had since her three-day tryst with Paul the pointer back on the *Gnat*. Not long after that, it was obvious that she was pregnant with her second litter.

Frank and friends were dumbfounded. Bets were placed on whether Judy would deliver a litter of tiger cubs, or perhaps goats. There hadn't been many dogs seen in the area, most having been killed for food by the natives or for sport. The only dog besides Judy that the men saw more than once was a scrawny, mangy mongrel they soon named Tick, as she was often covered by the insects. Tick toddled into camp following Judy one day after the pointer had disappeared to forage under the wire and remained a regular for weeks after that.

Tick's welcome in the camp came to an unseemly end one scorching hot and humid evening. Frank heard Tick crying in either fear or pain and went to investigate the sound. "I left the barracks just in time to see a guard outside of the fence hit the defenseless animal with his rifle butt," Frank remembered.

The guard kept slamming his weapon down on the helpless dog until he had broken her neck with the blows. Tick's friendliness, in contrast to Judy's wariness, proved her undoing. "Tick thought everyone to be her playmate, even the Koreans," Frank explained.

Before Frank could consider the ramifications of his actions, he had pushed through the wire, scratching himself, elbowed the guard out of the way, and reached down to cradle the dog in his arms. It was too late. Tick was gone.

"Seeing my face and hearing my voice, the guard must have thought I was going to attack him," Frank recalled. Indeed, Frank leapt to his feet, enraged, to confront the guard, who was startled by his presence outside the wire but ready for confrontation. Frank was larger, but he was weak from malnutrition, and anyway, the guard had a rifle. But to Frank's surprise, the guard had taken a few steps backward, and he tripped over a root or something else on the ground. The fall had two consequences—it probably saved Frank's life, for the guard wouldn't have hesitated to kill him too. But it also gave reinforcements racing to the scene the impression that Frank had somehow knocked the guard to the ground. And since he was outside the wire, naturally he had done so while attempting to escape. Tick's lifeless body and Frank's obvious dismay meant nothing to them.

"On my knees I held the body of the animal when it died in my hands, only to look up a moment later into the barrels of a bunch of rifles," Frank said.

Meanwhile, back in the prisoner hut, Judy's ears had twitched when she heard Tick's scream. Whether she recognized that her friend was in distress is arguable, but her reaction indicated something beyond curiosity. Judy pawed frantically at the door, baying to be let out to see what the situation was. She only got more frantic when Frank disappeared to investigate. But the other prisoners in the room wisely held her back. Whatever was going on out there, it involved guards, and letting Judy charge into their midst could only provoke a hostile reaction. So they barricaded the door from the inside.

Judy was safe, but Frank sat uneasily under arrest—"to wait for my trial for an attempt to escape." He could easily have been sentenced to death for his display of humanity and his unthinking reaction to hearing a dog in agony. Instead, he was taken for punishment, the standard penance, actually—two guards took turns beating him up for about eight hours. "I was bound with my arms backwards on a pole and beaten until my face was one bloody, raw mess," he later recounted. "Luckily I was released at dawn by the new officer of the guard, Takahashi, who did not know what I was accused for."

Once again, Judy was held back. When Frank's sentence was announced to the others, several prisoners lured Judy into a hut at the far side of the camp and locked her inside for the duration. She howled from within, perhaps out of concern for her best friend, perhaps merely because she was lonely and scared. But once again, it was for her own good—had she witnessed Frank being beaten, she would have charged right in and confronted the armed Japanese, as she had done so often before. She might well have been killed right in front of Frank as further punishment. "She would irrevocably have been shot on sight," was how Frank put it.

Luckily it didn't come to that, as Tick's death was tragic enough. And meanwhile, the mystery remained as to what animal had passed its seed along to Judy. That she was in heat was not something the men, even Frank, were likely to process. Judy probably had crossed paths with the father more than once before they mated, though it must have been far from the eyes of any of the POWs. Whatever dog fathered the litter, he was likely to have been as hungry and desperate as Judy, if not more so, making the social interaction required for mating even more improbable.

Perhaps in such a tenuous situation, normal behavior was superseded by an overpowering desire to procreate—the dog equivalent of "Eat, drink, and be merry, for tomorrow we may die!" But whoever the father and whatever the circumstances, Judy plumped and then gave birth to nine pups.

As with all pregnant canines, Judy was brooding and irritable in the days before she gave birth. Like a bird, she built a "nest" of branches and vines in order to make a comfortable home for the pups. Frank surmised the birth was imminent when Judy began licking herself madly. It was practice for the nonstop grooming she would perform on her pups to bond with them and, because the maternity ward was outdoors, to ward off pests.

The birth became a huge community event within the prison walls, a reminder to all that love and sentiment still existed in a world gone to hell. Simmonds recorded the occasion in his diary entry of November 18, 1942. "Judy gave birth to 9 puppies! Dr. Kirkwood and all the Dutch medical staff and supplies were at her disposal. Both Judy and her puppies are doing well!" Gifts of fruit and food were made to the proud mother, who tended to her pups as dutifully as she could in her weakened state.

Puppies are born blind and helpless, utterly reliant on the mother to live. Judy, like all dogs, reverted to her ancestral lupine ways and, as though a switch had been thrown, forgot all about her human friends in order to devote herself to her young. For a couple of weeks, even Frank was essentially ignored, though he was a regular presence at the nest.

Five of Judy's litter lived, a remarkable number given her malnutrition and the horrendous circumstances into which the pups were born. The ones who made it displayed the same notable grit and will to survive that their mother did. They put on weight despite the lack of food and made it to the one-month mark, a sign they would not die of hunger, anyway. Simmonds wrote, "Judy's puppies are growing up fine on bully [beef] and condensed milk"—supplied by the POWs combining their spare emergency victuals. "Judy's puppies are growing quickly to a nice interesting if amusing size. They are very loving." Persons, alluding to Judy's mascot days, recorded in his diary that "[Judy] is probably on Navy ration strength." And Simmonds later noted men "playing with Judy's lovable puppies," as did Stanley Russell, another diary-keeping POW. Russell even sketched the new mother bounding about with her offspring.

Amazingly enough, one of the cute little scampering bundles would play a critical role in the next stage of Judy's internment, when, through an extraordinary scheme devised by Frank, she would make military—and canine—history.

Lieutenant Colonel Hirateru Banno was sixty years old when he was put in charge of internment camps in Sumatra, operating out of the headquarters of the 4th Branch Malaya POW Command, a group of small buildings and huts that sat a short distance from the Gloegoer camp. (The 25th Army, based in Singapore and at Fort de Kock in Sumatra, had overall command over POWs in the area. Both officers in charge, Lieutenant General Yaheita Saito and Lieutenant General Moritake Tanabe, were sentenced to death after the war.) A retired lifer who saw little actual combat during his time in the Imperial Japanese Army, Banno had gone home to live the simple life of a gentleman farmer, only to come back to the military when the war with China broke out. Banno served in Manchuria for several years, then was transferred to internment service when his age made him too old for combat command.

Banno was from Kanazawa, a seaside town in the Ishikawa Prefecture on the west side of the main island of Honshu (almost directly across the country from Tokyo). A rainy, ghostly place, Kanazawa is best known in Japan for its winding, twisted roads that were laid out in haphazard fashion, and for its ancient architecture. Kanazawa is one of the few places where structures remained unvarnished from the Edo period, when samurai, geishas, and shoguns dominated the land.

A thoughtful, reserved type, the bespectacled Banno played against the stereotype of the loud Japanese officer who constantly spit bile. His elderly, lined face and gray mustache gave him an almost pleasant mien and a quite distinguished appearance. He was far taller than most Japanese soldiers, and lean, and while he was capable of harsh discipline when necessary, he generally gave off an air of remove from the creative cruelty on display in his camps.

Put simply, Banno was too old for that shit. He was generally too drunk as well—it was common knowledge that the old man put away copious amounts of alcohol, even while on duty.

He was also capable of crudeness, surely—Banno would gather his officers in their mess hut and put on great shows of civility, drinking iced tea and smoking cigarettes from ornate holders. Then he would rise from his overstuffed easy chair, stomp out to the garden, and urinate on the roses. Another of his favorite pastimes was to swing his heavy two-handed sword at prisoners, stopping inches from their heads. Those who flinched, which was most everyone, got a stern lecture on timidity. The one man who didn't, a Dutchman, was slapped on the back and given fruit and smokes as a tribute to his manliness.

Banno's lasting legacy to many POWs was the dank cellar used for storing fertilizer that he had converted into a punishment isolation cell, one that assaulted those unlucky enough to be kicked inside with an overpowering stench as well as dark loneliness. In the hole, prisoners were not permitted to lie down or sit during the day. The effort it took to stand for hours, days, sometimes weeks on end overcame all who were subjected to this punishment. At night, the only relief was a stone floor on which to collapse. Rations were cut as well, leaving the quaking mass inside so pitiable that even the Japanese guards were often moved to slip a banana or piece of chocolate through the bars.

Still, unlike many of the younger soldiers under his command, Banno didn't reflexively hate westerners, having served alongside them in World War I. Japan was an ally of Britain, France, and Australia during the Great War, and Banno served as a liaison officer on a destroyer that escorted troopships landing Aussie "diggers" in Egypt, a prelude to the ill-fated Gallipoli Campaign. Older Australian officers Banno would later encounter in POW camps would remark that he wore the same battle ribbons and stars that they wore.

He would become a complex, ill-starred figure over the course of the war. In April of 1943, just as he was getting used to Sumatra, he was called north as a last-minute replacement for an officer who had fallen ill. His new responsibility was to take over the so-called F Force, a large group of prison laborers tasked to help construct a railway across Siam and Burma. This would be the first and most famous of the Death Railways that would come to define Japanese POW camps in the public mind (mainly due to the movie *The Bridge on the River Kwai,* the classic adaptation of Pierre Boulle's fictionalized memoir of his time spent in the jungle suffering at the hands of his captors).

F Force left Singapore on a series of thirteen trains for the mountainous wilderness that was the border area between Siam and Burma in April 1943. The POW contingent numbered nearly seven thousand men, almost all of them British and Australian. Their job would be to build a railway between the city of Nieke in Siam and the Three Pagodas Pass that straddled the Burmese border. Compared to the railway construction at Kanchanaburi that encompassed the Kwai River Bridge, this task was far more formidable due to the terrain and the remote location of the site.

The POWs were force-marched some three hundred kilometers upon detraining, and matters only deteriorated from there. Disease, starvation, overwork, and the cruelty of the guards turned the area into an abattoir. Work began at seven in the morning and continued under arc lights far into the night, with no time to rest or wash. When progress fell behind schedule, prisoners were beaten by Banno's men with whips made from strands of fencing wire. The dead fell so fast, the funeral pyres could scarcely keep pace. They would be kept alight even in the pouring monsoon. Men who helped collect timber for the fires would themselves often be dead by nightfall.

By the time the work was finished, more than three thousand POWs of F Force were dead, a 45 percent death rate that dwarfed the toll in other sections of the railway, which averaged around 20 percent. Those who survived were essentially reduced to their skeletal framework, only technically alive.

As commander of the F Force guards, Banno was held responsible for the carnage and was brought to trial by the Singapore War Crimes Tribunal in the fall of 1946 (a simultaneous group of trials was taking place in Tokyo, which had far better coverage by the western press). Specifically, Banno was taken to task for his role in fostering a deadly outbreak of cholera. The POW doctors pleaded with Banno repeatedly to keep a group of sick men in place where they lay and not have them moved to where they would expose others. Banno, feeling pressure from above to complete what amounted to his final assignment in uniform, forced the party to push on as planned, transporting the sick POWs farther up the line to another camp. Sure enough, cholera spread like wildfire among the prisoners in the new camp, claiming countless more lives.

Banno defended his decision at his trial, calling the evacuated campsite where the cholera outbreak had begun "very dangerous."

> It was a narrow place surrounded by damp areas and there was no good water running and the only stream was lime water and it was not at all a suitable place for any person to stay. . . . The monsoon was also in and if the river over-flooded then the transport would come to a stand-still and the food rations have to be carried on men's shoulders; that means if we leave we have to suffer very unfit conditions and a great shortage of food for this large number of people. That is why I thought it was a greater disadvantage to the P.O.W. to stay there.

While the prisoners fell sick and perished, and others merely starved, Banno and the other Japanese always had plenty to eat. Still, the colonel was more humane and open to reason than many of his ilk. At one point, ten British prisoners attempted an impossible escape through the jungle.

After three weeks of wading across raging rivers, hacking through overwhelming bush, climbing steep terrain, and suffering under incessant rain, five men were dead, and the remaining five were rapping on the door. Having learned firsthand that what Banno had warned them about was true—that the jungle made escape attempts virtual suicide—the five men at last gave themselves up at a local village and were returned for reward to the Japanese.

The nominal sentence for escape attempts was death, but an extraordinary POW named Cyril Wild intervened and huddled with Banno. Wild, a Royal Army captain, had carried the white flag of surrender beside General Percival in Singapore and was now a captive member of F Force. Wild was fluent in Japanese and understood the culture (he would later be the official British interpreter to Lord Mountbatten during the unconditional surrender by Japan). Out in the jungle, Wild thrust himself into potentially deadly disagreements between prisoners and guards. He was so tireless in his intercessions on behalf of his fellow prisoners that the Japanese called him *nemuranai se no takai otoko,* translated as "the tall man who never slept."

Wild managed to persuade Banno to negate the death sentence by impressing upon him the severe disgrace that he would bring upon the emperor and the Imperial Japanese Army if he permitted the deaths of such brave men. Banno was moved to tears by Wild's eloquence. Amazingly enough, Wild's appeal to Banno's humanity and pride was successful; the men were instead removed to Singapore for brutal beatings and jail, but they lived to see the war's end.

Unlike in Sumatra, where his authority and the chain of command was clear, Banno's hands were tied by bureaucracy in Siam. While Banno was in charge of the guards and their day-to-day activities, the engineers of F Force were not subject to his orders, for reasons passing understanding. They were technically under the command of the POW administration in Singapore, not the commanding officer right there on the scene, as was the case in the other camps along the railway. So Banno, deep in the jungle, cut off from supply and communication, couldn't quickly sort out tangles (such as the one with the cholera-stricken prisoners) with a quick request for orders from a superior.

Meanwhile, later testimony from prisoners under Banno's ward suggested that he was afraid of these overzealous engineers, as well as many of the guards. While the highly respected Cyril Wild spoke up for Banno after the war (just before Wild died in a tragic plane crash as he shuttled between tribunals in Singapore and Tokyo), calling him "quite friendly" and acknowledging he had made "certain futile and totally ineffective attempts to ameliorate" conditions in the camps, others weren't so gentle. Banno was "unable to control the actions of his subordinates," sneered one witness. Other testimony smeared Banno as "negligent" and "an incompetent, fatuous old man." One survivor referred to Banno as "a doddering old donkey."

In large part, this weakness spared his life. When Banno came before the War Crimes Tribunal, he appealed that he had done "all he could in difficult circumstances" to prevent the deaths and that "lack of ability to impose his views on higher authority cannot be the basis of criminal responsibility." In other words, he argued it wasn't his fault.

Surprisingly enough, the tribunal saw it from his point of view, meting out a remarkably light three-year sentence, given the death toll in F Force. There were mitigating considerations: the prisoners were already considerably malnourished before they even left Singapore, and the unforgiving "climate and terrain were important factors that impeded the provision of adequate supplies," according to the official review of the case.

Banno spent most of his jail time in Singapore, then was transferred to the infamous Sugamo Prison in Tokyo, where political prisoners had been held (and tortured) before the surrender. Under General Douglas MacArthur's benevolent dictatorship of conquered Japan, Sugamo became the holding pen for war criminals. Banno wouldn't be there for long. He arrived in late January 1950, was fingerprinted but not photographed, and then was released less than a month later, on February 17, 1950, officially part of a group that had their sentences reduced, mainly to lower the expense of keeping them jailed.

He then returned to his farm near the sea, no doubt regretting the turn in history that had forced him to leave in the first place.

But before these events, Colonel Banno was at Gloegoer, halfheartedly attempting to squeeze in his administrative duties while spending most of his waking hours fanning the flames of a May-December romance.

Despite the hellish surroundings, Banno was in love, or at least lust. His inamorata was a much younger local woman. Whether it was true passion or merely an old man taking advantage of the spoils of war, Banno acted like a teenager with his local flame, visiting her often in her village and entertaining her in his officer's quarters whenever he could get away with it.

Frank knew that this woman loved Judy. She invariably cooed, "Judy, come," in her limited English when she encountered the dog, and was always trying to pet her, play with her, and nuzzle her ears. Judy was only too happy to oblige, unless Banno was standing next to her. For her part, Judy reviled Banno just as much as she did the other Japanese, going into her standard "back off" performance display whenever she encountered him.

Frank also knew that despite Banno's apparent hate for the dog, it was mostly for show. He enjoyed riling Judy up and getting her to snarl, so he would draw his sword and try to spear her when he encountered the pointer. Judy never enjoyed the joke and would growl angrily at the commandant. But he seldom seemed particularly upset or seriously attempted to turn the dog into a shish kebab.

That wasn't the case with the other guards. Whether due to the depletion of the food supplies, or the fact that the war was turning against the Axis after so much early success—or merely out of sheer orneriness—Frank noticed an alarming uptick in attempts on Judy's well-being. "The guards were malignant against Judy and many threats were made to kill her," was how he put it.

So in the early months of 1943, driven by the desire to protect his new best friend however possible, Frank launched an audacious plot. Through the camp grapevine he ascertained that Banno would be seeing his girlfriend one afternoon on an illicit call. Frank arranged to be on a detail that would take him outside the camp and close to the administrative offices. He managed to duck away from work and took up a spot in the bushes near Banno's living quarters. Frank watched patiently, tamping down the worry that his absence would be noted. As night began to fall, Frank could see through the window that Banno was alone, presumably relaxed after his liaison, now with a bottle of sake for company. It was time to play his trump card—a wiggling, drooling furry ace in the deck, the fattest, cutest of all of Judy's puppies, one named Kish.

Kish was the standout of Judy's second litter, but several of her other puppies were being enjoyed around the camp. The other four pups to survive were named Rokok, Sheikje, Blackie, and Punch.

Sheikje was the most attractive of the litter after Kish, in Searle's opinion. She wound up getting passed over to the women's camp—a place the prisoners scarcely knew existed, even though it was only a mile or so away. One day a native fruit vendor passed along a whispered message—the women wanted to know if they could have one of the puppies. Once Frank and the men got over their shock, they agreed, and managed to smuggle Sheikje over to their camp. The fruit vendor put the pup in her basket, covered her with several bunches of bananas, and walked out with the basket on her head. She then strolled into the women's camp in the same manner and delivered a now very sweet-smelling Sheikje to the grateful women. Years later, Len Williams heard from a woman who as a child was imprisoned in the women's camp and had lost her mother there. She had never forgotten the puppy and the woman who brought her in on her head.

There was a small drain hole in the wall of the compound, and it was through this passage that Rokok escaped the camp. As neutrals, Switzerland maintained a small consulate in the city of Medan, and though they could do nothing about the POWs, the message came through the grapevine that the Swiss would love to brighten the drab government dwelling with a puppy. Rokok was knocked into slumber with a whiff of chloroform and shoved through the hole to a waiting intermediary, who delivered the unconscious pup to the Swiss. Punch and Blackie hung around the camp, but both eventually died young. Blackie was beaten to death by a guard, while Punch disappeared altogether, his fate unknown.

Kish's impact would be far greater.

Frank approached Banno's quarters, ordinarily an executable offense on its own. Using sign language and an air of helpless submission, Frank managed to get past the guard and into Banno's room. If the officer was upset or shocked to see him, he was distracted by the combination of alcohol and the scrunchy puppy that Frank carried in and placed on his desk. Kish waddled to and fro, and played a game of balancing on the edge of a table, almost falling over before regaining his legs and moving toward Banno. Amazingly, the colonel roared with laughter and actually let the dog lick his outstretched hand.

"He was very drunk and seemed to forget that he was talking to one of the prisoners," Frank remembered later. "I had heard that alcohol put this normally very aggressive man in a good mood, and given enough to drink, he was likely to agree to anything."

It was time to test that theory. Frank said he had brought Kish not just as an amusement, but as a gift. The gift was not for Banno, though he was of course welcome to keep the pup. No, this dog was meant for Banno's lady friend from the nearby village.

Frank had feared that the mere mention of Banno's lover would be tantamount to suicide, and indeed, most other men in the commandant's position would have taken Frank's head on the spot. But the prisoner sensed Banno was different, betting his life on his reading of the man from afar (keep in mind this was a twenty-three-year-old kid from the shores of England, not, say, the worldly Cyril Wild), and he casually offered Kish to Banno as a gift he could then pass along.

Indeed, Banno was moved instead of insulted. He thanked Frank for his thoughtfulness. Yes, the pup would make a great gift and would go a long way toward establishing goodwill on his part.

So with rare good feelings in the air, Frank delicately brought up the pup's mother, Judy. He talked about the risk to her life from the guards, the natives, and the crocodiles; how brave and loving Judy was; and how important she was to morale.

After a while, he put his request on the table. He wanted Banno to officially make Judy a prisoner of war, which would offer her protection under the Geneva protocols and at least make the guards think twice about randomly or wantonly shooting her.

Banno thought it over for a while, as Frank refilled his sake glass. Your thoughtfulness and care for your friend is much appreciated, Banno said, but he couldn't do it. The Japanese, he explained, much like their German allies, were fanatical about precision in details, especially when it came to matters like the number of prisoners in a work camp. Much as Banno regretted not being able to help, he wouldn't be able to explain to his supervisors how there had come to be an extra prisoner in the Gloegoer camp. Many questions would be asked, and—though Banno didn't explicitly say as much—it was clear he feared his extracurricular, extramarital affair would be revealed to his superior officers. That simply wouldn't do.

Fortunately, Frank was steps ahead of the colonel and had anticipated this turn in the discussion. "That is a simple problem to avoid," he told Banno. "Simply add the letter 'A' to my number." Frank carried the prison number 81, or *hatchi ju-ichi*. By merely making Judy prisoner 81-A, she could be granted the official status while not raising suspicion back at imperial headquarters.

At this point Kish, sensing the pivotal moment, as his mother was so adept at, rolled over and plopped onto Banno's hand, looking impossibly cute with his big brown eyes, a trait inherited directly from his mother. Banno simply couldn't resist the puppy. Happily rolling Kish over and over on the table, he astoundingly agreed to Frank's request. Judy would hereby become the first—and only—canine prisoner of war in any theater of World War II, or in any known war before or since.

As Banno scrawled the official order, Frank looked at the puppy—and drew in his breath. Kish was relieving himself in an enormous puddle, mere inches from the commandant's elbow. Frank could envision the entire plan, which by some miracle was on the brink of success, going down in flames, ones that wouldn't be extinguished by dog pee.

But their fantastic luck held. Banno stayed dry, as did the order making Judy a POW. Frank bowed and thanked the officer obsequiously, then got the hell out of there as fast as he could, orders (and puppy) in hand.

Before the next dawn, Judy was proudly wearing a specially made attachment to her collar that read, "81-A Gloegoer Medan." If anyone needed another reminder that this pointer was unique, Judy now sported one on her collar.

CHAPTER 18

Subterfuge

Not long after Judy was placed on the official prisoner list at Gloegoer, Banno departed for his fateful command of F Force. His first replacement as top officer in the Sumatran camp was Captain Takahashi, the mild-mannered officer with the wry sense of humor. He immediately outlawed face-slapping as a means of punishment and told the imprisoned officers they would no longer need to bow to the lower-ranking Japanese troops, after the failure to do so previously meant a brutal beating. "He told us that while he did not like us particularly, he was going to see that we got the things we ought to have and that strict discipline would be maintained in the camp," remembered John Purvis. "This suited us very well and several months passed without any particular incidents occurring."

Takahashi seemed at times to be almost on their side. He would notice POWs staring longingly at airplanes that passed overhead, hoping against hope that they were Allied bombers. When they were gone, Takahashi would say, "Too bad, better luck next time."

"We could never work out whether he was pro-British, whether he was a more intelligent man than the rest of his compatriots and had seen the danger signal in the distance, or whether he was simply human," Hartley wrote. After the war, several prisoners would testify to his humanity at Takahashi's war crimes trial. "He was not a bad Nip," was the (qualified) praise offered by one liberated lieutenant.

Not even this small break would last for the POWs, however, and soon enough, Takahashi was transferred to Changi, the huge prison on Singapore. He was replaced by a Captain Meora, who scoffed at Takahashi's kindnesses, which he took as signs of weakness. Face-slapping was reinstituted, and the men were forced to count off at parade each morning in Japanese.

In June 1944, command of Gloegoer changed hands again. The new officer in charge was named Captain Nishi (in some accounts he is referred to as Nissi). From his first moments in charge of the camp, it was clear there was a new sheriff in town. He took the discipline reinstituted by Meora and ratcheted up the unpleasantness several notches. That attitude would ensure that Nishi played a brief but critical cameo in the lives of Judy and Frank.

On his first day, Nishi ordered all the prisoners into the common muster square in the center of the barracks area—and by *all,* he meant every single one of them. The wounded limped out or were carried out on stretchers. The sick leaned against comrades or slumped miserably in the heat. The dying were laid out in a row, not too close to any of the other prisoners, who were afraid to look at them.

As the prisoners formed up, Nishi stood in the center of the formations, impatiently smacking his cane on his polished boots, his uniform starched to a crisp perfection. He was of medium build, a little taller than average but not exceptionally so, with a somewhat bland countenance. In sum, there was nothing exceptional about him, save his strict military bearing and unbending attitude.

As he watched the men assemble, his gaze fell on Frank—and then down to his feet, where Judy stood at attention. Nishi was flabbergasted. There was not only a dog living here in this most unusual setting, but a prisoner's dog at that. The effrontery rendered him insensate for a few moments; then he shook off his shock and strode toward the POW and his pointer.

Frank's heart was pounding a rumba in his chest. The protection of the POW status he had managed to secure for Judy had lasted for more than a year, but it was apparent from the look on Nishi's face that it was about to come to a screeching halt unless he could think of something. As Nishi drew near, Frank was brought up short by his hard manner, so different from the affable Banno and the decent Takahashi. For her part, Judy's thin frame began to tremble, and as usual she snarled and growled in a low tone at the approaching Japanese soldier. The large group of prisoners was struck silent, realizing the magnitude of the moment.

Frank knew that if Nishi screamed out an order to kill or seize the dog before he could explain Judy's special status, all would be lost. The POW designation would carry little weight, and Judy's position would crumble before the officer's need to save face. So he hurriedly fumbled in his pockets to fish out the well-worn piece of paper he carried bearing Colonel Banno's official order to make Judy a POW. He held it out to the surprised Nishi, pointing at Banno's signature while saying over and over "It's okay, it's okay."

Nishi grabbed the precious document, and a bunch of other officers appeared, everyone examining the paper and Banno's signature, trying to comprehend exactly why the colonel would have signed the order, how Frank came to be in possession of it, and what the consequences would be if they followed their instincts, ignored Judy's POW status, and killed (and perhaps ate) the pointer, as they clearly wanted to do. There was much chattering and gesticulating in Japanese as Frank waited on edge, subconsciously moving Judy behind his knees as if they offered protection from the enemy's guns.

What Frank and all the prisoners knew was that "official" status as a POW meant very little, certainly in the context of a prison camp in the face of an angry Japanese officer. A piece of paper declaring Judy a POW wasn't really worth the document's weight, regardless of who signed it.

But it was a curiosity, and it had its desired effect. One member of Nishi's staff consulted a book of regulations during the examination of Judy's paperwork, and it was he who appeared to carry the day, apparently talking his commander out of killing anyone—or anything—that Colonel Banno had gone out of his way to protect. Nishi grunted, shot a hateful stare at Judy, and stomped back to the center of the formation.

Once again, Judy had slipped off the hook.

Many of the POWs had been working for some time by now at the disused Ford Motor Company plant (the same job mentioned earlier) and stripping it down for scrap to be transported to Singapore and reused in the Japanese war effort. It was a large job, and it went slowly, hindered in part by the physical decrepitude of the prisoners and in part by their deliberately slow work.

But within hours of his taking over the camp, Captain Nishi ordered the whole lot of them to the factory and gave them forty-eight hours to finish the destruction of the plant and its machinery. Why he gave them the short deadline wasn't known to the men, but it was clear he meant business when he had a couple of shirkers beaten within an inch of their lives on the first morning. The other prisoners rededicated themselves to the job.

They worked until nearly midnight, when, numb from exhaustion, they were at last trucked back to the barracks, only to be awoken at dawn the following day for a return to the plant site. The punishing pace dropped dozens of men and badly weakened many more. But by late in the afternoon of the second day, the last of the machinery had been stripped down and loaded onto trucks for Belawan, where Japanese transport ships awaited.

Nishi was pleased, and told the prisoners that as a reward for their hard labor they would be allowed to sleep in. But on the third day, the wake-up horns trumpeted before dawn as usual. When the men mustered in a daze on the square, Nishi had a surprise announcement: "According to the Imperial High Command," he read from a scroll wrapped around a bamboo rod, "all prisoners are ordered moved to Singapore."

The reason behind the suicidal pace of the work at the Ford plant had become clear. Nishi had been tasked to finish the job before the camp was moved, and he had done so, at a terrible cost.

Still, the prisoners who were still alive were buoyed by the news. Singapore may have been in enemy hands, but it was familiar terrain, and it surely had to be more comfortable than Gloegoer. Imprisonment in Singapore meant the likelihood of Red Cross packages, letters from home, a semblance of normalcy. They were likely to get news about the war, which they hardly ever received in the Sumatran jungle—for all they knew, the Japs were in London by now. "Cheer up, lads," Searle told a few buddies of his who had collapsed under the strain of the hardship over the last couple of days and were lying on stretchers. "You'll soon be out of this."

While the other prisoners were busy packing their meager possessions in readiness for the move, Captain Nishi himself appeared in the barracks. Frank rose from his usual spot, Judy between his legs. Nishi strode over to him in an imperious manner. His English was wanting, but his shouted orders were perfectly clear, regardless of language barriers.

Frank would be going to Singapore. Judy would not. The dog would be left behind in Sumatra to fend for herself.

Nishi may have been prevented by Banno's fiat from killing Judy outright, but now he ensured that he would do so in a de facto manner. Judy wouldn't last long on her own, that much was obvious. Frank was shaken, but the clever man who had worked so hard and risked so much to safeguard his dog via official POW status wouldn't cave in now. And he knew the problem was his and his alone. The other prisoners loved Judy, but Frank could hardly ask them to risk their lives over a dog, especially now that they had seemingly received some good news for the first time in ages.

He might have said the same thing about himself, but there was no way he would leave Judy behind—even if being discovered meant death for them both, which it surely would. He loved her too much—and after what they had been through, Frank could not imagine abandoning her now. It was an unthinkable act for a military man or a dog lover. Frank was now both.

So Frank decided to conceal his friend and somehow smuggle her on to the ship that would ferry the POWs across the South China Sea back to Singapore. His first thought was to use a brown suitcase that a Dutch prisoner had found in some remote corner of the camp. It would hide Judy easily enough, but the Japanese would rightly wonder why such an albatross was being dragged to the new camp. It would surely be searched before they left, and the game would be up.

Judy had already proven herself quite capable of learning tricks and repetitive techniques, and by then she was quite attuned to the sound and modulation of Frank's voice, whistles, clicks, and snaps. So Frank improvised a far more bold plan, one that relied on teaching Judy a new trick in the few hours left between lights-out and when the POWs would be mustered at dawn for their train.

Rice sacks were as common as flies at Gloegoer, and about as remarkable. If Judy could be secreted in one, she could slip under Nishi's radar. So Frank spent the wee hours of the morning teaching Judy to leap into and out of a cotton rice sack at the sound of the snapped click of his fingers. He kept the sound of the snap low, relying on her keen hearing, because it would be useless if it was too obvious. He also spent some time with the sack slung over his shoulder, indoctrinating Judy to the sensation of being held in such an awkward, claustrophobic condition. But there was no way to simulate the real thing perfectly, just as there was no way to guess how long she might be hanging upside down in the dark, stuffy bag. Frank would have to hope Judy could hide and scamper on cue. For her part, Judy quickly got the hang of this new demand, and by the time the first streaks of light pierced the darkness over the prison camp, Frank deemed the dog ready as she would ever be.

At dawn the prisoners were ordered to muster. The wounded and sick now numbered about one-third of the men and took up two long rows of their formation. Frank made a show of tying Judy with a long rope to a hut pole, surreptitiously ensuring that the slipknot he tied would loosen and release when pulled on. "Now you stay right here, girl," he said, a little louder than necessary, just in case any of the guards were taking an interest.

The guards counted and recounted the prisoners, and checked and rechecked the sacks of rice and packs of possessions they were taking with them. Frank had precious little to show for the two years and four months he'd spent in Sumatra, but since the plan required he be seen and known to possess a full sack of rice, he shoved a blanket into one and put it at his feet.

The guards were satisfied. Nishi himself then walked down the lines of prisoners, checking that all was in readiness. When he came to Frank, Nishi looked over the prisoner's shoulder at the dog tied up behind him and smiled. His war didn't contain any glorious banzai charges at the enemy. He didn't participate in any of the Imperial Japanese Navy's sweeping successes. He never flew a sortie, fired an artillery piece, or defended a beachhead. Crushing the spirit of helpless prisoners was about the only victory Nishi would achieve. And it appeared that he was on the brink of a memorable win in his pathetic corner of the war.

Then he gave the order to move out.

The seven hundred prisoners left alive, down from nearly a thousand when they made the long trek from Padang to Gloegoer, shuffled and limped toward the gates. Unlike popular depictions, there was no orderly march, no whistling of the "Colonel Bogey March," no lofty morale in defiance of their captors. The men simply stared straight ahead and put one foot in front of the other, as best they could.

Frank lingered near the rear, as far from the guards as he could get. Every now and again he snuck a peek back toward Judy, and was reassured to see she was watching him carefully. As soon as he cleared the gates of the camp, he whistled sharply, then coughed to cover it up, in case anyone noticed. He also made a small motion with his arm.

When he finally dared to look back at his dog, she had slipped her knot and disappeared. But Frank didn't catch sight of her until he was about to get on his train, and he was petrified that she either didn't know what to do, couldn't get close to the trains for all the guards, or had already been captured or killed.

But then he heard a low grumble and turned to catch sight of two familiar wet brown eyes and a black nose poking out ever so slightly from the shadows under a nearby wagon. Judy had made it!

So far, at least. Now came the riskiest moment yet. Frank kneeled down as if to tie his shoe. Several other prisoners, knowing what was required of them thanks to hastily whispered instructions, formed a loose protective cordon around him, leaving open a narrow gap. Frank then took the blanket from his sack and snapped his fingers.

Judy bounded over from her hiding spot, zipped into the gap between prisoners, and went straight into the sack. In one smooth movement, despite his physical wasting and the tension of the moment, Frank closed the sack and swung it and the now forty-five-pound dog onto his shoulder. Another man took his blanket. And without drawing any undue attention, Frank rose and stepped onto his train.

Stage one was complete.

For the moment, all was well. The train slipped its siding and made for Belawan, a journey of about forty-five minutes. When they arrived, Frank waited until the train was almost stopped, then opened the sack and bade Judy to make for cover. Without any good forest nearby that she could get to without being spotted, she instead doubled back and hid in the last place anyone would look—under the train itself.

The prisoners were lined up at the depot and marched the short distance down to the quayside, where again all their things were checked and counted. Frank had reloaded his rice sack with a blanket to match what he carried on the Gloegoer end of the journey. The ship they would board, a graying hulk, loomed above them but cast no shade for relief. The prisoners sweated unrelentingly in the heat. No one moved except the guards, who listlessly patrolled the perimeter of the formation, suffering as well under the equatorial sun.

Frank could hear nothing except the beating of his own heart. How would he get Judy to cover the two hundred or so yards between them and the train tracks unseen? Would he even be able to snap his fingers loud enough for her to hear? His hastily constructed plan had always contained this weak link—since he didn't remember the precise layout of the train depot and port at Belawan (he had been there for a very short time two years before), he didn't know where Judy would be in relation to the prisoners' formation. Now it appeared all would come undone.

There was no obvious sound, no clear statement as such, but a disturbance in the ranks made it apparent that something unusual was going on. Soon enough the word was passed to Frank by low sotto voce murmur—Judy was making her way to the formation. Frank desperately scanned his peripheral vision and spotted his dog creeping toward him. She was crawling on her stomach like a sniper inching into position, head low, not making a sound. Somehow she had managed to reach the edge of the column of prisoners without being spotted. A prisoner would later tell Frank that he had seen her stop and flatten several times when a guard neared, and she had made herself invisible enough not to be seen by them.

Now Judy crept between the rows of prisoners toward Frank. Not a man looked down to give away the game. No one spoke or even whispered encouragement. When she got to Frank's position in the ranks, he ensured that no one was looking directly at him. Then he casually dumped the blanket from the sack, held it open for Judy to hop inside, and deftly lifted it on his shoulder. Judy was at last out of sight.

Frank's exchange went unnoticed, but the ordeal wasn't over. It took ages for the ship to maneuver into the anchorage, for the gangway to be readied, and for the seven hundred men to board. Frank, as fate would have it, was among the last of the men to climb up to the ship. He had been out in the broiling sun, with his dog in a sack on his shoulder, not moving, for nearly two hours. It was only natural that after all this time he began to falter. Sweat beaded down his back, his limbs started to shake, and his vision started to blur.

A lanky Australian, his identity lost to history, stood next to Frank as he suffered. At last, he took off his wide-brimmed hat and put it on the head of his fellow prisoner.

"If I fall down," he whispered out of the side of his mouth, "someone will pick me up. If you fall down, you've had it, you and your dog."

Only about seventy-five men were left ashore, and Frank was one of them. The boarding continued. It was a race between the time it took for all the men to get aboard and Frank's stamina, but he was determined to hold out.

Then he saw a Japanese guard striding toward him.

The man's face flickered a note of suspicion. Eying Frank carefully, he asked, *"Ino murrasini noka?"* "Dog not come?"

Frank affected a look of deep grief, an acting job aided by the weight of Judy biting into his aching shoulder. He looked down at his feet and sadly shrugged. This seemed to satisfy the guard, and he moved on.

At last, his number was called, and Frank and his cargo were waved into a group forming up to board the ship. Incredibly, the plan worked. He and Judy had made it off the hellish island of Sumatra and onto the boat, away from the cruel Captain Nishi's sentence of death.

Frank shifted the weight of his burden and hauled his friend up the gangway and into what appeared to be a slightly brighter future.

CHAPTER 19

Hell Ship

Rust bucket. There was no other way to describe her.

The *Van Waerwijck* was heavy, an anchor chain or two over three thousand tons, tall, dwarfing the *Gnat* or the *Grasshopper,* and far more imposing than any vessel the prisoners had used to escape from Singapore. She was gray, with huge patches of rust from stem to stern. The only visible fresh paint was where the ship's name had been switched from Dutch to Japanese. She was as downtrodden and disheveled as the prisoners. She looked like a ship that had just been salvaged from the seafloor, which in fact she had been.

The Dutch had scuttled her in the harbor of Tandjong Priok in the northern section of Batavia, hoping to slow Japanese advances there, but the sunken vessel proved no more than a speed bump. The Japanese not only weren't impeded by the blockade, but also raised the *Van Waerwijck* for use as a cargo ship. They renamed her *Harukiku Maru,* and gave her one of the more nefarious jobs in naval history.

Of all the inhumane treatment visited on POWs by the Japanese, time spent on the "hell ships" may have been the worst. The IJA transported prisoners from island to island and camp to camp across the Pacific theater aboard these dilapidated craft. Men were stuffed into dank, reeking cargo holds from the Philippines to Java to Burma to Manchuria, and especially to and from the home islands of Japan. The *Van Waerwijck* was typical of the ships they used—usually aging or decrepit bulk carriers salvaged after poor attempts at scuttling—though occasionally a more modern liner was mixed in.

Needless to say, these ships weren't painted with a red cross to signal their special status and human cargo to Allied warships on the prowl. The Japanese didn't much care if the prisoners were killed by enemy attacks, which they were by the thousands. Precise numbers are difficult to measure, but Willem Wanrooy, whose *Prisoners of the Japanese in World War II* is a definitive account, puts the number at sixteen prison ships sunk, with over twenty thousand Allied prisoners killed. Wanrooy wrote his book (under the pen name Van Waterford) after surviving the sinking of the *Junyō Maru,* one of the hell ships, off Sumatra.

In addition to the 720 POWs brought over from Gloegoer, 454 more on board were from a camp near Belawan Harbor, one called Unie-Kampong. They were of a similar Dutch-British-Aussie mix to the Gloegoer prisoners, though there was also a single Norwegian imprisoned at this camp.

The mood among the prisoners was cleaved by nationality. The Brits and Aussies were relatively upbeat; the journey at least was a break from the relentless drudgery of their prison lives. By contrast, almost all of the Dutch were gloomy. They had spent most, if not the entirety, of their lives in Sumatra or the East Indies. Many were married and had families in Sumatra. This was no mere bad turn in the fortunes of war; it was a chilling trip into the unknown.

The POWs reached the deck, worked their way through a narrow companionway, and then were shoved down a series of steep iron ladders into several cargo holds. Deeper and deeper into the black void they descended, and more and more men piled in.

The holds of the *Van Waerwijck* were a Stygian scene of misery for the eleven hundred POWs. The sick and wounded prisoners were jammed into pigeonholes made of bamboo racks, about sixty inches by eighteen inches, slotted in as though already in the morgue. The rest of the men clambered well below water level into one of the dark holds of fetid air, scrambling down rope nets to reach the bottom. The hatches were then shut and battened down above them. Far more valuable machinery and bales of rubber took up the precious deck space, relegating the human cargo to steerage.

Frank carefully lowered his sack into waiting arms below, dropped down to the floor himself, and at last released Judy, who was gasping for air but otherwise seemingly unhurt by her long, uncomfortable stretch in the canvas. They pushed their way to a remote corner of the number three hold. Judy lay there, panting, stretching, looking as woebegone and bedraggled as the other prisoners. But the splotchy hunk of bones and fur was still with Frank, against all odds.

Close by, Peter Hartley gazed with wonder at the pointer. "I began to think dreamily about that dog," he wrote later. "What an adventurous life she had led in a few years of existence." It should be remembered that he wrote this without any particular knowledge of Judy's life in China, or he might have been even more amazed.

Phil Dobson lay close to Hartley, as usual. Walter Gibson, Len Williams, Les Searle, Jock Devani—they were all smashed together, along with the other Brits, Aussies, Kiwis, and Dutchmen.

It was the morning of June 25, 1944. Frank would turn twenty-five in a month's time, if he could live that long. Judy was well into her eighth year. By any measure, hers had been an exceptionally eventful and heartbreaking life—but there was still much more to come on both fronts.

The *Van Waerwijck* was untied and made off into the Strait of Malacca. She soon formed up with a convoy that consisted of three oil tankers, a pair of antisubmarine corvettes, and a minelayer. A scout plane circled overhead, on the lookout for enemy warships.

Frank knew Judy was an old naval sea dog, but it had been twenty-eight months since she had been on a boat. Concerned the pointer would struggle to find her sea legs, and worried for her well-being in the crushing heat of the hold, Frank made for the one place there was a hint of fresh air. A top corner platform in the stern offered not only a bit of headroom, which the lanky RAF man appreciated, but also a porthole. It was but ten inches across, smaller than a large pizza, but it could be shoved open a bit. Judy was able to gaze out at the calm passing sea.

If the pointer reminisced about her carefree days aboard the *Gnat* on the Yangtze, or her ocean voyages aboard the *Grasshopper,* she kept it to herself. A few yards away, Hartley and Dobson noticed a different porthole and managed to squeeze and shimmy their way to it, garnering a thimbleful of fresh air as a reward for their efforts.

The old steamer chugged along, hugging the Sumatran coast, making just eight knots, its speed kept down by the tonnage of human cargo in the hold and the inefficiency of her engines. Showing a hint of mercy, the guards removed a few hatches to allow some air into the belowdecks, but the effect was minimal. The punishing heat and the drone of the engines lulled them into a near-catatonic state. When the monotony of the dark waves ceased to interest her, Judy lay her head on Frank's legs and slept away the night hours. The convoy dropped anchor for the night only thirty miles into its journey.

A trio of Frank's other RAF mates sat with him and Judy. The men had helped to screen Judy's frame when guards popped their heads down into the hold to check up on things. The night passed uncomfortably but uneventfully. As the twenty-sixth dawned, the *Van Waerwijck* began zigzagging under the threat of Allied attack, keeping between roughly two and ten miles off the Sumatran coast. From his vantage, Frank could see the "thick, impenetrable jungle vegetation" gliding past. Many years later, the sinister beauty of the scenery was still fresh in his memory.

> Where ripe coconuts had washed ashore and had sprouted roots, the coastline was overgrown with coconut palm trees.... [Many] months ago we got to know these coastlines; the beauty of the flaming and shiny colored blossoms such as orchids; birds and butterflies with a wingspan of at least 15 cm. This was only Mother Nature's cover up. These mangrove jungles are the most dangerous and the least merciful jungles in the world, where shiny colors are used by nature as a trap to hide her true intentions. In these places a beneficent and fast death can be expected by crocodiles and snakes, or by a debilitating illness caused by insect bites.

All morning a handful of men at a time were allowed on deck for five-minute stretches in order to relieve themselves. This was accomplished by going over the side—when defecating, the men stepped out onto a small gangplank and held on to the rail with all their strength, while sticking their bottoms out over the sea. Toilet paper was a high-pressure seawater hose used to clean the decks.

Eight bells tolled on the ship's bell, signaling noon. The convoy was intact, though their air cover had disappeared. Les Searle was called to the deck, where he and a handful of other prisoners were given the task of emptying the Japanese latrines into the sea. Ordinarily a grim and ugly job, the men thanked their lucky stars for it, as the work got them out of the horrible hold and into the fresh air and sun.

Belowdecks, the midday heat had become so hellacious that men sat in pools of their own sweat. Frank wondered if "a couple of buckets would be distributed to catch our perspiration so that we would quench our thirst." The ship had traveled about one hundred miles from Belawan and was 260 miles northwest of Singapore.

At 12:42 p.m., Searle looked up from his spot amidships and uttered a strangled cry. There were no words he could muster that captured what he saw—the wake kicking up from a pair of torpedoes on the water's surface, homing in on the ship.

They had been fired by the HMS *Truculent,* a British submarine commanded by Lieutenant Robert L. Alexander. The sub was a veteran of the Norwegian Sea, transferring to the Indian Ocean late in 1943. *Truculent* was deep into her eleventh war patrol when the smoke of the *Van Waerwijck* convoy was sighted just before eleven thirty a.m. (the *Truculent*'s log shows this happening at ten a.m., the discrepancy due to the sub running on Ceylon time and the POW ship being on Tokyo time, a ninety-minute difference).

The sub stalked its prey for over an hour, closed to within thirty-five hundred yards, and fired its torpedoes. Such accidental friendly fire was common on both sides. For example, in November 1942, the *Nova Scotia,* a British troopship carrying 750 Italian POWs, was sunk by a U-boat off South Africa. The Nazi submarine surfaced and rescued a pair of survivors in order to determine the nature of the vessel. When told the majority of those on board were internees, the commander, Robert Gysae, apologized for the attack, and even more so for the fact that he had been ordered not to rescue any more men. The vast majority of the others sent into the water drowned or were taken by sharks.

Fortunately for the *Van Waerwijck* men, the Malacca Strait was much shallower, warmer, and less shark-infested than the Natal coast. But the Italians hadn't been crammed into the deep recesses of the *Nova Scotia.* Alexander clearly had no idea his quarry was ferrying his own POWs. The only notification of such was added after the fact to the *Truculent*'s official record, noting laconically, "The *Harukiku Maru* was carrying

POW's." In the ship's log, Alexander noted that his target "reminded me most of HMS *Titania,* as she was a two deck old passenger type, painted light greenish grey and looked like a depot ship of some kind."

Both torpedoes, each loaded with 250-kilogram charges, struck the *Van Waerwijck.* The first hit just behind the wall of the port-side heating plate. In the hold, there was a flash of light accompanying the loud explosion, then all went pitch-dark. Fire erupted in various spots. "Corrosive substances polluted the air," according to Frank. "The shock made the boat lean over to the starboard side and while she was recovering, a second torpedo ripped the number three hold with a deafening blow."

The *Van Waerwijck* was torn asunder by this second explosion. Dozens unluckily close to the blast were instantly killed. The fires in the hold were extinguished by torrents of salt water that poured in through the gaping hole in the hull. Thick smoke and steam from the damaged engine room asphyxiated the prisoners. "The harsh notes of the ship's siren penetrated plaintively through the uproar," Hartley recalled.

Slowly, the air was cleared enough by gusts howling through the ship's wound, and Frank could make out the scene. "The light passing through the shutters made it possible to perceive the ravaged hold. The area was one big mass of bent steel and splintered wood. The only thing that could be heard was the hissing noise of the escaping steam from the broken lines and the seawater pouring in. Below us the men were trapped and buried in a hopelessly distorted pile."

It was worse beneath the hatches, where the huge and heavy metal covers had blown inward and down on top of the POWs lying beneath, followed by the heavy crates on the dock, which broke free from their lashing and, as the ship heeled over, slid down the open hatch on top of the men as well.

Gazing upon the charnel, Frank was momentarily frozen. But then he felt Judy's wet nose sniffling upon his leg, and that "swept him back to reality." Gazing up at her friend, Judy "was incredibly calm and was motionlessly waiting for me to move." Her loyalty and instinct to safeguard her friends hadn't left her in other dire moments, and she stayed true even as the explosions sounded and the water filled the hold.

The destruction made impossible any thoughts Frank had of climbing down from his perch, maneuvering through the chaos, and climbing up and out the hatch while carrying Judy. "In a glimpse of an eye I could see that it was impossible to carry the animal through the mess," Frank said.

Instead he turned to the small porthole above them. Frank could never get through, but Judy might be able to squeeze out. Not stopping to consider the consequences, Frank opened it as far as it would go, picked up the pointer, "shoved her head and front paws though the hole and commanded her to 'swim!' 'Out you go old girl!' I yelled."

The drop to the sea was about fifteen feet. Before dropping, Judy "looked down and back at me with a sad look. I immediately understood her: she thought I was nuts! Then she wrenched herself with curled up rear paws through the porthole. The hole was just wide enough and with a last push she disappeared from sight. How Judy landed in the water must have been an amazing sight."

Now all Frank had to do was save himself.

Along with several men in the area, including Hartley, who had watched Dobson climb out a porthole in much the manner of Judy (and witnessed Frank push the dog out), Frank began to clamber over and under the hopelessly intermingled masses of wrenched steel and wood and bodies.

"After what seemed an eternity," Frank and the others reached a spot directly beneath the open hatch. There was a rope ladder, but it was "besieged by a mob of panic-stricken and desperate men," Hartley recalled. Instead, they climbed on top of a mountain of crashed crates. The summit still left them a few feet from the deck. "It was now or never," Hartley recorded. They simultaneously jumped for a handhold.

Frank records that he was able—somehow—to grab on and pull himself up. Only strength born from crisis could have allowed for such a thoroughly depleted man to perform such a feat. Hartley, several inches shorter than Frank, couldn't manage. Agonizingly, he hung on by his fingertips. "Tears of hopelessness welled up into my eyes, blinding me."

Then, a miracle—a hand from above reached down and pulled him on deck. Several hands, actually, belonging to Searle and the others on his latrine-dumping detail. After the torpedoes hit, Searle had found the rope ladder and lowered it into the hold. Then he and the others lifted as many as they could from the depths of the hold before the onrushing waves swept them all into the water.

"As far as the eye could see, the sea was filled with wreckage being dragged away by the fast currents," Frank remembered. "Somewhere in there, Judy was swimming." He worried about sharks, as much for his dog as for himself. She would be an easy lunch for the white tips and blues that marauded in the area. A few were spotted, but it seems there were so many corpses that the living swimmers were ignored in favor of easy pickings.

More explosions rocked the ocean. Two other ships of the convoy were struck by torpedoes. Frank watched transfixed as one fish zeroed in on its target:

> A tanker sailing at full speed was hit on its starboard side. The torpedo was apparently aimed low, because the hull above the Primsoll trading mark [a line on the hull beyond which cargo could not be loaded, so as to prevent overstuffing the hold, as the Japanese had done with the POWs] did not show any visible damage. With the prow down, the tanker plowed to the deep and sunk in a couple of minutes. It reminded me of a submarine performing an emergency dive.... Towards the [Japanese] crew of the ship I did not feel any compassion when they went down.

Another tanker exploded in a "blinding sheet of flame," according to Hartley, "leaving no trace that [it] had ever existed." Oil covered the sea in an enormous slick. Hartley's face was so blackened that he was unrecognizable to the friend, a New Zealander he called "Mac," who pulled him from the water and onto his overcrowded raft.

A Japanese corvette zigzagged to avoid being hit while randomly dropping depth charges (antisubmarine explosives), adding to the utter mayhem. Scout planes belatedly arrived to toss down bombs in an attempt to flush the *Truculent* to the surface, to no avail.

Frank glided down the steeply angled hull of the *Van Waerwijck,* which was "loaded with mussels," and began swimming as hard as his overtaxed body would let him to escape the ship's suction when it sank. He was comfortable in the water, dating to his Merchant Navy days, but he was exhausted. He flipped over onto his back to watch the reflagged steamer go under, sunk for the second time in the war. Her screw was still turning helplessly in the smoky air. "An imposing fountain sprayed in the air because of the exploding kettles [steam pipes] and the escaping steam," Frank remembered, and he patted himself on the back for swimming away from the ship so quickly.

Being so close to the coast (land was visible on both sides of the Malacca Strait), the depth was relatively shallow, only fifty-eight feet according to the *Truculent*'s log. Indeed, Dutch historian Henk Hovinga says part of the *Van Waerwijck*'s mast was still visible above the water when he visited the wreck site in 1983.

As the sun dipped toward the water, the corvette lowered its life rafts, but any POW who tried to get aboard was rewarded with a boot or a pistol butt to the head or hands. Only the Japanese were being rescued. The rest would have to wait.

Frank spent two hours swimming around, desperately searching for Judy while others grabbed hold of floating wreckage. "She remained without a trace," Frank recalled. "A Dutchman that held on to a rubber bale told me he had seen Judy swimming about. At that moment I knew she still had life in her."

After three hours, rescue vessels arrived, a handful of tongkangs and a tanker that had been part of the *Van Waerwijck* convoy and had scurried away when the torpedoes were swimming. Frank was pulled on board the latter. "I was still thinking about that submarine," Frank said. "Was it still lurking somewhere to strike again?" Some men recognized Frank and told him they too had seen Judy swimming through the wreckage. That was a shred of good news, but the scene on the tanker was grim. The deck was covered with the wounded and the dying. "They lay groaning," wrote Hartley, "and for the most part unattended, in pools of their own blood." A lone doctor, himself on the brink of keeling over, did his best without any medicines to offer. He begged the Japanese crew to take them to Sumatra or Malaya, which were close at hand, for immediate treatment. But the word came back that their orders were for Singapore, two days away, and that's where they were going.

As night fell, they suffered an unexpected agony. The steel deck became freezing cold to the touch, despite all the bodies upon it, and the nearly naked men were whipped by an icy wind that swept across the open space, urged on by the movement of the boat.

"The night seemed like it would go on forever," Hartley recorded. "The curses of the men who were thankful to be alive at all contrasted with the groans of the wounded who wished they could die."

Several men indeed passed on in the night. They were thrown over the railing and into the sea at dawn. Sharks trailed the boat in its wake and gorged themselves on the corpses. When the sun reappeared, the deck transformed from a meat locker to a coal oven, too hot to stand upon. The tanker steamed the rest of the distance to Singapore. Frank, nearly broken by the ordeal, streaked with oil and smoke, scanned the waters for Judy. He tried to weep, but no tears came. He was a shell. Hartley too was numb, "bereft of all feelings except an unquenchable desire for a cup of hot sweet tea." An Englishman to the last.

Finally, the tanker arrived at Keppel Harbor. Frank hadn't seen the place since evacuating aboard the *Tien Kwang,* as the city burned in his wake. Singapore still carried scars of the invasion, but much of the damage had been fixed, and the docks appeared to be in good shape. No ambulances stood ready to carry the wounded to emergency surgery.

Frank disembarked in a dazed shuffle while helping to carry men more wounded than he. "Japanese sailors and local stevedores stood goggle-eyed on the quayside" at their appearance, Hartley wrote. Many of the POWs had been badly burned in the torpedo explosion, others broken by falling debris. As they moved among the steamers and fishing boats docked in the harbor, they noticed an odd pair of ships that stuck out like Mercedes-Benzes in a junkyard. They were German U-boats, newly arrived in Singapore, fresh from stalking Allied shipping in the Indian Ocean, their huge red-and-white swastikas plainly marking them as part of the Kriegsmarine.

"From the command towers of the U-boats," Frank remembered, "the crew was watching us and shaking their heads when we passed them; they eluded our gazes." To Frank, this confirmed his (misguided) suspicions—the Nazis had sunk his boat, and to the best of his knowledge killed his dog. Any faint notion that an Allied sub had caused the destruction of the *Van Waerwijck* vanished when he saw the U-boats.

Moments later, one of the guards noticed the prisoners staring agape at the U-boats, whose sailors were out on deck cleaning equipment and sunning themselves, listening to a gramophone that played a German version of "Roll Out the Barrel." The guard yelled something and prodded the POWs with his gun. "In a flash," Frank said, "one of those crew members on the quay jumped up and hit the guard with a slap in the face to the ground, after which he returned to his U-boat without saying a word."

But this moment of compassion couldn't relieve the distress building inside Frank. Judy was nowhere to be seen. She hadn't made it. The reports of her swimming amid the wreckage had led to chimerical hopes.

His best friend was gone.

Frank numbly allowed himself to be herded onto a truck, which headed for the city center. The destination wasn't the Raffles Hotel, however. It was the River Valley camp. It was yet another, even more bleak prison, one that originally had been constructed to temporarily house refugees during the Japanese onslaught of the island. There was little left to keep Frank alive. The presumed loss of Judy had accelerated the decline started by imprisonment, malnourishment, and exhaustion. As Jock Devani put it, Frank was "headed for the end hut."

When the truck arrived at River Valley, Frank hopped down and was led to the gates of his third prison camp. It was June 27, 1944. After nearly two and a half years of captivity, it was his lowest moment yet.

In reality, Judy had proved to be unsinkable.

The last time Frank had seen her was when he shoved the pointer out of the porthole. According to various witnesses, Judy fell into the sea and popped up, stunned but alive. After that she began to swim strongly, head well above the water, perhaps thankful that the Malacca Strait was far more comfortable for a dip than the Yangtze River had been. Searle caught sight of her straightaway, seeing a man with his arm wrapped around Judy's shoulder, struggling to keep his head above the waves. "Why don't you shake him off, you crazy bitch?" he yelled out, as much to himself as to Judy, for she was too far away to hear him over the cacophony of the sinking. Surely she would be drowned by the weight of the man.

But she wasn't. She guided the man to a large piece of floating debris, where he managed to haul himself up, exhausted but alive. Judy then stayed in the water, looking for others to help. And help she did. No fewer than four men were seen and said later to have been rescued by Judy, and there may have been more beyond that. In each case, the method of operation was the same. The men reported thrashing about, either not able to swim or too beaten down by imprisonment and the shock of the sinking to muster the energy to save themselves. Out of the blue appeared Judy, acting like the aquatic version of a Saint Bernard. All that was missing was a life preserver around her neck.

The men would hang on to the swimming pointer, who would pull them either to flotsam or to the rescue ships that had begun to appear. Each time she approached one of the vessels, hands reached out to pull her from the water. Each time she pulled away from them to stay in the ocean and continue her rescue efforts.

When at last there were no more men alive in her vicinity, she allowed herself to be pulled into a boat. "She was more dead than alive," recalled one of the men who witnessed her coming on board. "She had totally given herself to the drowning men."

In all, 178 of the 1,174 prisoners on board the *Van Waerwijck* perished. Of the dead, 113 were Dutch, 48 British, 12 Australian, and 4 Indonesian. The lone Norwegian man on board was also killed. Henk Hovinga wrote that twenty-two of these men died later in Singapore, not in the water. An unknown number of Japanese and Korean soldiers and crew also perished.

Astonishing survival stories abounded. "Love, compassion, sincerity and selflessness were everywhere," said one survivor. Edward Porter, the English gunnery officer, was near the explosion and was trapped by a beam that fell across his legs. For a terrible moment, Porter couldn't move, but then the second torpedo hit, and the section of the hull attached to the beam was ripped open, freeing him. His legs were badly gashed, but he could move his upper body. Porter was washed into the ocean, where he drifted into a Korean guard who was clinging to a piece of wreckage. The guard helped him to safety.

John Purvis was clobbered by falling debris but managed to find his way topside. "I went to the open side of the ship and pulled myself up to look over and down below at a seething mass of bodies, some headless, others with limbs missing." Once in the water he hung on to a floating chicken coop, watching the swimming hens and rats that had been on board also desperately attempt to save themselves. At one point he grabbed a bobbing deck of cards he incredibly recognized as his own and was eventually pulled aboard the same steamer that saved Frank.

Also pulled on to that steamer was Farley, the injured stoker from the *Dragonfly* who had traveled with Judy all the way from Posic to Gloegoer. Still in a bad way, Farley was pushed into the sea by a fellow prisoner, who then held him above the waves for hours. That hero was, coincidentally enough, Sjovald Cunyngham-Brown, the same man who had ferried Frank and so many others off of Pompong Island.

Some opted to try to make it back to Sumatra. A dozen Dutchmen decided to swim for it, "a feat that makes the performances of the Channel swimmers who spend weeks in training seem pretty poor stuff," in Gibson's words. A Japanese patrol picked them up as they splashed ashore, which didn't make their effort any less gallant.

Local fishermen and other seafaring natives had been instructed by the Japanese to pluck any swimming prisoners from the sea. Japanese crewmen were to be given top priority, of course, followed by Indonesians, Dutch, English, and Australians, in that order. Any Americans found in the water were to be left to drown. Three prisoners were picked up by a tongkang and managed to make it back to Medan, where they were beaten up for the crime of having survived. They were then given food and money, as though by atonement, and put on a truck for transport to another camp. En route, their guard robbed them of the scrip at gunpoint.

The sinking of the *Van Waerwijck* was another cruel twist in Judy's life. She had now added being torpedoed to being bombed and sunk from the air, along with falling overboard into the Yangtze, being slashed by a crocodile, and surviving countless deadly encounters with the prison guards. She appeared to have even more lives than a cat's proverbial nine.

After being pulled from the ocean, Judy couldn't relax. The tongkang she was on carried a few Malay crew, several rescued prisoners, and two Korean guards who had been pulled from the wreckage, dead. A sail was turned into a makeshift shroud to cover their bodies. When the tongkang approached Singapore, several Japanese boats sailed out to meet it. Fortunately, one of the prisoners managed to recall that Judy was, as far as the enemy was concerned, still supposed to be back in Sumatra. Hurriedly, he pushed the weary dog under the sail that hid the dead, and she wasn't spotted by any of the Japanese who looked into their ship.

When it reached port, the prisoners were mustered into rank. Just because their transport had been sunk, it didn't change the fate of the survivors—they were still headed to the River Valley prison. Judy scooted into the crowd, looking for a familiar face. She soon found Les Searle, but Frank was nowhere to be seen. He had already been put on a truck for the camp.

Searle, however, was overjoyed to see Judy, and kept her close to him. In the confusion, she managed to remain unseen until the moment Searle picked her up to load her on his truck. In better shape, Judy might have remained hidden underneath the vehicle, only to dart aboard at the last moment. But she was totally spent, and Searle had to risk lifting her up himself.

"*Tomaru!*" Halt!

The sudden scream of rage came from the mouth of the last person Searle or Judy wanted to see—Captain Nishi. His boat had come in well ahead of the scheduled arrival of the transport steamer, and he waited patiently on the dock as the survivors of the sinking trickled in, ticking off exactly who had made it and who hadn't with ruthless efficiency. It was his job to ensure that the transfer of the Gloegoer prisoners to River Valley went off without a hitch. The sinking was a factor even Nishi couldn't account for, but he wasn't about to go home for the day.

Then he saw the dog he loathed, the animal he had explicitly ordered to be left behind on Sumatra. Instead it was here, drained but very much alive, and it was clearly headed toward the new camp, though it had been separated from its usual sidekick.

He bellowed another order, and two guards cocked their rifles, yanked Judy from Searle's arms, and brought her to Nishi. They threw her on the ground at his feet. That he even recognized her was surprising. She was gaunt, oil and muck covered her from nose to tail, and her cracked lips were pulled back to reveal yellow teeth, a parched tongue behind them. Her red-rimmed eyes glared in hatred at Nishi, who stood above her screaming epithets. Surely they didn't mean to eat her anymore, but now she would be killed on principle.

Then came a loud call of "Nishi!" Everyone turned in the direction of the voice. It was Colonel Banno, back from Siam, now based in Singapore. He had heard about the sinking and had come to the dock to meet survivors and check on the progress of the transfer to River Valley. Hartley remembered seeing him as the burned and broken passengers arrived at the dock. "His smile gave place to an expression which was surely the nearest any Japanese we had met could ever get to horror."

Upon seeing his subordinate challenge Judy, Banno rushed to action. Now he would play the role, once again, of unlikely savior. He yelled at Nishi that the dog was an official POW, and that he himself had signed the order giving her protection. Had Nishi not read it? Yes, Nishi began, but I ordered her to remain in Gloegoer.

Banno blew up anew, aghast that an underling questioned his orders. It was likely as much a matter of saving face as it was any affection for Judy—but whatever the cause, he had interceded just in time.

Searle took the opportunity to scoop Judy up, climb quickly into the truck, and bang on the cab window. The truck left the dock with a rumble, while Banno continued to dress down the insolent Nishi. Once again, Judy had slipped free of danger. She was on her way to another prison camp, but for the moment she had been spared.

CHAPTER 20

Reunion

The bombed and burning Singapore that Frank and Judy had left hurriedly behind in mid-February 1942 was a vastly different city under Japanese occupation than it had been under British colonial rule. Called *Syonan-To* ("Light of the South") by its conquerors, Singapore had been mostly rebuilt, thanks in part to POW labor. The city's large Chinese population was used as slaves, at least those who were still alive. Tens of thousands of ethnic Chinese were massacred by the *Kempeitai,* the Japanese secret police. One woman named Madam Wong Len Cheng, who survived the rampage, recalled this time as "a life of unremitting fear." While the Japanese conquerors toasted military successes across the Pacific at Singapore's nightspots, the locals did little but eat and sleep. "Sometimes we feared even having a light in the house, for fear it might attract a Japanese soldier to enter our home," recalled Madam Wong. One who came to her house bludgeoned her brother to death, and Madam Wong delivered four stillborn babies due to her malnutrition during this awful period.

The city's clocks were reset to Tokyo time. "If [the Japanese] told you it was midnight even when the sun was up in the sky, then it was midnight," said Madam Wong. Food stores were mostly reduced to tapioca and sweet potatoes. Pork was hugely expensive, and the lines to obtain it stretched for hours. Black markets proliferated even as the Japanese punishment for taking part in one was beheading. Western schools and influences had been systematically removed, and the once vibrant local press reduced to a propaganda arm of the Empire of the Sun. As at Gloegoer, a massive Japanese shrine had been built by POWs, at the cost of a huge swath of original primeval rainforest. After the war, it was swiftly demolished.

The River Valley Road prison camp sat near the center of the transformed city, along the west bank of a quiet stretch of the Singapore River. The "valley" was formed by a narrow drain that ran through the center of the camp area. The camp itself consisted of a dilapidated series of bamboo frame buildings, most of them merely roofs and beams with no side walls. The thatch used for the roofs had blown away on several of the structures, leaving them open from above as well. Some of the two-story huts had sleeping berths ten feet or so above the ground, but the ground platforms were so disintegrated that it left the men roosting like birds high above.

Even by prison camp standards, River Valley was ugly. It certainly contrasted poorly with the permanent concrete structures the men had left behind in Gloegoer. Singapore itself under the Japanese was unattractive as well, hardly resembling the carefree party scene it was a few years before. Desperation had replaced insouciance. On one occasion, Hartley carried the camp dustbin outside the gates for pickup. Before the Japanese could carry it away, a group of starving Chinese rushed over and picked through the trash, which already had been dissected for anything edible by the POWs.

Most of all, the men themselves were the epitome of squalor. Their faces were mattes of dirt, grease, and smoke debris. Their hair was unruly, caked in sweat and salt water. They were unshaven, hollow-eyed and -chested, scarred across their naked torsos. Many were still in shock, and all were at the brink of their endurance, pushed to their limits by recent events.

Upon arrival at River Valley, Judy refused to follow Searle into his hut. Instead, the pointer went on several circumnavigations of the camp. She went into every building, every pen, even the latrines looking for Frank. She quartered the area, leaving no inch unsearched. But he wasn't there. So she settled down on her belly just inside the front gate, hidden from obvious view by a slight incline, and waited. Her sad eyes scanned everyone who came in.

Frank's truck had stopped en route to River Valley for supplies in a native village. So although he had left before Judy got to the dock, he arrived in the camp well after she did. Her loyalty and patience were rewarded when she saw Frank stagger off his transport and into the camp.

Judy was overjoyed, and she displayed her pleasure by racing up to Frank and flattening him to the ground. "When I entered the camp, a ragged dog jumped me from behind with a great amount of force, flooring me," Frank remembered with a smile. "She was covered in bunker oil and her old, tired eyes were red." Somehow, some way, man and dog had been reunited, despite the best efforts of the British (if accidental) and Captain Nishi.

Frank was in tears when he finally got up from where Judy had knocked him down. "C'mon, old girl, and stop acting so daft," he said with typical English reserve. Moments before, he had been on the edge of a precipice. Now, with his best friend miraculously back at his side, his hope was renewed, his determination to survive restored. "His shoulders seemed to re-set," said Searle.

Peter Hartley and Phil Dobson had a similar reunion at River Valley. As with Frank and Judy, the last Hartley had seen of his close friend was when Dobson was working his way through a porthole on the *Van Waerwijck*. Hartley was an early arrival at River Valley, and he paced nervously as scores of POWs were trucked to the camp, waiting for his buddy to be one of them. He began to question why he had even bothered to fight to live. "So many of my friends had perished.... Why did I not give up when I had the chance, instead of making the struggle to survive?"

At last, after a sleepless night of worry, a truck carrying thirty prisoners arrived the next afternoon. Dobson was among them. "It was not until we were smiling joyfully into each other's faces and gripping each other's hands that I realized how great had been my sense of loss," Hartley wrote. "From now the outlook seemed to be so much brighter, as though a world of tarnished silver had been suddenly and miraculously polished."

Frank, Judy, Peter, and Phil were the lucky ones. Some of the friendships made at Gloegoer had been permanently rendered. And some of the survivors didn't make it to River Valley at all; the severely wounded from the *Van Waerwijck* sinking were moved to Changi to recuperate.

One of these more fortunate men was Edward Porter, whose legs were shattered by the beam that fell on him in the doomed ship's hold. Porter became well known at Changi for his skillful forgery of counterfeit watches and pens. His ability to engrave phony Rolex and Parker emblems on ordinary items was so amazing that he fooled the Japanese into not only believing they were the genuine article but into paying good money for them (the pull of the brands was so strong that the Japanese overcame any urge to simply confiscate the watches and pens). The money raised was used to buy medical supplies stolen from the Japanese and smuggled into the prison by locals.

Porter also spent much time in Changi composing songs and waltzes, most of which mirrored his lonely and mournful imprisoned state. His ditty "Always You'll Be Mine" could have been written by Frank during the hours he believed Judy to be lost at sea.

Parting brings much sadness
Hearts seem meant for pain
But who shall tell the gladness
When we meet again?
Thoughts of you dear keep returning
Thro' the lonely days
And my aching heart is yearning
For your fond embrace
Though we may be worlds apart
You're for ever in my heart
More beloved through being parted
Always you'll be mine.

When Frank, Judy, and the other survivors of the *Van Waerwijck* arrived in Singapore, they joined prisoners already in residence at River Valley. They were mainly POWs who had been held in Java and transported to this way station in anticipation of another move.

The Java men were, like the Gloegoer group, mainly Dutch and Commonwealthers, but there were at least a few Americans, the majority of them merchant marines. The most notable of the bunch was George Duffy. He was twenty-two when he was brought to River Valley, but he had had experiences over the last three years to last a lifetime.

Duffy had been a nineteen-year-old when he graduated from the Massachusetts Nautical School in late September 1941. His gruff New England accent and manner were offset by an easy smile and a twinkle in his eye. A week after graduation, he was in New York for his first contracted posting, aboard a brand-new diesel-powered vessel called, appropriately enough, the *American Leader.* Duffy and the crew had passed through Pearl Harbor just days before the attack, and they were fortunate to escape the Manila area when the Japanese bombed the American forces there. They worked as an escort vessel and hauled war matériel across the world's oceans until encountering a German raider off the coast of South Africa in September 1942.

American Leader was sunk by torpedoes, and Duffy went over the side, eventually clambering aboard a raft. After some time, another raft paddled to his craft and asked how many were aboard. When told there were twenty-three men, none badly wounded, the German-accented voice replied, "Gut, I will tow you."

Duffy was now a prisoner of the Nazis. He and the other surviving crewmen were held on board the German ship for several weeks until they were dropped off in Batavia, essentially traded to the Japanese. He was held prisoner in Java for nearly two years before being shipped to River Valley. Like the Gloegoer men, Duffy assumed this was not his final destination.

That was okay with them, for Singapore was little improvement over Gloegoer. The men had lost all the possessions they had accumulated in Sumatra, including utensils. Purvis remembered, "[I] managed to find a flat piece of tin which I bent into a plate and also a coconut shell which I cut in half and used as a mug. My spoon was made of a piece of bamboo." There was no mail, no Red Cross. If anything, there was less food, for the prisoners at least. The entirety of their diet consisted of small balls of rice and some dried fish and seaweed, "which both looked and tasted like dried rope," according to Hartley. The men quickly stripped leaves and bark from the trees to supplement their meager rations, but it did little to stave off the constant rumblings of their stomachs and the rapid spread of beriberi.

Even more cruel, in the estimation of many POWs, was the dire lack of tobacco. What had been so plentiful back on Sumatra was rare in Singapore, and the nicotine-addicted men keenly felt its absence. So did the Japanese, who eventually arranged for a vendor to sell some smokes to the hankering men, then noticed how their morale improved when they could light up. After that, the POWs never lacked for tobacco.

Another difference was the regular sight, albeit through the fence, of actual females. The women of Singapore went about their daily rituals in plain view of the prisoners, unaware of the fact they were being watched. "Tall, slender Malay and Chinese ladies in tight-fitting long gowns were a common sight," Duffy recalls. The men hadn't seen much of the fairer sex in over two years, save the occasional villager. One might imagine they would stare greedily at these well-groomed and fashionable young women, but at least in Duffy's case, the harsh treatment had quelled any sexual urge. "We had been poorly fed for so long, they had no physical impact on us," he writes. Les Searle would later say, "I, for one, shall never again believe that sex is the main urge; the motivating power; the driving force. Food without any doubt at all is the main target for man's arrows."

Worst of all perhaps was the teasing presence of civilization. From the camp windows, the neon glow of the city's downtown could be seen, close enough to almost smell the gin and hear the bands play. To the POWs, it appeared as though there was no war, or at least as though there was a war that the Japanese were winning comfortably. From a distance, the city at night appeared much the same as it had when the British were in control. The proximity of the fun available in the Lion City reminded them of what they had lost—and weren't likely to regain. And the men found it indecent that good times went on while they were cut off from it. One prisoner likened the situation to a woman remarrying before her husband was "properly dead."

So in some ways, it wasn't bad news when rumors began to circulate that most of them were going to be sent back to Sumatra. A special mission was at hand in some unknown part of the island—something to do with harvesting fruits and cereals. Only the fittest would be allowed to make the journey, those who passed a test to prove they were still in decent condition.

The test was a farce, though. The prisoners were lined up in groups of ten at one end of the compound. They were then marched at bayonet point to the other end. Everyone who made it without collapsing was deemed fit enough to join the traveling group. All but the very sickest of men were able to do it.

There was another, more humiliating test they had to pass. A van pulled up with a pair of Japanese doctors and a pair of Japanese nurses who were there to conduct a mass dysentery test. Each prisoner was made to pull down his shorts, bend over, and allow one of the nurses to insert a nine-inch glass tube in his rectum. No man was disqualified from being selected for travel, despite the fact that the large majority had at least mild dysentery.

The men were marched through Singapore to Keppel Harbor, where so many of them had left in desperate flight just under thirty months before. Here they were again, having transformed from despairing to utterly numb. No one cared much about the humiliating jaunt through town, the hostile stares from the crowds, or the guards shoving them onward with rifle butts. But a few Chinese flashed covert "V for Victory" signs to them, a gesture the more canny POWs took to mean the war was going less well for the Japanese than they had been bragging about.

There was certainly a note of unease about going back to sea. A great many of the men had abandoned ship at least once or twice in the very stretch of water they were now returning to. Even an old navy hand like Judy had to be skittish after her recent travails on the ocean main. Tramp paddle steamers had been chosen for their journey back across the strait, which was fortunate because these smaller vessels were unlikely to draw torpedoes from marauding subs. Even better, these were no hell ships—they didn't have dungeons belowdecks in which the prisoners could be crammed. The men were squeezed together on deck, but what they lacked in space was made up for by the fresh air.

Judy was smuggled aboard once again (her ship was called the *Elizabeth*), but this time there didn't seem to be much interest from the guards in ferreting her out. Perhaps this should have been a warning sign. Judy had spent most of her time in River Valley foraging like everyone else, catching some citified snakes and rats. But it was clear she was feeling the effects of hunger. Her weight had dropped from sixty pounds into the low forties. Her once rich brown spots turned a sickly tan, and her coat hung like a dappled curtain on her body. Her ribs were prominent, her eye sockets bulging. All Frank could hope was that this supposed mission to harvest food meant he and Judy could eat properly.

This time, Judy's boat made it across the water without being sunk. It wasn't until they reached the mouth of the Siak River and turned southeast that they knew for sure that they weren't headed right back to Gloegoer, that this all wasn't some elaborate ruse to mess with their heads. Instead, their destination was Pakan Baroe, the capital settlement of Central Sumatra.

They splashed ashore in late July. Immediately, they saw that there were other POWs here, but they didn't realize their new home and mission would have nothing to do with farming until they were put on a forced march through the jungle. Frank had been spared a previous tour of the Sumatran interior, but the trip was a sickening rerun for Judy, Searle, Devani, and the others who had done it already two years earlier.

Upon arrival, they had taken a short train ride, then disembarked and were told to get walking. After a while, the men encountered a ravine fifty yards wide, with a madly rushing river some sixty feet below. Instead of a legitimate bridge, the Japanese had jerry-rigged a span made of timber and wooden girders. There was no proper floor to walk on, just boards driven at intervals between enormous piles. There were no handrails either. Crossing was thus a terrifying ordeal, especially for beaten-down, starving men without shoes. One Dutchman refused to cross and began screaming hysterically. He was given the option of descending the ravine and swimming across. He was never seen again.

The rest managed to make it to the other side. There was a long wait while they picked their way carefully over the "bridge," and those who had made it already got a decent rest. Refreshed a bit, they marched the seven miles to their new home, singing "Roll Out the Barrel" and the popular soldiers' protest song "Bless 'Em All." But the good feelings quickly dwindled away back into hopelessness. Soon, the towering forest cut off all light. Swamp gas boiled up all around them, shrouding them in mist. Tongues swelled from thirst as the guards shoved them forward. Judy walked gingerly along, staying even with Frank's shuffling pace.

The men could eventually make out dim campfires along the sides of the trail in the distance. At last, they arrived at a clearing deep in the remote jungle. They had arrived at their new home. The pitch-black night obscured their frightening new reality. But not for long.

CHAPTER 21

Pakan Baroe

There had been warning signs. Radio Batavia had reported as early as October of 1943 on a labor conference held by the Japanese in Singapore. During the talks, the masters of the Greater East Asia Co-Prosperity Sphere used couched terms to advocate for the use of slaves and prisoners to undertake labor projects in the area. "Adequate measures were decided to meet the demand for labor in Malaya, Sumatra and Borneo. Other matters discussed were housing and transportation of the laborers."

Radio Berlin amplified the news the next day: "The newly established authorities for the mobilization of all available labor to intensify the war effort decided to increase war production on Malaya, Sumatra and Borneo still further than before, in view of the lack of labor in these three countries." A headline in the *Melbourne Argus* noted "Japs Are Rushing Defence Roads" in Sumatra, and went on to hint at an even greater project about to be undertaken on the massive Indonesian island.

By mid-1944, the time had come to begin this project—the construction of a railroad to connect the east and west coasts of Sumatra, thus providing greater flexibility for defending the island from Allied attack. While the manpower callously hurled at this Death Railway didn't match that of the better-known versions in Burma and Siam, the Sumatran version was equal in terms of cruelty—and was even more futile. As John Hedley points out in his oral history, "The Burma-Siam railway was built when the troops were comparatively fit. We had to build our railway in the last year of our incarceration. So we weren't fit to do anything."

The Dutch had considered such a transportation system during the

1930s, but ultimately passed on doing it for multiple reasons—mostly because of the scale of the work and the difficult terrain where the building would take place. A true cross-Sumatra railroad would pass through deep swamps brimming with malarial mosquitoes, over mountains as high as nine thousand feet, across rivers that flooded to twice their height in the rainy season, and in and around thick forests untouched by man.

Even the Japanese weren't mad enough to try to link the northern and southern edges of the island. Sumatra's northern half, scarcely populated and not nearly as blessed with resources as the south, was virtually ignored (the area is best known today for the coast city of Banda Aceh, which was wiped off the map by the tsunami of 2004). Instead, the Japanese planned to link the largest cities in Sumatra, after Medan—Padang in the west, Palembang in the southeast, and Pakan Baroe, which lies near the exact center of the island. There was already track between Padang and Sawah Luento, as the POWs well knew, having ridden trains on that route. That line ran farther east into the interior, to a hamlet called Moearo.

The initial stage of the Japanese plan was to build a railway between Pakan Baroe and Moearo, thus linking the former with Padang. This required laying track over roughly 140 miles of dense and deadly Sumatran wilderness (about the distance between Seattle and Vancouver). The extension to Palembang would follow, assuming the war didn't result in Japanese defeat before it could be built.

By the spring of 1944, the Japanese command surely realized their era of victory and expansion was over. There was much fighting ahead, but the strength of American industrial power made the outcome a foregone conclusion to all but the most delusional of warriors.

So in this context, the decision to use the POWs, along with more than a hundred thousand Indonesian and Malay slave laborers, seems like nothing more than a subtle "final solution." Unlike the Jews under the Nazis, the captured soldiers weren't to be killed outright—that would be a waste of ammunition and manpower the Japanese couldn't afford. Instead, the men would be worked to death in the jungle. Those who were strong enough to withstand the arduous labor, malnutrition, and disease would help the war effort. The rest would perish—and in the eyes of the Japanese, they should have died in battle anyway.

At first, the Japanese asked for the locals, called *romushas* ("laborers" in Japanese), to volunteer for the effort, promising decent food and good pay. When few signed up, they were enslaved by the thousands. Entire movie theaters and shopping markets were surrounded by troops, and all the men were taken away. At first, the majority came from Java, but later the Japanese took locals from their homes on almost all the islands of the Dutch East Indies to build the railway. In all about 120,000 *romushas* were taken to Pakan Baroe.

Only about 23,000 survived.

The slaves were brought in first to build a service road that would parallel the railway, a dangerous task that required monumental feats of terrain clearance, such as blowing up mountainsides and clearing the resulting piles of rubble. Some Allied POWs worked on this project as well, but the worst jobs went to the locals. Often, the dynamite went off even as the slaves were still setting charges. One blast killed thirty-six in an instant. The *romushas* were frequently left working under terrifying rock overhangs that were only partially blasted away. Often, these collapsed, killing all below. More *romushas* were then ordered to dig the corpses out of the rubble and continue the job.

Whereas the POWs who fell ill were at least taken away and given a semblance of care, sick and wounded *romushas* were left to die where they dropped. POWs often stumbled onto decomposing corpses while working, or found others who were still alive but who could not be helped.

The first mass of Allied prison labor was sent over from Padang on May 19, 1944. Their initial order of business was to build the base camp, aka Camp Two (Camp One became the Japanese headquarters and the main railway supply depot), as well as the first stretch of the railway out from the new railhead near the Siak River. Old, rotting barracks that had been built by a Dutch oil company served as the starting point. The buildings were about one hundred meters from the river. The frequent rain flooded the area with such thorough regularity that the entire Camp Two basin was a quagmire of knee-deep mud. The prisoners, many of whom were barefoot, gave the place the nickname "The Mud Resort."

Camp Two was close to the village of Pakan Baroe and various satellite hamlets, and in time would house a rotating cast of between eighteen hundred and two thousand POWs—mainly the sick, dying, or otherwise unfit to work. Among the first structures to be erected were a pair of hospital huts, one of which would later come to be known as the Death House.

At times officers were fortunate to pull light duty and work from here, although the proximity to those suffering in the hospital huts would temper their enthusiasm. Otherwise, the only permanent residents of the camp were some Japanese, a handful of poorly equipped Allied doctors, and a group of cooks (who were mostly Dutchmen).

Everyone else was posted for construction duty. The plan was to leapfrog gangs of workers as the line progressed, each establishing field camps in the jungle. From there the men would fell trees; cut them into sleepers, or wooden ties; lay them on the predetermined path (over, around, or through whatever natural barriers happened to be in the way); and drive steel dogs, or nails, to join the wooden planks to iron girders and form recognizable train tracks.

Pakan Baroe was exponentially worse than Padang or Gloegoer. The gnawing hunger and physical wasting remained, to which was added sadistically grueling manual labor and naked exposure to extreme wilderness. The open spaces may have been welcome after more traditional confinement elsewhere, but as Joe Fitzgerald, a POW who ended up working alongside Frank and Judy, put it, "Much freedom of movement was afforded but only a minimum of human dignity."

Eventually, there would number at least a dozen camps, with more than six thousand Allied POWs working the lines. As Len Williams said, "Every sleeper laid cost lives."

Frank and Judy woke up that first morning on the railway at their new home, Camp Five. It was near a speck on the map called Loeboeksakat, twenty-three kilometers out from Pakan Baroe and a shade under ten from Camp Three, which housed a large number of British POWs, including Searle and Devani. As a fellow POW in Camp Five recalled, "One look was enough to dampen the stoutest spirits." At its busiest, roughly one thousand men worked there, half Dutch, half British and Australian.

The ranking British officer in the camp was a Captain Gordon, and his *hancho* was Lieutenant Sparks. Both served under the senior officer in command of the British on the railway, RAF Wing Commander Patrick

Davis, a Londoner just past thirty years old. Like most of the air contingent, Davis had evacuated to Java from Singapore before the city fell, so he had spent time in POW camps there prior to his transport to Pakan Baroe in May 1943, when he suddenly found himself in command of a group of men brought to the jungle to be worked to death. Unlike the romantic portrayal of officers in POW camps, there were no escape attempts for Davis to plan, no authority for him to bravely defy in an ideological test of wills. The Japanese commander, Captain Ryohei Miyazaki, explained with a shrug that all hardships inflicted upon the men under Davis' command were ordered from above, and there was nothing he could do about them.

Meanwhile, as Davis pointed out in an official report to Lord Louis Mountbatten's Southeast Asia command headquarters, "It was extraordinarily difficult to run these camps, because the Japs did not give me the freedom to act as I saw fit and two-thirds of the personnel under my command were Dutch with a very limited understanding of English." Most communications were conducted in Malay, which few—English, Dutch, or Japanese—spoke fluently. And though Davis was the ranking officer, few Dutch actually considered him their leader.

Despite the difficulties he faced, or perhaps because of them, Davis would eventually receive a knighthood for his gallantry at Pakan Baroe. His citation, awarded October 1, 1946, read, "This officer, while a prisoner of war in Japanese hands, displayed remarkable integrity and bravery in the face of very adverse conditions. He tried everything possible to persuade the Japanese to improve the standard of living for the prisoners of war. Throughout his period of captivity Wing Commander Davis set a magnificent example to all."

While Davis certainly was brave and forthright, his efforts had little practical effect in sparing the POWs on the railway any suffering. About the only solace Davis and the other prisoners could take was that Miyazaki, like his superiors, would eventually be sentenced to death—in the junior officer's case, it was for blindly following inhumane orders to complete the railway at any cost.

"We worked all hours of the daylight," remembered Fred Freeman. "There were no rest days or anything." It was this endless toil under the punishing sun that sent the men to the edge of their limits, and sometimes past it. Building the railway was a grueling, never-ending job that made the temple project at Gloegoer and the motorworks demolition at Belawan seem like a leisurely stroll in the park.

Travel from camp to work site was usually made by train and took mere minutes in some places to over an hour in others, depending on progress and terrain. "When it was thought we spent too much time 'commuting' the camp would move up the line," remembered Fitzgerald. The journey back to their huts after a painful day of work "was anything but comfortable," Fitzgerald wrote, "and if it rained, sheer misery." These trains often derailed, especially come the rainy season, requiring the POWs to get out and push.

Frank and his fellow prisoners' first job at Camp Five was to create an embankment made of sand to shore up the path the track was to go through. During the previous rainy season it had washed away, a common failing along the entire line, as the Japanese had chosen a particularly soggy area in which to build. For weeks they filled wagons with "yellow-white sand," according to a Dutch prisoner named Fred Seljee, "sometimes for two kilometers." Some men were tasked with widening the road so cars could have passage while the railway was being built. Soon enough, construction began.

Every day, Frank took one of the nine separate jobs in the rail-laying process. The Rope Man placed colored rope on the track to mark the path. The Marker Man scratched a line in the sand under the rope with a steel hook attached to a four-foot pole. The twelve Rail Men carried the heavy rails (which rode to the work site along with the POWs each morning) from the train car to the proper spot on the track ahead. It was "really strenuous work," wrote POW Raymond Smith, who prepared a detailed accounting of life at Pakan Baroe for posterity. "A length of rail measures fifteen meters (almost fifty feet) and weighs 570 kilograms (1,266 pounds). Apart from the weight of the rail, the narrowness of the side footway and the soft soil made things exceedingly difficult. . . . The sun heated the steel to the extent they couldn't be handled with bare hands." Any padding on his shoulders and neck Frank may have had had long since wasted away, and the iron cut deeply into his flesh regardless of the makeshift buffers he used to ease the agony. His height was an issue too—the weight of the steel disproportionately fell on the taller men. "We tried to get teams of about the same height so that anybody tall would not be carrying most of the weight," a Camp Five POW named Ken Robson recalled, but that wasn't always possible. Fingers and toes were routinely crushed when men lost their footing.

Once the rails were painfully hauled to the right spot and the Sleeper Men laid their wood into place, the Dassi Man drilled holes in the sleepers with an auger, and the Bar Men crowbarred the steel into position. In came the Hammer Men, a role Frank also filled quite often. "Whilst the bar men held the sleeper solidly," Smith described, "he would hammer with a wood shafted steel hammer, fixing spikes into the pre-drilled holes until their flanges gripped the bottom of the steel rails." Said Robson, "He needed quite a good eye."

Once the spike was in tightly, the Noko Man, so-called for *nokogiri,* the large hacksaw he used, had the exhausting job of sawing the excess steel away. The blades often broke "for the simple reason that the Japanese saws cut on the stroke made toward you, while the Western version cuts on the forward stroke," Smith explained. When they did, the Noko Man caught a beating from the guards. Lastly, the Joint Men (also called Spanner Men) fit the plates to the rails with steel bolts using spanner wrenches.

"It all sounds terribly organized, and on paper it was so," Robson said, "but in practice everyone had to take part in all facets of the work." Frank mostly hauled steel and hammered it into the wooden sleepers, but he took part in every facet of construction, including felling timber in the forest and swamps, then cutting the wood into planks.

The guards were always hovering closely, yelling *"Hyaku!"* ("Hurry up!") or "Speedo!" (the pidgin version). Fitzgerald remembered one guard:

> "Black Joe" to his friends, had the habit of standing over the spanner men, yelling words of encouragement. His voice at close quarters let all know what is meant by the "threshold of pain." Should a bolting fail, he would immediately blame the spanner man, rewarding him with a tap on the head from the fishplate spanner he invariably carried. When he realized a replacement bolt was required, he would call, in his stentorian tones, for the peripatetic "Boltoman" to

attend with a replacement nut and bolt. When he did, he got the spanner treatment too.

The equipment was hardly first-rate. Many of the rails, bolts, and plates had been "filched from Java," in Fitzgerald's memory, "and some were believed to have been laid there before the turn of the century." Other, especially heavy rails were labeled "Broken Hole Point, Australia." When anything failed to operate properly, nearby POWs paid the price.

Sometimes they didn't work because the men had deliberately spiked the works. Guerrilla-style sabotage was an important part of the men keeping up a semblance of opposition against their captors, which in turn helped morale, at least a little. Engines were incapacitated by banana mush. Spikes were deliberately laid into soft sections of earth, causing the train engines to slide into the bush when they rolled over them. Spikes were also driven too hard until they broke, or not hard enough, so that the spike would split. Many spikes were broken so that only the heads remained—these were then driven into the earth so that it appeared a section of wood was connected by a proper spike. Once a train car went over it, however, it flew apart.

Frank laid out his attempts at disrupting the Japanese efforts on the official POW form he filled out upon liberation: he ensured the "destruction of petrol supplies by loosening bungs of petrol drums and stacking drums in inverted position" and "by burying spare parts of motor vehicles."

He made the Japanese vehicles less efficient by "adding sand and native brown sugar to aviation and transport petrols and lubricants."

He interfered with the railway building itself "by driving railway spikes into railway sleepers with the chisel edge of the spike in line with the sleeper wood grain, so the sleepers split when the weight of train and truck passed over them, sometimes causing derailment. Also by packing lines with decaying wood."

At times the sabotage attempts were far bolder. On one memorable occasion, a particularly crazy yet indomitable Aussie named Slinger spent days fixing a broken steamroller, earning plaudits from the Japanese and whispers of "traitor" from his fellow prisoners. But when the Korean guard fired it up, the machine exploded, along with the guard.

Regardless of the slowdowns, the men were expected to lay twelve hundred meters, or three-fourths of a mile, of track a day, though this was greatly affected by terrain and often came up short. As the men weakened drastically, the quota dropped to merely two or three hundred meters per day. The effort required to lay even a few meters was prodigious. Fitzgerald, a Welshman from Cardiff who was called "Japerin" by the Japanese for his Charlie Chaplin–style mustache, captured the scene in his short memoir of life at Pakan Baroe:

> Sweat rolled down our faces and bodies, sweat rags were soaking with it and our parched lips could taste nothing but the salt tang. . . . In with a peg, up with a hammer, down it comes, misses and clangs on the line. A screaming voice penetrates the mists, and as you straighten up from putting the peg straight, a fist, a piece of wood, a rifle, something, hits you on the side of the face, and in your weakness, the mind now a blanket of deadened misery, down you go. You pick yourself up, and somewhere through the blanket a glimmer of light; you try to explain but at the same time the voice screams again and the fist or whatever it was hits you on the other side of your face and down you go again. A redness, an unexplainable red that grows more vivid at the third time you are down and at the boot that kicks into your side . . . the red mist suddenly lifts and you become aware that you are standing on your feet again and that the voice is shouting again. But this time one of your own officers, who is seeing your plight, has come to help, and before long the incident is over. Keep going! It can't be long now! They must be stopping for food soon! Blast this sweat! Wipe it away! Sod it! Sod it! Sod it! Sod everything!

They slept in crude huts that had been built years earlier by coal miners. There was no electricity—light was provided by homemade lamps that were pieces of rags set ablaze and floated in a tin of coconut oil. The roofs and walls were merely palm leaves wrapped around poles. The POWs slept on wood platforms eighteen inches wide that ran the length of the exterior, with bare earth in the center of the hut. Nature owned this space, but the weeds and grasses also grew through holes in the platforms, totally unchecked. "Rats used to run up and down over our heads at night," wrote Robson. Insects were everywhere, flying in the men's ears, crawling on their legs, chewing on them in bed. The stench of rotting vegetation permeated the huts. Bullfrogs croaked incessantly from a nearby swamp.

A British bugler sounded reveille at seven a.m. Tokyo time, meaning the POWs rose at four thirty a.m., before the sun came up. Exhausted as they were after twelve, fourteen, even twenty hours of punishing exertion, sleep didn't come easily on their bedbug-ridden racks. Hunger pangs kept them tossing and turning. Many were actually afraid to sleep, lest the bugle sound for work more quickly. "Soon, much too soon, it was tomorrow, and we set off for a repeat of the previous day," Robson lamented.

Those for whom sleep was elusive heard the call of the wild all night long. "One could hear the roars of tigers answering each other, on the prowl for wild pig," said Robson. Both he and another POW, Rouse Voisey, recalled the incessant screams of monkeys from the jungle. "They screeched day and night, but you never saw them," Voisey says today, the sound still fresh in his ears after nearly seven decades. Robson said the POWs called them "siren-monkeys," due to their whoop, which reminded them of "a destroyer siren." Come dawn, Fitzgerald remembered, "another creature intrigued us by producing the first few bars of 'Rhapsody in Blue' each morning." The change in sounds was accompanied by what Fitzgerald called "a chilling mist reminiscent of those we disliked at home, but for now which we yearned." Soon enough, the sweat would be pouring freely again.

They went to bed in their work clothes: tattered shorts and, if they were lucky, a torn shirt or ruined socks. POW Harry Badger remembered, "I only had one shirt for most of the time which I kept for night. We had no shirts at all for the working parties and a simple loin cloth was the most comfortable clothing for the lower regions." The loin cloths were called *fundoshi,* or "Jap-happy," for reasons that elude the modern reader. Some of the men, especially the Royal Navy POWs such as Searle and Devani, were competent with a needle and thread and made clothes of whatever materials they could obtain. "We got hold of some canvas once and they turned it into shirts," Badger said. "The only problem was they were too damn hot to wear on other than cool nights." George Duffy, one of only a dozen Americans on the railway, owned four socks, all mismatched, a jacket he wore every night at dinner, and two pairs of shorts. "One is patched and threadbare and won't stand any more repairing. The other pair is just patched, but the condition is pretty good," he wrote of them. In his diary, he asked Mountbatten to hurry up and free him. "Lord Looie had better get a move on or most of us will be wearing grass skirts or leaves or something." For footwear, the men had two choices — going barefoot or teetering around on "Klompers," thick wooden platform shoes with fabric holding the toes in. This was a style familiar to most of the Dutch, but the others needed practice wearing them. "The [Klompers were] acceptable, once the knack of maneuvering them was acquired, whereas [going barefoot] involved many trials and tribulations," recalled Fitzgerald. He also said the barefoot brigade often walked on the railway itself until the sun made it too hot.

The *tenko,* or roll call, was an omnipresent fact of their lives. The men were counted upon awakening, before and after the train rides to the work site, upon arrival back at their huts, and before lights-out. "The number of times a POW was counted during the course of his captivity must be almost infinite," Fitzgerald noted. The guards would count the men by scratching slashes in the dirt with sticks.

Keeping up a modicum of hygiene was crucial, as much for morale as health. There were no morning ablutions upon wake-up; the men were taken directly from the huts to the work site. Teeth rotted from lack of fluoride and were stained dark. Rivers of sweat dried on the skin, adding body odor to the already formidable assault upon the olfactory senses.

In every hut, in every camp, there was a man who made a sharp implement and charged his fellow prisoners for hair cutting and beard trimming. Not everyone availed themselves of these services, however, letting their facial hair grow into shaggy beards and their locks reach their shoulders. Others, including Frank, kept the growth in check. "I had long since learned that self-respect and an interest in one's personal hygiene and appearance was one of the essentials of survival," recorded Hartley, who was among the more fastidious of prisoners. "Once having accepted defeat in this area, he went with increasing rapidity towards his lonely jungle grave."

Bathing was more difficult. The nearest fresh water at this camp was a long, difficult hike away, one that included a tiptoe across partially submerged tree trunks. The journey could only be made after the day's work, when most of the men were too exhausted to do so. So they waited—and prayed—for rain. A torrential downpour would be accompanied by hundreds of men standing naked under the eaves of the hut, washing in the runoff. The cold water would cause the men to tremble and their teeth to chatter, but at least the top layer of grime was removed. Then they would cluster in their huts, the room filling with the smells of men in from the weather, and for a brief moment the POWs could forget their plight.

The lack of food had been a serious concern at Padang, Gloegoer, and River Valley. At Pakan Baroe it was a dire threat. Rations barely reached the sustenance range for the indolent, much less for men engaging in such strenuous physical work. Breakfast was the familiar, vile tapioca and water glop, ongle-ongle. Lunch was a cup of rice, leveled off with a stick to ensure equivalent amounts for all, plus a cup of watery vegetable soup (a ladleful of grotesque brown liquid that congealed as it cooled). The evening meal was generally the same as lunch, augmented by whatever the men could forage during the day's work. As Fitzgerald put it, "This was little enough to get excited about... but there was always a chance some meat might be present." All was washed down with green tea or boiled swamp water.

"We tried to supplement the minimal daily diet in every possible manner with everything that was eatable, such as tubers, leafs, snakes, rats and sometimes even monkey meat," Frank remembered. Everything that could be caught or plucked was on the menu. The POWs adhered to the same maxim of the oft famine-struck Chinese—"If its back faces the sun, it can be eaten." They caught fish, salamanders, insects, and lizards; picked nuts, berries, toadstools, flowers, green leaves, and even stripped bark from trees, which Freeman said tore their stomach linings. "We used to take tin cans with us to collect jungle vegetables on the way to work," he added. "This entailed quite a risk, as if the Japanese caught us, woe betide us." They dumped handfuls of chilies onto their concoctions in order to make them more palatable to the taste buds. Cutlery was improvised from small pieces of zinc and tin.

But it was impossible to ever get enough. "We were all perpetually, agonizingly, hungry," Hartley recalled.

> Every organ in our bodies seemed to send out messages of pain, demanding to be fed. Our stomachs felt bruised and our knees trembled; we lived from meal to meal with a dumb hopelessness, knowing that even when the meal had been eaten the pains and the cravings would remain only partially and momentarily dulled. The food had as much effect on us as a short shower after a prolonged drought has on a garden. It did no more than wet the surface.

Thirst bedeviled the POWs too. Here the problem wasn't quantity but quality—the local water was rife with organisms carrying disease. "The Japanese supplied us with a petrol drum to boil water to prevent typhoid and we used to put our cans around the fire and cook it that way," Freeman recalled. The first order of business upon arriving at the work site each day was to boil the sixty-four-gallon drum. "As soon as this had boiled for a few minutes," a POW named J. D. Pentney described, "a whistle would be blown to signal that the drinking water was ready and we would dash like mad to get a container of it. We drank this off as soon as we could bear it in our mouths and it literally ran straight out of us through our pores, so we stood, drinking away at almost boiling water whilst the perspiration poured down our bodies in streams."

Intestinal issues plagued the POWs. Amoebic dysentery was a ruthless killer, and roundworm from poorly washed vegetables infected digestive tracts across the railway. One of Ken Robson's friends named Harry found out he had been infected in a most gruesome manner. "Harry suddenly shot up," Robson recalled, "sat on the edge of the bed boards and gave a cough. Putting his fingers in his mouth he produced a long worm, about as thick as a pencil and some ten inches long."

Meanwhile, the policy of reduced rations for the sick continued, preventing ill prisoners from getting enough nourishment to recover properly. As a result, many sick men refused to admit their illnesses and worked until they collapsed on the side of the tracks, left there to tremble until their fellow prisoners carried them back to camp at day's end. The Japanese told the men that if it were up to them, sick (and thus dishonorable) POWs would get no food at all; the half-rations came as a result of the emperor's mercy. Beriberi flourished, while the rampant dysentery was a double blow, hitting the men both physically and psychologically, as Ken Robson explained. "With no control over bodily functions there was not only the pain, but the humiliation of not being able to control oneself...the self-disgust at your own inability to prevent it."

Through it all, Judy suffered alongside the men.

While Frank toiled twelve, fourteen, sometimes sixteen hours on the railway, Judy stayed in the brush nearby, running around and playing a potentially deadly game of hide-and-seek. Her conversion from a pure "people dog," a ship's mascot who spent most of her time on the water and couldn't even reliably point despite her genetic predisposition, into a wilder canine capable of survival in untamed wilderness was ongoing—and quite remarkable. "She wasn't that tame, obedient dog anymore," Frank noted. "She was a skinny animal that kept herself alive through cunning and instinct."

With her nose attuned to this new environment, foraging was her main role, both for herself and for Frank and his friends on the line. She would catch snakes and rats for the grateful men, who would add the meat to their minuscule evening rations.

When she wasn't looking for food or hiding from other animals, she would simply lie in the brush and wait for the signal to rejoin Frank. While other camps were more open, the rail line extending out from Camp Five was mostly hemmed in by trees and bush, so Judy could keep her eyes on her best friend while remaining utterly invisible to whatever guard was nearby. "Another danger came from the local population," Frank recalled, but here again the remoteness of their work site was a boon. "Luckily she rarely came into contact with the inhabitants, because there were only a few villages near the railroad."

This wasn't the case elsewhere, and dogs were very scarce as a result. They were a delicacy to the Japanese and Koreans, a rare treat for the Sumatrans, and, as it happened, sustenance to the starving prisoners, who ate dog if and when they could get their hands on it—even the westerners. John Purvis was a good example. At one point later in the war he was transferred away from Judy to a different camp, but his experiences and relationship with the pointer didn't affect the rumbling in his stomach one iota. At this new camp, the Japanese officers were keeping a small dog, apparently to consume in celebration when the time was right.

Instead, the prisoners stole him one night and ate the dog themselves. "I had a bit of him," Purvis admitted. As it happens, Purvis didn't discriminate among domesticated animals. "In one camp there was a cat," he remembered. "The cat used to come and meow outside my hut each night and I decided it would be better in a pot. I tried night after night to catch it." Purvis would try to attract it by purring in a friendly manner, then making a leap, but the cat remained maddeningly out of reach. His frustration mounted when another prisoner managed to snag the cat and cook it. "However, he knew that I had been trying for so long that he gave me a nice piece," Purvis recalled decades later.

Stories of westerners consuming dogs in POW camps were legion, especially in camps in Japan, where canines were more plentiful. Even Englishmen, noted dog lovers who looked down with a condescending sneer upon the Asian custom of eating dog, were driven to eat the beloved animal, usually in its traditional form as soup or stew. As Pearl Buck once wrote, "A hungry man cannot see right and wrong. He just sees food." This was the operating principle among the men held by the Japanese.

As such, it behooved Judy to remain out of sight, which was helped by her extraordinary ability to communicate with Frank. "I only needed to click with a thumb and middle finger or whistle softly," Frank said later. "It was our language of understanding which she understood perfectly and without hesitation obeyed."

"The simple instruction 'go away' was enough for Judy to disappear," Frank said. "She calmly remained waiting, sometimes even for hours on end, until she received my signal to reappear. This didn't save her once—it saved her many times from certain death."

One man who often found himself on Frank's steel-carrying team, thanks to his similar height, was another radarman named Tom Scott. He gave this account of the relationship between man and dog:

> I was always fascinated at the complete understanding which existed between Frank and Judy—they were truly an amazing team. Judy was no longer a dog that anyone in his right mind would recommend as a suitable household pet. Thin, half-starved, always on the prowl, her eyes only softened when Frank touched her or spoke to her, or when she looked up at him. Whenever she found

herself too close to one of the guards, her lip curled back in a snarl, and her eyes seemed to glow with almost a red glare.

Sometimes this sort of thing would lead to trouble, and when a guard threatened to retaliate, Frank would click his fingers and Judy would disappear into the nearby jungle. We didn't see her and didn't hear her, yet the moment he gave a low whistle, she'd reappear at his side as if from nowhere.

That this tactic actually worked so well is difficult to believe, even—or perhaps especially—to men who survived Pakan Baroe but never witnessed Judy and Frank in action. This includes a good number of the POWs who spent their imprisonment at different spots along the railway. One of these nonbelievers is George Duffy. From his nursing home in Brentwood, New Hampshire, the crusty old sailor, still quite mentally agile at ninety-two, flintily dismisses the idea that a dog could have survived the same hellscape he did. "I don't know how it's possible," he says. "I can't imagine any animal living more than a day in that jungle. I only survived because I was tough and I was young. No dog could have done the same."

But one did. Judy's ability to remain alive in such an extraordinary manner would seem to indicate the guards on the railway were a slack, easily duped bunch. In fact, nothing was further from the truth, making her consistent skirting of danger even more remarkable.

Indeed, Duffy's skepticism, in the face of many direct eyewitness accounts, only underscores just how astonishing Judy's story of survival is. George Duffy saw all manner of scarcely believable happenstance during his wartime captivity, yet Judy's capacity to outlast the jungle and the Japanese is what gets him to shake his head and say "enough."

CHAPTER 22

Pig Face and King Kong

The Japanese soldiers who worked as guards and foremen on the railway were mostly an embittered, angry lot. By this point in the war, most able-bodied Japanese soldiers were considered too valuable for guard duty, especially in such an out-of-the-way place as Sumatra. The vast majority were shipped to Guam, Iwo Jima, and Okinawa, where they could more gloriously give their lives for the emperor. So the men who were assigned to the Sumatran backwater were stuck in what English-speaking soldiers would call a "shit detail." The more pragmatic of them realized they were less likely to be killed on the railway than battling Allied forces elsewhere, but even those men were cranky about the gig.

Some of the Japanese were more notably cruel than others, such as a dark-complexioned guard the prisoners called Black Bastard. He was a sullen, unsmiling gent who particularly loved to beat up on the *hanchos*. His preferred method was to issue orders in fast, guttural Japanese; when the POWs naturally failed to understand whatever was being said, the beatings ensued. Another guard enjoyed hurling tools such as axes and machetes at the prisoners, then demanded the prisoners pick up the implements and give them back to him.

But the main source of fear along the railway was not the Japanese—it was the Koreans.

There had been a handful of Korean guards at Gloegoer, but they were far more plentiful here at Pakan Baroe. So for many of the POWs, the railway was their first experience with Koreans, who were partly eager tormentors, partly dragooned subcontractors. Overall, they were much more violent, cruel, and unpredictable than the Japanese, who generally mistreated the POWs in a backhanded fashion, through malnutrition and deprivation.

Japan's relationship with its protectorate state of Korea was not unlike that of Britain's relationship with Malaya, or Holland's with the Dutch East Indies, albeit underscored with a deep vein of malice. In Korea, the Japanese owned much of the earth that provided the agricultural backbone of the economy, making Koreans tenants on their own land.

This power imbalance meant there was much ill will seething beneath the placid exterior of the average Korean, especially with the onset of the war. Korean men were conscripted into the Japanese fight en masse; nearly five and a half million either donned the uniforms of Imperial Japan or were sent to work in factories in the home islands. They were told they would only have to serve for two years, and be part of economic development projects. Instead, they were given jobs the Japanese didn't want to do.

Occasionally, Koreans fought alongside their Japanese "allies." At Tarawa, Korean troops made up roughly a fifth of the forces resisting the U.S. Marines, and fought as ferociously as the Japanese to hold the island. But for the most part, the Japanese didn't trust their Korean minions. On Tinian, the five-thousand-strong Korean labor force was kept in the rear and off the front lines. But as Gavan Daws writes in *Prisoners of the Japanese*, "So as not to have hostiles at their backs when the Americans invaded, the Japanese killed them."

And Korean females were not spared—countless were forced into becoming *ianfu*, "comfort women," made to sexually service Japanese soldiers and bureaucrats, a national scarring that still resonates today. Yet Korean men were equally complicit in the procurement and enjoyment of the licensed prostitution of their women. According to recent human rights scholarship, *ianfu* were enjoyed by South Korean military units during the Korean War, well after the Japanese had been defeated and scrubbed from Korean society—many of them the same women who had been forced into service during World War II.

The Korean soldiers who were forced into prison guard duty had a seemingly bottomless capacity to take out their frustrations on the POWs of the Pacific. "The Korean guards were the most abusive," wrote Eugene

Jacobs in his memoir of Bataan, *Blood Brothers*. "The Japs didn't trust them in battle, so used them as service troops; the Koreans were anxious to get blood on their bayonets; and then they thought they were veterans." Korean guards were alternately feared by POWs working on the Burma-Siam railway for their base cruelty and mocked for being "moronic," in the words of one survivor. Many of these same guards were moved to Sumatra when it came time to build that railway. "Those hard-liners cared not if we lived or died," wrote Duffy.

The Koreans in the IJA took out their anger across the Pacific theater with corruption and obstruction of the Japanese wherever possible. A secret report issued by the Japanese military warned, "The Koreans might riot at any time" or that "they might collaborate with the British or Americans against us at the front lines." The commanders at Pakan Baroe feared the Koreans would turn on their putative "masters" if strictly controlled, so they were allowed to, in Ray Smith's words, "pick the slightest argument against the POWs in order to vent their wrath." A Japanese corporal named Tokayama, recalled as "not wicked, but very stupid" by Dutch prisoner Chris Willemson, was nominally in charge of the Koreans, but he washed his hands of their behavior early on. Mainly, he simply didn't care what they did. This allowed the Koreans to run riot.

Korean guards were often drunk and always sadistic. They were forever face-slapping, rifle-butting, or shovel-whacking prisoners. That was just part of the average day, meant to hurry along slacking workers or merely vent some frustration. When the Koreans got truly angry, the punishment got exponentially worse. For example, POWs were typically forced to hold branches or sleepers overhead for hours in the broiling sun. If they dropped their arms, the beating was ferocious.

The prisoners knew the Koreans only by nickname: the Bully, Baby Face, Flower Pot, Fat Lip, Four Eyes, the Prizefighter, Fat Porky, Black Panther, Bawal, Wada, the Slime, John the Slapper, the Elephant, Cross-Eyed, Harimau, Slap Happy, Howling Monkey, the Battaker, Farmer's Son, Ohara, Wild Bill, Horse Face, Tapioca Jim, the Yid, the Dead End Kid, Neurotic, the Basher, Rubber Neck, the Wrestler, Gladys, the Aga Khan, the Chinaman. The humorous monikers gave the guards personality, while allowing the POWs to mock them behind their backs. But it didn't make them any less terrifying.

"I saw screaming, slavering Koreans beat up a Royal Navy lieutenant," an Australian doctor named P. M. Kirkwood reported after the war to the *Melbourne Age*. "Without provocation they beat him across the face with sticks until he fell. He was hauled to his feet and beaten again. It was the most sickening beating-up I have seen, but throughout the naval officer did not utter a word. He stood and took it."

One witness saw a POW get a pencil pushed into his ear, then punched in deeper, shattering the eardrum. Prisoners were deafened by whacks to the ears, requiring emergency surgery by the camp doctors. In several camps, the Koreans made great sport of pitting the men against each other, forcing them to fight. If they didn't whale on each other with enough gusto, the guards took over and hammered them both.

The guards experimented with their techniques. Raymond Smith wrote of taking a walloping—along with an officer named Upton—from a Korean called Inuee. "We were made to kneel next to one another. I was wearing Klompers which I kicked off to one side. As we both kneeled down he placed a bamboo rod in the angle at the back of the knees between the upper and lower legs. Then with a sickening laugh he applied downward pressure to both shoulders. The result was terrific spasms of pain in both knees. This he did to both of us. He then picked up one of my Klompers and promptly struck me on the forehead with it. As the blood ran into my eye I really thought I had lost my eye.... Inuee walked to the guardhouse table and picked up a small bottle of blue ink and poured it over [Upton's] head. As he had yellow 'malaria pallour' the combined effect was to make his face a brilliant green!"

Beatings generally increased near the end of the workday, when the race to fill the day's quota of felled trees and hammered ties grew tight. The guards would scream and prod the prisoners with abandon, the sore-shouldered men swaying under their heavy loads. It was worse in areas where teakwood was gathered, instead of wood from rubber trees. Teak was far too heavy for one man to carry, so teams of prisoners would haul the lumber from the jungle. If it dropped, the whole production was slowed while the man responsible, and his *hancho,* were beaten.

Illness only stoked their ire. The painful skin ulcers that were a common side effect of working in the swamps were a frequent target for the Koreans. Several men had to have their scarred limbs amputated after a guard went to work on the afflicted area. Meanwhile, the guards in the hospital hut of Camp Two would stub out cigarettes on bedridden men.

As was the case with the Japanese, some of the Koreans took the casual brutality of their countrymen to the next level. King Kong was the nickname for a particularly huge Korean guard. Being head-and-shoulders taller than the average sentry, King Kong was called upon to beat on men close to his own size, meaning mainly the lanky Dutchmen. Despite his size, he took unfair advantage by forcing them to kneel before raining blows upon them. He beat up one POW who was too injured to help build a soccer field for the guards. He beat another nearly to death for slipping a few *romushas* some bananas.

But not every battle went well for him. He once grew enraged with a Japanese soldier and challenged the man to a fight. But the smaller guard, clearly trained in martial arts, executed a nifty combat move, grabbing King Kong by the ankle and then running in a circle. Enraged, King Kong howled and tried to throw haymakers, but he was kept awkwardly out of position by the Japanese man. "Everyone roared with laughter," recalled a Dutch eyewitness.

Another especially barbaric Korean was called Porky or Pig Face by the POWs. He served in Camp Three early in the construction process, near a tributary of the Siak River called the Kampar Kanan. One day a Dutch friar named Jan Naninck went to the river to wash and found the incredible gift of a bar of soap, no doubt dropped by one of the guards. He shoved the priceless booty up between his buttocks to smuggle it into the camp—but at a crucial moment, it squirted free. Right at the feet of Pig Face.

The guard smiled monstrously, for now he had an excuse to torture a prisoner. First he beat Naninck, but that wasn't nearly enough. The POW's loincloth was yanked off, leaving him naked. He was then hung from a tree branch by his wrists, which were bound by rope. Naninck's toes barely scraped the ground.

Pig Face gathered up a bunch of fire ants and proceeded to insert them in several orifices, including Naninck's mouth, nose, and, horrifically, the opening of his penis. Pig Face walked away cackling, and Naninck was left in agony for twenty-four hours. When at last another guard cut him down, the Dutchman was delirious and barely conscious. He was taken to the huts, where he collapsed. When he came to, he saw Pig Face hovering above him, smiling in the same manner he had before. The sadistic guard was now carrying two bunches of bananas, which he thrust at Naninck as some manner of demented apology. Pig Face wouldn't leave until the POW had choked them all down.

As usual, the *hanchos* took the brunt of the beatings. While the Koreans whaled on everyone without discrimination, the Japanese generally singled out the *hanchos* for abuse. One time, Peter Hartley, much against his will, found himself named *hancho* on a work detail. A guard swung a blow at one of his men, and Hartley grabbed the guard's arm so he was unable to follow up with another strike. "I never did know what happened after that or how I got back to camp," he wrote later. "I was conscious only of the bandage on my head and later still of the fact that I was scarred for life."

One has to wonder how Judy could possibly have survived the wrath of the guards. The Koreans essentially had a free hand to kill and maim, had no regard for dogs other than as food, and saw Judy as a four-legged rejoinder to their superiority, a skinny, brown-and-white taunt aimed directly at them. They would have killed the pointer at any moment, if they could manage it.

But several factors worked against them. First and foremost was Judy's astonishing ability to disappear right in front of them. This was coupled with her unerring sense of brewing trouble, which always allowed her to bolt before matters got untenable. The enormity of the terrain, the plethora of hiding places, and the guards' unwillingness to push too far into the dark jungle all worked in the pointer's favor as well. And Frank pointed out that "because the guards were regularly being relieved, she had the luck that her assailants never remained too long nearby."

It's also helpful to take the point of view of the Koreans. The average Korean guard was a man brought against his will to a place far from home, with a terrible climate much different than his temperate homeland. Snarling predators and rapacious insects didn't care who held a rifle—the guards and POWs alike served as prey. He was caught up in someone else's war, one he didn't understand, didn't care about, and didn't actually fight. He took orders from a despised member of an army that dominated his country, yet who was so low in rank as to make his word barely worth listening to. His Japanese bosses considered this project little more than busywork, far from the action of the real war. The project itself was at a glance insane, a monumental tilt at nature's windmill that could never pay off in any meaningful way (certainly none of the Koreans would benefit even if the damn railway was ever finished). The POWs themselves were dehumanized chattel whose only role was to give the bottom-dwelling Koreans a level in the subbasement to look down upon.

In this context, Judy's existence didn't create any new absurdity for the Koreans. Their lives had already proceeded down a strange, twisted path. Besides, there were far more dangerous animals in the jungle to worry about. The camps in remote areas kept bonfires raging all night to keep the fauna away. Tiger and elephant spoor were regularly spotted. Elephants were a constant thorn in the side of the railway builders, not because they charged or tusked the men but because they trampled the tracks, smashing the sleepers like matchsticks and twisting the steel rails.

George Duffy twice saw footprints that reflected the enormity of what moved through the jungle darkness. Near Camp Five he saw a tiger print in the soft earth that was "as large as the palm of my hand." Near the end of 1944 he saw elephant tracks that "measured from the tip of my finger to the elbow. He had cut quite a wide swath through the jungle too."

On at least two occasions, tigers penetrated camps and stole provisions, one time taking some hogs the Japanese were keeping for a special occasion. The POWs took great satisfaction in this, until they were warned not to leave their huts at night unless they were in pairs. This was particularly hard on the sick men, especially the dysentery cases. Men who padded in agony to the latrine trenches at regular intervals in the night now had to wake up an exhausted comrade to join them—and the men feared for their lives with every crackle in the bush.

At times, the POWs turned this vulnerability to their advantage. One Dutchman named Jan De Quant, who was missing a lung thanks to a Japanese bullet sustained during the defense of Sumatra, was adept at imitating tiger roars, thanks in part to his breathing impediment. One night, he roared as loudly as he could, and the Japanese and Korean guards reacted as he'd hoped—by fleeing to their huts in terror. De Quant then slipped unnoticed into the guards' compound and stole one of their chickens, a theft then blamed on the "tiger."

The fear and inconveniences became worth it to the POWs when Pig Face was taken by a tiger outside of Camp Six, where Frank and Judy and most of Camp Five moved in March 1945 to build a bridge across a small river. On the day of his doom, the Korean had badly beaten a POW named Ben Snijders for the crime of stealing mangoes. Over and over he smashed Snijders in the face and kicked his shins bloody. "He hit me wherever he could," Snijders recalled to Henk Hovinga. "I could hardly see anymore. My mouth was full of blood. My face and ears had swollen up, beaten black and blue." He was helped back to his sleeping area, where he passed out.

The next morning, Snijders was greeted by excited shouts from his fellow POWs. "A tiger entered the camp last night!" one of them said. "And he took one of *them* with him. He screamed like a pig." The savaged guard wasn't identified. Later, however, a new Korean guard appeared, small and barely old enough to carry his rifle. Through the usual mixture of languages, he conveyed that he was replacing Pig Face. When asked where the tormenting guard had gone, the new arrival bent his fingers into claws, leapt forward, and imitated a roar. "We understood," revealed Snijders. "The tiger had picked the right one." Pig Face had beaten his last prisoner.

It's difficult to say that tigers were Judy's foremost concern, since the necessity of food-gathering beat out instinctual fear. But the great cats would have registered in her animal intuition. Certainly Frank was worried sick for Judy. "My main concern for her safety was when she went into the jungle, due to the presence of tigers in that thick vegetation. The Sumatran tiger is a big and silent killer," he said. "Although Judy was clever and quick, she would not be a match for this jungle inhabitant in his natural environment."

Elephants were less predatory, though still dangerous. As it happened, Judy's most memorable encounter with a pachyderm came near the end of the war. Night had fallen when Frank heard his pointer "growling in the brushwood." Frank roused himself to investigate and came upon a surprising sight. Judy was hauling the biggest bone he had ever seen, one "as big as herself." When she looked up to see Frank, she dropped it, grinned madly at him, and commenced to dig furiously at the ground, attempting to bury it. It was the leg bone of an elephant. The animal's decaying remains were scattered over a few hundred feet of bush.

Judy soon gave up her digging and began gnawing away on the femur, which was actually about three times her length. "Go ahead and enjoy it, girl," Frank muttered. After she'd gone hungry for so long, the huge bone must have tasted like the finest filet.

While the large mammalian threats were the stuff of nightmares, the endless, ever-present assault by Sumatra's insect hordes was actually much worse. The mosquitoes were direct killers via the malaria carried by females, but they were so thick and relentless that the men largely gave up combating them, save for the nets they strung up around their sleeping areas. Ken Robson remembered they "bit hard and fast, until very soon we admitted defeat and even the talk of roast beef or lamb or succulent chicken was unable to compete with the tiredness and the unerring dive bombing of never ending mosquito attacks." Even the nets were something of a double-edged sword—they trapped in the fetid, humid air, and many prisoners instead opted to sleep outside and offer themselves to the "mozzies" as a nightly buffet. Given that nearly all of them had malaria coursing through their systems, further damage seemed hard to fathom.

Beyond the mosquitoes, there were many other pests to hound them. Vicious ants of various colors attacked the men, including the leaf-cutters, who would pour from disturbed bark to deliver hundreds of bites at once. Flies were so thick that men relegated to light duty due to illness or injury were tasked with swatting as many of them as they could—they were even given daily quotas by the guards. Bluebottle flies laid eggs in the ulcers that festered on the men's limbs, making them living hosts to the larvae that would hatch, ghoulishly, inside their bodies. "Scorpions, spring steel blue in color, were treated with great respect, as were centipedes," recalled Fitzgerald, which hid in every nook and cranny of the POWs' huts. A Dutchman named A. Bruinooge recalled the infestations of jungle cockroaches. "Anything that was lifted up produced an army of the pests. And at night they ate the callused skin of our feet."

Even worse in some ways were the microscopic pests that devoured skin. Lice and bedbugs riddled the sleeping areas, chewing on scalps and soles. "The body lice had been partially thwarted by our shaven heads but they don't give up that easy," Smith wrote. "I don't have to draw you a picture to explain their next home." Mites spread scabies, the painful skin disease. The prisoners were driven mad by the constant scratching and slapping. Judy spent much of her time with her leg to her ear or shoulder, vainly attempting to relieve the incessant itch.

Maggots were found not only in the POWs' rice bowls (where many men, desperate for protein, ate them) but also in every latrine, by the thousands, breaking down feces in the stomach-turning sludge directly below the men as they relieved themselves. But even the shithouse maggots were consumed in some of the most desperate camps. The grotesque slime was often lit ablaze to kill the feeding larvae. The resulting smoke badly irritated the eyes of those using the latrines, causing tears. Smith remembered, "It was not unusual to see eight or ten grown men sitting there crying their eyes out."

Unlike most of the pests, the maggots were also put to good use in treating tropical ulcers. A rag would be filled with larvae and tied to the suppurating wounds. The maggots ate the infected area, cleaning it, and the afflicted would show considerable improvement.

Somehow, amid all the agony inflicted by both man and beast, the men found the intense suffering brought out their innate humanity. "The tenderness shown to mates who were ill, almost without exception, was remarkable," Robson wrote. "When a man was ill and couldn't eat his pals shared his food, when they were ill he had theirs. It was wonderful to see a man trying to force his sick pal to eat something, even though his whole body was crying out for every scrap he was offering after a hard day out on the line." Another POW noted, "Hunger tightened the bonds even as it weakened the body."

Amazingly enough, the capacity for the human spirit to rally, even in such thoroughly bleak conditions, was continuously on display at Pakan Baroe. As Robson wrote, "Faith is the greatest reservoir of energy . . . and faith in the future was something most of us had and was unexplainable." Rouse Voisey remembers that he "put his trust in his comrades to come and get him out of there, and they did."

The ever-hardy British soldiers performed regular cabarets, with over-the-top displays of singing and dancing. The Japanese and Koreans found this utterly incomprehensible—to them, there was never a cause for a prisoner to laugh or enjoy himself. He should, when it came down to it, be dead. But these men refused to stay defeated. "Campfire concerts would be held, and we marveled at the talent," recalled Fitzgerald. "One chap named Winstanley had a very powerful baritone voice and had quite a repertoire of rumbustious songs which were very popular. One was 'Legion of the Lost' which, though concerning the French Foreign Legion, was taken by many to refer to us."

The Dutch prisoners, being of more varied ages and fitness levels than the Brits, also scorned the rowdy entertainment. But that didn't mean they were lifeless. A group in Camp Two performed regular "Jungle Jamborees," complete with violin recitals, singing, and acidly funny spoken-word presentations by a POW named Jan Eggink.

"We were never cracking ordinary jokes," Eggink recalled in a documentary that aired in the Netherlands in 1997. "It was all meant as giving them something of a spiritual fighting spirit." Alas, even Eggink gave up his routines when the funeral services began piling up. But he came out of "retirement" for a performance on Christmas Day 1944.

"I will never forget that Christmas," he said in the documentary. "Singing was absolutely prohibited by the Japs. Suddenly, (POW J.) Bratu walked in with his violin. He played a medley of traditional Christmas songs. When he hit upon 'Silent Night, Holy Night' all those hollow-eyed skeletons in the audience hummed along, very, very softly.... I still get tears in my eyes when I think of it."

Eggink also read poetry to his fellow prisoners, mostly about keeping the faith to fight on and get back to the people who loved them. He wrote one poem dedicated to his wife:

I thought of you so many days, darling
And waited years in varied ways
to our liberation hour in a daze
though far away not yet in sight,
now still dark, I see no light,
I am ever close to you and nigh,

my darling...
When God gives you back to me to shine,
leaving worries behind, yours and mine.
Together once again we will be fine,
you and me, my darling.

Judy's ability to survive despite the incredible odds stacked against her was another element that brought the men together. She was, in modern terminology, an emotional support animal for the POWs. Even men in other camps, like Rouse Voisey, took heart when word was passed down the line of another of Judy's wondrous escapes. "We all knew of her existence, even when we didn't actually see her in action," he remembers. "It was a great thing to know someone was taking care of her, and that she was—somehow—still alive."

Judy's mere presence on the railway rallied men who had been pushed beyond the brink. Her effect was captured by an unknown poet, who added this quatrain to a longer poem written amid the grueling hours at the camps:

They would stagger to their workplace
Though they really ought to die
And would mutter in their beards
"If that bitch can, so can I"

Beyond his backbreaking work on the railway, Frank had an extra duty to perform at all times—looking out for Judy. As the calendar flipped to 1945, the pointer became even more aggressive toward the Japanese and Korean tormentors. Whereas before she would zip away from their kicks and do her best to hide from sight, she now often became openly confrontational, snarling and growling and standing her ground even in the face of shouts, bayonet thrusts, and drawn rifles. She would crouch a foot or two away from the boot that had just missed her, teeth bared and eyes flashing red. Only Frank's ever more urgent whistles would get her to retreat into the bush.

She was surely getting wilder, and her flight instinct was being slowly subsumed by her fight instinct. It was as though she was de-evolving back to her wolf days, and the effect made her more frightening. Alas, it also put her life in more danger.

One day, Judy's attitude almost made her a casualty. Work was proceeding apace on the railway when one of the prisoners dropped a piece of equipment down a small ravine; whether it was on purpose or due to exhaustion is unknown. A nearby guard suspected the former, or simply didn't care about the motive, and began beating the prisoner savagely over the head with a bamboo stave.

It was hardly an uncommon sight, yet as she so often did, Judy acted to protect her friend. When the prisoner fell backward from the assault, the pointer dashed in from the jungle unbidden by Frank and began barking fiercely and snarling at the guard. The guard kept his cool and very slowly, never taking his eyes off Judy, lowered his stave to the ground and exchanged it for his rifle, which lay ready at his feet.

This time there was no whistle from Frank, just a scared shout: "Go girl!" Judy saw the rifle come up and the muzzle flash, and she dodged out of the way in the nick of time. Frank took a few blows from the guards after the episode, then got back to work. A little later, when Frank had moved down the railway and judged enough time had passed, he called to her. Judy appeared, shaken and looking "abashed," in Frank's words.

On another occasion, the men had returned to their quarters after the evening meal when a guard began going after a prisoner. As usual, Judy got in between them and actually drove her body into the guard. Enraged, the guard chased after her. "Disappear!" Frank screamed. He later recalled that Judy "crawled through the hole in the wall of our barracks made out of palm leaves, and she was gone." All Frank could do when Judy was alone in the jungle was lie on his bunk, hold his breath, and hope.

Night fell. Gloom set over the hut.

Then Frank heard a shot ring out.

"Fearing the worst," Frank slipped outside and set out to look for his friend. "I crawled through the brushwood to find Judy," he remembered. "After a couple of minutes she appeared."

Examining her, Frank's hand came up red. There was a streak of blood on her shoulder. Indeed, the bullet had broken skin, but that was the extent of it, miraculously. Infection was always a concern in this septic environment, so Frank covered the wound with palm thatch. Quite literally, she had been a millimeter, or a nanosecond, from severe injury or death. But this was Judy, and she had survived so much over nearly nine years of life. A near-miss from a bullet was just another brush with the afterlife.

In both these incidents, Judy's interference meant the prisoner who was being beaten was forgotten about. The clamor of her barking and the guard's shooting at her had effectively saved these men from a horrible thumping, or worse. They would be added to the growing list of men who could say the same over the course of the war.

The men got together that night in the hut to discuss a way they could reward her, but they came up empty. They simply had no extra food to give her, no possessions to lavish on her, and no extra energy to do something special for her. All they had was the hope that they would soon be liberated, and that she would somehow survive to see freedom.

CHAPTER 23

Railway of Death

On March 23, 1945, Camp Five closed for good. Frank and Judy were moved up the line with several hundred men, first to Camp Six, then on to Camp Eight, 111 kilometers south of Pakan Baroe, and roughly 88 kilometers south from Camp Five, just outside the village of Kotabaroe and alongside the Singingi River. On a daily basis Frank and Judy were subjected to a terrifying train commute to the railway, crossing rickety bridges hastily thrown up across rivers and tracks that turned sharply at the edge of enormous cliffs and ravines. Because of the care needed to make the journey, Frank spent almost four hours on the train each day.

"The terrain was getting increasingly difficult," Fitzgerald, who moved up to Camp Eight to rejoin Frank and Judy, explained, "there being more small ravines to cross. These slowed the rail-laying process considerably, and did nothing to improve the temper of our tormentors." Camp Eight was among the roughest of any at Pakan Baroe. A Dutch POW named F. J. Pownall wrote of the place, "Heaviest work. Least food. Shortages every time. Working night shifts, many of the sick included." A. Bruinooge recalled the work done there as "murderous; we had to cut tree trunks for sleepers while standing in chest-high water and being eaten by leeches, ants, and other insects. We also had to haul tree trunks from the forest to build bridges with a Jap on our heels and pushing us to the breaking point."

POWs were on the verge of collapse up and down the railway. The goal of laying a completed track between Pakan Baroe and Moearo was only about halfway completed, so the pace was picked up considerably.

"The Japanese panicked," was how George Duffy remembered it.

Work parties were kept out longer, the guards grew more intense, and rest periods (called *yasumay* in Japanese) were shortened or eliminated altogether. Rations were tightened as well, in part because the rice sacks from Pakan Baroe seldom arrived full—quartermasters back in Camp One were busy selling them to the locals to line their pockets, and the corporals in charge of the remote camps were in no position to complain. Meanwhile, as POW Fred Seljee remembered, "the Japs robbed us of our food like scoundrels."

Higher-ranking officers from the base camp and even from Singapore began to arrive, demanding more work from both their underlings and the POWs. The usual threats were issued, of course, but also a carrot—if the railway was completed on schedule, the men would be sent to a "paradise camp," replete with running water, electric light, and no work. Few believed such a place existed, but their only option was to drive harder and harder. The expenditure of the last dregs of their reserves caused the death rate in these camps to skyrocket. For all the cruelty of the guards, their harshest blow came from simply blowing their whistles for work to begin day in and day out.

The reaper had been stalking the men for years now, but when they got to Pakan Baroe, he picked up the pace. George Duffy's diary spells out the cruel attrition rate exacted almost immediately after he arrived:

> July 30, 1944. A Dutch soldier named Jenxis, age 47, died in camp this morning from heart failure caused by overwork. And I came down with malaria. *(Duffy had been there fewer than two weeks.)*
>
> August 17. Dutch soldier Schipper, aged 50, died today.
>
> August 18. Dutch Sgt. Preiss, age 33, and Dutch Lieutenant van der Spek, also 33, died today.
>
> August 23. Dutch Adjutant Slikker, aged 42, died today.

By the spring of 1945, that death rate was a comparative trickle. At first, it was mostly the older, less fit Dutchmen, many of whom were civilians, not soldiers, who perished. But soon enough everyone was vulnerable.

After months and months of slave labor in the jungle, the flood tide of death was rising swiftly, and no one was immune.

"During the first months of 1945, death was a familiar part of our daily existence," Frank would later recount. "Each day friends and acquaintances died in growing numbers." And now, after a long period of relative fitness, Frank too began to succumb. He had gotten through occasional, comparatively mild attacks of malaria and dysentery, as virtually everyone on the line had. But hunger and hardship began to take their toll. "I noticed my ankles gradually started hurting and swelling," he said, the telltale early symptoms of beriberi, the illness he feared the most. "I realized I would be unable to survive for more than three to four months," he recalled. "Each day I saw the fluids passing through and up my body. When the process continues, fluid rises higher and higher until eventually the heart gives in."

Malnutrition had wasted both man and dog into mere caricatures. "Judy became a walking skeleton, a shadow of what she had been," Frank said. The two of them were sharing a handful of rice per day at this point—just enough to keep themselves alive. Judy was too exhausted to hunt for more than short periods, drastically reducing the amount of game she could catch. Even the rats that frequented the hut had mostly been caught and consumed by now. Frank dropped an alarming amount of weight. He told Neumann and van Witsen that he weighed but "36 kilograms" at his lightest, or a shade under eighty pounds.

"Not one of us was fit to crawl out of our blankets and certainly not fit enough to work for ten or twelve hours on the railway," remembered Tom Scott. "Judy was scraggly and bony. Frank was down to about half his weight—just as we all were. They were both, however, mentally strong and alert. They were both steel-tough and courageous, and between them there was a complete bond of understanding and affection."

That was the only thing keeping man and dog alive.

There were but fifteen Americans at Pakan Baroe. Eight had been prisoners in Java; most of them, like George Duffy and his buddies Bernard Hickey, Pat Paris, and Stan Gorski, were from the *American Leader,* the merchant vessel captured by the Germans. This number was almost doubled in September 1944, when a huge new group of prisoners arrived on the railway, including seven Americans. These were men from another hell ship, the *Junyō Maru,* which was sunk by a British submarine off the west coast of Padang in much the same circumstances as the *Van Waerwijck* months earlier.

The Americans were not treated well by the other POWs, an antipathy Duffy put down to simple "jealousy." "We were always in disagreement with the Dutch," he wrote in his memoir, noting as well that when it came to discussing their potential liberation, the Dutch always asked, "When are the Americans coming?" His Dutch commander, J. S. Rosier, made life difficult for Duffy in particular, complaining about him to the Japanese on multiple occasions (to the point that even those who sympathized with his anti-American leanings thought he went too far). Rosier's main sticking point was Duffy's officer status.

The officers were not required to work in some camps, which was a sore point among the rank and file. These men didn't lie about and get tans—often they dug graves and wells, or cleaned equipment. But some officers worked on the rails and in the jungle right alongside the enlisted types.

Duffy was an officer, but of the Merchant Marines, a branch of service the Dutch officers in charge of his camp didn't feel qualified him for lighter duty. So Rosier bitched about it. Even friendly gestures were loaded. At one point, Rosier noticed Duffy went around in hopelessly worn shoes and gifted him a fresh pair of Dutch army boots. Of course, the subtext was that Duffy should wear them while breaking his hump on the railway along with the other enlisted men and stop shirking in officers' country.

Duffy spilled out his frustration in his diary. "It will be great to get away from weak-sister, so-called brother officers, Dutch and English alike, and meet up with some two-fisted Yanks, who, if they've got something to say, tell you right to your face."

Instead of a mano a mano confrontation, Rosier instead had Duffy transferred to Camp Two, along with other "unfit to work" (mostly severely ill) men. Fellow Yank Stan Gorski went with him after falling off a bridge and badly dislocating his shoulder. Hickey had already been sent back to the hospital with chronic malaria, and Paris also wound up in the hospital tent.

They may have gotten away from their Dutch tormentors, but Camp

Two was home to the hospital hut the men called the Death House. They now faced life at a camp for the dying. Both Duffy and Peter Hartley spent considerable time at this camp. For the Brit, the camp was a hellish period spent combating dysentery and malaria, checking in to and out of the Death House. Ironically enough, Hartley had longed to be transferred out of the jungle, telling his camp commander, "If the base camp was a camp of dead men I would prefer to be alive among the dead than stay and be dead among the living."

The line between life and death at Camp Two was blurred and indistinct. Two large hospital huts serviced the infirm, with one for less serious cases. The intensive care hut was divided in half, with the ambulatory on one side, invalids on the other. In the middle were six actual rolling beds where the terminal cases were placed: their occupants changed virtually every night. The dead would be rolled out, and a new man would take his place when the bed was returned to the hut. Few who took up occupancy in the beds ever got up from them alive.

One man who managed to emerge from the darkness was J. D. Pentney, who originally came to the hospital after leaping off a truck barefoot and breaking a bone on a pebble. That healed, but he caught beriberi in the hospital and the dreaded swelling commenced. "I was grotesque and swollen," he remembered,

> resembling that well-known advert the Michelin Tyre Man. There was no pain, only pleasant lethargy, one drifted away out of life in POW camp and wandered in pleasant gardens or conversed with loved ones; the hallucinations were quite real and in 3D. . . . After about a week when my body passed no water and I was swollen to fantastic proportions, I suddenly sat up from the shelf where I was lying . . . and I began to pass water and kept on like that for about twelve hours and went down like a pricked balloon until all that was left was a pitiful bag of bones so weak I couldn't raise myself into a sitting position. It was nearly August—I had been hovering between life and death for nearly two months.

"The men lay on their backs, staring into space without seeing, while their hands were constantly moving as if they were pulling yarn from a ball of wool or handling a small rag," recalled Leo Hazebroek, a Dutch medic who lived in New York after the war. "That was mostly a sign they would not make it until morning. And that was the time when we had to make sure that the human vultures did not make a hit; there were always some who were itching to steal what few worldly possessions the dead and dying still possessed."

Another camp doctor, Otto de Raadt, wrote a technical book about his experiences, but some of his passages captured the capriciousness of the Death House. "On the one hand," he wrote, "there was often complete insight into their situation weeks and hours before death; they might discuss it and put their affairs right in an almost intelligent manner. Several times one could talk to a man with absolutely unclouded consciousness, who died within half an hour. On the other hand there were many who became delirious, a certain sign of impending coma and death."

The handful of doctors worked heroically despite lacking medicine and equipment to properly treat their patients. It was all they could do to not get sick themselves, or despair at their inability to keep the men out of the grave. Much of their day was spent making awful calculations about whom to treat and whom to let die. Whom to feed, and whom to let go so that others might live. A smuggled egg became a barometer of how close a man was to rapping on the pearly gates. "Don't give it to that man," the doctor would say. "He will die in a day or two. Give it to this man instead; we may be able to save him." Or the doctors were forced to judge via an awful triage who was "least sick," and thus able to be pulled from bed and made to work when the guards insisted upon more manpower.

The doctors caught revolting dysentery discharge with halved coconut shells. They drained beriberi swellings by piercing them with nails and catching the gushing fluid that poured out with oil drums, which filled to capacity with the horrible yellowish liquid. Amputations were performed without anesthesia, of course. Horribly infected limbs were sawed off with chisels while the patient screamed until passing out.

Placebos were commonplace, a last-ditch effort in the hopes that the mind would help cure what the doctors could not. What was needed most was quinine to fight the malaria, but there was none available. There was, however, a natural source on hand—cinchona trees, which grew in abundance in Sumatra. The Dutch and the British had smuggled seeds of this

South American evergreen from their native lands once the medicinal uses were known. Quinine is made from the tree bark of the cinchona. Several doctors at Pakan Baroe advised the men to pulverize and eat the bark whenever possible. Harry Badger, for one, refused, as it "tasted like sawdust and was hard to swallow." But those that choked it down generally warded off the dread ague, or at least tempered it.

This was still better than the medical care afforded the *romushas,* who received nothing at all. "After all, they are volunteers," was the twisted reasoning of one Japanese officer. Another medic, Adrian Duinhower, told Hovinga of a *romusha* who complained to a guard of stomach pains. "The guard said he had a good remedy for that. They tied him by his wrists and ankles to a ladder, cut open his belly, and gouged out his intestines."

In addition to the usual diseases, Hartley also suffered from scabies. The only cure on hand was to cover the afflicted with sulfur ointment, which was improvised by doctors who mixed the little sulfur they had with motor oil. Men were painted black head to toe, and stank to high heaven. Smokers like Hartley suffered even more than the others, as lighting up would have meant an explosive death.

When he was ill, lying in bed all day was torture. The lice and bedbugs ate him. Sleep was impossible after a day of inaction. His bed bruised him. All he had to read was a Bible, and even that failed to interest him after a while, despite his religious fervor. Pakan Baroe was certainly a place to persuade any man to doubt the existence of God.

But faith would ultimately get Hartley through the worst of his illnesses—though being up and about wasn't much better. He would encounter men he had known from Padang and Gloegoer and fail to recognize them because they were so malnourished. "Men who had once been strong and full of hope now wore beards and staggered about on sticks, too weak even to climb unaided up the gentle slope which led from the washing place." One unfortunate Dutchman was so ill with dysentery he actually fell into a latrine pit and drowned in the unimaginable filth (incredibly, one man leapt in and tried to save him—the redoubtable Sjovald Cunyingham-Brown). The five months Hartley spent at Camp Two were worse, in his mind, than all three years of his captivity elsewhere put together.

For Duffy, life at Camp Two was far more sanguine. To be sure, he battled malaria, four times between February and April, followed by a terrible case in June—"the full packet" of fever, sweats, and chills. But off the railway and away from the Dutch he was recognized as an officer without argument, a respect that placed him on the "wood party," a group of twenty to thirty officers who spent their days cutting trees for lumber to be used by the cookhouse and the locomotives. The work wasn't nearly as brutal as it was out in the jungle. Better still, there was only a single guard charged to the detail, meaning it was simple to arrange for meetings with the locals to buy food. "Bartering was supposed to be illegal," Ken Robson noted, "but of course went on all the time. The Korean guards were tough and would not allow any contact with the natives, but the railway Nips would mostly turn a blind eye, probably taking the view that it would make us happier and get more work out of us."

Duffy used burlap sacks to protect his shoulders while hauling out the felled trees. This gave him plenty of cover to smuggle in his haul—coconuts, peppers, peanuts, beans, coconut oil, eggs, salted fish, fresh fish, bananas, goat meat, water buffalo, tobacco. It was all acquired for cloth; the natives would take any clothing, no matter how worn or tattered. So in June, while fifty men in camp and another eleven out on the railway were dying from starvation, Duffy and his American pals Gorski and Hickey were eating heartily by comparison.

But there were downsides to being a member of the wood party, as the group was tasked with hauling corpses. Dead men were washed, then wrapped in a tatami mat. If the man had four friends in camp, they could request a service. Otherwise, the body was left outside a makeshift morgue. The wood party would return from tree chopping at lunch, swing over to collect the dead, and deliver them to grave diggers, "who would unceremoniously bury them," in Duffy's words. As the months went by, the toting of the lifeless increased. Forty-nine men died in Camp Two in March. One hundred and twenty more dropped in April, including ten on the emperor's birthday, April 29.

Hartley was numbed by the reaper's ceaseless touch. "Eventually death lost the power to move me." This was the attitude of so many of the thousands of POWs experiencing the horror by the railroad. The men were not only crippled physically, but their mental condition frayed badly as well. "Apathy threatened to break the mental resistance, inevitably ending in death," Frank said. "In the course of time this process had taken place with hundreds of men."

Frank did have a secret weapon to combat this apathy—a bag of bones with brown eyes and a cold nose. Years later, Tom Scott would testify to their unshakable bond. "Frank and Judy were never apart. Where Frank went, so went Judy. They lived for each other, and I dreaded to think what would happen if either of them fell seriously ill. Both, I felt sure, would die.... Without Frank, Judy would have died in any case—of a broken heart."

In the summer of 1945, probably in June, Frank fell seriously ill with malaria, much worse than the low-level sickness he had suffered through periodically since arriving in the jungle. He was, for the first time, sent off the line and into bed. Fortunately, he wasn't delivered to the terror of the Death House but to a far smaller adjunct camp not far from Camp Five. Judy was smuggled back with him, and because they were still out in the boonies, she was easily able to remain hidden, at least when she wasn't slipping into the hut where Frank lay trembling. According to one account, a Japanese officer caught a glimpse of the pointer and ordered that Judy not only be killed but also cooked and fed to the prisoners, "as meat was a luxury," with Frank being force-fed the first helping. But Judy, her sense of danger on high alert, remained out of sight, and the order was forgotten.

During his brush with death by disease, and even after he recovered and was sent back to work the railway, there were many nights when Frank would come close to realizing he and Judy had reached a point of no return. Riven with fever, prostrate with hunger, his joints swelling painfully, Frank would lie awake in his rack and ponder ending his suffering. And Judy's suffering.

"One started to wonder if it made sense to attempt to stay alive," he reflected years later. "Even if you would survive, what would the future hold? And even if there was a future, what should one live towards? Would our weakened bodies still respond to treatment if finally made available? And when would that be? Would blindness or paralysis be our fate for the rest of our lives?"

Every man on the line struggled with thoughts of suicide. They wished for the pain to end. They wished to stop casting a pall on others who might have a slightly better chance of survival with one less mouth to feed. They wished to die a death with a shred of dignity. After all, to be taken prisoner is a humbling moment for a soldier. In Frank's case, he hadn't fired a shot or contributed in any meaningful way to even a small moment of victory. His war consisted of ten weeks of humiliation in the face of the Japanese onslaught, followed by years of sustained existence as a POW. To control the manner in which he died, at least one slight aspect of what his life had become, would lend a touch of nobility to his tragic story.

But every time the urge to forever quell the pain threatened to overcome him, Frank would cast his eyes down at Judy. And a realization would sweep over him—his love for her *was* noble. His responsibility to stay alive and ensure she did too *was* looking toward a future. And the fact that they were both still alive, despite the overwhelming odds, despite the endless agony, *was* a victory.

This was his war. He couldn't lose it now.

But even if Judy unwittingly gave Frank the strength to stave off suicide, there was little either one could do in the face of the illnesses that scythed through the camps. What if Frank should die, not of his own hand but taken by disease?

"Looking at Judy," he would later say, "now a starving skeleton of a dog, I asked what would become of her when I would die. I instinctively felt that my passing would also mean her death. Maybe even starved to death, in some dark place, somewhere in the jungle."

This thought was more painful to Frank than reflections on his own mortality. And on nights even darker and bleaker than those that compelled him to contemplate taking his own life, he began to wonder if the merciful action to take, unthinkable as it may seem, was to kill Judy himself. Thinking about his dog dying without him "raised the question if there could perhaps be a simple way of killing her." Of course, the act itself was relatively easy, if Frank truly wanted to trod that path. Simply denying her the little food she received would go a long way toward this task. Or he could "forget" to whistle or speak a warning the next time a guard was onto her. He could probably even muster the physical strength to do it himself, as Judy was so weak by now.

"But would I have the courage to do this?" Frank asked. "Would I be able to take this decision and even if, how? A knife or a piece of wood? Whichever way, I would have to decide quickly as long as I still had the energy to move." One dreadful night, as the inky blackness consumed the jungle canopy, Frank made up his mind to do it. He would kill Judy in order to spare her.

But Judy, the ultimate survivor, was having none of it.

"One way or the other, this clever dog seemed to have guessed my thoughts," Frank said. "Curled at my feet she opened one bloodshot eye. and with that one glance, she rejected all my thoughts of despair." Judy had been defying death for so long it was second nature by this point. By staying alive through all her travails, Judy had kept many of the prisoners going, not just Frank. But there was no doubt who meant the most to her. Frank had wavered, but now he was reborn—and he was infused with the bitter tenacity it would take to survive.

"[Judy] strengthened me to hold on, regardless of what the future might bring," Frank said of that fateful night the pointer earned one more stay of execution. "We had defied so many dangers and looked into the eyes of death so often that we owed it to ourselves to hold on, in the hope that another miracle would present itself."

CHAPTER 24

Freedom

By mid-July, planes were seen overhead with some regularity, though exactly what they were doing remained a mystery. For the men below, the hum of the engines and the flash of sunlight on the wings could herald liberation, but they had been disappointed for so long that they dared not allow themselves to dream of freedom now.

They did think about the pilots of those planes, though, men who not only got to slip the surly bonds of earth and touch the face of God, but who then enjoyed life upon landing as well. One brutally hot afternoon, Duffy poured out his jealousy.

> For [the pilot], we had only envy.... He was free. Free to go to the canteen and buy a bar of soap and take a bath when he pleased. Free to drink a glass of pure water or coke or a ginger ale. Free to receive mail less than a year old, read a newspaper, and listen to today's news on the radio. Imagine the proper meal awaiting him on his return to base, with maybe a beer or two. Picture the decent, bedbug-free bunk he slept in that night. He probably took his good fortune for granted, at the same time griping about his particular situation. In our squalor and despair we waited.

The waiting was acutely frustrating for the men buried deep in the jungle interior. "We still did not have any clue as to what was happening in the rest of the world because we were completely secluded from the outside," Frank said of those endless summer days in 1945. "A lost bunch in these thick, tropical woods, where a place removed of all vegetation would be completely overgrown after a couple of weeks and would reveal nothing about the fact that it had been an empty clearance."

Men at war are as gossipy as a sewing circle, and even this group of POWs, shut away in such a remote backwater of the conflict, were rumormongers. The nervousness shown by the Japanese when the drone of a plane was heard above could indicate that the Allies controlled the skies. There were tales of landings across the Pacific, of retaking the Philippines and Singapore and Hong Kong, and of a terrible new bomb that completely destroyed whole cities. The native Sumatrans were flashing V signs out in the open. The USS *Missouri* was said to have anchored in Padang. Every man clung to the hope it meant that the end of their suffering was nigh.

But in the meantime, the struggles continued. On August 9, the day Nagasaki was destroyed by an atomic blast, seven men died, including a Dutchman who fell trying to cross a narrow bridge over a deep gully. An Englishman named Bromley died a short time later, after eating nuts from a rubber tree that hadn't been properly cleaned. He passed on in the cot next to the American Bernard Hickey, who was in the throes of malaria himself. "Get his beans and money," the sick man hissed out, remaining pragmatic in the face of death.

Hanging on to life at this stage became paramount. To die so close to the end would be the ultimate cruelty. Some thirty men would die in the time between the first atomic blast and Japan's surrender. Frank and Judy spent each day with a single purpose—to keep each other alive. Judy slept directly underneath Frank's bamboo slab and seemed to become even more alert than usual. Judy's increased awareness was fortuitous, for though she may not have known it, she had been officially sentenced to death.

It stemmed from an outbreak of lice in Camp Eight. The tiny bugs had been feasting on the prisoners since their arrival, so exactly why the Japanese and Koreans chose this moment to delouse the camp isn't precisely known. It's likely that Wing Commander Davis or another high-ranking prisoner had passed word along to the Japanese that a token attempt at improving conditions along the railway might alleviate what surely would be any liberator's first instinct—to massacre the guards as payback.

So heads were shaved, along with eyebrows, and all the bedding and most of the clothing was burned. Then came an additional order, which was likely made up on the spot by the guards: *Shoot the damn dog.*

At last, here was an opportunity to kill Judy that came cloaked in semi-official logic. We have to disinfect the camp, so—in the name of cleanliness—the dog has to die, her official POW status be damned.

But they couldn't find her.

The overeager guards had made a tactical mistake. Instead of simply walking over to Judy and shooting her before announcing why, they taunted Frank first, telling him all about the impending death of his beloved dog. This gave him the chance to shout to her the warning to disappear, and she hightailed it into the bush.

Judy disappeared for three days. On the first day, the guards were too busy enacting the anti-lice protocols to look for her, but on the second day, the hunt began in earnest. Several guards teamed up and began to sweep the area looking for Judy. Up and down the railway, on both sides, groups of men with rifles hunted for the dog. The prisoners waited and fretted. Frank was practically catatonic, scarcely believing that he was going to lose his soul mate at this late stage, all because the Japanese had belatedly "discovered their humanity," as he put it.

Every now and again, a shot would ring out, and he would hold his breath, waiting for the howl of pain. But it never came. The guards may have been shooting at Judy, or it could have been game for supper, or just at shadows. Late on the afternoon of the second day, a guard came sprinting out of the jungle and past a group of prisoners hanging around the train. Deeply frightened, he gasped out, *"Tora!"* as he ran past.

The rest of the guards soon appeared. Hunting for the dog clearly wasn't going so well, and it definitely wasn't worth getting eaten by a tiger. Still, Judy didn't appear that night, and Frank remained consumed with worry. He was sure he had seen the last of his best friend. And there was little doubt in his mind, or those of anyone who knew him: Judy's passing would surely be followed swiftly by his own.

Then the next morning, he heard a bark.

The barking got nearer and louder, and Frank and the other men raced outside their hut to see Judy standing in the middle of the clearing, happily barking and leaping in circles. Judy was ordinarily silent unless she was challenging a Japanese soldier or had spotted danger, so it was a shock to see and hear her barking her head off in the camp. And though Frank was overjoyed to see her, the others roared with relief as well.

It took them all of another moment to realize that their guards had disappeared.

There wasn't a uniform or rifle to be seen. The sun was high in the sky, yet there hadn't been a predawn bugle, no shouts of *"Kura"* or "All mens [*sic*] out to work!" as had been the case every morning of the last few years of their lives. They had actually slept in, only to be awoken by Judy. Frank noted later that the guards "had gathered in an area surrounded by barbed wire," hoping to be spared reprisals from the POWs.

A tall, emaciated Aussie prisoner said, "This way," and shuffled with what dignity he could muster, given the fact that he was stark naked, in the direction of an approaching noise. Judy happily led the way, barking loudly. The sound of an engine could be clearly heard on the other side of a copse of forest. A few moments later, two uniformed men stepped into the clearing, wearing the distinctive red berets of the RAF Parachute Regiment.

It was August 15, 1945. The great day had arrived—the war was over. The men and their dog were free at last. The widespread distance between camps meant the POWs outside of Camp Eight found out they were free in different ways and at different times. Farther up the line, the railway had at last been connected. Men working north from Moearo's Camp Twelve met up with workers building south from Camp Eleven. At about eleven thirty on a swelteringly hot, cloudless morning, the "golden spike" was hammered into place. There was a small, unenthusiastic ceremony to commemorate the occasion. The shouts of *"Banzai Nippon!"* failed to convince anyone present that the day belonged to the Japanese. The whole affair lasted barely half an hour.

The men in this area waited more than a week, incredibly enough, before being told they had officially been liberated. The now-recovered Duffy was one of them. As he took a train ride back to Pakan Baroe, he was overcome by the immensity of the task the POWs had accomplished, despite its toll.

He wrote in his diary, "If you could but see some of the cuttings, some of the fills, some of the bridges, the avenues hewn out of solid jungle, you would think it unbelievable that such a fantastic project could ever have been performed by man alone. Man, working almost barehanded. No trucks or tractors, bulldozers or steam shovels, pile drivers or power saws—just shovels and patjols [hoes or adzes] and baskets."

Duffy's pride was bitterly earned, but in truth the railway was barely usable. The workmanship was shoddy, either as a deliberate result of sabotage or as a result of the utter exhaustion of the laborers. Derailments were frequent. The path of the tracks ran up steep slopes that simply couldn't be summited by the underpowered engines in use. And the Japanese seemed unaware of (or didn't care about) the lack of staying power of rubber-tree wood. Away from its root structure, the wood turned rotten in a matter of months. The early bridges and embankments constructed near Pakan Baroe were totally unsafe by war's end. Even as the POWs were transported back from the far reaches of the railway to Camp Two, they had to disembark and watch as the train crept slowly across vulnerable stretches.

Camp Three remained the main British outpost on the railway. The ranking officer there, Captain Armstrong, and his translator, Ray Smith, were tipped off about the coming peace by a most unlikely source—King Kong, the hulking Korean guard. He led the POWs into the shadows and whispered, *"Hewa narumashita"* ("Peace has come"). When the Brits scoffed, he added, *"Ni no okino Bakudon Nihon"* ("Two very big bombs dropped on Japan"). The guard tried to get Armstrong and Smith to ensure he wouldn't be treated badly in the aftermath of freedom, then disappeared into the bush. Smith, unable to sleep nor comprehend the enormity of this gossip, woke his snoozing neighbor in the POW hut to tell him the news. "Have you gone off your rocker?" the man, known as Ginger, for his red hair, replied. "Don't be so bloody daft. Let's get some shut-eye." But to Ginger's amazement, it was true.

Back at Camp Two, the sight of the Japanese burning papers and calling off work duty had tipped off the POWs that something big was afoot. Rice rations increased, and Red Cross parcels were doled out. The men were assembled for a concert by a touring Japanese military band. For a while, they plinked their way through unrecognizable folk tunes. Then, with a suddenness that caught the room off guard, came a most familiar strain:

God save our gracious King,
Long live our noble King,
God save the King...

The rest of the anthem, long forbidden by the conquering Japanese, was drowned out by an explosion of joy. "There was a crescendo of rising voices, clamorous and chaotic," remembered Hartley. "Everybody was talking and shouting, voices shrill with excitement, hands working vigorously, patting friend and foe alike. Even the Korean guards received triumphant, joyful smiles and slaps on the back as they slunk disconsolately away. It was not their hour, but they needn't have been afraid, for no one was thinking of vengeance yet. It was a time for joy, ecstatic, uncontrolled joy, such as we had never known before."

The war in the Pacific had lasted 1,364 days, 5 hours, and 14 minutes, and now it was finally over. There was much laughing and cheering. Some men merely dropped to their knees in prayer. A great many deflated like tires that had driven over spikes, their resistance at last at an end. J. D. Pentney remembered the emotions years later:

> A simple ceremony was held in the centre of camp, where the Union Jack was hoisted to the top of a flag pole, which up til then had always flown the flag of the IJA. Every heart was full as it fluttered to the top and tears ran unashamedly down the faces of some of the toughest characters in the world.... Most of my original comrades were gone and I remembered them as I had known them, previous to our capture, young, boisterous, carefree but with a marvellous spirit that never deserted them, even in the face of the worst adversity. I was 23 and felt four times as old.

The Japanese guards were taken into protective custody. Wing Commander Davis, as it turned out, had known the war was over for at least two days, but agreed to keep things quiet until a peaceable transfer could be arranged.

All day and into the night, an assault from the air was carried out—except in this case, crates of food, equipment, and mail from home were dropped on the survivors. RAF Liberators had replaced their explosive payloads with nutritious ones. Harry Badger was out in the bush when the first parcels began to fall. "We saw planes coming from the east but because of the sun couldn't see the markings. When small dark things began falling, we all took to the bush in a bloody hurry, fearful they were bombs." "They flew back again," wrote Ken Robson, "so low we could see men in openings in the side waving at us. We waved back like crazy idiots, laughing, crying almost with excitement."

Instead of bombs, it was bounty, almost too plentiful to be grasped—cheese, meat, eggs, beer, chocolate, butter, bread, jams, tea, coffee. There was also milk in a tube, which resulted in confusion, according to Smith. "Most took this to be toothpaste and wound up with a mouthful of milk." The rich meals being prepared in the cookhouse were too much for the starving men to digest straightaway. Some wouldn't eat properly for weeks.

"Hey, you know something?" Frank said to Judy with a smile. "Now that this war is over, you can have your own rice ration. You won't need to share with me."

Clothing was dropped as well, and the exposed prisoners needed it all—from skivvies to boots to uniforms and hats. There was clean bedding, portable toilets, and, best of all, field kitchens and hospitals were quickly set up, improving conditions and preventing even further loss of life. In all, some fifteen thousand pounds of food and goods were dropped into the jungle.

All of these supplies came courtesy of a program called Operation Mastiff. This was the Asian segment of the Allied effort called Operation RAPWI, Recovery of Allied Prisoners of War and Internees. Mastiff fell under the auspices of Lord Mountbatten, and it began even before the documents of surrender were signed on August 28, 1945, aboard the USS *Missouri,* which was in Tokyo Bay, not Padang. The program provided far more than just food and clothing. There were frequent medical inspections, informal psychological sessions, and classes to bring the men up to date on what had been going on in the world over the last three years.

Unlike POW camps elsewhere, the very existence of the Sumatran camps was scarcely known to the majority of the Allied command, save the occasional report or rumor, mainly due to the difficulty of mounting intelligence operations on the island. "Clandestine organisations had little success in Sumatra," read a postwar account of spying in Asia, with considerable understatement. At least six British intelligence operations to penetrate the heart of darkness that was Sumatra during the war were failures. Occasional reports filed by Wing Commander Davis never reached his intended target, Mountbatten, having been intercepted and held by the Japanese. The first notification of the scope of the horror being inflicted at Pakan Baroe came only upon Japan's capitulation, thanks to an infiltration scheme code-named Operation Steel. A British major named Oliver Lodge was transported by submarine to a swampy marsh on the Sumatran coast and led a small team ashore roughly ten miles north of Pakan Baroe in early July to collect intelligence for a planned invasion of Sumatra, tentatively scheduled for mid-September. While secretly prowling the jungle, Lodge heard of the surrender on his shortwave radio, then brazenly strolled into a nearby Japanese outpost and demanded—then accepted—their surrender. These soldiers told of a railway being built by POWs deep into the country's interior.

Lodge's report shocked and electrified Allied headquarters in Ceylon. The Sumatran camps were hastily added to a propaganda operation, code-named Birdcage. The operation was launched to drop leaflets that warned the Japanese of severe repercussions should any further harm come to the POWs, and provided instructions for the prisoners themselves. Alas, due to the lack of hard information on the whereabouts of the camps, and the fact that the railway was so spread out, few of the leaflets were ever seen by their intended targets.

Plans to send massive support were put into action, but as an immediate response, Royal Marine Major Gideon François Jacobs, a South African, parachuted in virtually alone to accept surrender of the entire island and, more important, assess the POW situation. He met with Davis as soon as he reached Pakan Baroe and was shocked at the breadth of the barbarity on display. He was most moved by the beriberi cases in the Death House. He would later write of his impressions in his memoir, *Prelude to the Monsoon*. "In many cases, the men's bodies had become swollen to grotesque proportions, their limbs looking like water-filled balloons. In others the swelling had subsided and with the water drained away only the skeleton remained."

Efforts to arrange the safe and rapid evacuation of the POWs were hamstrung in part because of the backwardness of Sumatra. "Internal communications ... were completely non-existent," read the official report on Operation Mastiff. "The whole operation therefore had the necessity to be directed from Singapore, by wireless to a few sets with the clandestine personnel in Sumatra, and by daily messages sent in with the daily supply aircraft, which carried in food and clothing."

Mountbatten's efforts were also hampered by the conditions of the POWs. They were compared to the worst of the Burma-Siam railway survivors, and the daily situation reports from Sumatra attest to the hardship. "Indescribable ... PWs [*sic*] described as living dead ... all underfed and have no interest and are psychological problem ... 249 died of illness and malnutrition during last 3 months. ... Absolutely no attempt has been made by Japs to give medical treatment at any time and all PWs have been ill-treated and flogged."

Upon investigation, it was revealed that there was nowhere near the medical infrastructure to care for the sick and dying POWs in Sumatra, so it was decided to move them en masse to Singapore. But in the meantime, loads of medical supplies were airlifted to the camps. One report annotated the cache, which included "4 million units of penicillin, 100,000 tablets of Mepacrine [an anti-malarial drug], 1,000 blankets, syringes, needles, scissors (Shop, Straight Sharp, Straight Blunt), 20 stretchers, and 15 orderlies." Included among the food drops was a parachuting psychiatrist, one Major Blair, who landed and immediately began caring for traumatized prisoners.

Another report chronicled the "disease incidence" of the surviving men:

Chronic Malaria 100%
Relapses Malaria 70%
Beri Beri 50%
General Avitaminosis [Vitamin Deficiency] 100%
Tropical Ulcer 8%
Dysentery Bacillary 1%
Dysentery Amoebic 0%

Those last two numbers were so low because the men who caught those diseases were already dead.

On September 15, Lady Edwina Mountbatten, wife of Lord Mountbatten and officially the "Superintendent-in-Chief, Nursing Corps and Divisions, St. John Ambulance Brigade," as well as the point person for Operation Mastiff in the camps themselves, paid a two-day visit to Pakan Baroe, part of a weeklong trip to Sumatra. Upon landing, she was greeted by an excited POW who had lost his lone scrap of clothing—his loincloth—racing up to meet the plane as it taxied to a halt. It was the ubiquitous Sjovald Cunyngham-Brown. When a smartly dressed woman emerged from the Lancaster bomber, Cunyngham-Brown turned red with embarrassment. "I say, I do apologize," he muttered. The woman opened a cigarette case and said, "What you need is a cigarette!" It was only as they walked to camp, surrounded by the lady's retinue, that Cunyngham-Brown learned the identity of the famous woman he was chatting with while smoking away in his birthday suit.

Lady Mountbatten spent her stay "living in various buildings cheek by jowl with the heavily beswórded and be-armed Japanese officers," according to her report on her trip. She was in little danger—the officers were meek as kittens by this point, simply hoping to avoid prosecution and be allowed to return to Japan. Major General T. O. Thompson landed at Pakan Baroe with her, but upon taking in the railway camps "they found conditions so bad Thompson flew back to Singapore and arranged for the immediate evacuation of the prisoners by landing ships and [air]craft," according to the Mastiff situation report for the fifteenth of September.

Lady Mountbatten toured several of the camps, meeting just about every POW who was conscious. She was, Harry Badger noted, the first white woman they had seen in years. For the first time in ages, the men wore more than jungle attire. "We were wondering why suddenly we had been issued with a pair of shorts and a shirt, very ill-fitting and an off-white colour," remembered Ken Robson. But they remained sore-ridden, broken-bodied, and fever-drenched, mere caricatures of the men they once were. Many were weeping openly, including some of the toughest among them, who had kept stony facades through the worst of the beatings and deprivations inflicted upon them by the Japanese. One man, who had been consigned to a small cage for the last several weeks as punishment, stared at his hands, which held a piece of Nestlé chocolate. He didn't even look up as Lady Mountbatten passed, so enraptured was he by the incredible prize in his possession.

Rouse Voisey remembers being part of a group of POWs standing around her in a semicircle, and Lady Mountbatten assuring them, "My old man [her husband] will take care of you, don't worry." J. E. R. Persons wrote in his diary that "she spoke well and went down very well with the lads," perhaps thanks to comments like this one recorded by J. D. Pentney: "You boys will be pleased to know that when I left Singapore to come here the Japanese general formerly in charge of the prison camps was hard at work with his 'boots off.' " "She was obviously very moved by what she had seen," wrote Robson years later.

George Duffy wrote in his diary about Lady Mountbatten asking where he was from.

"Boston, Massachusetts," he replied.

Surprised at the presence of an American, she spluttered, "What are you doing here?"

"At the moment, ma'am, trying to get back to Boston."

She laughed and sat with Duffy for a full fifteen minutes, hearing of his capture by the "Jerries." Then she stood and told Davis to "put Americans at the top of the list" for evacuation.

The next day she toured the outlying camps, including Frank's camp in the jungle, where the POWs weren't so formal. Lady Mountbatten, resplendent in her all-white uniform, walked slowly up a line of survivors who had mustered for the occasion. Her escort trailed a step behind. "Their appearance and uniforms were in stark contrast with the groups of half-starved, emaciated persons with which they supported themselves," Frank recalled. She shook hands with some of them, and nodded to others. She then came to Frank, who was near the end of the column. Judy was, as ever, pressed up tightly against his legs. Lady Mountbatten glanced at Frank, then looked down to see his dog. Her face broke into a wide smile, one matched by Judy's trademark jowly grin.

When it was time to leave, Lady Mountbatten reflected on how close they had come to losing thousands more lives in Sumatra. "We had to do the whole of the evacuation of the prisoners of war before we had one single Allied soldier landed, or even the navy lying offshore.... Luckily, somehow it worked, and there is no doubt that had the war gone on a few more weeks there would have been no prisoners of war in these areas left alive at all." According to Raymond Smith, "Salvaged IJA orders... later confirmed beyond all doubt that if the pending landing of Allied invasion troops was to take place, all POWs and *romushas* were to be eliminated," so it wasn't a matter of conjecture on Lady Mountbatten's part, although any orders of the kind don't exist in any currently searchable format.

As it happened, given the horrible treatment, the death toll might well have been far worse. At liberation, the census at Pakan Baroe counted 4,772 prisoners. Some six thousand men, not including *romushas,* toiled on the railway at one point or another, but no one was transferred away—the only way out was through death. An estimated 677 men died, including 431 Dutch, 204 Brits, 38 Australians, 3 Americans, and 1 Norwegian. No formal accounting was made of the countless *romusha* dead—one hundred thousand is a conservative estimate. Of the Allied survivors, 3,185 of them were Dutch, with 722 Brits, including Frank but not counting Judy. There were 170 Aussies, 213 Indonesians, and a lone Dane and Norwegian. And there were a dozen Americans, including George Duffy. Duffy suspected Lady Mountbatten's order to let the Americans leave as soon as possible would be ignored once she left, and indeed, nothing happened at all for a couple of days after she reboarded her Dakota. So Duffy simply walked out of camp and headed for the airfield. There was no one there, but it was better than the camp, so he stayed overnight. The next day, a different Dakota landed and took him to Singapore. It was Duffy's first ever airplane ride. Duffy stayed at the Raffles overnight, then embarked on a dizzying world tour—Saigon, Calcutta, Agra, Karachi, Bahrain, Cairo, Tripoli, Casablanca, the Azores, Nova Scotia—before landing, on October 5, at long last, at Mitchel Field in New York.

"In 17 days," he later wrote, "I had been transformed and transplanted from an unbelievable, life-threatening existence to an awestruck state of wonderment. Colors! People! Traffic! Wow!"

As it happened, Duffy needn't have worried. Within a week, all of the non-Dutch POWs had been evacuated to Singapore (since so many Dutch lived in the area, they were not taken off Sumatra). The badly sick were flown out, while the plain old malarial and recovering beriberi cases—like Frank—were taken out by the landing craft ordered by General Thompson. Judy, of course, went with him. This time there was no need to smuggle her aboard. At long last, they could go for a sail in the South

China Sea without the fear of torpedoes slicing through the water or bombs arcing down on top of them. Judy's grin was as wide as the Malacca Strait as they made for Singapore.

Peter Hartley's turn to leave came suddenly. One afternoon, while moping around Pakan Baroe, waiting to leave the infernal island already, he achieved his long-held dream of tucking into a plate of six eggs with rice, a fantasy he had harbored since Gloegoer. At long last the opportunity presented itself, as there was still tons of food in the camp and few men to gorge on it. So he fixed himself his dream plate and settled in to wolf it down.

Just then, a runner approached. "Hey, Sarge, you're going on the next plane; they're all waiting for you in the truck. You'd better hurry or you'll miss it." Hartley grabbed his eggs and skedaddled. Yolk was still dripping from his face when the truck reached the airfield for the flight to Singapore.

A group of Australian POWs landed at the Singapore airport and were met by some reporters, including Athole Stewart, who had returned to his post in Singapore after his own difficulties escaping years earlier. He saw wizened, prematurely old men brought out of the landing planes.

"As stretcher cases were lifted out," he reported, "the men blinked at the strong sunlight and hid their heads beneath the blankets. They had the transparent pallor of men who have lain long in darkness without nourishment. Some were hardly better than skeletons clothed in skin. They were listless and motionless, their only movement being from their eyes as they received the nurses' ministrations."

The report from another correspondent, G. E. W. Harriott of the *Sydney Morning Herald,* was difficult for readers to stomach over their breakfasts.

> Yesterday I saw the first batch of liberated prisoners flown out of the green hell of Pakan Baroe (Sumatra). Their ravaged bodies repeated in the flesh the Belsen horror pictures from Germany. It was a sight almost too horrible to describe.
>
> I saw Indian stretcher-bearers with tears running down their faces as they carried these pathetic wrecks of humanity. I heard airmen and soldiers who had gathered to watch their arrival swearing bitterly and blasphemously at what was carried from the planes.

It isn't easy to convey what I saw without being suspected of exaggeration but it is certainly a story which should be told and which every Australian should read to learn just what sort of people the Japanese are.

About 100 of these living witnesses of fiendish brutality were flown out yesterday. Three and a half years ago they were fine fighting soldiers. Today they are bundles of skin and bones which hardly look human. Their faces have a dreadful similarity—the dreadful similarity that utter wretchedness, utter weakness and desperate illness stamp.

An RAAF nursing sister Margot Scott, who flew to Pakan Baroe with the mercy planes, told me, "These are the fittest of the sick, others are too bad to be flown. They are dying every day."

It was the worst camp she had seen, she added.

I helped to carry some of these men from the planes; they were so light that I could almost have carried one on each arm. The angry festering sores and the cruel ulcers which had eaten into their bodies and limbs had been skillfully bandaged by the flying sisters but they still wore their filthy prison rags and tatters. They were bearded, bareheaded, barefooted. Some had only the remains of a shirt and a loincloth and some had just indescribable rags.

Most of them were carried out on the stretchers on which they had travelled in the plane. Some who had been huddled on the floor of the plane essayed to crawl or hobble to the steps where willing hands lifted them down, but when they sat down or fell down they couldn't get up again.

Two Australians lying on stretchers croaked and whispered their tale of horror. One even essayed a joke which he and his companion in misery accompanied with a dreadful piping laughter which wrenched my heart to hear.

One prisoner put it best. "The Japanese took the last ounce of blood from us."

Men and women who didn't require urgent medical attention were brought to a place that represented the diametric opposite of their living conditions at Pakan Baroe—the luxurious Raffles Hotel. Prisoners from other areas in Sumatra, including the Padang cement factories and the women's camps at Medan and Palembang, were also there, sleeping between actual sheets for the first time in years.

Frank and Judy went straight to a hospital compound that had been set up for POWs. They stayed for a month, slowly regaining their weight and strength, and ensuring Frank's malaria was finally gone from his weakened system.

Many sick men were loaded onto transport planes for swift travel back home. Frank was a borderline case, as his recurring malaria was proving thornily resilient. But he knew that air travel would mean automatic separation from Judy. He had to secure transport on a ship at all costs. He was forced to "use my powers as an orator to make sure I did not qualify for transport via air"—and it worked.

One afternoon, an orderly found Frank playing catch with Judy out in the courtyard. Both had regained a fair amount of the weight they had lost in the Sumatran jungle. The orderly carried Frank's embarkation papers. "To leave for England aboard the troopship *Antenor,*" it said, which were the most glorious words Frank had ever read. Then he glanced at the footnote below. "The following regulations will be strictly enforced. *No* dogs, birds, or pets of any kind to be taken on board."

Incredibly, the fates were working against man and his best friend once more. But after all they had been through together, there was simply no chance Frank was going to leave Judy behind. It was time for one last clandestine operation.

On the day of departure, Frank enlisted four friends to help him smuggle Judy aboard. First, the dog had to avoid the military police who patrolled the docks. She did this easily enough, and found a hiding place between some duffel bags on the jetty, close by the gangway. Only her nose protruded from the heavy canvas.

Frank boarded the ship and waited until the right moment, when activity on the jetty fell away. Then he signaled to his quartet of coconspirators. They came up the gangway, showed their papers to the two men in charge of gatekeeping, and fell into extended conversation with them, which involved much pointing back in the direction of the city. The men got the guards to stroll away from the gangway for a moment. Their gazes averted, Frank, who was observing the scene from the edge of the deck, whistled once more to his crafty pointer. She zipped from her hiding spot, scrambled up the gangway, and in a blur of brown and white raced into the waiting bag Frank carried. In his familiar practiced motion, he closed the bag around his dog and lifted her to his shoulder.

He went below straightaway and hid Judy beneath his gear.

It was surprisingly easy, particularly compared to getting her on the *Van Waerwijck.* And so it was that after nine years in Asia, Judy was on her way to England for the first time.

CHAPTER 25

Hero

It took six weeks for the *Antenor* to travel to England, a most relaxing month-and-a-fortnight for Frank and his fellow survivors, including John Purvis, whose brother-in-law surprised him by coming aboard during a stopover in Colombo, and Rouse Voisey, the RAF man who remembers the trip fondly nearly seventy years later. These young men were still adjusting to life without exhausting labor, intense hunger and pain, and the terror of knowing death could come at any moment.

The slow passage at sea was particularly beneficial for Frank. While he related almost at a preternatural level with Judy, he was still a bit awkward with other humans, having pulled so deeply within himself to make it through his trial. If it weren't for Judy, he wouldn't have survived. Now, he was enjoying the fruits of making it to the other side, and for the first time as an adult (now twenty-six, he had spent most of the last decade in the service, at sea, or in prison) could experience the simple pleasure of making small talk with his peers. And he welcomed the chance to fully recover—by the time the ship approached home, he was back to nearly full health, at least physically. Judy had been slowly but surely fattened up by the *Antenor*'s cook, who was the only hand aware of her presence on board from day one.

As the ship neared landfall in Liverpool, Frank knew it was time to reveal Judy's presence to the top brass on board. The other passengers had kept her presence secret, and some of the lower-ranking members of the crew had either been told or stumbled upon her accidentally. But the captain was in the dark until three days out from England, when Frank briefed him apologetically.

Judy's first appearance on deck shook up the crew's ennui. "When she was roaming in front of me, a crew member that met us stood stiffly," Frank said. "Still staring in front of him he asked: 'It could be I'm just a bit groggy, but did you just see a dog pass by? And if so, how in the devil's name did she get on board?' "

The captain was angry at first, but when Frank detailed the incredible obstacles he and Judy had overcome together, he reversed course, so to speak, and became an advocate, calling ahead to insist on permission for Judy to make landfall, despite the fact that no dogs were allowed to be on the manifest.

One of the group of men who had helped distract the ship's guards at the gangway while Judy slipped on board was a fellow RAF POW named Brian Comford. His father was a London barrister of some influence, and after a barrage of phone calls, the path was cleared. A permit was granted, and Judy would be allowed to come ashore.

But there was one unavoidable part of the agreement. All animals, with no exceptions, that landed onto the shores of Great Britain had to undergo six months of quarantine to prevent rabies from spreading on the island. Even General Dwight D. Eisenhower, supreme commander of the European theater, had to board his beloved Telek, a Scottish terrier, for six months upon arriving in England to prepare for the invasion of France.

So when the ship anchored in Liverpool on October 29, 1945, what should have been an incredible moment of triumph for Frank was instead bittersweet to the point of tragic. He walked down the gangway, Judy of Sussex ranging ahead of him on a leash, her feet touching English soil for the first time in her nine years of life. Waiting to meet them was an official of the Ministry of Agriculture.

Frank hesitated. He had had a couple of days to get used to the idea of life without Judy, but that didn't make it any easier now that the time had come to say farewell. How to explain this abandonment, after the years in the jungle, surviving the torpedoing of the *Van Waerwijck,* the reunion in Singapore, and all the days they spent together? There was no way to do it, and Frank didn't trust himself not to collapse into tears, so he gave

Judy a quick tousle of the ears and told her to go on without him. He handed the leash to the government official.

"She stopped at the gangway," Frank remembered, "seemingly because she did not understand my command. Her questioning gaze and waggling tail suggested she expected me to summon her back. But as always on my command, she walked meekly toward the docks and jumped in the truck of the quarantine service."

Judy was a prisoner once more. And this time, she would have to burden it alone.

But life at the Hackbridge Quarantine Kennels in Surrey, about a twenty-minute train trip from London (passengers alighting at the Hackbridge Station were guided to the nearby kennels by the sounds of barking), was more pleasant than life in the various prison camps or even aboard the multiple ships she had called home. Upon arrival, she was thoroughly checked for disease and groomed in a way she hadn't been since at least the outset of the Pacific War, and perhaps ever. Frank visited often, and the seventy-member staff at the kennels, once briefed on Judy's story, went out of their way to comfort her.

Built after World War I to handle the influx of rescued and adopted dogs returning from the continent, Hackbridge could handle six hundred animals at capacity, but there were far fewer when Judy was there. No two dogs could come in contact with each other, in order to protect the quarantine. They couldn't even exercise together, so the complex needed plenty of room for every dog to have its own space. Set among the lush meadows and hedges of the Surrey countryside, the kennel offered a wealth of opportunity for Judy to explore. The rationing of food during the war had not extended to dog biscuits at Hackbridge, and now there were plenty of other morsels to go around, including fresh vegetables when appropriate. For Judy, it must have seemed an unimaginable luxury to have endless supplies of food delivered right to her every day. According to a photo essay published in the *Illustrated London News* in 1938, a "sun ray treatment" was used twice a day on the dogs (and presumably cats) to acclimatize them to the cold English winters, although why a cold sprinkler, instead of a sun ray, wasn't the apparatus of choice wasn't explained.

According to an essay in *Tail-Wagger* magazine, Judy would have been let out in her individual large paddock to run while her kennel was cleaned just after eight a.m., the exercise period lasting half an hour. At eleven a.m. she would have been fed her main meal of the day, "a sight for canine eyes," according to the essay, dog food either dry or "covered with delicious meat gravy." The afternoon brought more runs, along with a nap and whatever visitors turned up to give Judy's ears a scruffing. Then a smaller snack of biscuits, one last trip outside, and lights-out at seven p.m. In all, a dog's life, indeed.

But it wasn't easy. Even though life in the jungle had been difficult to the extreme, it at least came with a great deal of freedom. Here, despite the spoils and the long runs, that freedom—the independence she had shown since first tunneling out of the Shanghai kennel as a pup—was gone. Frequent visits from Frank, as well as legions of other returned Sumatra POWs, old navy friends, and just plain curious dog lovers, helped Judy pass the days, but the confinement must have felt strange.

Despite the highly unusual circumstances of Judy's quarantine, it didn't come for free—Frank was expected to pay for the cost of the boarding, which was about twelve pounds, or nearly fifty U.S. dollars (over six hundred dollars today). His RAF and POW back pay didn't go very far, so to help him out, the Tail-Waggers' Club put a notice in the December 1945 issue of the organization's magazine that they were "opening a small fund to defray the cost of Judy's stay in quarantine. Should there be any surplus it will be paid to Judy's owner as a help toward her future maintenance."

Plenty of readers answered the call for help. The next issue of the club's "Official Organ" detailed the contributions: eighteen pounds, eighteen shillings, and eight pence (a bygone method of denominations worth over one thousand U.S. dollars today), coming from sixty-one sources. More money poured in during the following months, including two Canadian dollars from an expat living in British Columbia. The total reached over thirty-five pounds in the end, far more than required.

It was a long six months for master and pet, but Judy was freed into Frank's care on April 29, 1946. Frank arrived looking dapper in his Royal Air Force uniform. Judy was sleek and well-groomed, having had a special long bubble bath that morning in anticipation of the big reunion.

Their meeting was as joyous as imaginable. "She was all legs and tongue," Frank remembered. Painful as it had been, the separation certainly did Judy some good; the time spent eating, resting, and playing in the fields was restorative.

There was a ceremony upon Judy's release, well attended by press photographers. The chairman of the British Kennel Club, Arthur Croxton Smith, presented Judy with a "For Valour" Medal of the Club and handed Frank a check for twenty-two pounds, one shilling, and four pence, or roughly ninety U.S. dollars in 1946 terms (over eleven hundred dollars today). This was the promised surplus from the fund-raising efforts of the Tail-Waggers' Club. The magazine noted that "Mr. Williams requests to us to convey his thanks to all the people concerned who have contributed so generously toward Judy's Quarantine expenses." A representative of Spratt's Patent Limited, a dog-food maker, also slipped a new collar on the pointer's neck, to go with her existing one that still sported her POW number 81-A, this one inscribed, "Presented to Judy, ex-Jap-P.O.W., by Spratt's."

While Judy was in Hackbridge, Frank had been busy. Shortly after handing Judy over, he boarded a train from Liverpool bound for the RAF base at Cosford, in Shropshire, about ninety minutes south in the Midlands. Cosford was the site of Personnel Reception Centre (PRC) #106, a reentry point for European POWs that was rather suddenly made to serve a similar function for the Far East POWs when the actual number of airmen coming home to the United Kingdom was fully realized.

While every detail of the war against the Germans was absorbed and memorized by the English populace, the suffering in the Pacific was far more a case of "out of sight, out of mind." The enormity of the terror faced by the POWs at the hands of the Japanese was only just being comprehended.

"The functional purpose of the unit is to receive, kit, medically examine and attend to the documentation of ex prisoner of war personnel," read the PRC mandate as written by the War Ministry. "After this procedure the ex prisoners of war proceed on 42 days leave, after which they return for a full medical board at the PRC."

The logs kept at Cosford report that two trainloads of former prisoners arrived on the twenty-ninth, a group of 340 at 1:50 and another of 341 at 3:10. Frank was interviewed, "kitted" out with fresh RAF uniform gear, given back pay, including combat and special service pay, and looked over by the doctors. Frank's condition was now improved enough after convalescence at sea to allow him to pass through the basic testing and debriefing and be turned out, free to go back to Portsmouth and his family for six weeks of leave, beginning as October turned to November.

Frank returned to his hometown, which was a far different place from the bustling port of his youth. The city had been thoroughly wrecked by Nazi bombs, most of the damage done during three major raids from August 1940 to March 1941. Frank's family home at 38 Holland Road had been bracketed by explosions during the Fire Blitz of January 10 and 11, 1941, although it appears the house miraculously suffered little damage. But that was the rare tale of good fortune. Approximately 930 people were killed by the bombings, with 1,216 more wounded. This was relatively light compared to other places across the country, but the physical part of the city was demolished. "Our principal shopping centres have been almost obliterated," wrote the *Portsmouth Evening News* in 1941. "There is not a part of the city which does not show hideous scars, in some places completely devastated areas." Thirty churches were leveled, as were eight schools and four cinemas. The George Hotel, where Nelson had stayed before sailing into history, was now rubble, as was the city's tallest building, the Centraal Hotel.

Far worse from Frank's perspective was some awful news. On June 6, 1944, while he had been at Gloegoer, shortly before smuggling Judy aboard the doomed *Van Waerwijck,* his older brother, David, a private in the Hampshire Regiment, had been killed during the D-day invasion of Europe. It wasn't until eighteen months had passed that Frank heard about the untimely death of another male family member in his life. He related none of the anguish publicly, but it must have been a savage blow that undercut the joy of his and Judy's homecoming.

At some point, Frank would have been handed a letter from King George welcoming him home. The date September 1945, a month Frank spent in Asia, indicates the boilerplate nature of the note, sent on Buckingham Palace stationery, but the sentiment expressed by the monarch is clearly genuine.

The Queen and I bid you a very warm welcome home.

Through all the great trials and sufferings which you have undergone at the hands of the Japanese, you and your comrades have been constantly in our thoughts. We know from the accounts we have already received how heavy these sufferings have been. We also know that these have been endured by you with the highest courage.

We mourn with you the deaths of so many of your gallant comrades.

With all our hearts, we hope that your return from captivity will bring you and your families a full measure of happiness, which you may long enjoy together.

Frank's leave in Portsmouth ended in mid-December, when he had to return to the air base at Cosford for a full medical evaluation. There is no record of any further treatment ordered for him, so Frank apparently met the standards set by the staff for a return to duty. That wasn't the case for many of his fellow ex-POWs. A situation report from Cosford points out the difficulty many had in leaving the Japanese camps behind. "Medical board action in respect of Far East POWs proved much more lengthy and complicated than was the case with prisoners ex-Europe, owing to the effect of malaria, dysentery, eye trouble and worms, and to the complete disregard which had been displayed by the Japanese in respect of all medical condition."

Fred Freeman experienced the doggedness of the malaria bug he contracted in the Sumatran jungle. He had returned to his prewar home in Brighton, but the attacks continued, to the point where he couldn't hold a job, and had to apply for a medical pension as a result. "The headaches persist," he wrote in his application. "In fact I had one all last night and this morning. Several times my employers have counted a day of illness as a day off to avoid losing cash."

Given the approaching Christmas holiday, Frank wasn't eager to spend any more time at Cosford than mandatory. The doctors too felt the pressure to get as many men cleared as possible so as to allow them to spend their first holiday at home after so many spent as captives. "To be home for Xmas," wrote one base doctor, "must have meant so much to these unfortunate people who had suffered so much in the cause of freedom." A handful of men (eighty-four, according to PRC records) didn't complete their exams in time and had to come back in January. Frank most likely was not one of them.

Once 1946 dawned, Frank was off to a new post—a POW rehabilitation (or "refresher," in RAF parlance) center called Sunninghill Park, located outside London, near Ascot. For three weeks the men sent here were given updates on developments in the service, taught how to reorient themselves into civilian life after their years in the jungle, introduced to important people in business and government who gave them pep talks, and taken to companies of all manner in order to give them a glimpse at how ordinary society—one that wasn't at war or dehumanizing them—worked. "Much time should be available for recreation and sports and games and gardening, music, amateur dramatics, farming, etc. etc," added an official Air Ministry report on the centers. There were visits by local symphonies, films shown in the station cinema, a "liberal supply of bicycles for officers and airmen," and plenty of "citrus fruit available," as many returned POWs were lacking in vitamin C. There were also courses in the history of the just-completed war, which Frank and so many others had missed while deep in the Sumatran jungle.

Rouse Voisey was there too. Frank struck him as a gentle sort, "a nice, quiet chap, quite average, really." For Rouse, the rehab center did the trick. He found a job in the local government near Norwich, where he grew up, and spent thirty-two years as a civil servant.

Frank's exact thinking on returning home is something of a cipher—he didn't give any interviews from this time, or provide any glimpses into what must have been a bewildering reintroduction into his native land. Rouse gives one reason why. "The government [in this case the War Ministry] told us not to talk about our experiences," he says some sixty-eight years after the fact. "We had just had to get on with it. No one wanted to make a fuss over us." When pressed on why the government would suppress, rather than celebrate, the incredible suffering and endurance these POWs showed in the name of king and country, Rouse can only laugh. "Who knows why politicians do anything?"

John Williams, who was on Pompong Island with Frank, wrote a brief memoir after the war, which also shines a small light on why the POWs were silent. Years later he revisited his work and found it wanting, which he explained in a note affixed to the front of the memoir. "At the time, it did not seem appropriate to write in more graphic prose about some of the horrors and barbarities which we had witnessed or experienced, especially having regard to the much worse happenings that had occurred at Belsen and other Nazi concentration camps."

The British military anticipated this to some degree. "Among the symptoms to be expected," read a report prepared for the Cosford medics, included "a sense of strangeness, shyness and reticence, a dislike of crowds, lack of concentration, mind changing, and a strong resentment against petty restrictions." Frank displayed all of these in some form or another.

His upper lip was as stiff as the drinks served at the Portsmouth waterfront pubs. He had also been beaten to a pulp by the guards after the Tick episode, put flat on his back by humiliating diseases such as dysentery and beriberi, and driven to contemplate ending his own life and that of his beloved dog. It was hardly an experience Frank wished to revisit.

One thing Rouse Voisey was sure of—Frank loved Judy. He remembers that Frank talked of little save his best friend. "He was peddling pictures of Judy to us at the rehabilitation center," he recalls. "They had information about her service and her adventures on the back. Somehow, Frank had gotten Judy's paw prints on there too. I bought a couple for a pound or two each, quite a small amount. The money was for charity. Frank was raising funds to give to the Dickin people [the People's Dispensary for Sick Animals, or PDSA]."

Upon leaving the rehab facility, Frank was assigned a new RAF base, for despite all he had been through, he was still an airman on active duty (another reason why he was discouraged from talking about his days as a POW). He was assigned to the Number 4 Mobile Radar Unit at the RAF base in West Kirby, near Liverpool. After a word to the base commander, Judy was officially assigned there too, in absentia. Like many returned POWs in the RAF, Frank was often invited for meals or tea to the homes of local residents near the base.

But Frank and Judy didn't spend much time at West Kirby. They had more important destinations, primarily London, where Judy's wartime exploits would at last be fully recognized.

During the six months of quarantine, the story of Judy's incredible journey and penchant for survival had made her a national heroine. The papers were filled with tales of her amazing adventures in the jungles of Sumatra and on the waters of the South China Sea and the Yangtze, as well as of her incredible defiance of the Japanese. The press called her "Gunboat Judy" and the "Precious Pointer." On May 3, 1946, there was a ceremony honoring her service in west London's Cadogan Square, an elite neighborhood akin to New York's Park Avenue. It was staged by the PDSA, for whom Frank was already raising money, as mentioned by Rouse Voisey. The PDSA was (and remains) a veterinary charity founded in 1917 by animal-welfare pioneer Maria Dickin, catering to the animals of the poor and suffering.

In 1943, with animals contributing to the war effort across all branches of the service, Maria Dickin established the Dickin Medal, the animal version of the Victoria Cross, the highest honor in the realm. Prior to Judy, thirty-five animals had won the award, including eleven dogs and myriad messenger pigeons, including Winkie, White Vision, and Tyke (aka George), all cited for "delivering a message under exceptionally difficult conditions and so contributing to the rescue of an Air Crew."

Now the seventy-six-year-old Dickin, much honored herself by the king, watched as Major Roderick Mackenzie, also known as the 4th Earl of Cromartie, also known as Viscount Tarbat, the chairman of the Returned British POW Association, stepped forward to bestow upon Judy the eponymous medal. The pointer sat casually as the medal was pinned to her collar, surrounded by former POWs and dog lovers.

The accompanying citation read:

FOR MAGNIFICENT COURAGE AND ENDURANCE IN JAPANESE PRISON CAMPS THUS HELPING TO MAINTAIN MORALE AMONG HER FELLOW PRISONERS AND FOR SAVING MANY LIVES BY HER INTELLIGENCE AND WATCHFULNESS

At the same ceremony, Frank also was given an award, the PDSA's White Cross of St. Giles, the highest award given to humans by the charity, for his special devotion to Judy. Major Mackenzie pinned it to his tunic, and man and dog beamed for the hordes of photographers there to mark the moment.

Honor followed honor during a whirlwind several weeks. Britain was at long last truly celebrating the victory over the Axis powers, and Judy was treated as a hero on the order of Field Marshal Bernard Montgomery, Britain's top-ranked officer in the war. The Tail-Waggers' Club, adding to their previous largesse, gave Frank a large (undisclosed) sum to ensure Judy never wanted for food or shelter again. She was feted at the Returned British POW Association in London, where she was enrolled by Major Mackenzie as an official member—needless to say, the only dog in the rolls.

Shortly thereafter came the Victory Day celebration on June 8. It was a massive celebration that included parades, fireworks, water cannons, orchestras providing music for dancing across the capital, and an appearance by the king. "This is your day—enjoy it," advised the *London Daily Mirror.* Frank and Judy were chosen to be part of a special episode of the popular BBC radio program *In Town Tonight,* along with servicemen from every theater of the war. Judy barked loudly on cue when prompted by host Roy Rich to say something to the listeners at home. "This happy barking echoed in a lot of houses all over the world," said Frank, who was there for all the pomp and circumstance. "Even in Singapore people could hear this dog 'talking.'" Later on, the duo appeared on another outlet of the Beeb, this time on television, on the show *Picture Page,* which aired in the afternoon and evening (Judy barked happily on both programs, while legendary songwriter Irving Berlin looked on).

One of the biggest extravaganzas Judy graced with her presence was a show at fabled Wembley Stadium called *Stars of Blitz and Battlefront.* Three other war dogs appeared alongside Judy to receive the love and ovations of up to eighty-two thousand spectators.

One of the other dogs was named Rob, "a sturdy collie crossbreed," in Frank's description. Rob was one of the dogs trained to be a paratrooper, jumping along with the elite Special Air Service commandos behind enemy lines on several missions. The two dogs had met frequently on the "hero dog" circuit and became friendly. They had bonded, like any good action-movie buddies, over a brawl. At a different appearance, Judy and Rob were waiting in the wings to go onstage when a quartet of tall brown borzois strutted past. Borzois are Russian wolfhounds, closely related to greyhounds, and like that speedy breed, borzois are quite high-strung.

When borzoi met pointer backstage, the Russian dog gave a preview of the coming cold war by biting Judy. "At that instance," recalled Frank, "the arena changed into a battlefield of fighting dogs." Rob jumped in to defend Judy's honor, while all four borzois attacked en masse. The two-against-four fight whirled behind the curtain while the show went on in front of it. Judy and Rob stood their ground valiantly, as "brown hair flakes flew in all directions," Frank remembered. When at last the dogs were separated, the borzois had lost the decision. Their performance had to be canceled.

Judy became a regular at fund-raising drives for all manner of causes, from the PDSA and other animal rights groups to the Federation of Boys' Clubs to postwar recovery bonds. She marched in one seemingly endless parade that stretched from the far north of Scotland to the shores of Brighton on England's southern tip. She took in dog shows, such as the large one in Bath that attracted "311 entrants and some 1,500 people," according to the *Bath Chronicle,* including the mayor of Bath. "The appearance of Judy, the 11-years-old English pointer... was the signal for crowds of spectators to leave the rings and go to the foot of the stage, where L.A.C. Williams, her owner, introduced Judy to her admirers." Indeed, Frank was by her side for every appearance, and Judy never strayed far from him, even as the masses pressed in to get a glimpse or stroke the heroic dog.

She met many stars of stage and screen along the way, who were all unfailingly charmed by her presence. David Niven reportedly called her the "loveliest bitch he had ever clapped eyes on." Frank would surely agree, as would Les Searle, George White, Tankey Cooper, and the many other servicemen who had befriended and fallen hard for Judy in Asia.

But her most valuable days were spent in children's hospitals and in the living rooms of other returned prisoners, or with the families of those who had not come home. She was invariably a tonic for the sick kids or the sorrowful relatives. She made these visits as an official member of the Royal Air Force, her naval background notwithstanding, wearing a coat with an embroidered RAF crest to match Frank's uniform. Frank made sure that Judy wore her other campaign ribbons honoring her service on these visits as well.

She was also a boon to those who had been held by the Japanese or the Germans for many years, as she had been, and who were having trouble adapting to civilian life and freedom. Though they were humans and she was a dog, Judy's apparent bonhomie and easy adjustment to a postwar life was a positive example for those once-imprisoned soldiers, sailors, and airmen. She had buoyed many men in the jungle by simply enduring. Now, by thriving, she set an ideal once more.

There was one other task Frank and Judy performed, this one far more difficult. Countless family members of POWs had received telegrams from the War Ministry informing them that the soldier or sailor or flier they loved dearly was missing or deceased. Now, many of them reached out to the suddenly famous pointer, sending her letters via the RAF or the War Ministry or sometimes simply to "Judy," with no address. Most if not all managed to find their way to Frank. All that these people wanted was more information about the husband or son or brother or father who had never come home from the war.

"Judy and I travelled throughout England to inform the mourning family that their family member was not rotting in the Sumatran jungle," said Frank. "It was not an easy exercise, explaining to someone the inhumane circumstances wherein a mate had died."

Most, though certainly not all, of the deceased hadn't actually been held in an area near Frank and Judy, but that really wasn't the point. Frank and Judy *had* survived and had come home. Often, the bereft families merely wanted to spend some time with this unlikely pair who had beaten the odds. As Frank noted, "The presence of Judy seemed in a way to soften the essence of these sad times and brought some comfort with many families that had lived for months or years in uncertainty about the facts."

It was a whirlwind few months for Frank and Judy, until the drawdown of forces and the embrace of peacetime—not to mention the postwar economic recession in the United Kingdom—forced the country to begin to move on. On July 22, 1946, Frank and Judy were demobilized. The exit ceremony took place at the RAF Technical Training Command Centre, out on the banks of the River Dee near Liverpool. Judy wore her medals and ribbons on her collar and stood at attention. The proceedings took a few minutes, and then the duo walked out past the gate and breathed in the sea air. They were now citizens, their military careers over.

Frank took Judy back home to Portsmouth, the southern naval town of his youth, where so many ships had been launched (including the *Gnat* and the *Grasshopper*), and wondered what he was to do with the rest of his life. Whatever it was, Judy would be part of it, that much he was sure of. And after all they'd been through, that was all that mattered.

CHAPTER 26

Africa

Life in Portsmouth was quiet and dull, which for a time suited Frank Williams and his dog. It isn't exactly known whether he moved back to his family's (still-shared) home at 38 Holland Road, but voting records indicate that while his mother, Agnes, as well as sisters Barbara and Jean Williams, cast ballots from that address in 1947, Frank did not. A Frank Williams did vote from an address in the northern part of the city, however, and it isn't hard to imagine Frank wanting a place of his own for him and his dog. The family home remained crowded and no doubt carried painful memories of his fallen older brother. This supposition is backed up by Frank's postwar memory of bringing Judy to his local pub, the Stamshaw Hotel, which was in the northern part of town and a fair distance from Southsea. While there, Frank would drop some beer in the dog's water dish as her "tot" after a hard day's work, which may have reminded the pointer of her drinking days aboard the gunships of the Yangtze. Judy was often the center of attention and the main topic of conversation in the pub, and she was invariably recognized around town. "Look, there goes the famous war dog," people would remark. But after a time, she faded into the everyday fabric of the city.

But life was unsatisfying after the epic struggle for life both man and dog had lived through the past few years. On the family memorial website, Frank's children say that "England's societal niceties seemed superficial and somewhat ridiculous to him after his experiences in the camps." This was hardly uncommon among returned POWs.

In addition, there were other factors in Frank's growing discontent.

Lizzie Oliver, a POW historian whose grandfather Stanley Russell sketched Judy in Sumatra, says that during that time "families either went overboard mollycoddling the returned men, or they went the other way and it was never spoken of again. Neither method really worked out well." John Hedley said that his family "had the perception that we had such a rough time of it that we wouldn't be normal. And they treated us as such—we were mollycoddled. And I had a hard time handling that. It's one of the reasons why after just under six months I was back in my old job in Malaya...to be understood, if you like, to feel normal." Indeed, Frank almost never talked of his experiences in the camps, though he was always happy to show off Judy and brag about her courage.

Meanwhile, many returning prisoners found the United Kingdom "quite grim and miserable," in Oliver's words, after a war spent in the tropics. Ironically, despite the circumstances of their time in Asia, many POWs missed the blue skies, green rainforests, and turquoise seas. "By contrast," says Oliver, "the bleak landscape of England in winter led many of them to wonder, 'Is this all there is?'" It didn't help that the winter of 1946–47 was particularly savage, requiring emergency power cuts across the country for weeks, which sent millions out of work when factories shut down. The country lived by candlelight for much of January and February 1947.

Portsmouth itself was very slow to rebuild after the war, adding to the general malaise. Shortages of material and manpower, along with the limp national economy, combined to keep the city in piles of rubble well into the 1950s. The first shop on Commercial Road didn't reopen until 1952. "For years after the war you were putting in reports that read, 'It was on the bomb site on such-and-such a road,'" recalled a frustrated local policeman of the years after the war. The historical homes that lent an inimitable character to Portsmouth and Southsea were gone, replaced eventually by bland, cookie-cutter "council flats," government housing that repulsed more than it inspired.

So Frank was stewing, holding everything inside, living in a cold shell of a town in a deflating country grappling with the loss of its empire, with few prospects save a life of looking backward. The jobs he held were work, not a career.

While it isn't known for sure if Frank suffered from any kind of post-war anguish, be it post-traumatic stress disorder (PTSD) or any variant of it, it would have been difficult for him to merely shrug off the awfulness of his war experience and the jarring transition back to "normalcy." Few had the capacity to deal with the suffering and imprisonment the way Rouse Voisey did—by essentially ignoring his time in the camps completely. "Perhaps nature has wiped it from my mind," he says today, "but I blanked out a lot of the worst of it. Sure, I have nightmares on and off, but I'm mostly okay with what happened to me. I think I actually learned how to do that in the camps—how to shut things out. There it was a necessity, you couldn't last any other way."

So it seems likely that Frank struggled after the wild ride with Judy slowed down (indeed, surely his feelings of discontent would have existed prior to that as well). What of his dog? Judy was outwardly fat and happy, up to her heaviest-ever weight of sixty-one pounds. A crewman from the *Gnat* and *Grasshopper* named John Hornley encountered Frank and Judy in 1948, many years after he had last seen the old ship's mascot. He recognized her instantly, though noted she "was much fatter than when I knew her on the gunboats." Her once solidly brown snout was turning white with age, but otherwise she was outwardly a healthy, loving dog.

But it is possible she too was having trouble dealing with the aftermath of the horror she survived. If humans like Frank were seldom diagnosed with PTSD at the time, canine trauma was utterly ignored. But recent science has confirmed that dogs indeed can and do suffer from a form of PTSD—by some estimates, between 5 and 10 percent of the nearly seven hundred dogs that have seen action in Iraq and Afghanistan have suffered from it. But the syndrome can also develop in household pets that have never heard a shot fired. Given everything that she had been through, dating all the way back to her travails on the streets of Shanghai as a cold, lost puppy, it would have been remarkable if Judy didn't have some form of PTSD. In recent years, dogs showing symptoms of canine PTSD have been prescribed antidepressants similar to the ones used to treat human sufferers, along with Chinese herbs. Of course, this was not an option for Judy. There was little to be done at the time, and few would even notice—except for Frank, of course.

Regardless of the severity of the aftereffects of imprisonment on both Judy and Frank, it was apparent that Frank was looking for an escape, an urge that he had felt since being a teenager, one that led him to join the Merchant Navy and then the RAF. In 1948, an opportunity came from seemingly nowhere that would offer him the chance to travel and take part in something far larger than a tedious job in his hometown—and Frank jumped at it.

The Groundnut Scheme was a plan to offset the food shortages in Britain by sowing tracts of land in Tanganyika (now Tanzania) with nuts—mainly peanuts, as most other nuts grow on trees. The area was among the dwindling regions of the British Empire still controlled by the crown, and it was seen as a way to bring some cheap and plentiful nutrition to the suffering isles. Frank applied for and was granted a position in East Africa with the Overseas Food Corporation, which was the chief organizing body in charge of the Groundnut Scheme.

Unfortunately, peanuts require a great deal of water for cultivation, and the areas chosen to plant were drought-stricken. The Groundnut Scheme collapsed after several years of failure and ultimately became a symbol of England's postwar decline. By 1960, Ian Fleming, in his James Bond story "Quantum of Solace," would have a character refer to a tragic figure who "after a lifetime of service gets shunted off into the groundnuts scheme."

But Frank didn't see it that way. He enjoyed his time in Africa, though at first it appeared the venture would accomplish what the Japanese, ocean, and jungle had failed to do—separate him from his friend. Try as he might, he couldn't get permission for Judy to accompany him. The *Evening Standard* of March 20, 1948, reported on the crisis, noting that "man and dog have not been parted for six years," excepting the quarantine, and that "young Frank Williams, who should be a happy man today... fears he will never see her again."

He appealed for help to the higher-ups at the PDSA, and someone there called the mastermind behind the plan, Lord Leverholme, whose firm Lever Brothers was underwriting the project. Once the big cheese heard that the famous Judy of Sussex wasn't to be allowed to participate in his brainchild, he threw a fit—and magically, all bureaucratic resistance to Judy's travel melted away.

The long flights—Judy's first—from London to Dar es Salaam were uneventful, save an incident in Egypt. While refueling at Wadi Haifa, a customs official came aboard the plane with a flit gun loaded with germ killer and proceeded to spray the interior of the aircraft. Judy was apparently dead asleep in the aisle, but at the approach of the man with a gun, she snapped awake and reverted to wartime footing. Baring her teeth and snarling, she chased the shocked Egyptian out of the plane, across the tarmac, and all the way to the door of the airport building. He managed to slam and lock the door just ahead of the mad dog.

Judy strolled back onto the plane, "grinning like the Cheshire Cat," according to Frank. It had merely been a show to liven up the proceedings, he surmised. Judy always did have a sense of the moment.

On the ground in Tanganyika, Frank was sent to the city of Kongwa for training. He was to be responsible for the successful sowing and harvesting of several large tracts of plantings, scattered across a huge swath of land centered in the Nachingwea District in the southeast part of the country.

From there on out, Judy and Frank were perpetually in a Land Rover. Frank was routinely spending hours each day traveling between growing sites and the villages in between. There were up to a dozen passengers crammed into the extended safari vehicle, but room was always made for Judy.

It was easy to readapt to life in the bush; if anything, snakes, monkeys, and elephants made more sense to Judy than did taxicabs, trolleys, and manicured lawns. "She was at her best when traveling through unsoiled nature," Frank recalled. "She was able to live her hunting instincts by chasing a diversity of wild animals." Incredibly enough, her first action upon seeing a herd of elephants trumpeting through the savanna was to point them out in the classic pointer form excelled at by her breed. Oh, if the men from the *Gnat* could have seen her then! Her paw perfectly raised, her head and tail straight as a ruler in a direct line toward the pachyderms.

"Stop showing off, Judy, I see them," Frank muttered.

Judy became quite aware and wary of the enormous creatures in Africa. But she wasn't scared of them, a fact she proved late one night outside Frank's hut. The footman, Abdul, had taken the bathing tub outside so it could be emptied in the morning. At around two a.m., man and dog were awoken by what sounded like a giant vacuum cleaner operating just outside. Judy raced out the door and started barking furiously. Frank looked and saw a big bull elephant noisily sucking the water in the tub down his trunk, the large full moon perfectly illuminating the scene.

Judy was racing back and forth, barking and leaping at the elephant's trunk, then the tail, as though unable to decide where she wanted to concentrate her fire. The animal, tired of the irritant at his feet, lumbered away without any further incident. That wasn't victory enough for the pointer, however. She seized the tub in her teeth and hauled it back inside the hut. With a final deep bark of warning back out into the night, she lay down, her job finished for the evening.

Judy had less luck chasing the baboons that frequented the area. Her encounters with primates had been unpleasant, dating back to Mickey the monkey on board the *Grasshopper* in Singapore. These baboons came at her in waves, entire families up for a game of tag Judy could never win, as they had the advantage of being able to disappear into the trees at will. A group of the animals would jump all about her, turning Judy this way and that, thoroughly flummoxing the dog. Judy played along for a while, but when the apes began hurling corncobs and sticks at her, she gave up and ceased playing their games.

At one point, Frank took Judy with him on a flight to Dar to handle some business in the capital. He was worried about her—Judy would be forced to fly in a small kennel for the first time, unlike the flights to Africa, where she could roam the aisles at will. As it turned out, Judy was perfectly silent for the length of the flight. Frank discovered why when he went to retrieve her. The kennel had a hole cut at the top so she could stick her head out, and someone had placed a slab of fresh beef within chewing distance.

Indeed, Judy ate virtually the entire portion, leaving only a ring of meat that she couldn't reach. From Shanghai to Sumatra, Judy had learned the hard way that she shouldn't ever pass up a meal, any sort of meal, regardless of how much she ingested at once. The huge lunch left a visible bulge in her belly, making her resemble an anaconda after devouring a goat. Frank picked her up and raced off the plane and into his Jeep before the owner of the beef discovered it had disappeared down Judy's gullet. He tried to take a stern approach but could hardly keep from laughing.

There was another surprise to come during Judy's period in Africa. For the third time in her life, she became pregnant. The father remained anonymous, though unlike at Gloegoer, there were many obvious local possibilities. Seven pups were born to her in 1949, making her total litter twenty-nine pups across eleven years spanning three countries on two continents. She became a mother aboard a warship, in a prison camp, and while farming in the bush. Her progeny brought untold joy to adults and children along the Yangtze riverside and in African villages, as well as to fellow prisoners of war and the mistress of her captor in Sumatra. While the family tree of Judy of Sussex has become hopelessly obscured over the years and miles, it is still worth celebrating that her extraordinary DNA had been passed along so fruitfully.

Hopefully, her pups didn't have to prove their tenacity in quite the same fashion their mother did.

On January 26, 1950, Frank loaded up Judy in his Land Rover and headed out from his home into the bush about twenty kilometers. Frank was to inspect a mining operation that had been created alongside the groundnut planting, as the powers in charge had begun to realize the futility of their agricultural scheme. Judy hung around the area for a little while, but as was her wont, she soon "went hunting on her own," according to Frank.

Judy's liver-and-white coat was getting increasingly gray, her fourteen years also showing in her face and her gait. But she remained happiest when she ranged far and wide in nature—the years in the Sumatran jungle had not soured her or robbed her of this love. She was, at heart, still the wild descendant of wolves, and she yearned to be free. But she was also the domesticated species who always returned to meet Frank at his Jeep when it was time to go.

But on this day, she didn't answer his whistle. She was nowhere to be found, not having "returned from her safari," as Frank put it. He whistled again and again, but no pointer came streaking in from the bush.

"It was about four o'clock in the afternoon when I went looking for her together with some of the remaining workers in the mining area," Frank remembered. "Unfortunately, without any result. At dusk we had to stop our efforts in finding her. We made as much publicity about Judy's disappearance as possible and offered a reward for anyone that could find her."

An intensive subsequent search turned up her tracks, and, worryingly, leopard tracks intercutting them, but no sign of either animal in the flesh. Frank combed the countryside with Abdul, but to no avail. He offered villagers rewards of five hundred shillings if they came across the wayward dog. The days passed, and all gave up hope, except Frank.

Finally, a group of native tribesmen showed up at his door. The men surrounded Abdul and gesticulated wildly. Excited, he got the message.

"They've seen Judy!" he cried.

Judy had been spotted near the village of Chumbawalla, a few hours away. The sun was already setting, and soon night would drop like an anvil, as it did on the African plain. It only made sense to wait until morning, but Frank was far too frantic. He jumped in his Jeep and set off straightaway.

He drove madly into the darkness, going far too fast for the primitive roadways. He crossed roaring rivers, including one where the bridge had been washed away. The engineering required to get across stole hours from him, but still he pushed on. At last, a short time before dawn, he arrived in the village.

Frank gave more than one account of what happened next, each many years apart and long after the fact. In the 1970s, he said that he encountered the headman of the village, who took him to a low thatched hut. Inside was Judy, who was in bad shape. She got up, excited to see Frank, then collapsed with a whine.

A decade later, Frank told the Dutch researchers Neumann and van Witsen that "after a conversation with the chief and the village eldest they agreed to organize a search party. This time with success, because Judy was grabbed the next day and held until I came to get her. She looked awful and was exhausted due to malnourishment." Either way, Judy and Frank were together again.

Why Judy, who had so successfully navigated the deepest, darkest, most impenetrable jungles without incident, suddenly got lost and badly shaken is a mystery. It is quite possible she was spooked by or perhaps chased by a leopard or some other predatory animal. Her usually unerring sense of navigation, keyed by her nose, had been scrambled. At her advanced age she was unable to bounce back easily. She was clearly in bad condition when she stumbled into the village, and had resisted attempts to comfort her. Most likely, she was still trying to sniff out a familiar smell that would lead her back to Frank.

Frank spent hours bathing her, removing the numerous cattle ticks that had affixed themselves to her coat. Judy got a healthy meal of chicken and milk to restore some protein to her system. She was too old and slow to be able to reliably hunt and catch game by this point, and she had likely spent all her reserves searching for her friend.

After devouring her dinner, Judy rolled over and slept for twelve hours straight. "After a couple of days, she seemed to be recovering perfectly," Frank said, and indeed, Judy regained some of her old bounce.

But on the evening of February 16, she awoke and began to cry. Frank stayed with her and tried to lull her back to sleep, but she would wake up and cry at least once an hour. She could scarcely walk and was clearly in terrible pain. In the morning, Frank carried her to the Nachingwea veterinary hospital, the dog still crying in his arms. Overcome with the reality of the situation, Frank couldn't reply to the many welcomes and wishes of good luck. He barely could control his voice when the chief surgeon of the hospital, a Dr. Jenkins, came to see them.

Upon examination, it turned out the awful pain was from a mammary tumor. "It was a race against time to get her up to strength as quickly as possible so that she could undergo the surgery to remove the tumor," Frank recalled. Dr. Jenkins operated as soon as he dared and excised the malignant growth.

In the immediate aftermath, all seemed well, but soon a tetanus infection set in, and Judy was in even worse pain. She began shuddering with convulsions that racked her entire frame, and she was again beginning to resemble the skeleton that survived Sumatra. There was little the undersupplied hospital could do to ease her suffering.

Dr. Jenkins went to see Frank, who was sleepless on a small couch in the waiting room. The doctor had been friendly with Frank and Judy since the day they arrived in Africa. Much as it pained him to say it,

Judy's extraordinary life was in its final moments. Despite his sentiment, and Frank's, it was time to be firm.

"Let me end it, Frank," he said.

Frank could only nod and turn away, tears rolling down his cheeks. Wordlessly, he followed Dr. Jenkins into the small room where Judy struggled to recover from the infection. He watched the vet prepare the hypodermic that would sever the intensely felt bond he and Judy shared, one that stretched across three continents and countless reversals of fortune.

Judy was put down via injection at five o'clock in the afternoon, local time, on February 17, 1950. She was almost exactly fourteen years old, ninety-eight in human terms.

She was buried in her RAF jacket, in a grave close to Frank's hut. She also wore her citations—the Pacific Star campaign medal, the 1939–45 Star, and the Defence Medal, awarded to all participants of the war. Stones were placed over the grave to keep the hyenas away. Frank then began his last service for his beloved dog.

Day after day, hour after hour, he would venture out into the bush looking for white marble after putting in a long workday on the groundnut project. He would cover wide areas of ground without raising his gaze from the dirt, searching for that telltale gleam of white catching the sun. The marble came in large chunks, which Frank laboriously broke down into small bits, hammering away into the wee hours of the night. He then mixed the pieces with concrete, poured it over Judy's grave, and spent many more weeks shaping the contours of the marble slab. His goal was to make a monument for Judy that he thought equaled her love and extraordinary devotion. In his own words, it was to be a "worthy monument for an exceptionally brave dog who was an example of friendship, brave and courageous in all, even the most difficult, circumstances and who meant so much for so many when they lost courage."

He then etched a metal plaque to affix to the side of the monument.

IN MEMORY OF
JUDY DM CANINE VC
BREED ENGLISH POINTER

BORN SHANGHAI FEBRUARY 1936
DIED FEBRUARY 1950
WOUNDED 14TH FEBRUARY 1942
BOMBED AND SUNK HMS GRASSHOPPER
LINGGA ARCHIPELAGO FEBRUARY 14TH 1942
TORPEDOED SS VAN WAERWIJCK
MALACCA STRAIT JUNE 26 1944
JAPANESE PRISONER OF WAR
MARCH 1942–AUGUST 1945
CHINA CEYLON JAVA ENGLAND EGYPT BURMA
SINGAPORE MALAYA SUMATRA EAST AFRICA
THEY ALSO SERVED
"A REMARKABLE CANINE . . . A GALLANT OLD GIRL
WHO WITH A WAGGING TAIL GAVE MORE IN
COMPANIONSHIP THAN SHE EVER RECEIVED . . .
AND WAS IN HER SHORT LIFETIME AN INSPIRATION
OF COURAGE, HOPE AND A WILL TO LIVE, TO
MANY WHO WOULD HAVE GIVEN UP IN THEIR TIME
OF TRIAL HAD IT NOT BEEN FOR HER EXAMPLE
AND FORTITUDE."

But such an extraordinary creature, and such an exceptional life, lived on past physical death. More than a half century later, Judy's bravery and service still earned plaudits and inspired others. Her story lay dormant until the men of the Yangtze gunboats decided to resurrect her memory, leading to the book *The Judy Story* in 1973. Periodically after that, Judy was recognized in the United Kingdom in print and, most notably, by the Imperial War Museum (IWM) in London. In 2006, the IWM mounted a retrospective of animals who served bravely in wartime, and Judy was front and center in the display.

Perhaps the most poignant tribute to the wonderful pointer came on February 27, 1972, during church services in naval towns across the country, including Portsmouth. Judy's name was read aloud in remembrance for the dead, and church bells pealed in her honor. The *Times of London,* in noting the tribute, called Judy "the shaggiest and saltiest seadog that ever howled in an ancient mariner's nightmare," making the friendly liver-and-white pointer sound more like a kraken than a mascot. The article also quoted old *Gnat* shipmate Bill Wilson, the medical attendant who, decades before, had treated Judy's hangovers and called her friend.

"It is right that she should be remembered for her magnificent valour at sea; she is an inspiration to all sailors."

Wilson's only mistake was in limiting the scope of Judy's example to merely sailors.

Epilogue

Shortly after burying Judy, Frank Williams nearly joined his late dog in the everafter. His contract finished with the Groundnut Scheme project, he boarded a flight leaving Tanganyika, the first leg in a long journey back to England. Incredibly, the plane crashed on the slopes of Mount Kilimanjaro. But Frank had survived too much to perish now. He walked away from the crash unhurt and made it back home in one piece.

By that point, Frank had much to live for. He had once again found a close companion, this time of the human variety. An Englishwoman living in Tanganyika had heard about a compatriot who was searching far and wide for matériel to build the proper memorial for his deceased dog. Intrigued, the woman sought out the grieving man and persuaded him to lead her on several guided tours of the countryside surrounding his home. She was a striking, curly-haired brunette almost as tall as Frank, and something sparked during those treks through the bush.

About a year later, with both of them back in England, Frank married the new Mrs. Doris Williams. The couple started a new and peripatetic life together, one that included a son. Frank Alan Williams was born in Yorkshire in 1954. But once again, the crushing weight of home impelled Frank to flee England. In Frank's obituary, his first son (who goes by Alan) said that "the stuffiness and artificial formality of postwar England didn't suit Frank." Remembering how the beauty of Vancouver had struck him when he docked in western Canada as part of the Merchant Navy, Frank persuaded Doris to immigrate there in 1955. Alas, jobs were difficult to come by in British Columbia, so when his old foreman from the Groundnut Scheme, who remembered Frank's competence in Africa, reached out to Frank and offered work in Pakistan, the Williamses packed their bags once again.

After three years in south Asia, where Frank and Doris had another son, David, the family returned to Canada in 1958. A third child, Ann, was born in 1959, completing the immediate clan. This time British Columbia stuck. Frank had trained to become a mechanical engineer, and he was hired to work with a variety of large construction firms, including Laing Construction and Chemetics International. His work took him on a number of overseas assignments, feeding his travel bug, but he also contributed to numerous projects at home, including Vancouver's huge Pacific Centre mall and the downtown Four Seasons Hotel. Most important was the family home he built from scratch in the suburb of Burnaby, where he would live for the next four decades. The family called it Fort Williams. True to his motto—"If a job is worth doing, it's worth doing well"—the house was of the finest craftsmanship.

Frank retained not only his love of animals but also a tangible kinship with them. In 2004, his daughter, Ann, wrote of her father's touch with nature. "He had a way with animals that I have not experienced with anyone else. They always understood him, and always adored him. If an animal was found hurt or suffering, they knew somehow to put their trust in him, and could relax at the sound of his voice, or his caring touch." Ann kept ponies as a girl, and they would invariably follow Frank around the field and crowd around him as he fixed up a fence. He once found a lost skunk and kept it as a pet, often taking it on long walks. "He would wake us up as kids in the middle of the night because he discovered something cool," Alan told the *Vancouver Sun*—once to show the children a giant toad he had found in the backyard.

His children would remember two Franks—one a lighthearted storyteller, the other practical, conservative, and "downright stubborn at times." His love of flight stayed with him despite his negative experience in the RAF, and he maintained pride in his English heritage even though he'd taken every chance to leave the United Kingdom.

Of course, his special relationship with Judy was one his family knew all about. "He didn't advertise it by any means," Alan told the *Burnaby Now* newspaper in an obituary, "but he was happy to talk about it. If you got him going about it, he wouldn't stop. Probably the folks he worked with knew about it, but he didn't go out of his way to say, 'By the way, did you know I had a dog who was a heroine?'

"I think personally the bond he created saved his life," Alan continued in the obituary. "I think she added an element to his life that gave him more reason to live. She took care of him, and he took care of her."

In 1992, at the age of seventy-three, Frank underwent minor surgery, but while recovering in the postoperative ward, he fell out of his bed, with disastrous results. He lost feeling in the lower half of his body and spent the next year in the hospital. When he finally went home, he was a paraplegic, cruelly confined to a wheelchair. His memorial website reads, "He had always been an agile, active, and self-reliant man. The loss of freedom and independence was probably the hardest thing of all." What the Japanese had failed to do was accomplished by a mere slip from bed.

Frank lasted for ten years after the accident, mixing good times with bad, keeping his humor and high spirits around his nurses and his friends but understandably lapsing into melancholy in quiet moments. Infections and sores, aftershocks from the fall that took his mobility, no doubt brought him back to the Sumatran jungle, to the painful skin ulcers and the awful creep of the crippling beriberi.

Frank finally passed away on February 16, 2003, one month past his eighty-fourth birthday. On display in the chapel at Frank's funeral service at the Forest Lawn Chapel in Burnaby was a picture of Frank and Judy. His second son, David, wrote on the memorial website devoted to Frank's memory this touching eulogy: "The only thing that helps me to overcome my grief is the knowledge that you are strolling leisurely along the warm sands of some heavenly beach . . . laughing at Judy, while she valiantly defends the shoreline from yet another impending wave."

Frank lived for fifty-three years after Judy died. He never again owned a dog.

Acknowledgments

One day in the summer of 2013, I was partaking in one of my favorite pastimes since childhood—idly flipping through the pages of *The People's Almanac,* David Wallechinsky and Irving Wallace's massive book of lists, factoids, and esoterica. As I skipped through accounts of "Great Detectives and Their Most Famous Cases" and biographies of fictional characters such as Mr. Spock, my eye was caught by a brief paragraph or two concerning a dog that had become a POW during World War II.

Since that fateful day, Judy and her adventures with Frank Williams have accounted for most of my thoughts and energy. Piercing through the fog that has enshrouded her story after these many decades wasn't easy, and to do so I am thankful for the help of many. My researcher, Dr. Kevin Jones, was instrumental in scouring the archival record and helping me pursue tangents large and small. Without him, this book would be much the poorer (and he provided this rabid *Raiders of the Lost Ark* fan an excuse to address someone as "Dr. Jones").

Several people helped to shed light on the mostly forgotten POW experience in Sumatra. Henk Hovinga not only wrote a book on the subject but was quite helpful in answering my numerous follow-up questions. In the UK, historian Lizzie Oliver not only was kind enough to meet with me but pointed me to the sketches of Judy her grandfather made while held captive. I'd also like to thank Robin Rowland, Meg Parkes, Keith Andrews, Noel Tunny, Kamila Szczepanska, Allan Sheath, Gavan Daws, Bernardine Fiddimore, and Jacqueline Ford.

I was fortunate to get help from any number of excellent research staffs, especially the group at the Imperial War Museum, the UK National Archives, the Portsmouth City Archives, the Southampton Government

Archives, the Greenwich Maritime Museum, and the University of Houston Libraries. Jeff Walden at the BBC Written Archives Centre was also quite helpful. Donald Degraen provided vital translations from Dutch to English. David Lambert drew the maps that help guide the narrative.

John Rosengren and, as always, Mark Sternman read the manuscript and offered invaluable advice. My great friend Ben Wolf and his family provided support, both logistical and emotional, as did my brother, Mark Weintraub, and his family. Thanks as well to Tricia and Amy Burnett, Drew and Karen Voetsch, Rob Spears, Beth Buyert, Yael Sherman, Barry Steig, Jason Kurtz, and Robert Beck. A research journey to England would have been much more difficult without the good graces and warm support of Michael McKinley and Jason Bradley, who, among other charities, provided their beautiful South London flat, which would surely fetch hundreds of pounds per night on Airbnb, for no charge.

I had the great honor of speaking directly with two men who not only survived Pakan Baroe (not to mention several other hellish experiences) but, as of this writing, remain alive and well—dare I say feisty. To George Duffy of New Hampshire, USA, and Rouse Voisey of Norwich, UK, I salute you, and I hope this book does justice to your experiences.

I have had the great fortune of having the sturdy John Parsley edit all three of my books, and they are infinitely better for it, in particular this one. My agent, Farley Chase, was instrumental as always in not just closing deals but helping to shape the narrative and find the story line. My thanks as well to Reagan Arthur, Karen Landry, Shannon Langone, Heather Fain, Sabrina Callahan, and the invaluable Malin von Euler-Hogan for their help from the newly open offices of Little, Brown.

Most of all, I'd like to thank my family, especially my wife, Lorie Burnett, for their patience and loving embrace.

Notes

On a cold night in February 1970, a group of British sailors gathered for a reunion in the proud naval city of Portsmouth, England. They had all served in China in the 1930s, on the Yangtze River, part of the gunboat fleet that served the interests of the crown in that faraway land. As they got to reminiscing, they began to talk incessantly not of adventures on the high seas or especially rowdy shore leave, but of their ship's mascot.

After much consumption of spirits, they decided to find out more about her life, beyond her service on the gunboats. As dogs don't write memoirs, they decided the least they could do was to pen one for her. The mascot, Judy the pointer, left such an impression upon them that even after the men sobered up, they pressed on with their project.

So several of them hunted down more information about Judy's life. They talked to old mates who served with her, wrote letters, scoured the archives. When they were finished, they handed over their findings to an editor named Edwin Varley, who assembled them into a small book called *The Judy Story,* which was published in Britain in 1972.

Thanks to these men—George White, William Wilson, Les Scarle, and Vic Oliver—the full measure of Judy's adventures and extraordinary life, in war and out, found its way out of the murky backwater of untold history. And it is thanks to them that this book is possible.

But there were numerous gaps that needed to be filled in, in order to properly account for Judy's full story. Her "best friend," Frank Williams, as mentioned in the narrative, wasn't the most forthcoming of men when it came to his experiences during the war. While he could have written a fascinating memoir, he chose to remain mostly silent about his life with Judy, at least publicly. He made two exceptions: a long letter he wrote to the Dutch authors H. Neumann and E. van Witsen for their 1984 book about Pakan Baroe called *De Sumatra Spoorweg* (*The Sumatra Railway*), a work not translated into English, and a chat with the gunboatmen who put *The Judy Story* together.

As such, some but not all of Frank's experiences and innermost thoughts, in particular the many decades of his life that didn't involve Judy, are something of a cipher. I filled in the gaps as best as possible through archival and obituary material, but there are some things that, alas, went to the grave with him. Exhaustive efforts to contact his surviving family in Canada, including the hiring of a private investigator and cold calls in the hundreds, were unsuccessful. Hopefully this book finds them, and Frank's descendants will help to complete the picture of their extraordinary father.

Otherwise, source material and asides to the narrative are as follows.

Chapter 1: Mascot

Information on Judy's adoption, episode on the streets of Shanghai, and early days aboard the HMS *Gnat* is from the memories, diaries, letters, and ship's logs collected by Vic Oliver, Les Searle, George White, and William Wilson in *The Judy Story.*

The story of the Japanese sailors' attack on Mr. Soo's shop and the punting of Judy is likewise from *The Judy Story.*

Famine has visited China in outbursts great and small throughout its history. The 1928–30 famine, brought on by severe drought in the north, killed an estimated three million people. In 1936, drought was again the cause of vast famine across the nation, made worse by severe flooding when the rains at last came. Five million people were estimated to have perished in this single, horrible year. In both cases, the poorly coordinated relief efforts served to exacerbate the suffering, rather than end it. The Three Years of Famine at the time of the Great Cultural Revolution, from 1958 to 1961, was even worse, killing anywhere from fifteen to forty-three million people, depending on various estimates.

The saying "If its back faces the sun, it can be eaten" has a southern Chinese, or Cantonese, origin. Denizens of northern China, such as those in Beijing, say of their southern cousins, "The Cantonese will eat anything that swims, except the submarine. Everything that flies, except the airplane, and everything that has legs, except the table."

After their stunning victory over the Russian fleet in 1904, the Japanese set their sights on creating a navy capable of defeating the U.S. fleet in the Pacific. A key thinker was Admiral Satō Tetsutarō, who came up with the "70 percent doctrine"—Japan should have a fleet 70 percent as large as the American Navy, one capable of winning an engagement against the enemy Pacific forces, as well as a follow-up battle against American ships from the Atlantic that would inevitably be sent to reinforce. Soon, Japan was eagerly involved in the dreadnought arms race that swept the great sea powers in the decade before World War I, one that began with England and Germany but expanded to include not only Japan but the United States and France.

Shanghai's Bund (rhymes with *fund*) is known locally as the Zhongshan Dong Yi Lu, or the Zhongshan East First Road. Upon the advent of the British settlement in Shanghai, the Bund was paved and its banks reinforced to keep the Huangpu River at bay, which gives the Bund its name (a bund is an embanked levee wide enough for commercial or pedestrian use). It swiftly became the heart of the city, economically as well as culturally. The area was picturesque, with a radical mix of architectural styles thrown together, and romantic, with lovers strolling arm in arm along the water or canoodling against the floodwall. Commercially, the Bund was home to bank and trading company headquarters, consulates and embassies, and newspaper and publishing houses. Today, it is the first stop for tourists of all nationalities, and while much of its old-world charm has been leached away, it is still a symbol of the city.

Japan invaded Manchuria, the huge region in far northeast China and far eastern Russia, on September 18, 1931. The area swiftly fell under the control of the aggressors, but when the fighting slipped south to the Shanghai area, Japan pulled back, and a United States–brokered peace proposal quelled the fighting for a few years.

Shanghai, which translates to "city on the sea," was a sleepy fishing village until the British named it a treaty port in 1842, after the First Opium War granted the empire access to trade concessions in the Middle Kingdom. After that the strategically placed city's status grew exponentially in both population and import.

Vital statistics on the gunboat fleet, including the specifications, are taken from Angus Konstam's invaluable monograph *Yangtze River Gunboats.*

There were twelve Insect-class gunboats in the Royal Navy on station in China. In addition to the *Gnat* these included the *Aphis, Bee, Cicala, Cockchafer, Cricket, Glow-worm, Ladybird, Mantis, Moth, Scarab,* and *Tarantula.*

The Second Opium War is also called the Arrow War. It was much the same as the First Opium War, in that it pitted western commercial interests, chiefly English and French, against the Chinese rulers, in this case the Qing Dynasty, who chafed under the foreign influence over its trade. The *Arrow* was a British ship seized by Chinese officials in Canton, an incident that precipitated the war, which swiftly escalated out of control from the Chinese perspective. The Qing military was routed, and the sacking of the Forbidden City discussed by the western powers, who settled instead on the burning of the Summer Palaces in Beijing. The Treaty of Tientsin (also called Tianjin) was ratified in 1858, opening the way for the gunboat navy to be deployed on the Yangtze.

The Sand Pebbles was a classic novel written by Richard McKenna before it was turned into a Hollywood production. Paul Newman turned down the starring role of Jake Holman in *The Sand Pebbles,* which was taken by Steve McQueen and resulted in his lone Academy Award nomination for best actor. The movie also features a nineteen-year-old Candice Bergen.

In recent times the use of the term *warlord* to describe the regional strongmen of this period has fallen into politically incorrect sand traps. But that obscures the basic truth that these men were motivated by money and territory, and were not freedom fighters in any capacity, as some revisionists would paint them.

Yang Sen may have been a provincial warlord, but that only scratches the surface of his remarkable, and long, life. He was loyal to Chiang Kai-shek and served in various roles in the Kuomintang regime, mainly as a military governor. During World War II, he was a deputy commander in chief and fled to Taiwan with Chiang after the ascension of the Communists under Mao Tse-tung. A humanist despite his fearsome reputation and activities, Yang believed in the arts and higher education, only hiring college graduates for his staffs and funding parks, museums, and schools throughout his fiefdom. Yang was a dedicated mountaineer and sportsman, and carried the Taiwanese flag into the Olympic Stadium in Mexico City during the Opening Ceremonies of the 1968 Summer

Games. He also became a Taoist master and a bigamist, believing men should have as many wives as they wished (he had at least five, and multiple children from each). He encouraged these women to get an education and become active in community affairs outside of the home. Yang died in 1977 at the age of ninety-three, extraordinary longevity for a man of his time and career path.

The Wanhsien Incident was triggered by Yang's objections to English and American gunboats denying him and his soldiers passage upriver on their ships, a service the Italian and Japanese boats provided for him. English and American skippers pled neutrality, which was rather hypocritical given their mission.

The history of the pointer breed, limned in the narrative, is told at length by Ernest Hart in *Pointers.*

Chapter 2: Dog Overboard

Information on Judy's adventures on (and over) board the *Gnat* is from the memories, diaries, and ship's logs collected by Vic Oliver, Les Searle, George White, and William Wilson in *The Judy Story.*

The life of the average seaman on the gunboats is documented in *Yangtze River Gunboats.*

The concept of the *umwelt* began with Jakob von Uexküll but was pushed into the public arena by Thomas Sebeok, a professor of semiotics at Indiana University. Sebeok saw that the German's work concerned "biological foundations that lie at the very epicenter of the study of both communication and signification in the human animal," not to mention other animals. Where *umwelt* is specific to canines is well described by Jennifer Arnold in *Through a Dog's Eyes.*

Chapter 3: Shore Leave

Judy's love of shore leave, including her induction into the Strong Toppers' Club and her difficulties in training to be a hunting dog, come from memories, diaries, and ship's logs collected by Vic Oliver, Les Searle, George White, and William Wilson for *The Judy Story.* More general stories of shore leave and hijinks along the river are from *Yangtze River Gunboats.*

After nearly four decades of sterling service in the Royal Navy, Admiral Sir Charles Little took over as commander in chief of the China Station in 1936. His next posting, in 1938, was as second sea lord, one of the top positions in the Admiralty. Little was also head of England's staff mission to Washington in 1941, when joint sea operations were discussed, and took over command of the fleet at Portsmouth in 1942.

The idea that it was sound vibrations from an airplane that Judy picked up on aboard the *Gnat* isn't necessarily true. Dogs, like most animals, are indeed better equipped than man to detect vibrations; for example, they are often credited with sensing earthquake tremors in the ground before we do. But airborne vibrations operate at a different pitch. It might have been that Judy was picking up on the airplane engine's whine at a distance far greater than our capacity to hear. The auditory sense of a canine can capture sounds at far higher frequencies than human ears, hence the high-pitched dog whistle. It stands to reason that Judy simply heard the plane before the *Gnat*'s crew.

The term *gwailo* stems from the Cantonese *gwai lo,* or "ghost person."

Gould Hunter Thomas was a New Yorker known to his friends as Jim or Tommy. He graduated from Yale in 1934 and traveled to China shortly afterward. He meant to continue on an around-the-world journey, but a steamship strike marooned him in Shanghai, where he found work with Texaco, selling oil for lamps. While there he kept journals of his three years in Shanghai, which were collected in his wonderful book *An American in China: 1936–39.*

Chapter 4: War

Information concerning the *Gnat*'s operations after the eruption of the Sino-Japanese War is from memories, diaries, and ship's logs collected by Vic Oliver, Les Searle, George White, and William Wilson.

The Marco Polo Bridge predates the famous explorer of China. Built about fifteen miles southwest of modern-day Beijing, it was first constructed in 1189. The simple stone affair built over the Yongding River was washed away and rebuilt in time for Polo to see it and declare, "Over this river there is a very fine stone bridge, so fine indeed, that it has very few equals in the world." Recent rerouting of the Yongding means that at present there is little to no water under the bridge.

Notes on Shanghai during the Japanese onslaught come from contemporary sources, including Gould Hunter Thomas' *An American in China: 1936–39* and Edgar Snow's *Red Star over China,* as well as various quotes gathered by English writer John Gittings at johngittings.com.

Further reading on the breadth of Japanese atrocity in Nanking is available in Iris Chang's *The Rape of Nanking: The Forgotten Holocaust of World War II.*

The interplay between the HMS *Gnat* and the USS *Panay* is revealed in *The Judy Story.* Movement of the gunboats prior to, during, and after the *Panay* bombing comes from *The Judy Story* and *Yangtze River Gunboats,* as well as information from the Naval History and Heritage Command website (history.navy.mil) and multiple contemporary accounts.

Chapter 5: *Amour*

Judy's friendship with local Chinese and details of her love affair with the pointer on the *Francis Garnier* are courtesy of the memories of Vic Oliver, Les Searle, George White, and William Wilson in *The Judy Story.*

The Flying Tigers, officially the 1st American Volunteer Group of the Chinese Air Force (CAF), began when Claire Chennault, a retired Army Air Force officer, accepted an offer from Madame Chiang Kai-shek to make a confidential survey of the CAF on the cusp of the Sino-Japanese War in 1937. Chennault went on to organize a web of airfields and an early-warning system that allowed the CAF to stay competitive in the air with the far superior Japanese Air Force. "All over Free China these human ant heaps rose to turn mud, rocks, lime and sweat into 5,000 foot runways to nest planes not yet built in Los Angeles and Buffalo factories," Chennault wrote in his memoir, *Way of a Fighter.* Of the alarm network he helped form, he wrote, "The Chinese air-raid warning system was a vast spidernet of people, radios, telephones, and telegraph lines that covered all of Free China accessible to enemy aircraft. In addition to continuous intelligence of enemy attacks, the net served to locate and guide lost friendly planes, direct aid to friendly pilots who had crashed or bailed out, and helped guide our technical intelligence experts to wrecks of crashed enemy aircraft."

American pilots began to arrive in China to fly for Chennault in July 1941. They made the American Volunteer Group famous due in part to flying skill (they were credited with downing 296 Japanese airplanes to only 14 lost pilots) and in part to painting their P-40 Curtiss Warhawk airplanes with the ferocious fangs and stripes of the tiger. "Our pilots copied the shark-tooth design on their P-40's noses from a colored illustration in the *India Illustrated Weekly* depicting an R.A.F. squadron in the Libyan Desert with shark-nose P-40's," Chennault wrote. The Flying Tigers disbanded on Independence Day 1942, replaced by the 23rd Fighter Group, also under Chennault.

Stanley Cotterrall's story, as well as the story of Jack Law throwing a Japanese soldier into the Yangtze, are related in *The Judy Story.*

Chapter 6: War Dogs

The *Gnat* wasn't sent directly to beach defense in Egypt—she was hit by a torpedo first. At half past three in the morning on October 21, 1941, the gunboat was nearly destroyed by the German submarine *U-79* off the North African coast, near the border between Egypt and Libya. The bow was blown away, but her forward gun still functioned, so the badly damaged vessel was towed to Alexandria's harbor and used as an antiaircraft weapon until she was scrapped in 1945.

Judy's seasickness and recovery en route to Singapore is recorded in *The Judy Story.*

In the seventh century, around the same time dogs were being used in combat by the Magnesians against the Ephesians (in what is now Turkey), war dogs also were used by the ruler of the Kingdom of Lydia, Alyattes. He reportedly had his soldiers release the hounds upon troops from Cimmeria in a battle. One contemporary source recorded that the Lydian attack dogs were especially effective against cavalry. Some historians believe this occurred before the Magnesians set their dogs upon the Ephesians. Others believe that Hammurabi used dogs as early as 1760 BC, though there is little evidence for this. Alas, there is no single "bible" on the subject of war dogs.

The Spanish conquistadors brought battle mastiffs to the New World. Fully armored and with teeth bared, they served some battlefield functions against the Aztecs but were mainly used to cow the local citizenry. According to Cynthia Jean Van Zandt in *Brothers Among Nations,* the Spanish conquistador and explorer Hernando de Soto used his mastiffs "by pretending to release Indian captives, only to let the dogs loose to hunt them as hounds would chase a fox or other game animal in Europe." Juan Ponce de León used the animals to assist in the quelling of slave rebellions, while Vasco Núñez de Balboa took the mastiffs to Panama, having them rip local chieftains to shreds as an example to others not to resist.

Sallie the Boston terrier was given to the 11th Pennsylvania Volunteers as a puppy and took part in all the regiment's battles, standing on the end of the battle line and barking furiously at the enemy. Wounded at Gettysburg, Sallie was separated from her unit but was later found, weak but alert, standing vigil over several of the dead and wounded from the 11th. She was killed at the Battle of Hatcher's Run in February 1865. Despite heavy Confederate fire, members of her regiment stopped fighting to bury her.

Sallie is one of two dogs depicted on memorials at Gettysburg. The other is an Irish wolfhound that symbolizes the bravery of the Irish Brigade, a group of five regiments—three from New York, one from Pennsylvania, and one from Massachusetts—that fought valiantly at Gettysburg despite heavy blooding in previous engagements at Antietam and Fredericksburg.

War dog service during the American Civil War is nicely chronicled on the website the Loyalty of Dogs, loyaltyofdogs.com.

The Battle of Shiloh is also known as the Battle of Pittsburg Landing, due to the fact that the North tended to name battles after local landmarks or bodies of water, such as Pittsburg Landing on the Tennessee River, while the South named them for the closest town or rail junction, in this case Shiloh, Tennessee. The more commonly used name is generally determined by popular usage; in this case, Shiloh apparently was more memorable or sounded better than Pittsburg Landing. Both General U. S. Grant and General William Sherman refer to "Shiloh" in their respective memoirs, for example.

The Battersea Dogs Home honored the dogs that served from their kennels in World War I at the Collars and Coats Gala Ball in London on October 30, 2014.

Information about Stubby, the World War I hero mutt, comes from several sources, including an article in the *New York Evening World* of July 8, 1921, called "Stubby, Hero Mascot of Seventeen Battles, Showing Decorations for Bravery," as well as a profile on the website Badass of the Week (badassoftheweek.com/sgtstubby.html), information from the History Learning Site (historylearningsite.co.uk/sergeant_stubby.htm), and the children's book *Stubby the War Dog* by Ann Bausum. The dog is often referred to as "Sergeant Stubby," but actually he was never promoted.

A great deal of information about war dogs during World War II can be found in the overview and history *Dogs and the National Defense*, written in 1958 for the U.S. Army by Anna M. Waller.

William Putney's memoir about serving with the war dogs of Guam, *Always Faithful,* provided information about not only the heroism of the dogs but also the bond they formed with their marine handlers, Putney in particular.

Putney's efforts to detrain the war dogs of Guam and place them into civilian homes is mirrored by modern treatment of military dogs that have served in Iraq and Afghanistan. Until very recently, such animals were considered "surplus equipment" and put down after their service. It wasn't until President Bill Clinton signed into law H.R.5314, aka "Robby's Law," that suitable homes for MWD, or military working dogs, were required to be facilitated. Robby was a Belgian Malinois who served in the U.S. Air Force for eight years as a patrol and detection dog. Increasingly arthritic, Robby was scheduled for euthanasia. His handler pleaded with the brass for him to be spared and took his fight public when they refused. The matter came to the attention of the U.S. Congress, resulting in the new codicil enforcing adoption when possible. Unfortunately, the law came too late to save Robby, who was put down in early 2001.

Despite Robby's Law, military dogs remain difficult to place into civilian homes. Anyone interested in adoption of these animals can learn more at websites such as Pets for Patriots (petsforpatriots.org) and the U.S. War Dog Association (uswardogs.org), among others.

Sinbad's heroic, if oft-drunken, service is recounted thanks to an article in the *U.S. Coast Guard Retiree Newsletter* from July 1988 called "Sinbad the Four-Legged Sailor," and the USCG website (uscg.mil/history/faqs/sinbad.asp).

Gander the Newfie's story is told in loving detail in Isabel George's book *The Dog That Saved My Life.*

Chapter 7: Frank

George White recounted his tale of boarding the *Grasshopper* for the first time and of meeting Judy the pointer and Mickey the monkey in *The Judy Story.*

The chronology of the *Grasshopper*'s bridge officers can be found, ironically enough, at the website uboat.net (uboat.net/allies/warships/ship/13127.html).

Frank Williams' background is, alas, only partially known. Much information can be gleaned from the memorial website his family prepared upon his passing in 2003, frankwilliams.ca. The Portsmouth in which he grew up is detailed through tax, death, and voting records held at the Portsmouth City Archives, as well as *The Portsmouth That Has Passed* by William Gates; *Sunny Southsea* by Anthony Triggs; "People of Portsmouth," a collection of oral histories by John Stedman; and Wally Greer's oral history "Pompey Boy in the 1930s and '40s," the latter two held at the Portsmouth City Archives. The author's visit to the seaside city also informed the passage.

Information about Frank's Merchant Navy (MN) service is likewise scant. The basic information comes from his official MN records held at the Southampton Government Archives. Further details were provided by the National Maritime Museum in Greenwich and by Frank's memorial website.

When Frank referred to his complexion as "fresh" in his Merchant Navy records, he most likely meant it as a synonym for "Caucasian."

The SS *Harbledown,* upon which Frank served in the Merchant Navy, came to an unfortunate end during World War II. On April 4, 1941, she was sunk by the U-boat *U-94* off the Icelandic coast while in a large convoy bringing wheat from Portland, Maine, to England. Sixteen men perished, while twenty-five more were plucked from the sea and brought to safety in Liverpool.

John "Cat's Eyes" Cunningham became a national hero thanks to his performance in the skies during the Battle of Britain. When he told reporters his success was due to eating carrots, a generation of kids began to eat their vegetables.

In addition to radar, the Tizard Mission to Washington passed several other advanced scientific programs across the Atlantic, including Commodore Frank Whittle's jet engine idea; designs for gyroscopes, gun sights, and plastic explosives; and the Otto Frisch–Rudolf Peierls memorandum, which outlines the technical possibility of the atomic bomb. Yes, Frisch and Peierls were Germans, but they had immigrated to England and conducted their research at the University of Birmingham.

The particular breakthrough shared in the radar realm during the Tizard Mission was the cavity magnetron, a high-powered vacuum tube that created microwaves by blasting electrons past a series of open metal cavities, creating an effect not dissimilar to sound waves emanating from an electric guitar. It was invented in 1940 at the University of Birmingham in England, but since the United Kingdom was prostrate from fighting the Nazis, it was given to American scientists by Tizard. The magnetron was enhanced and mass-produced, and its performance was significantly greater than that of more rudimentary German and Japanese radars.

Frank Williams' precise military service history cannot be known without obtaining his service records, which can only be done by family members. But the important movements can be determined by his recollections in *The Judy Story* and to Neumann and van Witsen, as well as remembrances from other members of the RAF radar units in Singapore, mainly Stanley Saddington and Fred Freeman. The former's memoir, *Escape Impossible,* is held at England's National Archives; the latter's private papers are at the Imperial War Museum.

The history of radar operations in Singapore comes from RAF files held at the National Archives, in particular "Signals Vol. IV—Radar in Raid Reporting" (RAF AIR 41/12), "RDF Stations Overseas Policy" (RAF AIR 20/3032), and "History of the RDF Organisation in the Far East" (RAF AIR 20/193).

Memories of prewar Singapore come from various contemporary sources as well as the private papers of J. Cuthbertson, held at the Imperial War Museum; Cecil Brown's memoir *Suez to Singapore;* and *Singapore's Dunkirk* by Geoffrey Brooke.

Details of British overconfidence vis-à-vis the Japanese threat come from Brown's memoir as well as John Dower's *War Without Mercy.*

On May 23, 1941, the German super battleship *Bismarck,* the pride of the Kriegsmarine, had made its attempt to break through the Royal Navy blockade of German ports and wreak havoc in the Atlantic. Stationed off Iceland for just such an engagement, the largest British battleship, HMS *Hood,* steamed to intercept, along with *Prince of Wales.* The ships exchanged heavy fire with *Bismarck* beginning a few minutes before six a.m. The *Hood* was destroyed in a matter of moments, exploding with the loss of all 1,419 on board save but three lucky survivors.

Wales sustained several hits as well, and Captain John Leach, an austere, rail-thin forty-seven-year-old Australian, made a controversial decision to break off and recover, rather than continue the fight. It was the proper move, given the damage she had suffered, the strength of the enemy force, and the deflating sight of the *Hood*'s demise moments before. Yet some in the Admiralty felt Leach should have been court-martialed.

Dozens of warships and planes chased the *Bismarck,* which was damaged in the *Hood/Wales* encounter and was racing to safety. A torpedo from a warplane destroyed *Bismarck*'s steering gear, and a sustained bombardment from British ships finished her, killing all but 114 of 2,200 crewmen.

The concerted attack upon the *Bismarck* is the stuff of naval lore. There was a popular film based on the engagement, *Sink the Bismarck!,* released in 1960, which led to a country music hit of the same name (except the ship was misspelled as *Bismark*) by Johnny Horton and Tillman Franks, which reached number three on the charts. A particularly good documentary on the sinking aired on the Military Channel series *Dogfights,* which provides a three-dimensional perspective.

Chapter 8: Force Z

The British experiences with their war dogs are reported in the American War Department's official history *Dogs and the National Defense,* written by Anna M. Waller in 1958.

In addition to Pearl Harbor, Singapore, and Siam, the Japanese struck several other places on December 7 (or 8, depending on the international date line), 1941, including Guam, Wake Island, Hong Kong, and, most infamously, the Philippines. Several hours after Pearl Harbor, the Japanese destroyed the U.S. Army Air Force B-17 bomber fleet at Clark Field in the Philippines on the ground, as well as a third of the fighters based there and the lone radar system. Why the planes hadn't been scrambled or sent to safety upon word of the Pearl Harbor attack reaching General Douglas MacArthur's headquarters is a subject of much controversy, then and now.

The incredible story of Ian Forbes comes from his private papers held at the Imperial War Museum, as well as "The Real-Life Uncle Albert," a piece in the *London Daily Mail* published June 14, 2013. The Uncle Albert in the headline references a character on the popular BBC sitcom *Only Fools and Horses,* which aired between 1981 and 1991. On the show, Uncle Albert Trotter served during World War II on seven different ships that were sunk by torpedoes or bombs, including two during peacetime. But he lived on to pursue a lucrative postwar career staging falls down the cellar stairs of pubs across London in order to collect insurance claims.

Cecil Brown's extraordinary experiences aboard the HMS *Repulse* are recounted in his memoir, *Suez to Singapore.*

Personal details of Brown's life are further pulled from his *Los Angeles Times* obituary from October 27, 1987. Brown had left his newspaper job in Ohio for the sea, craving adventure and the salt-packed life. He worked on a freighter for a spell, but when his ship sailed into Soviet waters in the early 1930s, he felt the old twitching of the reporter's urge to share what he witnessed with the world. Besides, there was money to be made. So Brown filed several stories from the Black Sea ports he visited, commenting acidly on the Communists, who had closed themselves off from the world.

Upon returning to the States, the lanky, long-faced Brown (who bore a resemblance to the actor Anthony Edwards) fell back into reporting, and when conflict began bubbling to the surface in Europe, he returned as a freelancer. In 1940, CBS hired him, at Edward R. Murrow's urging (Brown was one of the fabled Murrow Boys), and he covered Mussolini's Italy from Rome. Typical of Brown's commentary was his observation of "a comic-opera army preparing for slaughter under orders of a Duce with a titanic contempt for his own people."

Brown was disappointed he wound up aboard the *Repulse* rather than the *Prince of Wales,* and gloomily assumed he would miss all the real action taking place in Siam and Malaya. The *Repulse* too had an animal mascot—a black kitten, which was weakened from rickets but playful. Brown dangled a string over her head as he moaned to a Royal Marine, "What the hell are we going to do for four days?" "Oh, we may have something," the young lieutenant answered. "We might even have movies. We had a picture last night—*Arise, My Love,* with Claudette Colbert." Instead, Brown witnessed history when the Japanese attacked.

Even as the race to construct ever-larger and heavily armed battleships gripped naval departments from Washington to London to Berlin and Tokyo, U.S. Army General Billy Mitchell and British Air Commodore Charles Rumney Samson were early, and loud, proponents of the changing doctrine in naval warfare. Both men spent the years after World War I proselytizing on the way airpower would utterly transform oceanic combat. Both were, in the main, ignored. And both would wind up resigning their commissions in order to make plain their beliefs (Mitchell labeled the American investment in battleships rather than aircraft carriers "almost treasonable administration of the national defense" and was court-martialed for his trouble). The action of December 10, 1941, would prove them utterly correct.

The aircraft carrier meant to be sent with Force Z to Singapore was the HMS *Indomitable.* She served in the Indian Ocean; the Mediterranean, where she was slightly damaged; and finally in the Pacific, where she was hit by a kamikaze attack on May 4, 1945. *Indomitable* survived and went on to support the liberation of Hong Kong, her final action of World War II. In 1947, she carried the British national rugby team to a series of test matches in Australia, thus giving the team its nickname, the Indomitables.

In response to the arrival of *Prince of Wales* and *Repulse* in Singapore, Japanese Admiral Isoroku Yamamoto deployed an extra three-dozen medium-range Mitsubishi bombers to the landing force he planned to use in an invasion of Malaya. The pilots began training specifically for a potential attack on the capital ships.

The poor performance of the radar systems is illuminated by Frank's recollections to Neumann and van Witsen, along with Stanley Saddington's memoir and the RAF report "Signals Vol. IV—Radar in Raid Reporting." A Chinese businessman offered British pilots a bottle of champagne for every Japanese plane they shot down. He gave few away.

The loss of Singapore remains a tremendously controversial episode in British military history. Scapegoats abound, as in any colossal battlefield failure, although in this case one may have to tip the cap to the attacking Japanese under General Yamashita before calling out any of the British commanders or even Winston Churchill. Even a better-prepared British defense would almost certainly have been forced to surrender eventually, especially once Japan took control of the skies over Singapore and Malaya.

For more reading on the British side of the disaster at Singapore, pick up *Singapore Burning* by Colin Smith, *The Fall of Singapore* by Frank Owen, and *Singapore: The Chain of Disaster* by S. Woodburn Kirby. Geoffrey Brooke also provides some interesting perspective in his memoir, *Singapore's Dunkirk.*

The majority of operational details about the *Grasshopper*'s movements in the days before the fall of Singapore were destroyed in the Japanese onslaught. Some information is related in *The Judy Story* by George White and Les Searle. More comes from other Royal Navy files held at the National Archives, including "HMS *Grasshopper* Packet" (WO 361/404), although the larger segment of this information concerns the actions of *Dragonfly* and *Scorpion.*

Details of Singapore's last days before the fall come from multiple contemporary sources, the books about Singapore's loss referred to above, and official reports written by the War Ministry held at the National Archives.

Frank's escape to the docks, along with the general chaos of those last days, is informed by his recollections to Neumann and van Witsen, as well as Stanley Saddington's *Escape Impossible,* Arthur Donahue's *Last Flight from Singapore,* and Geoffrey Brooke's *Singapore's Dunkirk.*

C. Yates McDaniel's final filing from Singapore appeared across the United States and elsewhere under the Associated Press banner on February 12, 1942, with the headline "Last Message from Singapore."

The Vickers Vildebeest (often Anglicized as Wildebeest) dated to 1928. The ones McDaniel saw flying were among the last ones to see combat with the RAF.

Chapter 9: Flight

Details recounting the hellish scenes at Keppel Harbor as the British abandoned Singapore are from multiple sources, including Frank's recollection to Neumann and van Witsen; George White in *The Judy Story* and in an interview he gave to the *Portsmouth Evening News* on July 27, 1945; Leonard Williams' (no relation to Frank) obituary in the *Times of London* of January 22, 2007; Geoffrey Brooke's *Singapore's Dunkirk;* contemporary accounts by C. Yates McDaniel and Athole Stewart; Stanley Saddington's *Escape Impossible;* Frank Owen's *The Fall of Singapore;* and Colin Smith's *Singapore Burning,* along with dozens of accounts collected by the Ministry of War in documents stored at the National Archives, and the private papers of J. A. C. Robins (5153) and Ian Forbes (18765), which are held at the Imperial War Museum.

Needless to say, accounts concerning numbers and identities of the people embarking on the rescue ships vary wildly. I have quoted those whose accounts are most trustworthy and, as the British themselves did in the postwar aftermath, gave rough figures where no precision exists.

Wong Hai-Sheng's famous photograph is also known as "Bloody Saturday" and "Motherless Chinese Baby." Wong owned a camera shop in Shanghai, and on August 14, 1937, he responded to particularly heavy bombing by racing out to capture the carnage. At about four p.m., Japanese planes attacked Shanghai's South Station, ripping apart refugees trying to escape the city.

Wong told competing versions of how his photo came to be, leading some (especially in Japan) to claim it was faked or staged. In August 1945, Newsreel Wong shared the story of his famous shot with syndicated columnist Lowell Thomas. In this account, Wong was at the station under bombardment and noticed another wave of Japanese planes coming:

> I only had about fifty feet of unexposed film left, and thought I'd better use it up and put in a fresh roll to be ready to shoot when the bombs fell. So I pointed my camera at whatever happened to be nearby, and shot the rest of the film. Nearby was the track, covered with litter, wreckage, and horror, and I pointed my camera that way. I didn't notice anything in particular.... As it happened, the plane that approached did nothing in particular, so my hurry was needless.

Wong sent the film undeveloped to his usual newsreel company in the United States, the Hearst Company, and forgot about it. "Weeks later," Wong continued to Thomas, "an

American officer I knew came over and remarked, 'Say, Newsreel, that baby picture was sweet.' "

"What baby picture?"

"The one you made at the Shanghai bombing, the one at the railroad track."

I couldn't remember any such thing.

The American pulled out a copy of *Life* magazine and showed it to Wong for the first time:

> I looked at it and still scored a blank... obviously I had shot the picture... quite by accident the camera had happened to make a perfect shot of a crying child, which in the haste and chaos of the horror, I hadn't noticed.
>
> It really is quite a picture.

But years later, the National Press Photographers Association put out a book called *Great Moments in News Photography,* compiled by John Faber. In this version, Wong states that he was photographing the bombing with not only his movie camera but also a Leica still camera, and saw a man place the crying baby on the platform. The man then moved off to rescue another child, at which point Wong snapped the image. "I ran toward the child, intending to carry him to safety, but the father returned," Wong said. He then took the film to the offices of the China Press and excitedly pointed out the baby image to an editor there, exclaiming, "Look at this one!"

Whatever the genesis of the shot, it remains one of the definitive war images of the century. Estimates of how many people viewed the baby wailing amid the nightmare range from 80 to 136 million. Frank Capra used the film in his 1944 documentary *The Battle of China.* Andy Warhol painted a version of the image in the 1960s. Lowell Thomas himself compared the image to that of Joe Rosenthal's fabled photo of marines raising the American flag over Iwo Jima. Wong survived the war and died at his home in Taiwan in 1981.

The image is easily found on the Internet—an example is at oldhistoricphotos.com/bloody-saturday-a-crying-chinese-baby-amid-the-bombed-out-ruins-of-shanghais-south-railway-station-saturday-august-28-1937/.

Details of the incredible story of the *Vyner Brooke* are from Ian W. Shaw's *On Radji Beach,* Noel Tunny's *Winning from Downunder,* Barbara Angell's *A Woman's War,* and Betty Jeffrey's memoir *White Coolies,* as well as numerous contemporary articles in the Australian press.

There is no relation between Sir Vyner Brooke, the last rajah of Sarawak, and Geoffrey Brooke, the naval officer who escaped death aboard the *Prince of Wales* and while escaping Singapore.

The liner *Empire Star* carried well over two thousand people out of Singapore on February 11, despite having cabin accommodations for just sixteen. Most were military personnel and nurses, but roughly 135 were Australian army deserters, who shot and killed the Royal Navy Captain of the Dockyard, T. K. W. Atkinson, and forced their way on board at rifle point. The *Empire Star* was attacked by Japanese airpower on the twelfth but survived the damage and made it to Batavia, where the Aussies were arrested. After repairs, she sailed for Fremantle, Australia, on the sixteenth, bringing those on board to safety.

The name of the capital city of Java, Batavia, was also in its final days. When the Japanese conquered the Dutch, Indonesian nationalists joined with their fellow Asians in a propaganda triumph for the Greater East Asia Co-Prosperity Sphere, and tossed aside the colonial name in favor of the pre-Dutch nomenclature, Jakarta. Actually, the original name of the city was Jayakarta, but it was shortened for modern times.

Chapter 10: Day of Destruction—February 14, 1942

The story of the sinking of the *Grasshopper* and her sister ship *Dragonfly* is informed by George White's, John Devani's, and Les Searle's recollections in *The Judy Story;* Ian Forbes' (18765) and J. A. C. Robins' (5153) private papers at the Imperial War Museum; Forbes' statement held at the National Archives (ADM 1/30/600); Geoffrey Brooke's *Singapore's Dunkirk;* and dozens of accounts held at the National Archives, notably "Various Reports on Sinkings of HMS *Grasshopper* and *Kung Wo*" (ADM 199/622A), as well as collected at kinnethmont.co.uk/1939-1945_files/thos-ingram/hms-grasshopper.htm.

At the outset of the war, there was great confusion in identification of Japanese planes, as there was no standard set by the Allies. Each country had different names for enemy planes, and even the American Army Air Force and U.S. Navy used different verbiage. Finally, an Army Air Force intelligence officer named Captain Frank T. McCoy simplified and unified the identification effort. Fighters were given boys' names, every other type of plane given girls' names. A Tennessean, McCoy livened up the process by using hillbilly names, like Rufe and Zeke, the original name for the fabled Mitsubishi A6M navy fighter, better known as the Zero. Few in the military cottoned to calling such a potent weapon by such a goofy name, so Zeke was put out to pasture. McCoy used a personal touch when possible, naming planes after his friends; for example, the Mitsubishi G4M bomber, whose large gun turrets resembled female breasts, was called the Betty after a busty pal of McCoy's.

Lieutenant Sidney Iley's death remained unannounced and unofficial for a long period. His wife, Betty, a reserve in the Women's Naval Service back in England, only knew that her husband had gone missing in the mad race away from Singapore. Betty attempted to maintain her poise, aware that loved ones were missing all over the world. For more than a year she woke up in the morning expecting to find out the truth about Sidney, one way or the other. Finally, she couldn't take it anymore. On July 28, 1943, Betty placed an ad in several newspapers across England begging readers for information.

> ILEY, Sidney L, Lt RN; missing since the fall of Singapore. Any information gratefully received by his wife, third Officer Betty Iley, W.R.N.S. 22 Barkston Gardens S.W.5.
>
> (Australian papers please copy)

Alas, no one taking the paper in either England or Australia had been in the Lingga Archipelago that fateful Valentine's Day of 1942. It wouldn't be until December 8, 1945, that the death notice was released by the military into newspapers across the United Kingdom:

> ILEY Missing since fall of Singapore now officially presumed killed in Feb. 1942 Sidney L. Iley Lieut., Royal Navy, H.M.S. *Dragonfly,* beloved husband of Betty (nee Foulk), Stokesley, Middlesbrough, Yorks.

The details of the sinking of the *Tien Kwang* and the *Kuala* are taken from Frank's recollections to Neumann and van Witsen, Stanley Saddington's *Escape Impossible,* Geoffrey Brooke's *Singapore's Dunkirk,* the private papers of John Williams (no relation to Frank or Leonard) held at the Imperial War Museum (17378), and dozens of accounts held at the National Archives, especially "Various Reports on Sinkings of HMS *Kuala* and *Tien Kwang*" (CO 980/237). As the *Tien Kwang* carried far more military personnel than the *Kuala,* especially RAF servicemen, the majority of accounts pertaining to her sinking are from documents prepared for the RAF; others are in more general files. Also helpful was the remembrance of Brian Napper, a boy at the time of the flight from Singapore, who told his story to the BBC website bbc.co.uk/history/ww2peopleswar/stories/55/a7697055.shtml.

The story of the massacre of the Australian nurses on Bangka Island is recounted in *On Radji Beach, Winning from Downunder, White Coolies, Singapore's Dunkirk,* and multiple news accounts in the Australian press. Good details come from an account at angellpro.com.au/Bullwinkel.htm#Massacre. Also helpful is the Australian War Memorial account of Vivian Bullwinkel's life at awm.gov.au/exhibitions/fiftyaustralians/5.asp.

The Bangka Strait was nicknamed Bomb Alley due to the huge number of ships destroyed there by the Japanese—some seventy boats of varying sizes and flags were sunk in the area in the forty-eight-hour period from the morning of the thirteenth.

Amid the civilian refugees on the *Vyner Brooke* were a sprightly four-year-old boy named Mischa Warman and a haughty woman who called herself Dr. Goldberg. Both were Jewish refugees of the war in Europe. Mischa was beloved by the nurses for his eager energy. The Warman family had fled Poland ahead of the Nazi onslaught, traversed the Soviet Union, come down through China to Shanghai, and fled to Singapore roughly one year after Judy and the *Grasshopper* had traveled the same route. Now they were fleeing war once more, hoping to get to Australia. He survived the sinking, and the war, and afterward was sent to Shanghai, where some relatives had stayed.

Dr. Goldberg, by contrast, was full of attitude, and her strong Berlin accent didn't win her many friends. Rumors abounded that she had been detained by the British on suspicion of spying in Singapore, but obviously she had been cleared, given her evacuation permit and presence on the ship. Upon jumping into a lifeboat, the pompous Dr. Goldberg remained arrogant as ever, insisting that she was "a mother of three and therefore more important" than anyone else on the raft. A nurse named Veronica Clancy couldn't stand any more of this attitude and began raining blows upon the astonished doctor. At length they were separated, and an uneasy peace settled in. The boat carrying Dr. Goldberg and her pugilistic enemy thought rescue was at hand when a small launch carrying, astonishingly, two Australian airmen, pulled up and took them aboard. They offloaded at a small jetty on what appeared to be a deserted stretch of Bangka. One airman went ahead for a look, only to come tearing back to the launch. He and his buddy cast off and disappeared into the murk, leaving the nurses, most of them either stark or nearly naked, to be captured by a Japanese patrol almost as nonplussed as the group they had just taken into custody.

Captain Borton was also taken captive, having not gone down with the ship.

The possibility that Vivian Bullwinkel and the other nurses on Radji Beach were sexually assaulted before they were slain is the subject of intense study by historian Barbara Angell in *A Woman's War.* Clues in the damage to Vivian's uniform are part of her argument, as is a Japanese soldier quoted in an Australian War Crimes inquiry by a Captain James G. Godwin. The soldier said the nurses had been "raped incessantly" before they were herded into the water and executed. And later in life, the surviving nurses would obliquely mention a secret never to be revealed. While there is no definitive evidence, this particular horror certainly wouldn't be surprising. Soldiers sexually assaulting captured women is an abuse of power and a terrifying aspect of war that has been going on since the dawn of conflict.

Geoffrey Brooke passes along the detail that the Japanese officer responsible for the massacre killed himself in Manchuria later in the war in *Singapore's Dunkirk.*

Chapter 11: Posic

Much of what happened on Posic comes from George White, John Devani, and Les Searle's memories recounted in *The Judy Story;* Ian Forbes' (18765) and J. A. C. Robins' (5153) private papers held at the Imperial War Museum; *Singapore's Dunkirk;* and multiple accounts given to the Royal Navy in documents held at the National Archives.

Canine licking behavior stems from pups cueing their parent to regurgitate freshly killed meat, a scientific fact George White likely cared not to know as Judy happily licked his face.

An account of Judy's water-finding heroics appeared in the September 1975 edition of *Look and Learn,* a British periodical aimed at young adults. In this article, the story of Judy's discovery of water on the island is told this way:

> Each time the men asked her to search she ran down the beach barking excitedly. Eventually one of the sailors grew so intrigued by her curious behavior that he dug a hole where Judy was scratching in the sand. As the hole deepened it began to fill up with water and more water.

Dogs have a sense of smell that is estimated to be millions of times more sensitive than that of humans. The skin tissue inside the nose of a dog is replete with receptors that identify smell with far greater detail than we are capable of, as we have nowhere near so many receptors. According to experiments, a dog can sniff out a teaspoon of sugar in a million gallons of water, roughly the equivalent of two Olympic-size swimming pools.

Of course, water is odorless, at least to humans, and if Judy could truly "smell water" she would have been overwhelmed by the fragrance at all times, especially given that she had spent most of her life to that point aboard boats (and the Yangtze was a particularly smelly body of water). Indeed, it was probably her long experience and familiarity with the smell of organisms that live in water that allowed her to so readily find it underground, in particular fresh water that clearly smelled different to her than the seawater in which she had just been immersed.

The Spanish Civil War of 1937 was fought in a crucial commercial location, lying astride major trade routes, and both the Nationalists and the Republicans ignored maritime law when it suited them, often capturing internationally flagged vessels and relieving them of their cargo. In response, much of the British Home Fleet and the French Navy took up operations off the Iberian coast. George White probably served on one of the five class B destroyers the Royal Navy sent to the area, though precisely upon which one he delivered an infant isn't exactly known—unless one of his descendants steps forward and contacts the author to allow his service record to be closely examined.

Chapter 12: Pompong

The doings on Pompong Island are taken mainly from Frank's recollections to Neumann and van Witsen; *Escape Impossible; Singapore's Dunkirk;* John Williams' private papers held at the Imperial War Museum (17378); and multiple accounts in National Archives documents, in particular "Report of Charles Baker" (NA 199/357) and "Various Reports on Sinkings of HMS *Kuala* and *Tien Kwang*" (CO 980/237).

Molly Watts-Carter's statement on her incredible survival at sea is recounted in the National Archives document "Singapore and Far East Personal Experiences" (WO 106/2550).

William Caithness would make it all the way back to South Africa, managing to avoid the fate of so many others who jumped off his boat at Pompong. After the war, one Royal Navy officer commented, "If ever a man deserved a distinction it was Lieutenant Caithness.... He was responsible for the lives of more than six hundred men, women and children. Despite agonizing wounds and partial paralysis, he directed the rescue of the survivors and the treatment of the wounded. Unfortunately, the custom of the Service in these circumstances is that the Captain remains silent. Deeds and not words." When victory was at hand in 1945, his esteem in Singapore was remembered. He captained the flagship of the Straits Steamship Company that led the Royal Navy ships back into the recaptured island harbor, and he was accorded the honor of leading the victory parade through the streets of the Lion City.

Other ships to take survivors of the *Tien Kwang* and the *Kuala* sinkings were the *Plover,* a small log-burning launch, the junk *Hung Jao,* the coastal ship *Numbing,* and the barge *Heather.*

Chapter 13: Sumatra

Details of the various mad dashes from Singkep to Padang are taken from a legion of materials, including Frank's recollections in *The Judy Story* and to Neumann and van Witsen; George White's, John Devani's, and Les Searle's accounts in *The Judy Story, Singapore's Dunkirk,* and *Escape Impossible;* Peter Hartley's *Escape to Captivity;* the private papers of John Williams (17378) and Ian Forbes (18765) held at the Imperial War Museum; and myriad documents stored at the National Archives, in particular "Evacuation from Singapore Across Sumatra" (WO 141/100), "Far East Anglo Dutch Operations" (HS 1/272 and 1/273), and "Report of Charles Baker" (NA 199/357).

Thorium (atomic symbol Th, atomic number 90) has been eyed by countries, in particular the United States, for decades as a wonder fuel. Thorium atoms don't split but absorb neutrons when irradiated. A tiny fraction of the material then becomes fissionable (as uranium 233) and can be used for nuclear devices. But it never did work well enough to replace plutonium as the more reliable activator of nuclear chain reactions, a fact that cost the United States untold millions in research and development programs, and continues to hemorrhage waste-containment dollars. Alvin Weinberg, the longtime director of the Oak Ridge National Laboratory, lost his job in large part because he favored thorium over plutonium. The element remains a holy grail for dreamers and thinkers in the scientific realm; "Thorium-Fueled Automobile Engine Needs Refueling Once a Century" reads a recent, wondrous headline in an oil industry newsletter (industrytap.com/thorium-fueled-automobile-engine-needs-refueling-once-a-century/15649).

The Battle of the Java Sea was the largest naval engagement since the Battle of Jutland in 1916, but unlike that stalemate between British and German navies, the combat of late February 1942 was one-sided. Japanese forces sank two cruisers and three destroyers, including *Stronghold* with Hoffman and Forbes aboard, and killed twenty-three hundred sailors. Japan suffered only light damage to a single vessel. The victory paved the way for all of the Dutch East Indies to fall rapidly into the expanding Empire of the Rising Sun.

George White tells of his miraculous journey across the Indian Ocean to safety in an appendix in *The Judy Story,* as well as in an interview in the *Portsmouth Evening News* of July 27, 1945, entitled "Portsmouth Petty Officer's Escape from Singapore."

Unbeknownst to White, he had been listed as missing in the Portsmouth-area press since the sinking of the *Grasshopper.* Shortly after he arrived in India he managed to get word to his wife of three years and his parents that he was alive and well, a fact that also appeared in the local newspapers.

Captain William Bligh was set adrift by the HMS *Bounty* mutineers on April 28, 1879. Bligh navigated the twenty-three-foot launch with nothing but a quadrant (an instrument that measures angles) and a pocket watch, with no charts or a compass, for an incredible 3,618 nautical miles. Forty-seven days after being cut loose, Bligh piloted the boat into the harbor at Timor in the Dutch East Indies, the island on the western edge of the archipelago, closer to Australia than Sumatra or Singapore. Bligh returned to Britain and reported the mutiny to his superiors, just over two years after he set sail from England on the *Bounty.*

Details of Judy's trek across the Sumatran interior come from Les Searle and John Devani in *The Judy Story* and by Taff Long's recollections in *Singapore's Dunkirk.*

Incredibly, the multiple rescues in the waters around Sumatra weren't the end of Bill Reynolds' contributions to the war effort. In the fall of 1943, he helped conceive and lead an attack on Japanese warships docked in Keppel Harbor called Operation Jaywick. The invaluable *Krait,* perfectly camouflaged as a Japanese fishing vessel (which it was), slipped near the harbor and put ashore several commandos, who used canoes to row to the warships and attach limpet mines to their hulls. Seven ships were sunk or seriously damaged, and all the raiders got away scot-free. Unfortunately, the Japanese assumed the mission had to have been carried out by local saboteurs, and began a wave of reprisals on the Chinese and Malay inhabitants of Singapore, as well as Allied POWs held nearby. The resulting deaths and torture took place on October 10, 1943, a date that ensured it would become known as the Double Tenth Incident.

Chapter 14: Padang

The details of the chaos at Emmahaven Harbor in Padang and the wait for Japanese capture are sourced by Frank's recollections in *The Judy Story* and to Neumann and van Witsen; Les Searle's and John Devani's memories in *The Judy Story; Escape Impossible; Singapore's Dunkirk; Escape to Captivity;* John Williams' private papers held at the Imperial War Museum (17378); and multiple documents at the National Archives, in particular "Personal Statement RAF F/O R. Knowles" (RAF AIR 20/5577), "Evacuation from Singapore Across Sumatra" (WO 141/100), "Far East Anglo Dutch Operations" (HS 1/272 and 1/273), "Various Reports on Sinkings of HMS *Grasshopper* and *Kung Wo*" (ADM 199/622A), "Singapore and Far East Personal Experiences" (WO 106/2550), "HMS *Grasshopper* Packet" (WO 361/404), and "Various Reports on Sinkings of HMS *Kuala* and *Tien Kwang*" (CO 980/237).

The account of the ship captured by the Dutch and returned to Padang comes from John Purvis, who over a ten-year period in the 1950s recorded his wartime experiences on a tape recorder, which his secretary typed up. It was recovered in 2011 by Purvis' son Malcolm and subsequently passed along to Lieutenant Colonel (Ret.) Peter Winstanley, who maintains the website pows-of-japan.net, which is where the author saw it.

Many of the pertinent details about Walter Gibson's incredible story of survival after the sinking of the SS *Rooseboom* are from his memoir, *The Boat.* Others come from the National Archives document "Far East Anglo Dutch Operations" (HS 1/272 and 1/273) and from *Singapore's Dunkirk.*

Geoffrey Brooke was among the last men ordered to leave Padang by Colonel Warren. "Personally, I think you have a sporting chance," Warren said before the men left on the fishing ketch, straight into the teeth of the monsoon season and Sumatra's notoriously tricky-to-sail west coast. For weeks they sailed in much the same direction as George White would shortly afterward, and were plagued with difficulties. A waterspout tossed their boat; two "immense blue-nosed whales" nearly rammed them, missing the vessel by a few feet; and they were strafed by Japanese airplanes. The sails tore, batteries died, passengers fell ill. Finally, after nearly a month and 1,690 miles of sailing, the helmsman called out with serious understatement, "I don't think you'll be disappointed if you come up here and see what I see." It was land, Ceylon, and salvation.

Another ship was sent from Ceylon to pick up the remainder of those stranded in Padang, the steamship SS *Chilka*. But on March 11, 1942, about 340 miles away from Emmahaven, a Japanese submarine surfaced and sank the *Chilka* with shell fire from her deck guns. Seven men were killed; around a dozen more, including the wounded ship's captain, Walker Bird, survived five weeks at sea before being rescued by a Greek freighter.

John Williams noted the earthquake that hit Padang before the Japanese arrival in his private papers (17378), held at the Imperial War Museum.

Chapter 15: Imprisoned

Key sources for this chapter include Frank's recollections in *The Judy Story* and to Neumann and van Witsen; Les Searle's and John Devani's memories collected in *The Judy Story; Escape Impossible; Escape to Captivity;* the private papers of A. B. Simmonds (21578), J. A. C. Robins (5153), J. E. R. Persons (18760), and John Williams (17378) held at the Imperial War Museum; and the oral history by John Purvis reprinted at the website pows-of-japan.net.

While the Germans treated escape attempts by POWs quite harshly, in general they were kept in somewhat humane conditions in the stalags. Malnutrition was the general complaint, but there was relatively little torture or beatings. Of course matters were far different in other camps operated by the Nazis.

Chapter 16: Gloegoer

Main sources for this chapter include Frank's recollections in *The Judy Story* and to Neumann and van Witsen; *Escape to Captivity;* Les Searle's and John Devani's memories in *The Judy Story;* the private papers of A. B. Simmonds (21578), J. A. C. Robins (5153), J. E. R. Persons (18760), F. G. Freeman (14046), W. R. Smith (8443), and John Williams (17378), and an oral history recorded by John Hedley, all held at the Imperial War Museum; Captain Edward Porter's biography as it appears at roll-of-honour.org .uk/p/html/porter-edward.htm; John Purvis' history as reprinted at pows-of-japan.net; and the National Archives document "Evacuation from Singapore Across Sumatra" (WO 141/100).

Most of the details concerning the temple building project at Gloegoer come from Hartley's *Escape to Captivity.*

What Les Searle unscientifically called a radar system wasn't far off, in that Judy was able to "see" things from far away, and in ways we humans not only cannot match but can scarcely fathom. Her sensitive nose could sniff out subtle changes in emanations from people; as the bromide goes, dogs can indeed "smell fear," along with pressure, anger, depression, and joy.

The item about the depressing sameness of many diary entries from the POWs comes from the author's conversations with Lizzie Oliver, the British historian who carefully studied written records of the Sumatran prisoners.

The idea that Judy could understand what Frank was thinking isn't especially surprising, given the subtlety and complexity of social interactions between man and dogs. The canine species evolved from its wild lupine state specifically because it was able to persuade the human who had the regular food supply that dogs were worth keeping around and even feeding. That was a special and unique display of cross-species communication, and as any dog lover will tell you, it is their ability to understand, and act upon, our actions and desires that separates them from other domesticated animals.

Chapter 17: POW #81-A

The main sources for this chapter are Frank's recollections in *The Judy Story* and to Neumann and van Witsen; Les Searle's and John Devani's memories in *The Judy Story; Escape to Captivity;* the private papers of A. B. Simmonds (21578), J. E. R. Persons (18760), F. G. Freeman (14046), W. R. Smith (8443), and John Williams (17378), and an oral history recorded by John Hedley, all held at the Imperial War Museum.

Tick's sad tale was recounted by Frank to Neumann and van Witsen.

With the survival of five puppies in the Immaculate Conception at Gloegoer, Judy was now the mother of fifteen offspring.

Judy's pregnancy was also unusual in that dogs who imprint early in life onto adults, rather than other dogs, as the kennel-escaping pup had done in Shanghai, are often ill-equipped to socialize and breed properly. Back on the *Gnat,* Judy had displayed this wasn't an issue, at least once. But it is rare for such dogs to successfully mate multiple times, especially when factoring in the hunger and exhaustion she suffered in the prison camp. Throughout her life, save the episode with Paul, her French suitor, Judy seldom had the opportunity to "practice" social behavior with other canines. So the fact that she found a way to reproduce in the POW camp was even more exceptional.

Lizzie Oliver showed me the sketches her grandfather, Stanley Russell, drew in his diary but, citing privacy concerns, preferred they, along with any quotations from the diary, not be reproduced in this book. The sketches that appear in the photo insert are an exception.

Hirateru Banno's story is informed by details from Robin Rowland, a scholar of the Japanese prison camps. His book *A River Kwai Story* and paper "Sugamo and the River Kwai: The American Occupation of Japan and Memories of the Asia-Pacific War," presented at Princeton University on May 9, 2003, were invaluable, especially concerning Banno's command of F Force and subsequent war crimes trial. Conversations with Robin further assisted the author in filling in this fascinating officer's background. More on Banno comes from *The Judy Story;* Frank's letter to Neumann and van Witsen; *Escape to Captivity;* an article in the *Sydney Morning Herald* of September 24, 1945; a file on Banno held in the U.S. National Archives, "Banno, Hirateru," 8th Army Sugamo Released Prisoner 201 Files, RG 338, Folder 20, Box 4, 290/66/21/1; and the UK National Archives document "Hirateru Banno and Six Others" (CO 235/1034).

The plane crash that prematurely ended Cyril Wild's remarkable life is shrouded in controversy. Some historians speculate his plane was sabotaged, either by sympathizers to the Japanese on trial (reams of records and documents pertinent to the cases were destroyed in the crash) or perhaps even by Americans, who didn't want the earnest Wild to secure lighter sentences for the Japanese they wished to see given death for their crimes. Such theorizing is commonplace with tragic and random deaths, and there is no evidence that points to anything other than an accident.

Chapter 18: Subterfuge

Main sources for this chapter include Frank's recollections in *The Judy Story* and to Neumann and van Witsen; *Escape to Captivity*; Les Searle's and John Devani's memories in *The Judy Story;* and John Purvis' history as reprinted at pows-of-japan.net.

Captain Nishi appears as "Nissi" in *The Judy Story,* but most other sources use Nishi. There is precious little about this officer in the historical record, so his name isn't known for sure, but Nishi is a common Japanese surname, while Nissi is rare, so it seems more likely the former is correct. Probably the most well-known Nishi is Colonel Takeichi Nishi, who won an Olympic gold medal for Japan at the 1932 Olympics in Los Angeles in the equestrian competition. He was killed during the Battle of Iwo Jima in 1945.

Chapter 19: Hell Ship

The death of the *Van Waerwijck* and the scenes at sea are recounted by Frank in *The Judy Story* and to Neumann and van Witsen, by Les Searle and John Devani in *The Judy Story,* Peter Hartley in *Escape to Captivity,* Edward Gibson in *The Boat,* John Purvis' history as reprinted at pows-of-japan.net, Captain Edward Porter's biography as it appears at roll-of-honour.org.uk/p/html/porter-edward.htm, and Captain J. G. Gordon's testimony in a document "Statement by Capt. J. G. Gordon" (WO 361/1592), held at the National Archives. The accounts of multiple Dutch survivors are recounted in *The Sumatra Railroad,* whose author, Henk Hovinga, goes into great detail about the tragic voyage.

Willem Wanrooy's *Prisoners of the Japanese in World War II* (written under the pen name Van Waterford) is not only a key source for information about the hell ships, but also a testimony to survival, as Wanrooy wrote the book several years after surviving the sinking of a hell ship, the *Junyō Maru,* off Sumatra.

By some estimates, the Japanese used more than two hundred hell ships to transport POWs during the war, though a precise number is impossible to figure. Besides the *Van Waerwijck* and the *Junyō Maru* (see chapter 23), at least eight were sunk by Allied forces:

Arisan Maru—carried 1,781 POWs, mainly Americans; sunk by submarine USS *Snook;* only nine people survived.

Asama Maru—sunk by submarine USS *Atule* in South China Sea.

Chichibu Maru—sunk by submarine USS *Gudgeon* while carrying approximately 2,500 Japanese troops and civilians; 465 were rescued from the wreckage.

Chuyo—sunk by submarine USS *Sailfish* while carrying 1,250 POWs, many of them Americans. All perished.

Oryoku Maru—carried 1,620 American POWs along with 1,900 Japanese; sunk by American bombers from the carrier USS *Hornet.* Two hundred men died at the scene, and the rest were brought to the Philippines, where hundreds more died of mistreatment and neglect. Several more were reportedly beheaded and thrown in a mass grave.

Enoura Maru—carried the survivors of the *Oryoku Maru* bombing. Bombed in harbor at Taiwan; 350 more POWs died in the attack.

Hofuku Maru—carried 1,289 POWs, mostly British and Dutch. Sunk by carrier-based planes off of Corregidor; all but 242 killed.

Awa Maru—Carried 2,004 passengers, some of them POWs, though on this trip the number is unknown and thought to be relatively few. She was rumored, however, to be carrying billions in gold, diamonds, plutonium, and other precious metals. She was sunk by USS *Queenfish* on April 1, 1945, in the Taiwan Strait—only a single survivor was pulled from the water, Kantora Shimoda, who also had survived two other sinkings at sea, making him a Japanese counterpart to Ian Forbes. In 1980, the Chinese underwent a massive salvage operation to try to recover the supposed fortune that went down with the *Awa Maru,* but found nothing. A later investigation by the U.S. National Security Agency determined no treasure had been loaded aboard the ship, but a large cargo of gold and diamonds left by road just before the *Awa Maru* departed Singapore, bound for Japan.

The voyage of the submarine HMS *Truculent* and her fateful encounter with Frank and Judy's transport vessel is detailed at the website uboat.net:8080/allies/warships/ship/3514.html and in her daily logs for those critical days, accessed in documents at the National Archives, "HMS *Truculent* Patrol Report, 12th June to 5th July, 1944" (ADM 199/1868 Pt. 1).

HMS *Titania* was a submarine tender between the wars, operating mostly out of Hong Kong.

Information about the tragedy of the HMS *Nova Scotia* can be found at wrecksite.eu/wreck.aspx?16429.

The amazing reappearance of Sjovald Cunyngham-Brown, the hero of Pompong Island, to save yet another life in the wreckage of the *Van Waerwijck* is recounted by his close friend Geoffrey Brooke in *Singapore's Dunkirk*.

Chapter 20: Reunion

The main sources for material about the River Valley Road prison camp are Frank's recollections in *The Judy Story* and to Neumann and van Witsen; Les Searle's and John Devani's memories in *The Judy Story; Escape to Captivity;* George Duffy's *Ambushed Under the Southern Cross;* John Purvis' history as reprinted at pows-of-japan.net; and Captain Edward Porter's biography as it appears at roll-of-honour.org.uk/p/html/porter-edward.htm.

The ship that sank George Duffy's Merchant Marine vessel *American Leader* was a "raider," a German ship called the *Michel* that flew a false flag. The *Michel* appeared to be a neutral cargo vessel until moments before an attack, when the German crew (all trained members of the Kriegsmarine) would hurriedly drop the false flag, raise the Nazi swastika, and capture or sink the enemy.

The Allied version of these decoys were called Q-ships. These were cargo ships that pantomimed un-navylike panic on deck in order to lure German U-boats into surfacing and commencing an attack. The Q-ships would then turn their camouflaged weapons upon the subs. But they were essentially defensive, whereas the German raiders actively sought prey.

Michel was commanded by a notorious figure, Hellmuth von Ruckteschell. A highly decorated seaman during World War I, the German was one of the raider fleet's most successful captains in terms of gross tonnage sunk. But he was alleged to have repeatedly fired upon ships that had already surrendered, and in the wake of the Axis defeat von Ruckteschell was brought before a war crimes court. He was found guilty and sentenced to ten years in prison; he died in jail in 1948.

Ironically enough, Duffy's weeks aboard von Ruckteschell's ship would lead to lifelong postwar friendships with some of the enemy crewmen.

After internment on the *Michel,* Duffy was moved to Java, where he was held at camps in Tandjong Priok, the so-called Bicycle Camp, and Soni before being transferred to Singapore aboard the hell ship *Chukka Maru,* which made it safely to port, unlike so many of her counterparts.

Details about the steamship that ferried Frank and Judy back to Sumatra from Singapore are from *The Sumatra Railroad.*

The soldier protest song "Bless 'Em All" is actually a cleaned-up version—the original title is "Fuck 'Em All," which neatly captures the average grunt's viewpoint about war, the enemy, and his superiors since the dawn of conflict. The song began its life among RAF personnel serving on the Indian North West Frontier in the 1920s. Singers such as Gracie Fields and others released it commercially, using the bowdlerized title, subtly changing its meaning to imply patriotism. But British and Commonwealth soldiers sang the original version throughout World War II, using blue lyrics:

Oh they say there's a troopship just leaving Bombay
Bound for old Blighty's shore
Heavily laden with time-expired men
Bound for the land they adore
There's many a twat just finishing his time
There's many a cunt signing on
You'll get no promotion this side of the ocean
So cheer up my lads fuck 'em all!
Fuck 'em all!
Fuck 'em all!
The long and the short and the tall
Fuck all the Sergeants and WO ones
Fuck all the corporals and their bastard sons
For we're saying good-bye to them all
As up the CO's arse they crawl
You'll get no promotion this side of the ocean
So cheer up my lads fuck 'em all!

American soldiers had their own versions, including one that went:

They called for the army to come to Tulagi
But Douglas MacArthur said no
They said there's a reason
It isn't the season
Besides there's no USO
Fuck 'em all!
Fuck 'em all!
The long the short and the tall
Fuck all the Pelicans and Dogfaces too
Fuck all the generals and above all fuck you!
So we're saying good-bye to them all
As back to our foxholes we crawl
There will be no promotion on MacArthur's blue ocean
So cheer up Gyrenes fuck 'em all!"

Chapter 21: Pakan Baroe

The main sources for details of Pakan Baroe are Frank's recollections in *The Judy Story* and to Neumann and van Witsen; Les Searle's, Tom Scott's, and John Devani's memories in *The Judy Story; Escape to Captivity; Ambushed Under the Southern Cross; The Sumatra Railroad;* the private papers of J. F. Fitzgerald (8209), Ken Robson (11338), W. R. Smith (8443), J. D. Pentney (20664), and F. G. Freeman (14046), and John Hedley's oral history (23219), all held at the Imperial War Museum; National Archives documents including "Recommendations for POW Awards" (RAF AIR 2/3775) and "POW Information Cards" (WO 345); the author's interview with Rouse Voisey; Leonard Williams' obituary in the *Times of London* on January 22, 2007; Harry Badger's oral history, as captured by his son Rick Badger and published on the website pows-of-japan .net/articles/63.htm; and John Purvis' history as reprinted at pows-of-japan.net.

Preparations for the use of POWs and slave labor to build the Death Railway at Pakan Baroe are described in *War, Nationalism, and Peasants,* as well as in numerous contemporary accounts, mostly in the Australian press.

After the war, Rolex built a worldwide advertising campaign around Edward Porter's story to show how it lent testimony to the power of the Rolex trademark.

Geographic and camp details are mostly taken from *The Sumatra Railroad,* as is information about the forgotten holocaust of the Indonesian *romushas* used as slave labor by the Japanese.

Wing Commander Patrick Davis kept something of a low profile at Pakan Baroe, and afterward as well. He never left a service memoir or anything other than his turgid reports that chronicle the organizational life at the railway, which are kept at the Hague Historical Museum in the Netherlands. This is unfortunate, as he seemed to have been a brave and competent officer. Those who worked with him in the camp command structure praised him for his ability to negotiate with the Japanese. But many others, in particular those out on the railway, found him "haughty," in Henk Hovinga's words. This likely stems from the fact that Davis, quite naturally, tended to favor the Brits over the Dutch when issues between POWs of the two nationalities arose.

The report Davis filed to South East Asia Command is held at the NIOD Institute for War, Holocaust, and Genocide Studies in Amsterdam, document IC 072256.

The chief Dutch officer at Pakan Baroe was Lieutenant Colonel W. C. M. Slabbekoorn. According to Hovinga, he was sickly, "an old, conservative gentleman, totally worn out and showing early signs of dementia. He even had to be bathed by his aide Pinchetti, who was so badly disfigured during an air raid on Surabaya in 1942 that he even scared the Japs." Soon enough, a much younger man, Lieutenant Henk Vennik, took over as the Dutch top kick. Other Dutch officers outranked Vennik, but the lieutenant's natural command authority cowed all save Captain De Vries, who also plagued George Duffy. One day, Vennik told the tetchy De Vries, "If you know it all so damn much, here is my chair. Take my seat and do the work. If you do not want it, then keep your mouth shut and find yourself a place in the barracks." De Vries meekly complied.

Each POW was required to detail his attempts at sabotage, along with his escape attempts, upon release on his POW Information Card, a remnant from the European POW experience, where such resistance was expected. Many of the Sumatran POWs left this part blank (or wrote "nil," like J. G. Gordon did), as there was little effective resistance possible. Frank was an exception in this case. The sabotage attempt by the Australian POW Slinger is detailed in *The Judy Story*.

In some of the more outlying camps at Pakan Baroe, the strict adherence to Tokyo time was relaxed.

Judy's ability to navigate the jungle was due in part to her keen vision. Dogs see the color green (and blue) exceptionally well. Red presents far more of a problem—dogs don't see that color well at all.

For the curious epicurean, dog meat is very lean and chewy, somewhat similar to goat.

The original Camp Three drowned when the Kampar Kanan River overflowed. The replacement, built on higher ground, was populated on November 8, 1944.

Chapter 22: Pig Face and King Kong

The main sources for this chapter were Frank's recollections in *The Judy Story* and to Neumann and van Witsen; Tom Scott's and Les Searle's memories in *The Judy Story; The Sumatra Railroad; Escape to Captivity; Ambushed Under the Southern Cross;* the private papers of J. F. Fitzgerald (8209), Ken Robson (11338), W. R. Smith (8443), and J. D. Pentney, (20664) and John Hedley's oral history (23219), all held at the Imperial War Museum; and the author's interview with Rouse Voisey.

There were roughly three thousand Koreans working as guards in POW camps across the Pacific theater. Hovinga and Smith are the sources for the repository of nicknames the men had for the guards.

Details of the Japanese conscription and mistreatment of Koreans is taken from several sources beyond those listed above, including Gavan Daws' *Prisoners of the Japanese* and *Blood Brothers* by Eugene Jacobs. An example of the Koreans' sabotage from within was the planned mutiny of the 30th Korean Division against the Japanese in 1944, details of which can be found in the *Asia-Pacific Journal: Japan Focus* online at japanfocus.org/-Kiriyama-Keiichi/3151.

One sidebar to the Korean conscription into the war was the Japanese goal of reducing ethnic Koreans. A school of thought in Japan was that the deaths of so many ethnic Japanese would open the door for the Koreans "to pose a serious threat in the future," especially given "their formidable power to reproduce," according to *An Outline of the History of the Army System* by Masao Yamazaki.

Information about the Koreans continuing the odious policy of *ianfu*—comfort women—even after World War II has been highlighted in recent years by the scholarship of Korean sociologist Kim Kwi-ok, who closely studied the South Korean military official record, *Hubang Chonsa* (War History on the Home Front), as well as the memoirs of many retired soldiers and officers for a paper entitled *The Korean War and Women: With a Focus on Military Comfort Women and Military Comfort Stations,* presented in Japan in 2002. According to Kim, the Korean military used specially designated units of comfort women, along with mobile units and local prostitutes.

Jan Eggink remembered the poignancy of the playing of "Silent Night, Holy Night" on Christmas 1944 in the documentary *Eindstation Pakan Baroe 1943–1945,* which aired in Holland in 1997. The poem he dedicated to his wife is reprinted in *The Sumatra Railroad.*

At one point, a touring Japanese military band arrived at Pakan Baroe. All were invited to witness them perform in a nearby village. This invitation was universally declined, so some men were ordered to go, including Peter Hartley. After a typical backbreaking day of work, the concertgoers crossed a river by ferry and trekked a long way to the village. A large bamboo shelter had been erected for the musicians, but the men sat on the ground. Japanese officers surrounded them on chairs and benches.

The band had just picked up their instruments when an ominous crash of thunder rolled over the village. The band went on, playing "strange Jap compositions which were supposed to tell the story of the [Japanese] Air Force dropping bombs on New York," Hartley would write in *Escape to Captivity.* Then the storm broke with a fury. Huge lightning bolts struck all around, but the men were ordered to remain in place until the concert finished. The grass where they sat quickly became a pond as the monsoon came down, and the music could barely be heard over the downpour.

At last, with everyone drenched and shivering, the festivities came to an end. The POWs slogged back through a sea of mud. When they reached the river, it was churning even faster than before, and the ferryman had disappeared. With no other choice, the men risked their lives and piled into the boat, managing to get across to the other side without flipping. It was past midnight when the prisoners returned to Camp Five, soaked, muddy, and freezing. They were greeted by peals of laughter from the other POWs who had stayed behind.

Elsewhere in Sumatra the importance of music among POWs was underscored by the women and children held at the prison camp at Palembang, including Helen Colijn. Six hundred prisoners were crowded into the barracks there; some two hundred would die of starvation and disease before liberation. To fend off misery and hopelessness, these

POWs turned to music. They formed a large choir, arranging the vocals of famous works from memory. They had no instruments, so they simulated the sounds of the various sections with their voices. "It seemed a miracle that among the bedbugs, the cockroaches, and the rats, among the smells of the latrines, among the fever, the boils and the hunger pangs, women's voices could recreate the surging glorious music of Debussy, Beethoven, and Chopin," Colijn wrote in her memoir of the camp, *Song of Survival*. When the Japanese discovered the secret rehearsals, they were furious, but punishment soon gave way to collaboration, and by war's end some of the guards sat in with the choir to perform. Colijn's memoir was turned into a 1997 movie, *Paradise Road,* starring Glenn Close.

The most famous example of musicality among POWs is undoubtedly the *Quatuor pour la fin du temps* (*Quartet for the End of Time*) by Frenchman Olivier Messiaen. Imprisoned by the Germans at Stalag VIII-A, Messiaen, a composer and organist before the war, found among other POWs a violinist, a cellist, and a clarinetist. Messiaen wrote a quartet of movements for the group to play behind the barbed wire, and they practiced under trying conditions and frigid weather. Performed originally for an audience of POWs and prison guards, the quartet has become an acknowledged masterpiece of modern European classical music.

Chapter 23: Railway of Death

The main sources for this chapter were Frank's recollections in *The Judy Story* and to Neumann and van Witsen; Tom Scott's and Les Searle's memories in *The Judy Story; The Sumatra Railroad; Escape to Captivity; Ambushed Under the Southern Cross;* the private papers of J. F. Fitzgerald (8209), Ken Robson (11338), W. R. Smith (8443), and J. D. Pentney, (20664) and John Hedley's oral history (23219), all held at the Imperial War Museum; the author's interview with Rouse Voisey; and John Purvis' history as reprinted at pows-of-japan.net.

Frank and Judy's movements up the railway are approximates in terms of timing—men were forever being shuttled between camps for various reasons. In the main, man and dog stayed at Camp Five until it was closed and the majority of men were moved to Camp Six, then Camp Eight. Joe Fitzgerald was among a group of men who detoured to Camp Seven first, there to help complete a bridge across the Kampar Kiri River. Work began in mid-December, on the cusp of the monsoon season. By Good Friday, heavy rains had washed the bridge away. Frank never talks about working on the ill-fated bridge built there, so presumably he wasn't in the subsection of men sent to Camp Seven.

Exact locations of the Pakan Baroe camps are finely detailed by Hovinga in *The Sumatra Railroad.*

The *Junyō Maru* was sent to the bottom of the ocean on September 18, 1944, by the submarine HMS *Tradewind,* skippered by Lieutenant Commander Stephen Maydon. *Junyō Maru* carried some 6,500 POWs, including Americans, Brits, Dutch, and Aussies, plus a multitude of *romushas*. But Maydon was unaware of her human cargo, and slammed two torpedoes into the steamer. At least 5,620 people went down in the disaster. Maydon didn't find out about the human cost of his action until over two decades had passed, when he had retired from the navy and become a member of the British Parliament. The discovery that he was responsible for the deaths of so many innocents on his side of the war would haunt him until he died in 1971.

Rouse Voisey was on the *Junyō Maru* when it was sent to the bottom: "I climbed up a rope ladder and jumped overboard," he recalled to me of that horrible day.

> I spent hours upon hours in the water, from Monday evening until Wednesday morning. I held on to debris, along with two Dutchmen. At some point both of them slipped away and disappeared under the water, and I was left alone. It all felt like a dream in a way. I hallucinated much of the time. At last a Japanese sub chaser drifted by and dropped a rope ladder over the side. They didn't help you up, but if you could hang on they hauled you up and over like a net of fish. They gave me water and a sea biscuit. One Dutch survivor went berserk, so the Japanese simply threw him over the side to his doom. That was sobering, and made you behave yourself.

Rouse wound up at Pakan Baroe shortly afterward. He survived it all and still lives, at age ninety-four, on his own in Norwich, England. He is quite sharp mentally, as evidenced by his reaction when I mixed up a name or a date during our conversation in the fall of 2014. "Keep up, Bob!" he reprimanded me, quite correctly indeed.

Of the 114 men who died at Pakan Baroe in March 1945, 54 of them had survived the sinking of either the *Van Waerwijck* or the *Junyō Maru.*

The only American of the twelve at Pakan Baroe who told his story was George Duffy in his memoir.

The chief medical officer among the British was RAF Wing Commander C. W. Coffey. At some point during his headlong plunge into the miasma of disease and suffering at Camp Two he contracted beriberi. According to the citation later awarding Coffey the Order of the British Empire, Coffey "spent five months in the hospital, paralyzed below the waist. Immediately he was able to move, he volunteered to take over the daily British Sick Parade, which was attended by approximately 200 men. At all times Wing Commander Coffey showed a complete disregard of his illness and, through his untiring efforts and hard work, in spite of the extreme shortage of medical supplies, he did all in his power to alleviate the pain and suffering of the sick. His example in this connection had an excellent effect on the morale of the prisoners."

Sjovald Cunyngham-Brown, the man who dove into the unholy filth of the latrine to try to save the drowning Dutchman, among other wartime exploits, was also a close friend of John Purvis while at Pakan Baroe. His full name was actually John Sjovald Hoseason Cunyngham-Brown. He went on to become a government figure in the beautiful Malaysian city of Penang for years after the war. Sadly, SCB never wrote a memoir detailing his incredible story, but did pen a pair of books in the early 1970s, *The Traders—A Story of Britain's South-East Asian Commercial Adventure,* and a novel, *Crowded Hour.*

The account of a Japanese officer ordering Judy's death while Frank was sick comes from the December 1945 issue of *Tail-Wagger* magazine. The article, "Judy (Ex-POW Sumatra) Is Now in England," goes on to declare that the Japanese officer "was the same as at Medan, who had forbidden the dog to go aboard" the *Van Waerwijck,* i.e., Captain Nishi. There is no evidence that Nishi was ever at Pakan Baroe, and the only Japanese officers in the camp with that high a rank are well documented. So while such an order is likely to have been given, there is reason to be skeptical as well. One presumes the fact-checking at *Tail-Wagger* magazine didn't reach the standards of, say, the *New Yorker.*

Frank's thoughts of killing himself and/or Judy come from his letter to Neumann and van Witsen. Interestingly, according to Lizzie Oliver, the Pakan Baroe historian, such contemplation wasn't pervasive among the prisoners, many of whom essentially figured they were already dead, so why bother expending the energy to make it official? But Judy's presence complicated matters for Frank.

Chapter 24: Freedom

The main sources for this chapter were Frank's recollections in *The Judy Story* and to Neumann and van Witsen; Les Searle's and Tom Scott's memories in *The Judy Story; Escape to Captivity; Ambushed Under the Southern Cross;* Harry Badger's oral history, as captured by his son Rick Badger and published on the website pows-of-japan.net/articles/63.htm; the private papers of J. D. Pentney (20664), Ken Robson (11338), J. E. R. Person (18760), and W. R. Smith (8443) held at the Imperial War Museum; and documents held at the National Archives, including "Royal Air Force Operations Record Book" (RAF AIR 29/153), "Operations Birdcage and Mastiff Sortie Reports" (RAF AIR 23/2664–2667, 2669–2670, 4800), "RAPWI Sitreps" (RAF AIR 23/2669), "Operations Record Book Appendices Sept–Oct 1945" (RAF AIR 24/938), "Recommendations for POW Awards" (RAF AIR 2/3775), "Evaders and Prisoners of War" (RAF AIR 49/385), "Movement and Evacuation of P.O.W." (WO 203/3800), and "Secret Supplement to Report to Combined Chiefs of Staff by Rear Admiral Mountbatten of Burma, 1943–46" (CAB 106/77).

George Duffy wrote movingly about his jealousy of those who remained free men in his diary/memoir *Ambushed Under the Southern Cross.* He also wrote about the poor Brit who passed away in front of Bernard Hickey, with liberation at hand, and the story of his not finding out he was free until close to a week after the other POWs.

Raymond Smith actually didn't speak much Japanese, but the little he did understand put him head and shoulders above most of the POWs, thus Wing Commander Davis placed him in the key role of translator at Camp Three. At first, Smith told Davis he didn't want the job. "I have thought it over, and I'm not going," he told his superior officer. Davis replied, "I have thought it over too, and you are going."

The exact number of deaths at Pakan Baroe in the final months is difficult to discern with precision. W. R. Smith, in his private papers, said thirty men died between liberation and evacuation. Other estimates run up to one hundred, which seems a bit high. The official War Ministry report says that "249 died of illness and malnutrition during the last three months," though it isn't known if that counts the men who died once rescuers arrived on the scene.

The guards had good reason to fear retribution, but as it happened, so did the Dutch. Years and years of colonial resentments had built up among the people of Sumatra, and while liberties were seldom taken while the Japanese held the island, its liberation ironically freed locals to take out their frustrations on their once and (hopefully not) future masters. In an internment camp in Medan, a howling mob stormed the fences and murdered twenty people, including women and children, believing them to be Dutch. In fact, they were Swiss.

Major Gideon François Jacobs came to Pakan Baroe on a near-solo commando mission called Force 136. There were only four other men with him: two Aussies, a Dutchman, and a Javanese originally from China. While sussing out the entirety and hideousness of the POW situation in Sumatra, they discovered a POW camp at Belalau rubber plantation, where sixty women, including two dozen Australian nurses, most notably Vivian Bullwinkel, were being held in secret. It was Bullwinkel herself who saw the two Aussies, identified only as Sergeant Bates and Sergeant Gillam, approach the camp. She yelled out, "The Australians are here!" The Japanese had taken the nurses from the camp at Palembang, where they had been held for most of the war, to the secret site at the rubber plantation in order to improve their physical condition before handing them over to the Allies. Gillam was so outraged at the condition of the nurses that he lined up all the Japanese guards in sight along a fence and threatened to shoot them all before he was talked out of it by Jacobs.

Airdrop memories come from Frank's recollections as well as the private papers of J. D. Pentney, Ken Robson, W. R. Smith, and Harry Badger.

The press release announcing Operations Mastiff and Birdcage called the joint operation the "greatest mercy mission of the war."

The leaflets dropped over the POW camps in Southeast Asia—more than thirty-three million of them in all—read as follows:

TO ALL ALLIED PRISONERS OF WAR
THE JAPANESE FORCES HAVE SURRENDERED
UNCONDITIONALLY AND THE WAR IS OVER.

We will get supplies to you as soon as is humanly possible and will make arrangements to get you out but, owing to the distances involved, it may take some time before we can achieve this.

YOU will help us and yourselves if you act as follows—

1. Stay in your camps until you get further orders from us.
2. Start preparing nominal rolls of personnel, giving fullest particulars.
3. List your most urgent necessities.
4. If you have been starved or underfed for long periods DO NOT eat large quantities of solid food, fruit or vegetables at first. It is dangerous for you to do so. Small quantities at frequent intervals are much safer and will strengthen you far more quickly. For those who are really ill or very weak, fluids such as broth and soup, making use of the water in which rice and other foods have been boiled, are much the best. Gifts of food from the local population should be avoided. We want to get you back home quickly, safe and sound, and do not want to risk your chances from diarrhea, dysentery, and cholera at this late stage.
5. Local authorities and/or Allied officers will take charge of your affairs in a very short order. Be guided by their advice.

Total stores dropped on Pakan Baroe during Operation Mastiff, according to the official Recovery of Allied Prisoners of War and Internees history, were 46,850 pounds of food, 4,820 pounds of clothing, and 1,350 pounds of medical supplies.

One airplane flying a mission for Operation Mastiff crashed, with all aboard killed, on September 1, 1945.

Many of the POWs were "distressed about ill-timed publication of Sumatra atrocities" by the press upon their evacuation to Singapore, according to an official Recovery of Allied Prisoners of War and Internees report. "PWs anxious consideration of their relatives," it read. This tied in to the later reticence to discuss their experiences once home.

Details of the Allied effort to treat and evacuate the POWs in Sumatra are taken from the official Recovery of Allied Prisoners of War and Internees history written for the Ministry of War, as well as daily situation reports and official documents.

Lady Mountbatten's visit was recalled by Frank, Badger, Robson, Voisey, Persons, Pentney, and Duffy, as well as in the Recovery of Allied Prisoners of War and Internees official history and reports from the lady herself. Sjovald Cunyngham-Brown's embarrassing story of greeting the lady's plane in the buff is recounted in *Forgotten Wars.*

Smith, in his private papers, writes about the recovered Imperial Japanese Army documents that proved the POWs were to be exterminated if all was lost, but never specifies his evidence.

Athole Stewart documented the horror of the POW survivors coming to Singapore in the *Melbourne Argus* of September 17, 1945. G. E. W. Harriott's articles ran in the *Sydney Morning Herald* on September 17 and September 18, 1945.

A monument to the men killed at Pakan Baroe was erected in 2001 in the National Memorial Arboretum at Staffordshire, near Lichfield.

Chapter 25: Hero

Information about the sailing of the HMS *Antenor* comes from the recollections of Frank in *The Judy Story* and to Neumann and van Witsen; the author's interview with Roise Voisey; and the oral history of John Purvis, along with records of the ship's voyage kept at the National Archives (BT 26/1212/20).

Information about Hackbridge Kennels comes from *Tail-Wagger* magazine, the *Illustrated London News,* and correspondence with Bernardine Fiddimore, the daughter of Hackbridge's former superintendent. Hackbridge closed in 1970.

The British Isles maintained its six-month quarantine policy for incoming animals until 2011. Animals landing on British soil from most countries now only require proof of a negative blood test for rabies before entry. Dogs from certain countries, including South Africa, India, and Brazil, still must be quarantined, though for only three months, not six.

The complicated pre-decimal pound/shilling/pence monetary system (or £sd) was used in much of the British Empire until the 1960s and early 1970s. Nigeria became the last country to abandon it in 1973. There were twelve pence to a shilling, and twenty shillings (240 pence) to a pound. The United States got rid of the system upon declaring independence in 1776.

The ceremony upon Judy's release from Hackbridge Kennels was well covered by the press, in particular the *London Daily Mirror* and *Tail-Wagger* magazine.

Frank himself relays little about the death of his older brother, David, on D-day. The simple fact it occurred is mentioned by his family on Frank's memorial website, and confirmed by the Commonwealth War Graves Commission website (cwgc.org/find-war-dead.aspx).

Information about the RAF refresher centers and Personnel Reception Centre 106 at Cosford is from RAF documents held at the National Archives, including "Repatriation of R.A.F. Ex-Prisoners of War from the Far East" (RAF AIR 49/386), "P.O.W. Resettlement and Refresher Course" (RAF AIR 49/388), "Report on the Recovery of Allied P/W and Internees After the Collapse of Japan, 1945" (RAF AIR 23/1980), "RAF Station Cosford 1940 Jan–1945 Dec" (RAF AIR 28/173), and "Personnel Reception Centres Cosford 106" (RAF AIR 29/1102), as well as the author's interview with Rouse Voisey.

Fred Freeman's account of postwar medical difficulties is from his private papers (14046) held at the Imperial War Museum.

The Portsmouth City Archives hold exceptionally detailed bombing maps, showing exactly where and when Nazi bombs landed on the city, and the damage caused. The Portsmouth and Sunderland newspapers put together a book, *Smitten City,* encompassing its coverage of the Blitz, which helped with details of the bombings.

The letter all returning POWs received from King George is reprinted in full on Frank's memorial website.

Joe Fitzgerald talks about POWs being welcomed into the homes of locals living near RAF bases in his private papers (8209) at the Imperial War Museum.

Details of Judy's Dickin Medal ceremony come from Frank's memories in *The Judy Story*, his recollections to Neumann and van Witsen, and numerous contemporary news accounts.

There have been sixty-five Dickin Medal honorees in all, thirty-two pigeons, twenty-nine dogs, three horses, and a cat, Simon, awarded for his service during the Yangtze Incident of 1949, when the Royal Navy frigate HMS *Amethyst* was trapped and shelled by Chinese Communist forces for three months before escaping. Simon's medal came for "disposing of many rats despite being wounded by a shell blast." The most recent animal to win the medal is Theo, a springer spaniel with the Royal Army Veterinary Corps, 104 Military Working Dog (MWD) Squadron, an arms and explosives search dog killed in Afghanistan in March 2011. A full accounting of the Dickin Medal winners, along with the fascinating history of Maria Dickin, is available at pdsa.org.uk.

Judy and Frank's appearances on the BBC were on June 10 and September 5, 1946. The host of the radio program *In Town Tonight,* Roy Rich, was renowned for being one of Britain's first disc jockeys, hosting the show *Housewives' Choice* in 1946. The host of the television show *Picture Page* was Wynford Vaughan-Thomas, one of Britain's most famous broadcasters, akin to Edward R. Murrow in his excellence on both radio and TV and in covering topics both serious and light. Information about the shows and Frank and Judy's appearances on them comes from the BBC Archives Center.

The People's Dispensary for Sick Animals remains the largest animal charity in the United Kingdom, carrying out more than one million examinations every year. My source for information on the organization comes from its website, pdsa.org.uk.

Frank discusses the backstage dog brawl between Judy and the borzois in his letter to Neumann and van Witsen.

The history of Britain's paratrooper dogs, or the "Luftwoofe," is well-chronicled by Andrew Woolhouse in his book *13—Lucky for Some: The History of the 13th (Lancashire) Parachute Battalion.* The dogs that went in on D-day trained for skydiving by spending hours upon hours acclimatizing themselves to air travel and parachute jumping. They were coaxed from the aircraft by their handlers, who carried steaks to feed them upon landing. The dogs were very successful in sniffing out mines, booby traps, and enemy positions. A life-size replica of one paradog, Bing, an Alsatian-collie mix, in full jumping gear is preserved at the Parachute Regiment and Airborne Forces Museum in Duxford, near Cambridge.

Information about Judy's "hero tour" comes from Frank's recollections in *The Judy Story* and to Neumann and van Witsen, as well as contemporary news accounts in the *London Daily Mirror, Evening Standard, Bath Weekly Chronicle, Bath Herald, Tail-Wagger* magazine, *Western Daily Press,* and *Bristol Mirror.*

It should be remembered that Frank himself was largely unaware of Judy's adventures in China and aboard the *Grasshopper.* He was briefed more fully about the details when he traveled to England and shared his stories with the gunboatmen who were gathering information for *The Judy Story.*

Chapter 26: Africa

Voting records and household information in postwar Portsmouth are taken from the Kelly's Directories and voting rolls, all kept at the Portsmouth City Archives.

Frank recorded his memories of postwar Portsmouth in *The Judy Story.* Other details on postwar Portsmouth are taken from various remembrances collected in the "People of Portsmouth" series kept at the Portsmouth City Archives, as well as *The Portsmouth That Has Passed* by William Gates and *Sunny Southsea* by Anthony Triggs.

John Hornley's memory of encountering Judy after the war appears in *The Judy Story.*

Postwar malaise, be it PTSD or some other syndrome, was a common theme among returned POWs. Frank was typically mum about the subject, but his family talked of it on his memorial website. Lizzie Oliver discovered it often in her research of Pakan Baroe POWs. Rouse Voisey talked about it in an interview with the author. John Hedley's oral history recording, which details his difficulty with postwar Britain and his salvation at returning to Asia, is kept at the Imperial War Museum, and is available online at iwm.org.uk/collections/item/object/80023021.

Most cases of canine PTSD come not from combat but from the everyday mistreatment, abuse, and abandonment of dogs everywhere. Medications such as Prozac seem to have a similar affect in alleviating the symptoms of traumatized dogs. Interestingly, according to research by animal scientist and psychologist Jaak Panksepp at Washington State University, rough-and-tumble outdoor play has been shown to vastly help as well. The action apparently releases large amounts of brain-derived neurotrophic factors (BDNFs), which are associated with new neuronal growth—replacing the part of the brain that houses bad memories with new growth, and hence, new memories. Lee

Charles Kelley, a prolific author and trainer, has written extensively on the subject at canineptsdblog.blogspot.com.

The star-crossed Groundnut Scheme is finely accounted in Alan Wood's *The Groundnut Affair.* Details of Frank's experiences there come from his recollections in *The Judy Story* and to Neumann and van Witsen, as well as his memorial website, frankwilliams.ca.

The memorial to Judy's service in 1972 at churches across Britain is recounted in the *Times of London* edition of February 28, 1972.

Epilogue

The information about Frank's life post-Judy comes from his memorial website, frankwilliams.ca, as well as from obituaries in the *Burnaby Now* and the *Vancouver Sun.*

Bibliography

Books

Angell, Barbara. *A Woman's War.* Chatswood, New South Wales, Australia: New Holland, 2003.

Arnold, Jennifer. *Through a Dog's Eyes.* New York: Random House, 2011.

Barnett, John L. D. *The Sea Is My Grave.* Bloomington, IN: Xlibris, 2011.

Bausum, Ann. *Stubby the War Dog.* Washington, DC: National Geographic Children's Books, 2014.

Bayly, Christopher Alan, and Timothy Norman Harper. *Forgotten Wars.* Cambridge, MA: Harvard University Press, 2007.

Brooke, Geoffrey. *Singapore's Dunkirk.* London: Leo Cooper, 1989.

Brown, Cecil. *Suez to Singapore.* New York: Random House, 1942.

Churchill, Winston. *Memoirs of the Second World War.* New York: Houghton Mifflin, 1991.

Colijn, Helen. *Song of Survival.* Ashland, OR: White Cloud Press, 1995.

Daws, Gavan. *Prisoners of the Japanese.* New York: William Morrow, 1994.

Dower, John W. *War Without Mercy.* New York: Random House, 1986.

Duffy, George W. *Ambushed Under the Southern Cross.* Bloomington, IN: Xlibris, 2008.

Fogle, Bruce. *The Dog's Mind.* New York: Macmillan, 1990.

Gates, William. *The Portsmouth That Has Passed.* Portsmouth, UK: Milestone Publications, 1987.

George, Isabel. *The Dog That Saved My Life.* London: HarperCollins, 2010.

Gibson, Walter. *The Boat.* London: W. H. Allen and Co., 1952.

Hammond, Kenneth James, and Kristin Eileen Stapleton, eds. *The Human Tradition in Modern China.* New York: Rowman and Littlefield, 2008.

Hart, Ernest. *Pointers.* Neptune City, NJ: TFH Publications, 1990.

Hartley, Peter. *Escape to Captivity.* London: Hamilton and Company, 1952.

Horowitz, Alexandra. *Inside of a Dog.* New York: Scribner, 2009.

Hovinga, Henk. *The Sumatra Railroad.* Leiden, Netherlands: KITLV Press, 2010.

Jacobs, Eugene. *Blood Brothers.* Whitefish, MT: Kessinger Publishing, 2004.

Jacobs, Gideon François. *Prelude to the Monsoon.* Cape Town, South Africa: Purnell, 1965.

Jeffrey, Betty. *White Coolies.* Sydney, Australia: Angus and Robertson, 1954.

Jewkes, Stanley. *Humankind? Planet Earth's Most Enigmatic Species.* Bloomington, IN: Authorhouse, 2002.

Kirby, S. Woodburn. *Singapore: The Chain of Disaster.* New York: Macmillan, 1971.

Konstam, Angus. *Yangtze River Gunboats 1900–49.* Oxford, UK: Osprey Publishing, 2011.

Morison, Samuel Eliot. *The Oxford History of the American People.* London: Oxford University Press, 1965.

Neumann, H., and E. van Witsen. *De Sumatra Spoorweg* [*The Sumatra Railway*]. Middelie, Netherlands: Studio Pieter Mulier, 1984.

Owen, Frank. *The Fall of Singapore.* New York: Penguin, 2001.

Pisani, Elizabeth. *Indonesia, Etc.* New York: Norton, 2014.

Putney, William W. *Always Faithful.* Washington, DC: Brasseys, 2001.

Rowland, Robin. *A River Kwai Story.* Sydney, Australia: Allen and Unwin, 2008.

Saddington, Stanley. *Escape Impossible.* Stockport, England: A. Lane Publishers, 1997.

Sato, Shigeru. *War, Nationalism, and Peasants.* Sydney, Australia: Allen and Unwin, 1994.

Shaw, Ian W. *On Radji Beach.* Sydney, Australia: Macmillan Australia, 2010.

Smith, Colin. *Singapore Burning.* New York: Penguin, 2006.

Snow, Edgar. *Red Star over China.* London: Victor Gollancz, 1938.

Stedman, John. *People of Portsmouth.* Portsmouth, UK: Breedon Books, 2002.

Thomas, Gould Hunter. *An American in China: 1936–39.* New York: Greatrix Press, 2005.

Triggs, Anthony. *Sunny Southsea.* Devon, UK: Halsgrove, 2001.

Tunny, Noel. *Winning from Downunder.* Moorooka, Queensland, Australia: Boolarong Press, 2010.

Van Zandt, Cynthia Jean. *Brothers Among Nations.* Oxford, UK: Oxford University Press, 2008.

Varley, E., ed. *The Judy Story.* London: Souvenir Press, 1973.

Wallechinsky, David, and Irving Wallace. *The People's Almanac.* New York: Doubleday, 1975.

Wanrooy, Willem (Van Waterford, pseud). *Prisoners of the Japanese in World War II.* Jefferson, NC: McFarland, 1994.

Wood, Alan. *The Groundnut Affair.* London: The Bodley Head, 1950.

Yenne, Bill. *The Imperial Japanese Army: The Invincible Years 1941–42.* Oxford, UK: Osprey Publishing, 2014.

Newspaper and Magazine Articles

Baker, Larry. "Sinbad the Four-Legged Sailor." *U.S. Coast Guard Retiree Newsletter,* July 1988.

"Bath Dog Show." *Western Daily Press and Bristol Mirror,* January 20, 1947.

"Chief Petty Officer Leonard Williams (Obituary)." *Times* (London), January 22, 2007.

"Dog POW Wins Dickin Medal." *Dog World,* May 10, 1946.

"Ex-POW 'Judy' Is Dead." *Dundee Courier and Advertiser,* March 21, 1950.

Folkhart, Burt A. "Cecil Brown; Noted War Correspondent, Scholar." *Los Angeles Times,* October 27, 1987.

"The Four-Legged Heroine." *Look and Learn,* September 1975.

Fryer, Jane. "Judy, the Dogged POW Who Defied the Japanese." *London Daily Mail,* August 12, 2010.

Gardner, Tom. "The Real-Life Uncle Albert." *London Daily Mail,* June 14, 2013.

"The Hackbridge Boarding and Quarantine Kennels." *Tail-Wagger,* January 1950.

"Heroine Dog's Medal Goes on Display." *Western Mail* (Cardiff), August 26, 2006.

Howard, Philip. "Navy Will Pay Tribute to Judy the Pointer." *Times* (London), February 25, 1972.

"Jap Gaoler Defended." *Sydney Morning Herald,* September 24, 1945.

"Judy (Ex-POW Sumatra) Is Now in England." *Tail-Wagger,* December 1945.

Locke, Michelle. "War Dogs Who Died for Our Men Finally Get Their Day." Associated Press, June 19, 1994.

"A Man and His Dog." *London Evening Standard,* March 20, 1948.

McDaniel, C. Yates. "Last Message from Singapore." Associated Press, February 12, 1942.

"Missing, Now Safe." *Portsmouth Evening News,* May 4, 1942.

"More Help for Judy." *Tail-Wagger,* February 1946.

"Our Judy Fund." *Tail-Wagger,* April 1946.

"Portsmouth Petty Officer's Escape from Singapore." *Portsmouth Evening News,* July 27, 1945.

"Presentation to Judy." *Tail-Wagger,* June 1946.

Read, Nicholas. "Prison Camp Heroine Judy Was History's Only Bow-Wow POW." *Vancouver Sun,* March 12, 2003.

"Readers' Help for Judy." *Tail-Wagger,* January 1946.

Reilly, Tom. "VJ Day—Bravery of POW Dog." *London Daily Mirror,* August 15, 2005.

Shute, Joe. "Dogs of War: The Unsung Heroes of the Trenches." *London Daily Telegraph,* October 29, 2014.

Stewart, Athole. "Mercy Planes Fly POWs to Singapore." *The Argus* (Melbourne), September 17, 1945.

"Stubby, Hero Mascot of Seventeen Battles, Showing Decorations for Bravery." *New York Evening World,* July 8, 1921.

Turnau, Amber. "The Incredible Tale of Frank Williams." *Burnaby Now,* March 19, 2003.

"VC Dog Was Popular." *Bath Weekly Chronicle and Herald,* January 25, 1947.

Wolf, Tom. "Dogs Sent to England Are Put in Quarantine Kennels for Six Months." NEA Syndicate, March 13, 1944.

Internet Articles

Alvarez, Robert. "Thorium: The Wonder Fuel That Wasn't." Bulletin of the Atomic Scientists, thebulletin.org/thorium-wonder-fuel-wasnt7156 (accessed October 30, 2014).

"Auction for Medals of RAF Hero Nicknamed 'Cat's Eyes' Who Downed a German Bomber Without Firing a Single Shot." Daily Mail, dailymail.co.uk/news/article-2193429/How-carrots-helped-RAF-hero-nicknamed-cats-eyes-German-bomber-firing-single-shot.html (accessed July 9, 2014).

Bibliography

Backovic, Lazar. "Britain's Luftwoofe: The Heroic Paradogs of World War II." Spiegel Online, spiegel.de/international/zeitgeist/the-parachuting-dogs-of-the-british-army-in-world-war-ii-a-939002.html (accessed October 23, 2014).

"The Bangka Island Massacre." Angell Productions, angellpro.com.au/Bullwinkel.htm#Massacre (accessed March 6, 2014).

Becker, Marty. "Can All Dogs Swim?" Vet Street, vetstreet.com/dr-marty-becker/can-all-dogs-swim (accessed August 2, 2014).

"A Brief History of the Flying Tigers." Flying Tigers Association: American Volunteer Group, flyingtigersavg.com/index.php/avg/history/28-history-of-the-flying-tigers (accessed October 29, 2014).

"The Canine Senses." Responsible Dog and Cat, responsibledog.net/canine_senses.html (accessed July 7, 2014).

Catchpoole, David. "How the Dingo Confirms Genesis." Creation Ministries International, creation.com/the-australian-dingo-a-wolf-in-dogs-clothing (accessed July 25, 2014).

Cleveland, Les. "Soldiers' Songs: The Folklore of the Powerless." Buffalo State, faculty.buffalostate.edu/fishlm/folksongs/les01.htm.

Coyle, Jim. "End of World War II Leaflets." The Star, thestar.com/news/canada/2011/11/10/end_of_world_war_ii_leaflets.html (accessed October 27, 2014).

Creer, Commander H. V. "The Loss of HMS *Kuala,* 1942." Naval Historical Society of Australia, navyhistory.org.au/the-loss-of-hms-kuala-1942 (accessed March 11, 2014).

Deely, John. "*Umwelt.*" Internet Archive, web.archive.org/web/20060221134707/http://www.ut.ee/SOSE/deely.htm (accessed October 28, 2014).

Dodman, Nicholas. "Canine Maternal Behavior." Pet Place, petplace.com/dogs/canine-maternal-behavior/page1.aspx (accessed March 31, 2014).

"The Dogs of War: A Short History of Canines in Combat." Military History Now, militaryhistorynow.com/2012/11/08/the-dogs-of-war-a-short-history-of-canines-in-combat (accessed October 29, 2014).

Dunnell, Tony. "War Dogs of the Spanish Conquistadors." Suite, suite.io/tony-dunnell/47jm2j7 (accessed October 29, 2014).

Gamble, Mark. "Statements Made by Witnesses Regarding the Loss of HMS *Grasshopper.*" From UK National Archives, ADM 267/122. Kinnethmont, kinnethmont.co.uk/1939-1945_files/thos-ingram/hms-grasshopper.htm (accessed March 2, 2014).

Gittings, John. "A Brief Survey Written in Shanghai, April 2003," johngittings.com/id65.html (accessed March 28, 2014).

Henning, Peter. "An Anzac Story: Finding the Nurses in Sumatra." Tasmanian Times, tasmaniantimes.com/index.php/article/an-anzac-story-finding-the-nurses-in-sumatra (accessed October 27, 2014).

"Heroines of the *Empire Star:* The Perilous Journey." Angell Productions, angellpro.com.au/Hamilton.htm#Empire%20Star (accessed March 6, 2014).

Hope, David. "Stanley Saddington Ex RAF, Tien Kwang Survivor and Former POW." Singapore 1942, singaporeevacuation1942.blogspot.co.uk/2010/11/stanley-saddington-ex-raf-tien-kwang.html (accessed March 11, 2014).

Huntingford, Janice. "Post-Traumatic Stress Disorder in Dogs." IVC Journal, ivcjournal.com/articles/post-traumatic-stress-disorder-in-dogs (accessed July 7, 2014).

Jackson, Allan. "*Nova Scotia*." Facts About Durban, fad.co.za/Resources/Nova/novascotia.htm (accessed April 4, 2014).

"Japanese Conquest of Manchuria 1931–1932." Mount Holyoke, mtholyoke.edu/acad/intrel/WorldWar2/manchuria.htm (accessed October 28, 2014).

"Koreans in the Imperial Japanese Service." WWIIF, ww2f.com/topic/15019-koreans-in-the-imperial-japanese-service (accessed October 27, 2014).

"The Loyalty of Dogs." The Loyalty of Dogs: A Tribute to the Dogs of the American Civil War, loyaltyofdogs.com/ReadTribute.htm (accessed March 20, 2014).

"Memorial to Sumatra Railway Dead." BBC, news.bbc.co.uk/2/hi/uk_news/1492191.stm (accessed August 24, 2014).

Napper, Brian. "Escape from Singapore—4. My Parents' Fate." WW2 People's War. BBC, bbc.co.uk/history/ww2peopleswar/stories/55/a7697055.shtml (accessed March 11, 2014).

Pereira, Mathew. "Living in Distrust and Constant Fear." Headlines, Lifelines, ourstory.asia1.com.sg/war/headline/torture2.html (accessed November 4, 2014).

Porter, Brian. "Tribute to Ted," roll-of-honour.org.uk/p/html/porter-edward.htm (accessed March 17, 2014).

Putney, William W. "The War Dog Platoons: Marine Dogs of World War II." Converted from *Always Faithful: A Memoir of the Marine Dogs of WWII.* World War II History Info, worldwar2history.info/Marines/dogs.html (accessed March 21, 2014).

"Quarantine Laws to Be Relaxed in UK." BBC, bbc.com/news/uk-16347725 (accessed April 4, 2014).

Schilling, David Russell. "Thorium-Fueled Automobile Engine Needs Refueling Once a Century." Industry Tap, industrytap.com/thorium-fueled-automobile-engine-needs-refueling-once-a-century/15649 (accessed October 30, 2014).

"Sgt. Stubby." Badass of the Week, badassoftheweek.com/sgtstubby.html (accessed March 20, 2014).

"The Side Effects of Dogs Drinking Salt Water." Vet Info, vetinfo.com/dogs-drinking-salt-water.html (accessed July 23, 2014).

"The Sinking of the *Vyner Brooke*." Angell Productions, angellpro.com.au/vynerbrooke.htm (accessed March 6, 2014).

"Treating PTSD with Natural Dog Training." Canine PTSD, canineptsdblog.blogspot.com (accessed October 24, 2014).

"The Truth About the Numbers in Singapore!" Never Forgotten: The Story of the Taiwan POW Camps and the Men Who Were Interned in Them," powtaiwan.org/archives_detail.php?THE-TRUTH-ABOUT-THE-NUMBERS-IN-SINGAPORE-3 (accessed August 17, 2014).

"*Van Waerwijck*." Oo Cities, oocities.org/frans_taminiau/vanwaerwijk.htm (accessed April 4, 2014).

"The Wah Sui Incident." Angell Productions, angellpro.com.au/Wahsui.htm (accessed March 6, 2014).

Waller, Anna M. "Dogs and National Defense." Department of the Army, Office of the Quartermaster General. U.S. Army Quartermaster Museum, qmmuseum.lee.army.mil/dogs_and_national_defense.htm (accessed March 22, 2014).

Whiston, Robert. "International Naval Intervention and Protection Force 1936." Robert Whiston's Weblog, rwhiston.wordpress.com/2010/02/17/1 (accessed October 30, 2014).

Wingate, David. "The Story of the *Tanjong Pinang*." Malayan Volunteers Group, malayanvolunteersgroup.org.uk/node/341 (accessed March 21, 2014).

Websites

clydesite.co.uk/clydebuilt/viewship.asp?id=1452
cofepow.org.uk/pages/ships_list.html
fleetorganization.com/1937rnforeign.html
forcez-survivors.org.uk/biographies/listothershipscrew.html#HMS%20GRASSHOPPER
frankwilliams.ca
historylearningsite.co.uk/sergeant_stubby.htm
history.navy.mil/photos/sh-usn/usnsh-c/ap5.htm
ibiblio.org/chineseculture/contents/food/p-food-c01s03.html
scoutdogpages.com/content/robby.htm
stonesentinels.com
uboat.net/allies/merchants/1174.html
uboat.net:8080/allies/warships/ship/3514.html
willysthomas.net/AuthorPage.htm
wrecksite.eu/wreck.aspx?105041
wrecksite.eu/wreck.aspx?58402

Archives

United States National Archives

"Banno, Hirateru." 8th Army Sugamo Released Prisoner 201 Files. RG 338. Folder 20, Box 4, 290/66/21/1.

Imperial War Museum

Baxter, Arthur Leonard. Oral History, IWM 13278.
Cuthbertson, J. Private Papers, IWM 21579.
Fitzgerald, J. F. Private Papers, IWM 8209.
Forbes, I. D. S. Private Papers, IWM 18765.
Freeman, F. G. Private Papers, IWM 14046.
Hedley, John. Oral History, IWM 23219.
Lawrence, Peter. Oral History, IWM 18282.
Oliver, A. C. W. Collection, IWM HU43990.
Pentney, J. D. Private Papers, IWM 20664.
Persons, J. E. R. Private Papers, IWM 18760.
Robins, J. A. C. Private Papers, IWM 5153.
Robson, Ken. Private Papers, IWM 11338.

Saddington, Stanley. Collection, IWM 2010-02-04.
Simmonds, A. B. Private Papers, IWM 21578.
Smith, W. R. Private Papers, IWM 8443.
Williams, J. F. Private Papers, IWM 17378.

UK National Archives

RAF Files

"Evaders and Prisoners of War." RAF AIR 49/385.
"History of the RDF Organisation in the Far East," RAF AIR 20/193.
"Malaya Operations Signals 1941/42," RAF AIR 20/5576.
"Operations Birdcage and Mastiff Sortie Reports," RAF AIR 23/2664.
"Operations Birdcage and Mastiff Sortie Reports," RAF AIR 23/2665.
"Operations Birdcage and Mastiff Sortie Reports," RAF AIR 23/2666.
"Operations Birdcage and Mastiff Sortie Reports," RAF AIR 23/2667.
"Operations Birdcage and Mastiff Sortie Reports," RAF AIR 23/2669.
"Operations Birdcage and Mastiff Sortie Reports," RAF AIR 23/2670.
"Operations Birdcage and Mastiff Sortie Reports," RAF AIR 23/4800.
"Operations Record Book Appendices Sept–Oct 1945," RAF AIR 24/938.
"Personal Statement RAF F/O R. Knowles," RAF AIR 20/5577.
"Personnel Reception Centres Cosford 106," RAF AIR 29/1102.
"P.O.W. Resettlement and Refresher Course," RAF AIR 49/388.
"RAF Station Cosford 1940 Jan–1945 Dec," RAF AIR 28/173.
"RAPWI Sitreps," RAF AIR 23/2669.
"RDF Stations Overseas Policy," RAF AIR 20/3032.
"Recommendations for POW Awards," RAF AIR 2/3775.
"Repatriation of R.A.F. Ex-Prisoners of War from the Far East," RAF AIR 49/386.
"Report on the Recovery of Allied P/W and Internees After the Collapse of Japan, 1945," RAF AIR 23/1980.
"Royal Air Force Operations Record Book," RAF AIR 29/153.
"Signals, Vol. IV: Radar in Raid Reporting," RAF AIR 41/12.

Admiralty Files

"Deaths Aboard HMS *Dragonfly, Grasshopper,* and *Scorpion,*" NA ADM 358/2875.
"HMS *Gnat* Packet," NA ADM 267/122.
"HMS *Truculent* Patrol Report, 12th June to 5th July, 1944," NA ADM 199/1868, Pt. 1.
"Statement of Ian Forbes," NA ADM 1/30/600.
"Travel Operations RAPWI," NA ADM 1/19324.
"Various Reports on Sinkings of HMS *Grasshopper* and *Kung Wo,*" NA ADM 199/622A.

General Files

"Account HMS *Dragonfly* by Comm. C. C. Alexander," NA WO 361/178.
"Ernest Fisher Lodge Registry," NA HS 9/933/6.

"Evacuation from Singapore Across Sumatra," NA WO 141/100.
"Far East Anglo Dutch Operations," NA HS 1/272.
"Far East Anglo Dutch Operations," NA HS 1/273.
"Force 136," NA WO 20B/H332.
"Fourth Supplement to the *London Gazette,*" September 27, 1946.
"Hirateru Banno and Six Others," NA CO 235/1034.
"HMS *Grasshopper* Packet," NA WO 361/404.
"Japanese POW Index Card: Frank Williams," NA WO 345/56.
"Liberated POW Interrogation Questionnaire: Frank Williams," NA WO 344/409.
"List of POWs Pakan Baroe Area," NA WO 361/2013.
"List of Ships Sunk, Damaged, or Captured Near Bangka Strait," NA 199/607A.
"Mastiff Control Sitreps," NA WO 203/3029.
"Movement and Evacuation of P.O.W.," NA WO 203/3800.
"POW Information Cards," NA WO 345.
"Report of Charles Baker," NA 199/357.
"Report of R. A. Stuart of Hong Kong and Shanghai Bank," NA WO 222/1378.
"Secret Supplement to Report to Combined Chiefs of Staff by Rear Admiral Mountbatten of Burma, 1943–46," NA CAB 106/77.
"Singapore and Far East Personal Experiences," NA WO 106/2550.
"Special Operations Report on Clandestine Activity in Holland," NA HS 7/161.
"Statement by Capt. J. G. Gordon," NA WO 361/1592.
"Summary of MI9 Activities in India, South East Asia, and China," NA WO 208/3251.
"Third Supplement to the *London Gazette,*" January 25, 1946.
"Various Reports on Sinkings of HMS *Kuala* and *Tien Kwang,*" NA CO 980/237.

Portsmouth City Archives

Greer, Wally. "Pompey Boy in the 1930s and '40s." Oral History, Portsmouth WEA Local History Group.
Kelly's Directory of Portsmouth, Southsea, Etc., 1932–38, 1946–48.
"People of Portsmouth," selected memories of the city history.
Portsmouth Bombing Maps.
Smitten City: The Story of Portsmouth Under Blitz. Report on WWII bombing in Portsmouth by Portsmouth and Sunderland Newspapers, Ltd.

Southampton Government Archives

"Frank Williams #163338," Merchant Navy Records.

Official Reports and Historical Papers

Kim, Kwi-ok. *The Korean War and Women: With a Focus on Military Comfort Women and Military Comfort Stations.* Paper presented at the Fifth International Symposium on Peace and Human Rights in East Asia. Kyoto, Japan, February 22–25, 2002.

Kirby, Major General S. Woodburn, with Brigadier M. R. Roberts, Colonel G. T. Wards, and Air Vice Marshal N. L. Desoer. *The War Against Japan, Vol. 5: The Surrender of Japan,* 1948.

Rowland, Robin. "Sugamo and the River Kwai." Paper presented to Encounters at Sugamo Prison, Tokyo 1945–52, Conference on the American Occupation of Japan and Memories of the Asia-Pacific War. Princeton University, May 9, 2003.

Waller, Anna M. *Dogs and the National Defense.* Department of the Army, Office of the Quartermaster General, 1958.

Index

Note: Italic page numbers refer to maps.